The Palestine Yearbook of International Law, Volume 22 (2019–2020)

# The Palestine Yearbook of International Law

*Editor-in-Chief*

Nimer Sultany

*Consulting Editor*

Anis F. Kassim

*Editors*

Reem Al-Botmeh
Ata R. Hindi

*Editorial Board*

Anis F. Kassim          Camille Mansour
Nimer Sultany           Ata R. Hindi
Reem Al-Botmeh

*Advisory Board*

Georges M. Abi-Saab       Ahmed Abouelwafa
Abdallah Alashaal         Badriya Al-Awadhi
Mohammed Bedjaoui         Salah Dabbagh
Riad Daoudi               Nabil Elaraby
Awn Al-Khasawneh          Mahmoud Mubarak
Mohammad K. Al-Musa       Anis M. Al-Qasem†
Muhammad M. Al-Saleh      Moufid M. Shehab
Muhammad Y. Olwan         Muhammad Aziz Shukri

VOLUME 22

The titles published in this series are listed at *brill.com/pyil*

# The Palestine Yearbook of International Law, Volume 22 (2019–2020)

*Edited by*

Nimer Sultany

BRILL
NIJHOFF

LEIDEN | BOSTON

The *Palestine Yearbook of International Law* is published in cooperation with the Birzeit University Institute of Law, under whose auspices it is edited. Established in 1993, the Institute of Law is research based and aims to contribute to the modernization of Palestinian legal structures both at the academic and professional levels.

All e-mail correspondence concerning the Yearbook should be sent to the Editor-in-Chief at: iol.pyil@birzeit.edu. Posted correspondence may be sent to: Attn: *Palestine Yearbook of International Law*, BZU Institute of Law. P.O. Box 14, Birzeit. Palestine. Telecommunication may be directed to the Institute of Law, at: Tel: (972) (2) 298-2009; Fax: (972) (2) 298-2137.

Typeface for the Latin, Greek, and Cyrillic scripts: "Brill". See and download: brill.com/brill-typeface.

ISSN 1386-1972
E-ISSN 2211-6141 (e-book)
ISBN 978-90-04-49912-6 (hardback)

Copyright 2021 by Koninklijke Brill NV, Leiden, The Netherlands.
Koninklijke Brill NV incorporates the imprints Brill, Brill Nijhoff, Brill Hotei, Brill Schöningh, Brill Fink, Brill mentis, Vandenhoeck & Ruprecht, Böhlau Verlag and V&R Unipress.
All rights reserved. No part of this publication may be reproduced, translated, stored in a retrieval system, or transmitted in any form or by any means, electronic, mechanical, photocopying, recording or otherwise, without prior written permission from the publisher. Requests for re-use and/or translations must be addressed to Koninklijke Brill NV via brill.com or copyright.com.

This book is printed on acid-free paper and produced in a sustainable manner.

# Contents

List of Contributors   VII
Introduction, Vol. 22 (2019–2020)   IX
  *Nimer Sultany*


### PART 1
## *Articles*

Using the Master's Tools to Dismantle the Master's House: International Law and Palestinian Liberation   3
  *Ralph Wilde*

Fact and Fiction: The Nation-State, Colonialism, and International Minority Law   75
  *Sally Shammas*

Systemic Economic Harm in Occupied Palestine and the Social Connections Model   112
  *Shahd Hammouri*

Restrictions on Freedom of Movement in the West Bank: A Policy of Apartheid   141
  *Costanza Ferrando*


### PART 2
## *Case Commentaries*

Will the German Judiciary Protect the Right to Boycott, Divestment, and Sanctions?   179
  *Nadija Samour and Ahmed Abed*

**PART 3**
*Review Essays*

A Hundred Years of Settler-Colonialism: History, Law, Horizons Beyond
*Rashid Khalidi, The Hundred Years' War on Palestine: A History of Settler Colonialism and Resistance, 1917–2017* (2020) & *Noura Erakat, Justice for Some: Law and the Question of Palestine* (2019)    203
  *John Reynolds*

The "Visible" and "Invisible" College of Legal Advisers
*Andraž Zidar and Jean-Pierre Gauci eds., "The Role of Legal Advisers in International Law"* (2016)    217
  *Ata R. Hindi*

**PART 4**
*Book Reviews*

Rouba Al-Salem, "Security, Rights and Law: The Israeli High Court of Justice and Israeli Settlements in the Occupied West Bank"    235
  *Diana Buttu*

Marco Longobardo, "The Use of Armed Force in Occupied Territory" (2018)    241
  *Omar Yousef Shehabi*

Angélica Maria Bernal, "Beyond Origins: Rethinking Founding in a Time of Constitutional Democracy" (2017)    251
  *Alicia Pastor y Camarasa*

Index    256

# List of Contributors

*Diana Buttu*
is a Haifa based lawyer and analyst. She previously served as an advisor to the Palestine Liberation Organization (PLO).

*Alicia Pastor y Camarasa*
is a PhD candidate at the Research Centre on State and Constitution, University of Louvain (Belgium).

*Costanza Ferrando*
is a junior researcher in international law. She earned her law degree at the University of Turin and her Masters in Human Rights at Université Saint Joseph de Beyrouth. She is a committed humanitarian worker with field experience as a refugee law expert. She has been a visiting researcher at Birzeit University in 2019, where she conducted ethnographic field research addressing freedom of movement in the West Bank.

*Shahd Hammouri*
Lecturer at the University of Kent.

*Ata R. Hindi*
Research Fellow in International Law, Institute of Law at Birzeit University. PhD Candidate in Law at Tilburg University.

*John Reynolds*
Associate Professor, Department of Law, National University of Ireland, Maynooth.

*Nadija Samour and Ahmed Abed*
Both authors are lawyers in Berlin.

*Sally Shammas*
acquired her LLB from the University of Kent and her LLM in International Law from SOAS, University of London.

*Omar Yousef Shehabi*
JSD Candidate, Yale Law School; Legal Officer, United Nations; Former legal advisor to the Palestinian negotiating team (2013–2014).

*Ralph Wilde*
Associate Professor of Law at University College London, University of London, where he teaches general international law, including the law of statehood and self-determination, international human rights law, and the international law on the use of force.

# Introduction, Vol. 22 (2019–2020)

At the time of submitting this volume to the publisher in May 2021, a ceasefire had just recently been agreed to between the Israelis and Palestinian armed groups. During the course of Israel's brutal attack on Gaza, the Palestinian Center for Human Rights reported that 247 people were killed, including 66 children and 39 women in addition to 1417 wounded, including 277 women and 412 children.[1] The repeated onslaughts on the Gaza Strip, and the ethnic cleansing in East Jerusalem that had sparked them, exemplify a colonial setting in which colonial wars seek to maintain colonial "peace" through pacification and merciless attacks on civilians. As such, the ceasefire does not end the unjust status quo that denies Palestinians their right to self-determination, refugees their right to return, and Palestinian citizens inside Israel their right to equality.

These repeated onslaughts place in the foreground the question of the role and limitations of international law in limiting the powerful and holding them to account for their crimes. Since its first volume in 1984, the Palestine Yearbook of International Law, the Institute of Law at Birzeit University, and Birzeit University overall – published a wide range of cutting-edge analysis to various aspects of the "Question of Palestine."[2] Much of this analysis anticipated recent developments. In April 2021, Human Rights Watch released a report identifying the crimes of apartheid and persecution throughout historic Palestine.[3] While the report is welcome, it is unfortunate that it took such a long time for the international human rights community and western academic scholarship to heed the call of Palestinians and critical scholars who had laid bare, in excruciating detail, the reality of colonialism and apartheid in Palestine in the past decades, including within the pages of this Yearbook.

Continuing with this tradition, this volume seeks to nurture critical approaches to international law relevant not only for Palestine, but also the Arab World, and the Global South more generally. In the first article, Ralph Wilde invokes Audre Lorde's: "… the master's tools will never dismantle the master's house." Inspired from his visit to Khan Al-Ahmar – a Palestinian

---

1  Palestinian Center for Human Rights, *Cease-fire Reached After 11 Days of IOF Aggression on Gaza* (May 21, 2021), https://pchrgaza.org/en/cease-fire-reached-after-11-days-of-iof-aggression-on-gaza/.

2  *See* Ata R. Hindi, *The Palestine Yearbook of International Law: A Medium for a Principled International Law on Palestine and the Palestinian People*, 50 Neth. Y.B. Int'l L. 253 (2019).

3  Human Rights Watch, *A Threshold Crossed* (Apr. 27, 2021), https://www.hrw.org/report/2021/04/27/threshold-crossed/israeli-authorities-and-crimes-apartheid-and-persecution#.

Bedouin village outside of Jerusalem, home to refugees and the subject of forced transfer – he provides a critical evaluation of international law in the context of the Palestinian struggle. He examines the key areas of international law invoked in the Palestinian context by various persons – *e.g.* international humanitarian law – and the genuine constraints it places on Palestinian liberation. For Wilde, the law has its limits and international law may very well be part of the problem in emancipating Palestinians, such as in the marginalization of self-determination based on the parameters of the two-state solution and the push for "negotiations."

In her contribution to this volume, Sally Shammas finds international minority law similarly wanting. Shammas looks at the ways in which the legal entrenchment of minority/majority categories overlooks the nature of legitimacy in the nation state-model. She assesses international minority rights within this context by pointing to their colonial origins and their tenuous relationship with the universal human rights regime. She also considers the ways in which power-sharing mechanisms adopted in the aftermath of conflict in Iraq and Syria continue to encourage divisive identities by limiting political participation to the expression of group belonging, making the case that this serves to restrict minority participation and social acceptance, rather than attempting to integrate the different segments of society into a universal and inclusive civic identity. The categories create, or at least exacerbate, the very problem they seek to solve with respect to equality, sectarianism, and power sharing.

Shahd Hammouri then discusses the lack of adequate recognition and treatment of systemic economic harm under occupation. In light of international law's limitations in this regard, Hammouri applies the perspective of the "social connections model" to the reality of an occupation. Zeroing in on the situation in occupied Palestine, Hammouri posits that this context is ripe for applying such a model, in order to deal with systematic economic harm premised on the idea that remedying injustices requires holistic perceptions of causality so as to trace connections sustaining dire economic conditions. Hammouri examines the international community's efforts to deal with systemic economic harm, including the United Nations business and human rights framework, and its database listing companies benefitting from the settlement enterprise in occupied Palestine.

Finally, Costanza Ferrando similarly argues for a holistic perspective with respect to the applicability of the apartheid legal paradigm to the situation in Palestine. In the context of growing recognition of the reality of apartheid – including from national and international NGOs (such as B'Tselem and Human Rights Watch) – this article zeroes in on a detailed analysis on restrictions

INTRODUCTION

XI

to the freedom of movement in the West Bank. These restrictions and other violations are symptomatic of an institutionalized system of domination and should be understood in reference to this system as opposed to disparate violations of international law.

In their case commentary, attorneys Nadija Samour and Ahmed Abed discuss the role of the German judiciary in restricting or protecting the right to free political speech and activism as in the advocacy for BDS. Samour and Abed show that officials and judges across Germany have used a non-legally binding Bundestag motion that stigmatized BDS as "anti-semitic" to justify encroachments upon pro-Palestinian political speech and activism. They illustrate this by discussing a range of cases related to access to public and private venues as well as seeking entry visas to invited speakers.

The volume also includes two review essays. In the first, John Reynolds looks at two texts – Rashid Khalidi's *The Hundred Years' War on Palestine: A History of Settler Colonialism and Resistance, 1917–2017*, as well as Noura Erakat's *Justice for Some: Law and the Question of Palestine*. As Reynolds explains, both texts highlight Zionism's settler-colonial nature as a foundation to understanding the question of Palestine. Moreover, in tracing the history, and the law in the course of that history, Reynolds points to the authors' realization of the shape-shifting complicity of international law in Israel's settler-colonial project. Applauding both texts, Reynolds shares the perception of other authors in the need to take a step back and realize international law's shortcomings and setbacks.

Ata Hindi then reviews Andraž Zidar and Jean-Pierre Gauci's *The Role of Legal Advisers in International Law*. While commending the authors for compiling an overview of the work of legal advisers in international law, Hindi argues that the volume oversees the "invisible" college of international lawyers in its shortcomings of more diverse geographic and thematic contributions. In order to highlight the interplay between law and politics, Hindi examines the role of the Palestinian legal adviser as an adviser guided by a cause rather than attached to a particular institution.

In addition, this volume includes three book reviews. Omar Shehabi reviews Marco Longobardo's *The Use of Armed Force in Occupied Territory*; Alicia Pastor y Camarasa reviews Angelica Maria Bernal's *Beyond Origins: Rethinking Founding in a Time of Constitutional Democracy*; and Diana Buttu reviews Rouba Al-Salem's *Security, Rights, and Law: The Israeli High Court of Justice and Israeli Settlements in the Occupied West Bank*.

Last, but certainly not least, we would like to thank the various peer reviewers who supported us throughout this process, including: Michelle Farrell (University of Liverpool), Kevin Jon Heller (University of Copenhagen), Ardi

Imseis (Queen's University), Michelle Staggs Kelsall (SOAS), Mazen Masri (City University London), Eva Nanopoulos (Queen Mary), Paul O'Connell (SOAS), and Robert Wintemute (King's College London). The development and strength of this volume's submissions are a testament to their contributions.

*Nimer Sultany*
*Editor-in-Chief*

# PART 1

## *Articles*

# Using the Master's Tools to Dismantle the Master's House: International Law and Palestinian Liberation

*Ralph Wilde*

## Contents

I   Introduction
II  Occupation and Occupation Law
III Law on the Use of Force, Including its Interface with the Law on Title to Territory
IV  Self-determination as a Legal Right
V   Self-determination Delayed and Potentially Dropped
VI  Self-determination Obscured
VII Erosion of Legal Standards?
VIII Conclusion

## I Introduction

In 2018, Al-Haq and the Muwatin Institute organized two international law conferences at Birzeit University in Palestine.[1] Al-Haq took some of the attendees at the first conference, including the present author, to meet the Jahalin Palestinian Bedouin community of Khan al-Ahmar, in al-Quds Governorate of the West Bank. The Jahalin settled there in the 1950s, when the West Bank was under Jordanian control, having been expelled from al-Naqab by the Israeli army in 1948. After Israel captured the West Bank in 1967, the Israeli settlements of Ma'ale Adumim and Kfar Adumim were established in the adjacent areas to Khan al-Ahmar. Israel treated the Jahalin as illegitimate

---

[1] See Al-Haq, *International Conference: The Threshold from Occupation to Annexation*, Oct. 3–4, 2018, https://www.alhaq.org/advocacy/6155.html; and Birzeit University, *Annual Muwatin Conference reviews seven decades of the Universal Human Rights Declaration* (Oct. 10, 2018), https://www.birzeit.edu/en/news/annual-muwatin-conference-reviews-seven-decades-universal-human-rights-declaration.

© KONINKLIJKE BRILL NV, LEIDEN, 2021 | DOI:10.1163/22116141_022010_002

residents, refusing to connect them to utilities, notably water, sanitation, and electricity. This created a situation of acute material deprivation. Eventually, Israel forcibly evicted residents and demolished their houses. At the time of the visit, the remaining residents were under threat of forced eviction and relocation to an area near the refuse dump of Abu Dis, in a different part of al-Quds Governorate.[2] At the meeting, community leader Amran Reshaq stated that it is a common misconception to think that Palestinian communities like his want merely to improve their humanitarian conditions in their place of residence – for example, by having proper access to water. Instead, he insisted, their primary demand is to return to the place from where they were displaced.

Amran Reshaq's crucial distinction between the underlying situation and improving conditions within the situation is the focus of this article. The theme of Al-Haq conference was the threshold from occupation to annexation.[3] The theme of the Muwatin conference was the 70th Anniversary of the Universal Declaration of Human Rights (UDHR).[4] These themes implicate the three main areas of generally-applicable international law commonly invoked in relation to the situation of the Palestinian people. Legal "tools" deployed to dismantle the "master's house" of colonial oppression, to borrow from Audre Lorde.[5] First is the law on the use of force, including the interface between this area of law and the law on title to territory.[6] Second is the law of armed conflict/international humanitarian law (IHL), including occupation

---

2 *See, e.g.,* Al-Haq, *Al-Haq Urgent Appeal to the United Nations Special Rapporteur on Adequate Housing as a Component of the Right to an Adequate Standard of Living, and on the Right to Non-Discrimination in This Context* (May 28, 2018), https://www.alhaq.org/advocacy/6194.html; *Khan al-Ahmar: Israel court approves demolition of Bedouin village,* BBC News (Sep. 5, 2018), https://www.bbc.com/news/world-middle-east-45420915; Alice M. Panepinto, *Jurisdiction as Sovereignty Over Occupied Palestine,* 26 Soc. & Legal Stud. 311 (2017); B'Tselem, *Communities facing expulsion: The Khan al-Ahmar area* (Oct. 10, 2017), https://www.btselem.org/communities_facing_expulsion/khan_al_ahmar; Al-Haq, *Plight of Palestinian Bedouin depicts impact of illegal Israeli occupation and practices in Palestinian Territory* (Dec. 17, 2014), https://www.alhaq.org/publications/8068.html.

3 *See* above n1.

4 *See* above n1. Universal Declaration of Human Rights, U.N. Doc. A/RES/3/217A (Dec. 10, 1948) [*hereinafter* UDHR].

5 Audre Lorde, *The Master's Tools Will Never Dismantle the Master's House,* in Sister Outsider: Essays and Speeches (1984) [*hereinafter* Lorde (1984)].

6 The authorities are voluminous and references to them readily available. For helpful lists, *see* Oxford University Press, *Oxford Bibliographies-Use of Force in International Law* [*hereinafter* OUP UoF list (2020)], https://www.oxfordbibliographies.com/view/document/obo-9780199796953/obo-9780199796953-0005.xml; Oxford University Press, *Oxford Bibliographies-Territorial Title* [*hereinafter* OUP Territorial Title list (2016)], https://www.oxfordbibliographies.com/view/document/obo-9780199796953/obo-9780199796953-0004.xml. Further particular sources on these areas of international law are cited below.

law.[7] Third is international human rights law (IHRL), including the right of self-determination.[8] Thus, Amnesty International UK invokes IHRL as central to the work of Amnesty International generally,[9] and describes this work in the Palestinian context as aimed at bringing an "end" to the "oppression" of the Palestinian people.[10] Related to this common association of international law with emancipatory objectives is the idea that if only the law were enforced, emancipation would be realized. Or, put differently, that the lack of Palestinian liberation is due to the violation of the law with impunity. Thus, for Amnesty, the oppression of the Palestinian people has occurred despite its "campaigning hard ... for the last 50 years."[11] What is being implied is that if such a campaign were to be successful, the objective of bringing "oppression" to an "end" would be realized.

But the international legal system is embedded with the ideology and techniques of imperialism and colonialism.[12] This includes in its operation through, and assumption of the legitimacy of, the division of the world into sovereign states, and, often, the basis on which it determines how boundaries are drawn.[13] Is international law not, then, part of the "master's house"? Would

---

7    The primary and secondary authorities are voluminous and references to them readily available. For helpful lists, *see* Oxford University Press, *Oxford Bibliographies – International Humanitarian Law* [*hereinafter* OUP IHL list (2017)], https://www.oxfordbibliographies .com/view/document/obo-9780199796953/obo-9780199796953-0146.xml; Oxford University Press, *Oxford Bibliographies-Military Occupation* [*hereinafter* OUP Occupation list (2017)], https://www.oxfordbibliographies.com/view/document/obo-9780199796953/obo -9780199796953-0077.xml. Further particular sources on these areas of international law are cited below.

8    The primary and secondary authorities are voluminous and references to them readily available. For a helpful list, *see* Oxford University Press, *Oxford Bibliographies-Human Rights* [*hereinafter* OUP HR list (2017)], https://www.oxfordbibliographies.com/view/ document/obo-9780199796953/obo-9780199796953-0056.xml. Further particular sources on these areas of international law are cited below.

9    *See* Amnesty International UK, *Human rights law* (July 20, 2018) [*hereinafter* Amnesty International UK (2018)], https://www.amnesty.org.uk/human-rights-law.

10    *See* Amnesty International UK, *Help end the 50 year oppression of Palestinians* [*hereinafter* Amnesty International UK (2019)], https://web.archive.org/web/20210516051751/https:// www.amnesty.org.uk/campaign/palestinian-crisis-appeal-carousel.

11    *See id.*

12    *See, e.g.,* Antony Anghie, Imperialism, Sovereignty, and the Making of International Law (2005) [*hereinafter* Anghie (2005)]; B.S. Chimni, *Third World Approaches to International Law: A Manifesto,* 8 Int'l Comty. L. Rev. 3 (2006) [*hereinafter* Chimni (2006)]; James Thuo Gathii, *TWAIL: A Brief History of its Origins, its Decentralized Network, and a Tentative Bibliography,* 3 Trade L. & Dev. 26 (2011); and, on borders in particular, *see* Makau Mutua, *Why Redraw the Map of Africa: A Moral and Legal Inquiry,* 16 Mich. J. Int'l L. 1113 (1994) [*hereinafter* Mutua (1994)].

13    *See* the discussion below, text accompanying n121.

the implementation of international law necessarily bring about Palestinian liberation? More fundamentally, is the conservative social institution of law compatible with transformatory emancipation? Lorde insists that "... the master's tools will never dismantle the master's house."[14] She cautions that "they may allow us temporarily to beat him at his own game, but they will never enable us to bring about genuine change."[15]

Given these challenges, the present article provides a critical evaluation of what is at stake when international law is invoked in the context of the Palestinian struggle.[16] How and to what extent does it speak to Amran Reshaq's claim?

The article is divided as follows. Section 2 identifies a predominant, and at times exclusive, focus on IHL, including occupation law, when international advocates address the Palestinian struggle. Relatedly, there is an exclusive focus on the occupation itself. This excludes key elements of the Palestinian struggle arising out of the creation of Israel in 1948. Specifically, it bypasses the question of the situation of the Palestinian people vis-à-vis the territory of Israel, whether they are Israeli citizens or refugees displaced during the Nakba (such as the Jahalin). Moreover, even within this limited focus, the exclusive invocation of occupation *law* ignores entirely, because of the narrow scope of that law, the question of the existential legitimacy of the occupation itself.

The article then discusses the two areas of international law that address this existential legitimacy – the law on the use of force and the law of self-determination – and how they interface with the law on title to territory

---

14  Lorde (1984), above n5.

15  *Id.*

16  The focus is on general international law only, not also the specific legal arrangements that are also relevant to the Palestinian situation, such as United Nations Security Council (UNSC) and General Assembly (UNGA) resolutions, the Oslo Peace Accords, etc. (although such resolutions are mentioned when they are significant to the general international legal framework). For critical evaluations encompassing further features of the legal framework, *see, e.g.*, Ardi Imseis, *The United Nations and the Question of Palestine: A Study in International Legal Subalternity* (Sep. 2018) (doctoral thesis, Cambridge University) to be published as *The United Nations and the Question of Palestine: Rule by Law and the Structure of International Legal Subalternity* (CUP, forthcoming 2022) [*hereinafter* Imseis (2018/2022)]; F. Yahia, *The Palestine Question and International Law*, Palestine Liberation Organization Research Center (1970) [*hereinafter* Yahia (1970)]; Ardi Imseis, *Negotiating the Illegal: On the United Nations and the Illegal Occupation of Palestine, 1967–2020*, 31 Eur. J. Int'l L. 1055 (2020) [*hereinafter* Imseis (2020)]; Noura Erakat, Justice for Some: Law and the Question of Palestine (2019) [*hereinafter* Erakat (2019)]; Hani Sayed, *The Fictions of the 'Illegal' Occupation in the West Bank and Gaza*, 16 Or. Rev. Int'l L. 79 (2014) [*hereinafter* Sayed (2014)]; Conference report, *"Law and Politics: Options and Strategies of International Law for the Palestinian People" – Birzeit* [*Proceedings*], 17 Palestine Y.B. Int'l L. 141 (2014) [*hereinafter* 2014 Birzeit Conference]; John Reynolds, *Anti-Colonial Legalities: Paradigms, Tactics & Strategy*, 18 Palestine Y.B. Int'l L. 8 (2015) [*hereinafter* Reynolds (2015)].

when it comes to annexation. Section 3 begins with annexation. International law provides a seemingly clear repudiation of the legitimacy of this as far as Israel and the West Bank (including East Jerusalem) is concerned. However, despite what some commentators suggest, such a position does not necessarily delegitimize the continuance of the occupation. To completely address the applicable normative framework, one must account for the self-defense component of the law on the use of force. Regrettably, most commentators seem unwilling to appraise the occupation's legitimacy in these terms. Yet such an appraisal, provided herein, reveals that the occupation is an illegal use of force – aggression – and must therefore be terminated. The problem, however, is that engaging with this crucial argument requires the Palestinian people to frame their case in terms of the legitimacy, or otherwise, of Israel's security requirements in justifying the occupation. The focus is thus on Israel's needs, not their own situation.

Section 4 turns to the law of self-determination, which provides in its "external" manifestation an alternative basis for framing arguments, ostensibly orientated towards freedom for the Palestinian people. However, the right is commonly presented as restricted to the model of sovereign statehood as the basis for collective Palestinian identity. Moreover, this statehood is itself limited to the territory of West Bank and Gaza. The territorial limitation excludes (like the earlier limited focus on the occupation) the situation of the Palestinian people with respect to the rest of the land between the river and the sea.

Even within the limited exclusive focus on the West Bank and Gaza, Palestinian self-determination has not been realized in over half a century of occupation. Experts and commentators tend to make that point, sometimes (but not always) call for the occupation to end, then conclude their analysis. But there are additional relevant factors to the denial of Palestinian self-determination *beyond* the basic fact of the occupation. And these factors can be identified in aspects of how international law is understood and applied.

To appreciate this, it is helpful to broaden the focus to other situations where people entitled to external self-determination have also been denied the realization of this – for example, the Sahrawi, who have been under Moroccan occupation since 1975. This is done in Section 5. A link is made to these practices and the racist, patriarchal concept of trusteeship over people: the idea that a people are granted freedom only if they are deemed "ready." The notion of a conditional entitlement to freedom has been identified by Ardi Imseis in the UN treatment of Palestinian liberation.[17] Here, freedom is contingent on the reaching of a peace agreement. However, international law ostensibly framed self-determination as a repudiation of trusteeship over people and its racist

---

17    Imseis (2018/2022), above n16; Imseis (2020), above n16.

underpinnings. According to this, independence was supposed to be realized immediately. How, then, has this idea been re-introduced in the "post-colonial" era and applied to the Palestinian people?

One explanation is the failure to appreciate the full significance of the law on the use of force. Section 6, however, offers additional explanations. Three factors have the effect of downgrading and even bypassing the question of realizing Palestinian self-determination. In the first place, is the exclusive focus on occupation law, and the characterization of the situation as an "occupation." In the second place, further features of the application of the trusteeship-over-people concept are relevant. These include distinctions sometimes made between situations designated as "colonial," and those designated as "occupations," with the concept somehow applying differently between the two categories. In the third place, is the jurisprudence of IHRL that includes self-determination as a "human right" in the two main global human rights treaties. Section 6 evaluates the practice of the two United Nations (UN) committees monitoring the implementation of those treaties, and the positions taken by leading international human rights NGOs: Amnesty International and Human Rights Watch. This analysis reveals a tendency to ignore the existential legitimacy of the occupation and the significance to this of the self-determination right. Relatedly, they treat the right of return of the Palestinian people in a problematic way. Moreover, these bodies' approaches to the Palestinian people's "internal" self-determination within Israel implies an affirmation of the collective self-determination entitlement of the people of Israel. The ironic nature of the bypassing of the collective Palestinian self-determination entitlement – in the context of an implied affirmation of this right for the people of the very state responsible for preventing the entitlement from being realized – adds insult to injury.

Finally, Section 7 considers whether the foregoing might not be understood only in terms of the existing international legal status quo – that self-determination is being violated and this violation is being ignored. Alternatively, might it suggest that the norms themselves are being altered? The Trump administration's recognitions of Israel's purported annexation of the Syrian Golan Heights and Morocco's purported annexation of Western Sahara, and the moving of the United States (US) Israeli embassy to Jerusalem (maintained by the Biden administration), potentially suggest an effort at normative challenge. The Section considers the issues at stake here, including the implications for the silence of the international human rights committees and NGOs on external self-determination.

Throughout the article, the discussion makes comparative references to other relevant situations of occupation/denial of self-determination/illegal annexation, such as the occupations of Germany, Austria, and Japan after the

Second World War;[18] the Moroccan occupation and purported annexation of the Western Sahara;[19] the Indonesian occupation and purported annexation between 1975 and 1999, and subsequent UN administration, between 1999 and 2002, of Timor Leste;[20] the Russian occupation and purported annexation of Crimea since 2014;[21] the US-United Kingdom (UK)-led Coalition Provisional Authority (CPA) occupation of Iraq 2003–2004 and subsequent military presence;[22] and the Israeli occupation and purported annexation of the Syrian Golan Heights.[23]

## II    Occupation and Occupation Law

The UDHR, whose 70th anniversary was the theme of the Muwatin conference, was adopted in 1948 as part of the broader post-1945 law-making efforts on humanitarian issues which included the 1949 Geneva Conventions.[24] These treaties, notably the Fourth Convention, contain key rules on occupation

---

18    *See, e.g.*, the sources cited in Ralph Wilde, International Territorial Administration: How Trusteeship and the Civilizing Mission Never Went Away (2008) [*hereinafter* Wilde (2008)], at 21, 23–5, 275 n140, 295, 309, 323, 328–9, 369–70, & 428.

19    *See, e.g.*, Western Sahara, Advisory Opinion, 1975 I.C.J. Rep. 12 (Oct. 16) [*hereinafter* ICJ Western Sahara Advisory Opinion]; Wilde (2008), above n18, Ch. 5, Section 5.6 (and sources cited therein); Rainer Hofmann, *Annexation*, Max Planck Encyc. Pub. Int'l L. (Jan. 2020) [*hereinafter* Hofmann (2020)], para. 37 (and sources cited therein), https://opil.ouplaw.com/view/10.1093/law:epil/9780199231690/law-9780199231690-e1376; and the UNSC resolutions discussed below, text accompanying n148 *et seq.*

20    *See, e.g.*, Wilde (2008), above n18, *passim* (*see* the index entry for East Timor, at 580), and Sources list, at 514 *et seq.* On the Indonesian occupation in particular, *see* International Law and the Question of East Timor (Catholic Institute for International Relations, 1995).

21    *See, e.g.*, Thomas D. Grant, *Annexation of Crimea*, 109 Am. J. Int'l L. 68, 68–95 (2015) (and sources cited therein).

22    *See, e.g.*, Adam Roberts, *Transformative military occupation: Applying the laws of war and human rights*, 100 Am. J. Int'l L. 580 (2006) [*hereinafter* Roberts (2006)]; Stefan Talmon, The Occupation of Iraq (2020); Matilda Arvidsson, The Subject in International Law: The Administrator of the Coalition Provisional Authority of Occupied Iraq and its Laws (2016); David J. Scheffer, *Beyond Occupation Law*, 97 Am. J. Int'l L. 842 (2003) [*hereinafter* Scheffer (2003)]; Eyal Benvenisti, The International Law of Occupation Ch. 9 (2nd ed., 2012) [*hereinafter* Benvenisti (2012)]; Kerry Rittich, *Occupied Iraq: Imperial Convergences?* 31 Leiden J. Int'l L 479 (2018).

23    *See* Hoffman (2020), above n19, para. 33 (and sources cited therein).

24    UDHR, above n4. Geneva Convention (I) for the Amelioration of the Condition of the Wounded and Sick in Armed Forces in the Field, Aug. 12, 1949, 75 U.N.T.S. 31 [*hereinafter* First Geneva Convention]; Geneva Convention (II) for the Amelioration of the Condition of the Wounded, Sick and Shipwrecked Members of Armed Forces at Sea, Aug. 12, 1949, 75 U.N.T.S. 85 [*hereinafter* Second Geneva Convention]; Geneva Convention (III) Relative to the Treatment of Prisoners of War, Aug. 12, 1949, 75 U.N.T.S. 135 [*hereinafter* Third Geneva

law, implicating the theme of the Al-Haq conference. They form part of the international law regulating the conduct of warfare – the *jus in bello*. The Geneva Conventions supplemented the occupation law norms of the Hague Regulations of 1899 and 1907.[25] This is understood to form part of a broader paradigm shift, from a state-centric, bombs-and-bullets "law of armed conflict" paradigm to a supposedly human-centered, humanizing approach.[26] Hence the alteration in the name being associated with this area of law, "international humanitarian law." The general assertion of humanitarianism is then associated with occupation law in particular. So, the legal department of the International Committee of the Cross (ICRC), the self-appointed guardian of this body of law, asserts that "the law of occupation is primarily motivated by humanitarian considerations."[27]

This association with humanitarianism paves the way for the predominant or exclusive focus on IHL, including occupation law, in discussions of legal questions and advocacy strategies aimed at vindicating the Palestinian people's rights. Such an approach is typically followed by "internationals" working in Palestine, whether for foreign states, international organizations, or NGOs. For example, the Swedish NGO Diakonia, which states that its international work generally is concerned with ending "poverty and oppression," conducts its work in Palestine exclusively within an IHL-orientated framework.[28]

---

Convention]; Geneva Convention (IV) Relative to the Protection of Civilian Persons in Time of War, Aug. 12, 1949, 75 U.N.T.S. 287 [*hereinafter* Fourth Geneva Convention].

25    Hague Convention (II) with Respect to the Laws and Customs of War on Land, annex: Regulations concerning the Laws and Customs of War on Land, July 29, 1899, 26 Martens Nouveau Recueil (ser. 2) 949 [*hereinafter* 1899 Hague Regulations], especially Section III; Hague Convention IV – Laws and Customs of War on Land, annex: Regulations concerning the Laws and Customs of War on Land, Oct. 18, 1907, 3 Martens Nouveau Recueil (ser. 3) 461 [*hereinafter* 1907 Hague Regulations], especially Section III.

26    For this evolution, *see* the sources cited in: OUP IHL list (2017), above n7.

27    ICRC, *Occupation and international humanitarian law: questions and answers* (Aug. 4, 2004), https://www.icrc.org/en/doc/resources/documents/misc/634kfc.htm.

28    On the general international work of Diakonia, *see* Diakonia, https://www.diakonia.se/en/. On its work in Palestine, *see* Diakonia, *Israel and Palestine (oPt)* [*hereinafter* Diakonia (2021)], https://www.diakonia.se/en/where-we-work/middle-east-north-africa/israel-and-palestine-opt/. I should declare that I worked as an independent consultant for Diakonia, writing the following: Ralph Wilde, *Expert opinion on the applicability of human rights law to the Palestinian Territories with a specific focus on the respective responsibilities of Israel, as the extraterritorial state, and Palestine, as the territorial state*, Diakonia (Feb. 2018), https://www.diakonia.se/ihl/download/download/applicability-human-rights-law-palestine-expert-opinion-wilde/ [*hereinafter* Wilde (2018)].

This is done through its "Diakonia International Humanitarian Law (IHL) Resource Centre."[29]

As Hani Sayed observes, "the focus on the legality of the occupation [as a matter of IHL] is not politically neutral ... it implicitly incorporates a specific substantive position on the future of the Palestinian people and the nature of the political solution to the conflict."[30] In occupation law, "occupation" denotes a situation where a state administers territory that is not its sovereign territory.[31] Thus as a matter of *law*, deploying the terminology of the "Israeli

---

29    Diakonia (2021), above n28.

30    Sayed (2014), above n16, at 105–106 (fn omitted). The present article complements the analysis by Sayed, addressing different matters. *See also* 2014 Birzeit Conference, above n16.

31    On occupation law generally, *see* 1899 Hague Regulations and 1907 Hague Regulations, *passim* and especially Sections III, above n25; First Geneva Convention art. 2, above n24; Second Geneva Convention art. 2, above n24; Third Geneva Convention art. 2, above n24; Fourth Geneva Convention arts. 2, 27–34 & 47–78, above n24. For academic commentary, *see, e.g.,* the sources contained in the OUP Occupation list (2017), above n7; Adam Roberts, *What is A Military Occupation?,* 55 Brit. Y.B. Int' L. 249 (1985) [*hereinafter* Roberts (1985)]; Benvenisti (2012), above n22; Commentary on Geneva Convention (IV) Relative to the Protection of Civilian Persons in Times of War (J.S. Pictet ed., 1958); Gerhard Von Glahn, Law Among Nations: An Introduction to Public International Law Ch. 25 (7th ed., 1995) [*hereinafter* Von Glahn (1995)]; Arnold Wilson, *The Laws of War in Occupied Territory,* 18 Transactions Grotius Soc'y 17 (1932) [*hereinafter* Wilson (1932)]; Allan Gerson, *Trustee-Occupant: The Legal Status of Israel's Presence in the West Bank,* 14 Harvard Int'l L. J. 1 (1973) [*hereinafter* Gerson (1973)]; Hans-Peter Gasser, *Protection of the Civilian Population,* in The Handbook of Humanitarian Law in Armed Conflicts (Dieter Fleck ed., 1999); Adam Roberts, *Prolonged Military Occupation: The Israeli-Occupied Territories Since 1967,* 84 Am. J. Int'l L. 44 (1990) [*hereinafter* Roberts (1990)]; Scheffer (2003), above n22; Ardi Imseis, *On the Fourth Geneva Convention and the Occupied Palestinian Territory,* 44 Harvard Int'l L. J. 65 (2003) [*hereinafter* Imseis (2003)]; Nehal Bhuta, *The Antinomies of Transformative Occupation,* 16 Eur. J. Int'l L. 721 (2005); Roberts (2006), above n22; Valentina Azarova, *Towards a Counter-Hegemonic Law of Occupation: On the Regulation of Predatory Interstate Acts in Contemporary International Law,* 20 Y.B. Int'l Humanitarian L. Ch. 4, 113 (2017) [*hereinafter* Azarova (2017)]; Fionnuala Ní Aoláin, *The Gender of Occupation,* 45 Yale J. Int'l L. 338 (2020) [*hereinafter* Ní Aoláin (2020)]. As for the definition of occupation implying control over non-sovereign territory, this is implicit in the treaty definitions, which describe occupation as being "of the territory of a High Contracting Party" (*i.e.* of the territory of *another* party to the treaty other than the state engaged in the occupation). 1907 Hague Regulations art. 42, above n25; First Geneva Convention art. 2, above n24; Second Geneva Convention art. 2, above n24; Third Geneva Convention art. 2, above n24; Fourth Geneva Convention art. 2, above n24. Adam Roberts states that, "[a]t the heart of treaty provisions, court decisions and legal writings about occupations is the image of the armed forces of a state exercising some kind of domination or authority over inhabited territory outside the accepted international frontiers of their State and its dependencies." Roberts (1985), above, at 300. Eyal Benvenisti defines occupation as

occupation" or the "occupied Palestinian territories" (oPt), or focusing exclusively on occupation law when it comes to the situation of Palestine and the Palestinian people, necessarily implies the following two elements. First, Israel is a state. Second, an exclusive focus on the land that is not the sovereign territory of Israel, and the people in that land, is to be adopted. The first element is essential. Occupation law only applies to states.[32] Moreover, the concept of an occupation in this law presupposes a sovereign/non-sovereign distinction regarding the status of the occupying state and the occupied territory. Palestine is only "occupied," legally, if it falls outside the sovereign territory of Israel.[33]

---

"effective control of a power (be it one or more states or an international organization, such as the United Nations) over a territory to which that power has no sovereign title." Benvenisti (2012), above n22, at 37. This non-sovereign-territory definition of occupation is presupposed by the prohibition on the annexation of territory through occupation (it is only relevant if occupied territory is not already the sovereign territory of the administering authority). This prohibition is addressed below, text accompanying n74 *et seq.* Equally, the prohibition on annexation is seen as the reason for the norms of occupation law, which, as discussed more below, are aimed at constraining the conduct of occupation in order to preserve the rights of the displaced sovereign over the territory in question. On this reason see below, text accompanying n49 *et seq.* Eyal Benvenisti states that "[t]he foundation upon which the entire law of occupation is based is the principle of inalienability of sovereignty through unilateral action of a foreign power, whether through the actual or threatened use of force ... Effective control by foreign military force can never bring about by itself a valid transfer of sovereignty." Put differently, it is *because* occupation cannot transfer sovereignty over the territory to the occupier, that "international law must regulate the inter-relationships between the occupying force ... and the local inhabitants for the duration of the occupation." *Id.*, above n22, at 42. *See also* Roberts (2006), above n22, at 582–585. The non-sovereign status of occupied territory is similarly presupposed by the conception of the relationship between occupier and occupied territory and population as one of "trust." On this, see the discussion below, text accompanying n174 *et seq.*

32  As far as occupation law presupposing that the actor engaged in the occupation is a state, this is because the relevant treaties, cited above n31, are only open to states as parties.

33  There is also the separate question of whether the treaty definition of occupation references to the territory of a "High Contracting Party" (*see* the treaty extracts above n31) limit the concept of occupation, and so the applicability of occupation law, to territory that falls under the sovereign territory of states who are contracting parties to the relevant treaties. This has potential implications for the Palestinian territories, bearing in mind their legal status. Most experts do not take the view that the legal definition of occupation has this limitation, the only issue, as far as the legal status of the territory in question is concerned, is whether or not it falls under the sovereign territory of the occupying state (and also, for some, whether or not it is inhabited by people, and whether it falls outside a state's colonial territories). *See* the general sources cited above n31; and, for examples

As for the second element, the UN, most states, and independent experts of international law, generally follow the ceasefire "green line" from the 1967 war. This determines the boundaries between the sovereign territory of Israel and potentially occupied territory.[34] Hence the focus on Gaza and the West Bank, meaning the territory of Mandatory Palestine from the west bank of the River Jordan to the green line. It therefore includes East Jerusalem, but otherwise stops at the borders of the state of Israel (West Jerusalem is a different matter, bearing in mind the "Corpus Separatum" issue).[35] Within this framing, the question is what is "occupied" of this non-sovereign territory, *i.e.*, what meets the legally required threshold of Israeli control triggering the application of occupation law.[36] The standard view is that the threshold is certainly met in all of the West Bank. There is some debate about whether Gaza, post-"withdrawal," meets the threshold.[37]

Thus, the aforementioned exclusive focus on IHL generally, and occupation law in particular, has the following effect, as Hassan Jabareen, the Director of Adalah (the Legal Center for Arab Minority Rights in Israel), pointed out at

---

    of this definition of occupation, *see* Imseis (2003), above n31, *passim*, and the quotations from Roberts (1985) and Benvenisti (2002), above n31.

34    On the legal status of the oPt, *see, e.g.,* Roberts (1990), above n31; Imseis (2003), above n31; Imseis (2018/2022), above n16, *passim*; Erakat (2019), above n16, *passim*; Benjamin Rubin, *Israel, Occupied Territories*, Max Planck Encyc. Pub. Int'l L. (Oct. 2009), https://opil .ouplaw.com/view/10.1093/law:epil/9780199231690/law-9780199231690-e1301.

35    For a review of the legal issues relating to the status of Jerusalem in general, *see, e.g.,* Antonio Cassese, *Legal Considerations on the International Status of Jerusalem*, in The Human Dimension of International Law: Selected Papers of Antonio Cassese Ch. 12 (Antonio Cassese et al. eds., 2008) (and sources cited therein). It is also addressed in the sources cited above n16. On East Jerusalem in particular, there is a question, beyond the scope of this article, as to whether or not Israel has purported to annex this territory, bearing in mind the extension of Israeli law to it (*see* Law and Administration Ordinance-Amendment No. 11 Law 5727-1967 (1967) (Isr.)); Municipalities Ordinance (Amendment No. 6) Law, 5727-1967, (1967) (Isr.)). On this question, *see* generally the aforementioned sources. For an example of the view that through the extension of its domestic law Israel has purported to annex East Jerusalem, *see* Orna Ben-Naftali, et al., *Illegal occupation: framing the occupied Palestinian territory*, 23 Berkeley J. Int'l L. 551, 573–574 (2005) [*hereinafter* Ben-Naftali et al. (2005)].

36    On the definition of occupation as far as the exercise of territorial control is concerned, *see, generally,* the sources cited above n31, in particular 1907 Hague Regulations arts. 42–43, above n25; First Geneva Convention art. 2, above n24; Second Geneva Convention art. 2, above n24; Third Geneva Convention art. 2, above n24; Fourth Geneva Convention art. 24, above n24; Roberts (1985), above n31, at 251–252, & 300.

37    *See, e.g.,* Iain Scobbie, *Gaza*, in International Law and the Classification of Conflicts 295 (Elizabeth Wilmshurst ed., 2012) (and sources cited therein).

the Al-Haq conference, and I am paraphrasing: it excludes crucial elements of the Palestinian struggle – the Nakba, the position of Palestinian people in the land between the river and the sea outside the West Bank and Gaza, and the refugees.[38] Accordingly, the focus in the case of the Jahalin is only on the situation in the West Bank, including efforts to forcibly relocate them to near the garbage dump in Abu Dis. The original displacement from al-Naqab is off the table. Amran Reshaq's wish to return is ignored.

The Palestinian struggle is legally framed in a way that excludes these aspects of it. What is claimed to be a humanitarian effort to vindicate the needs of Palestinian people in the oPt erases the struggle as it relates to all other Palestinian people, both on the other side of the green line from the oPt, and beyond.[39] It also ignores the Palestinian people in the oPt insofar as their links, including of land and property, with the other side of the green line are concerned, as in the case of the Jahalin. Put differently, the exclusive focus on the IHL/occupation framework denies, through omission, the right of return and the rights of Palestinian people on the other side of the green line from the oPt to equal treatment as citizens of Israel. More fundamentally, this framing excludes any questioning of the "green line" as an organizing principle for the question of the status of the land between the river and the sea and the people who have a relationship to it. Because occupation law's applicability presupposes Israeli statehood, invoking it as a regulatory framework effectively takes a position on this more fundamental matter, and what follows, that the horizons for Palestinian liberation are limited to the West Bank and Gaza. What is on its own terms only concerned with how Israel treats the Palestinian people in these territories has direct implications for more fundamental matters such as the one state/two state "solution."[40]

---

38    Confirmed in an email from the speaker, on file with the author and this Yearbook. *See also* Hassan Jabareen, *How the Law of Return Creates One Legal Order in Palestine*, 21 Theoretical Inquiries L. 459 (2020). On these issues and the areas of international law relevant to them, *see, e.g.,* and the sources cited therein, Yahia (1970), above n16, at 106–115 (on the Nakba and the refugees), at 115–124 (on Palestinian people within Israel); Imseis (2018/2022), above n16; Erakat (2019), above n16; and, on the refugees in particular, Francesca Albanese & Lex Takkenberg, Palestinian Refugees in International Law (2nd ed., 2020) [*hereinafter* Albanese & Takkenberg (2020)]. *See also* below, text accompanying n215 *et seq.*

39    On these themes, *see also* Darryl Li, *Occupation Law and the One-State Reality*, Jadaliyya (Aug. 2, 2011) [*hereinafter* Li (2011)], https://www.jadaliyya.com/Details/24275/Occupation-Law-and-the-One-State-Reality.

40    On further aspects of the problematic nature of starting in 1967, and "the exclusion of 1948," *see* the critique in: Nimer Sultany, *International Law's Indeterminacy and 1948*

## USING THE MASTER'S TOOLS TO DISMANTLE THE MASTER'S HOUSE                    15

Thus an Amnesty International UK webpage on the Palestinian situation asks readers to "HELP END THE 50 YEAR OPPRESSION OF PALESTINIANS."[41] It boasts that "When we see people suffering, we don't back down – we act."[42] This action is described as "campaigning hard to end the human rights abuses suffered by Palestinians under the Israeli occupation for the last 50 years."[43] Such a timeframe and related exclusive focus on the "occupation" ignores or necessarily assumes as settled all that happened prior to 1967. Moreover, it limits the focus from the entire land from the river to the sea to whatever was left of this land after the creation of Israel in 1948. It reflects how, as Samera Esmeir observed at the Muwatin conference, "the project of human rights has configured the horizons of political and ethical possibilities under conditions of colonial destruction, [and] has charted new itineraries for political life by diminishing the pursuit of collective freedom adequate to a non-colonial future."[44] In its general statement about IHRL forming the "bedrock" of all Amnesty International campaigning, Amnesty International UK insists on the relevance of the UDHR as an instrument to guide Amnesty International's work despite the long passage of time ("although it is now over 60 years old this document remains fundamental to our work").[45] However, it is not prepared to adopt a similar time span – indeed, the same time span, since the beginning of the Nakba and the creation of Israel, on the one hand, and the adoption of the UDHR, on the other hand, happened in the same year – when then it conducts this work in relation to Israel and Palestine.

Moreover, even within the distorted focus exclusively on the occupation and the territory and people covered by that, the exclusive IHL/occupation *law* approach is only concerned with the "humanitarian" conditions in the oPt. As will be explained, the occupation itself is not placed into question. Whereas Israel's position as a state has been affirmed, Israel's right to control the oPt has not been questioned. Occupation law, then, requires Palestinian people to affirm Israeli statehood in order to invoke a regulatory regime that

---

*Palestine: two comments on Aeyal Gross's The Writing on the Wall*, 6 London Rev. Int'l L. 315, 320–324 (2018).

41     Amnesty International UK (2019), above n10 (emphasis in original).

42     *Id.*

43     *Id.*

44     Samera Esmeir, paper presented at the Muwatin conference (unpublished), on file with the author.

45     Amnesty International UK (2018), above n9. This statement could be found on the website at the time of writing, 2021, which is, of course, more than 70 years since the UDHR was adopted (the Muwatin conference commemorated the 70th anniversary).

is not concerned with the corresponding question of their own right to collective freedom.

IHL, including occupation law, regulates war/occupation when it happens.[46] It does not also challenge the legitimacy of occupation itself – whether it should be in existence. It is presumably for this reason that at the Al-Haq conference, Munir Nusseibeih of Al Quds University said, to paraphrase: occupation is not illegal, it is simply regulated by international law.[47]

Some have tried to challenge this by arguing that the law of occupation rules out a "prolonged occupation."[48] This argument proceeds as follows. Occupation law addresses a situation after war, when a victorious state ends up in control of the defeated state's territory.[49] The situation has to be regulated, it is said, to ensure that the rights of the temporarily displaced sovereign are preserved.[50] A regime is introduced to preserve the *status quo* and provide basic guarantees, until the displaced sovereign returns, and the occupation ends. All of this assumes it is a temporary situation.[51] Some take the existence of this assumption to conclude that, given that a prolonged occupation would operate contrary to it, such an occupation would be illegal in occupation law.[52]

However, just because those who sought to regulate occupations saw such occupations as temporary does not mean that the temporary nature of occupations is thereby rendered legally obligatory by that regulatory framework. This is a *non sequitur*, transforming a regulatory regime only concerned with the operation of occupations into one that also addresses the existential matter of whether occupations should be in existence. The requirement that an occupation be temporary arises out of the entitlements of the displaced sovereign in *general international law* to resume control of its territory, and the limits of the

---

46   *See* the sources cited above n7 & n31.

47   Confirmed in an email from the speaker, on file with the author and this Yearbook. *See also* the reported comments by Allegra Pacheco, in: 2014 Birzeit Conference, above n16.

48   *See, e.g.*, in the context of the oPt, Ben-Naftali et al. (2005), above n35. *But see* below when it comes to their proposal for how the Israeli occupation might end, text accompanying n159.

49   *See* the sources cited above n7 & n31. For a discussion about this aspect, *see, e.g.*, Ben-Naftali et al. (2005), above n35, at 592 *et seq.*

50   *Id.*

51   *Id.* In the words of Benvenisti: "Because occupation does not amount to sovereignty, the occupation is also limited in time and the occupant has only temporary managerial powers, for the period until a peaceful solution is reached. During that limited period, the occupant administers the territory on behalf of the sovereign." Benvenisti (2012), above n22, at 6. On temporariness, *see also* Ben-Naftali et al. (2005), above n35; Salvatore Nicolosi, *The Law of Military Occupation and the Role of De Jure and De Facto Sovereignty*, 31 Polish Y.B. Int'l L. 165 (2011).

52   This is seemingly the argument put forward by Ben-Naftali et al. (2005), above n35.

belligerent occupant's right to prevent this, which are determined by a test set by the *international law on the use of force* – the *jus ad bellum*. These normative considerations will be returned to in the next two sections. Treating the *in bello* regime of occupation law as if it had *ad bellum* characteristics in this way is to make a category error.

But might, at least, the full implementation of IHL including occupation law remove any benefits to an occupier derived from continuing the occupation?[53] So, for example, in the case of Palestine, what if the settlements were removed, there was proper freedom of movement for Palestinian people, the end of resource exploitation etc.?[54] Would this eliminate the advantages Israel gained from the occupation? In particular, Israel would no longer be able to create "facts on the ground" to assist it in successfully asserting/acquiring sovereignty over parts of the West Bank. Israel would also be prevented from doing things understood to constitute the *de facto* exercise of sovereignty (annexation is addressed in the next section). It might be suggested that although occupation law does not directly require an occupation to end, the things it *does* require directly of the occupying state might have an indirect effect in removing the advantages, for sovereignty-asserting/annexationist ambitions, gained through maintaining the occupation. If so, when it comes to how occupation law does or does not address the existential legitimacy of the occupation, the issue might be not only whether this is covered by some sort of implied rule based on the temporary nature of occupations. It might also be a matter of the constructive effect of the obligations being fully complied with.

The significance of compliance in this regard is potentially illustrated by the occupation of Iraq. There, the CPA, through which the US and the UK conducted the occupation, aimed at the economic, political and legal transformation of the country – "transformatory occupation."[55] Key changes would be made, notably concerning how natural resources would be exploited and owned. Administrative authority would then be transferred to the Iraqi people. The US and the UK separately, and as part of the UN Security Council

---

53 I am grateful to Anna Mykytenko of the NGO Global Rights Compliance, based in Ukraine (the subject of another occupation, that of Crimea by Russia) who raised this point and discussed it with me at the Al-Haq conference.

54 On the rules of occupation law relevant to these practices, *see, generally*, n31; and, on the settlements in particular, *see* Fourth Geneva Convention art. 49, above n24; and, as far as violations concerning settlements constituting war crimes, *see* Rome Statute of the International Criminal Court art. 8.2.b.viii, July 1, 2002, 2187 U.N.T.S. 3, as amended (through resolution RC/Res.6 of June 11, 2010) [*hereinafter* Rome Statute].

55 On the occupation of Iraq generally, including commentators who use the "transformatory occupation" term, *see* the sources cited above n22.

(UNSC), acknowledged that this was an occupation, thereby accepting that occupation law applied to it.[56] Some legal experts working for those states, and some academic commentators, identified this law as an impediment to the intended changes, given its general "preserving the status quo" orientation.[57] It was argued that there was a need to move "beyond occupation law."[58] They expressed concern that if this law was followed, the changes would not be possible.[59] The objective served by maintaining the occupation beyond a short period necessary to transfer power to the Iraqi people – to profoundly alter the economic and political character of the state – would be legally impermissible. We might see in these arguments compliance with occupation law being understood as significant to the existential question of the duration and termination of an occupation.

As two (permanent) members of the UNSC, the US and the UK were able to work within that body to pass resolutions that supposedly gave them the authority to engage in the transformation of Iraq.[60] This process was, moreover, discussed as potentially, through the operation of the trumping norm in UN Charter article 103, somehow modifying any inconsistent norms of occupation law.[61] There is much that could be said about what was intended in and/or what the legal effects of this process were.[62] For present purposes, the example is given to illustrate how occupation law can be viewed as an impediment to doing the sorts of things that would have necessitated prolonging that occupation.[63]

However, the crucial difference between the occupation of Iraq, and the Israeli occupation of the Palestinian territories, is that the US and the UK did not aspire to formally incorporate Iraqi territory into their sovereign territory. They wanted to transform its economic and political system only. Without an ability to do this, there would have been little purpose served by maintaining control beyond the time it took to temporarily fill the vacuum in

---

56    *See* S.C. Res. 1483 (May 22, 2003), pmbl., referencing the US and UK as "occupying powers" and being in receipt of a letter from these states acknowledging this.

57    *See, e.g.,* Scheffer (2003), above n22.

58    *Id.*

59    On the broader question of what is permitted by way of transformation under occupation law, *see* the sources cited above n31; and, in particular, Benvenisti (2012), above n22, Ch. 4; Roberts (1985), above n31.

60    *See, e.g.,* S.C. Res. 1483 (2003), above n56, *op cit.*

61    *See, e.g.,* the authorities cited above n22.

62    . *Id.*

63    Whether it actually has this effect is a subject of debate. On this, *see, e.g.,* the sources cited above n22 & n31.

# USING THE MASTER'S TOOLS TO DISMANTLE THE MASTER'S HOUSE 19

governance created by their removal of Saddam Hussein, before handing over to local representatives.

When, however, a state has sovereignty-related ambitions, as with Israel, Morocco (in Western Sahara), Russia (in Crimea), and, in the period between 1975 and 1999, Indonesia (in East Timor), the situation is different.[64] Full compliance with occupation law would remove the ability to alter facts on the ground in order to support these ambitions, *e.g.* implanting settlements. But there would still be a purpose served in maintaining the occupation itself – "facts on the ground" in a more elemental sense – for leverage purposes to gain an advantage when the question of sovereignty was being addressed. Similarly, insofar as ensuring security for Israel is a factor, maintaining an occupation even when complying fully with occupation law serves a purpose.[65]

Here, the contrast with Gaza is instructive. Israel withdrew its "boots on the ground" presence because it did not want the territory and could maintain its security through the siege and control exercised by air, sea, and at the borders.[66] The West Bank is the subject of territorial sovereignty assertions/ aspirations and is understood to pose a different security proposition.[67]

It is not possible, therefore, to place faith in the notion that full compliance with occupation law would somehow necessarily end the conditions that incentivize Israel to maintain the occupation in order to further its sovereignty-related aspirations.

Indeed, treating the situation as one of "occupation" governed by occupation law can be advantageous to Israel, given that its sovereignty aspirations relating to the West Bank have to reckon with the existence of the Palestinian population there.[68] A formal annexation of the entire West Bank would necessarily raise the question of granting those people Israeli citizenship. Doing this would place the sustainability of the majority-Jewish character of Israel

---

64  On Morocco and Western Sahara, *see* the sources cited above n19. On Russia and Crimea, *see* the source cited above n21. On Indonesia and East Timor, *see* the sources cited above n20.

65  In Iraq, the US and UK pursued their security objectives through a continued military presence after handing over formal administrative control to local representatives. "Consent" for this presence was supposedly provided by those representatives, whose position as such owed much to what happened during the formally proclaimed occupation period. The continued presence may actually have constituted occupation either generally or in parts of the country. *See, e.g.*, S.C. Res. 1546 (June 8, 2004), *passim*; and more broadly the commentary above n22.

66  On this, *see* the source cited above n37 (and further citations contained therein).

67  Annexation is addressed in the following section.

68  On these issues, *see also* Li (2011), above n39.

under strain. The alternative would be to conduct mass forcible expulsions, as in 1948; or to treat the people as second-class persons without citizenship, *i.e.* an apartheid regime, as in Israel's treatment of Palestinian people in (potentially purportedly annexed) East Jerusalem.[69] In contrast, treating the situation as an occupation (outside East Jerusalem, if Israel has purported to annex that area) enables Israel's exercise of control over an inhabited territory to avoid these challenging alternatives. It provides a patina of basic protections to the subordinated population and "humanizes" this subordination without affording equal rights. Israel can then benefit from the "facts on the ground" advantage for its sovereignty claims that such control provides. It could pave the way for "land for peace" swaps involving the depopulation of some of this territory of its Palestinian population and the conferral of Israeli sovereignty over that territory.

To address the existential question of bringing occupations to an end, it is necessary to *depart* from occupation law;[70] to go "beyond" it, as certain commentators wanted to do in Iraq. But not, as in that case, to enable a different, "transformatory" occupation. Rather, to be able to make arguments that would transform the situation triggering the application of occupation law – the occupation itself – to one of liberation. Sticking only to the frame of reference covered by occupation law necessarily means addressing only how "humanitarian" occupations are. It is not possible to address whether and when they should end. The debate is only about the merits and legality of "transformatory" occupation. It is not a discussion about whether occupation itself can be "transformed" out of existence.

---

69 On apartheid, *see* below n113. On the question of whether Israel has purported to annex East Jerusalem, *see* above n35.

70 See also Azarova 2017, above n31. Hani Sayed also argues that there are other reasons why the focus on occupation/occupation law is a distraction, rooted in the problematic way it characterizes the situation faced by the Palestinian people in their relations with Israel. Sayed (2014), above n16. At the end of his piece, Sayed states: "The challenge is ultimately to imagine a legal framework for understanding the situation in the WBGS [West Bank and Gaza Strip] that does not link the Palestinian right to self-determination to the law of occupation." *Id.*, at 148–149. For different, complementary reasons, I am also arguing herein about the problems of linking the self-determination of the Palestinian people to the law of occupation. But also, more broadly, I am suggesting some of the problems in seeking to approach self-determination through any legal framework, insofar as the options for such a framework are those that exist within international law as currently conceived. And, relatedly, I am concerned with some of the problems with the focus only on the "WBGS" when it comes to the question of the self-determination of the Palestinian people. For additional analysis on further problems with the focus on IHL, and on law generally, *see* Reynolds (2015), above n16.

Two areas of international law do, it is claimed, speak to the existential legitimacy of the occupation in the oPt: the law on the use of armed force and self-determination. The following sections address each in turn.

## III    Law on the Use of Force, Including Its Interface with the Law on Title to Territory

The existential legitimacy of war, including the conduct of associated military occupation, is the subject of the "law on the use of force" – the *jus ad bellum*.[71] Israel's presence in the oPt stems from the 1967 war, and is, therefore, a "belligerent" occupation and falls to be determined, as a use of force, under this legal framework.[72] Legality depends on two factors. In the first place, (a), is whether there is a legally-acceptable "just cause," defined as the existence of particular type of threat and/or use of force necessitating a defensive response involving the threat/use of force.[73] In the second place, (b), is whether the defensive response taken is a necessary and proportionate means of responding to that threat/use of force. Before turning to this as a general matter, it is necessary to addresses the related question of the legitimacy of that which the occupation is commonly associated, as reflected in the title of the Al-Haq conference: annexation of all or part of the oPt.

Annexation – the acquisition of title over territory whether or not that territory is the sovereign territory of another state – is not a legally-acceptable "just cause" under (a).[74] Thus, the use of force – including an occupation – for this purpose is illegal *ab initio*. Relatedly, the use of force cannot by itself be the

---

71    On the law on the use of force, *see* Michael Wood, *Use of Force, Prohibition of Threat*, Max Planck Encyc. Pub. Int'l L. (June 2013) (and sources cited therein), https://opil.ouplaw.com/view/10.1093/law:epil/9780199231690/law-9780199231690-e428; OUP UoF list (2020), above n6; Christine D. Gray, International Law and the Use of Force (4th ed., 2018) [*hereinafter* Gray (2018)] (and sources cited therein).

72    *See* the sources cited above n31 & n34.

73    Note the emphasis here is on "legally-acceptable" in order not to confuse this requirement with what might be understood to be justified through a (potentially broader) non-legal "just war" theory.

74    Because it is absent from the permitted bases for using force and is, indeed, embedded in the prohibition on the use of force (*cf.* the reference to "territorial integrity" in UN Charter art. 2(4)). *See* the sources cited in: OUP UoF list (2020), above n6; and, in particular, Sharon Korman, The Right of Conquest: The Acquisition of Territory by Force in International Law and Practice (1996) [*hereinafter* Korman (1996)]; and below, the following note.

basis for the acquisition of territory (again, whether or not that territory is the sovereign territory of another state), what is referred to as "conquest" or "subjugation" under the law of title to territory. In the words of the UNSC, it is "inadmissible," *i.e.*, any claim to title over territory made on this basis is invalid.[75]

---

75  *See, e.g.*, the following statements made by the UNSC in the particular context of the oPt: "inadmissibility of the acquisition of territory by war" (S.C. Res. 242 (Nov. 22, 1967), pmbl.); the "acquisition of territory by military conquest is inadmissible" (S.C. Res. 298 (Sep. 25, 1971), pmbl.); the "acquisition of territory by force is inadmissible" (S.C. Res. 476 (June 30, 1980), pmbl.); the "inadmissibility of the acquisition of territory by force" (S.C. Res. 2334 (Dec. 23, 2016), pmbl.). The Friendly Relations and Co-operation Declaration of the UNGA asserted that "no territorial acquisition resulting from the threat or use of force shall be recognized as legal". G.A. Res. 2625(XXV), *Declaration on Principles of International Law concerning Friendly Relations and Co-operation among States in accordance with the Charter of the United Nations* (Oct. 24, 1970). This statement was affirmed in the context of the Israeli occupation of the Palestinian Territories in the Wall Advisory Opinion, where the ICJ describes it as a "corollary" to the "principles as to the use of force," "entailing the illegality of territorial acquisition resulting from the threat or use of force." Legal Consequences of the Construction of a Wall in the Occupied Palestinian Territories, Advisory Opinion, 2004 I.C.J. Rep 136 (July 9), para. 87 [*hereinafter* ICJ Wall Advisory Opinion]. Article 4 of the CSCE Helsinki Final Act proclaimed that "the participating States will ... refrain from making each other's territory ... the object of acquisition by means of [occupation]. No such ... acquisition will be recognized as legal." Conference on Security and Co-operation in Europe, Helsinki Final Act, Aug. 21, 1975, 14 I.L.M. 1292, 1294–1295 [*hereinafter* Helsinki Final Act]. For academic authority, *see, e.g.*, Robert Y. Jennings, The Acquisition of Territory in International Law (1963/2017), 2017 reprint, section IV, at 68–85 [*hereinafter* Jennings (1963/2017)]; W. Schätzel, *Die Annexation im Völkerrecht*, 2 Archiv des Völkerrechts 1 (1949); Hoffman (2020), above n19; Roberts (2006), above n22, at 582–585; Korman (1996), above n74. For academic authority specifically on annexation and the West Bank, *see Open Letter to the Israeli Government Condemning Annexation by International Law Scholars*, Opinio Juris (June 11, 2020) [*hereinafter* Annexation Letter (2020)], http://opiniojuris.org/2020/06/11/an-open-letter-to-the-israeli-government-con demning-annexation/. For Robbie Jennings, because of the legal prohibition on the use of force, "it seems impossible ... to concede that the successful seizure of another's territory by force, i.e. conquest, or subjugation, may be itself a lawful title to the territory." Jennings (1963/2017), at 84. In the words of Masaharu Yanagihara, "conquest is incompatible with the prohibition of the use of force in international relations." OUP Territorial Title list (2016), above n6. Eyal Benvenisti describes the position as "the principle of inalienability of sovereignty through unilateral action of a foreign power, whether through the actual or threatened use of force ... Effective control by foreign military force can never bring about by itself a valid transfer of sovereignty." Benvenisti, above n22, at 42. *See also, id.*, at 169. As indicated by the language of "another's territory," "conquest," and "sovereignty" used by Jennings, Yanagihara, and Benvenisti, the implication of these positions on the non-forcible-annexation of title to territory is that the territory in question is either the sovereign territory of another state (or more than one state), or a non-state territory that is not *terra nullius* and so where the rights of the local population to self-determination would be a bar. This is addressed further below, text accompanying n138. In the law of title to territory, the term "occupation" is used to denote a head of title based on effective

## USING THE MASTER'S TOOLS TO DISMANTLE THE MASTER'S HOUSE 23

This is the case even if the use of force/occupation might be lawful as a matter of the law of self-defense (to be addressed further below).[76]

Thus, the designation of the Palestinian Territories as "occupied" has two cumulative effects. Impliedly, the territories are not the sovereign territory of Israel. Consequently, the law on the use of force prevents Israel from founding a legally valid claim to sovereignty based on the control exercised over the territories. Moreover, it prohibits Israel from conducting the occupation on the basis of founding such a claim. Put more simply, an assertion of annexation based on the occupation would be both illegal (as a prohibited use of force) and without legal effect, as far as territorial acquisition is concerned. (It is important to acknowledge that this presupposes that the territories do not form part of territory which Israel either enjoys or somehow has the right to enjoy title over. Annexation is a matter of forming a new root to title, not asserting control over territory in relation to which the state already has or is entitled to title).[77]

As with occupation law, this legal position on annexation presupposes that the relevant areas of international law – the law on the use of force, and the law on title to territory – apply to Israel as a state. To make these arguments about the illegality of annexation is to presuppose Israeli statehood and the "green line" framework. Necessarily, the exclusive focus on Israel annexing new territory is not concerned with other matters such as Palestinian return to the land that since 1948 has been in the territory of Israel. For the Jahalin, then, Israel is prevented from annexing the land on which Khan Al-Ahmar is located (*e.g.* as part of a broader move encompassing the surrounding settlements). Amran Reshaq's concern to return to al-Naqab is not addressed.

---

      control of *terra nullius*. *See. e.g.*, Jennings (1962/2017), above n75, at 33–37. The significance of this is addressed below, text accompanying n138.

76    Jennings (1963/2017), above n75, at 71–72. In the words of Christine Gray, "the use of force in self-defence has not been accepted as a valid root of title to territory." Gray (2018), at 164 (citing Jennings (1963/2017), the 1963 publication, at 203 (in the 2017 reprint, the book only has 160 pages – the relevant pages on this point are cited at the start of this note); Korman (1996), above n74; Allan Gerson, Israel, The West Bank And International Law (1978) [*hereinafter* Gerson (1978)].

77    In the words of Robbie Jennings, "although closely linked ... title and the use of illegal force are distinct questions ... the putative aggressor may be in fact the one who is entitled;" Jennings (1963/2017), above n75, at 85. *See also, id.*, at 82–84. Thus, to apply this framework it is necessary, for example, to have rejected the notion that, via the Balfour Declaration and the League of Nations Mandate Agreement for Palestine the entire territory of Mandatory Palestine (so including the oPt) was somehow determined to be allocated to the future state of Israel, and that this determination was internationally-legally-effective, and in operation with such legal status on and after 1967.

Robbie Jennings, a canonical authority on this area of international law, once posed the following question in relation to a situation where a state retains control over territory captured in war: "is there any point in denying title to the thief if there is little hope of being able to deny him the thing itself?."[78] Jennings posed this question to highlight the problem of the lack of enforcement of the prohibition of force-enabled annexation. This is clearly relevant to the Israel-Palestine situation. That said, his question, as befits the context of a study of title to territory, discusses only *title* as that which could determine the legitimacy of the control exercised over the "thing." However, there is an alternative potential basis for such legitimacy, which, moreover, presupposes that the territory is indeed not the sovereign territory of the state concerned. This covers all of the West Bank, not just the part(s) that Israel may have purported to annex. It is the right of self-defense.[79] Even if Israel cannot annex all or part of the West Bank through the occupation (which would transform legally the legitimacy of Israel's control to that conducted by a state within its own territory), this is not by itself necessarily dispositive of the legality of Israel's exercise of control there.

Self-defense has been a justification for the occupation put forward by Israel.[80] However, commentary on the legality of the occupation tends to ignore the relevance of the law on the use of force (other than as far as annexation is concerned).[81] Or, to invoke this area of law, only to then dismiss its relevance (other than to annexation).[82] Or, to address the occupation's legality in these terms in a cursory fashion.[83]

---

78  *Id.*, 76–77.

79  Or authorization by the UNSC, which is not relevant to the occupation of Palestine. The potential significance of UNSC Resolution 242 is addressed below n100. On UNSC-authorized force, *see* the sources contained in OUP UoF list (2020), above n6. On the link between lawful use of force and occupation, *see, e.g.*, Stephen M. Schwebel, *What Weight to Conquest?*, 64 Am. J. Int'l L. 344 (1970) [*hereinafter* Schwebel (1970)]. On the subject of the self-defense right and the occupation, *see, e.g.*, sources in the following fns, and Yahia (1970), above n16, at 147–77 & 184; John Quigley, *The Oslo Accords: International Law and the Israeli-Palestinian Peace Agreements*, 25 Suffolk Transnat'l L. Rev. 73, 81 (2001); Imseis (2020), above n16, at 1073 (and sources cited therein).

80  On Israel invoking self-defense to justify the occupation, *see, e.g.*, Antonio Cassese, Self-Determination of Peoples: A Legal Reappraisal 235 (1995) [*hereinafter* Cassese (1995)] (and sources cited therein).

81  *See, e.g.*, 2014 Birzeit Conference; and Reynolds (2015), both above n16.

82  *See, e.g.*, Ben-Naftali et al. (2005), above n35, in particular at 559, 573, & 613.

83  *See, e.g.*, Yael Ronen, *Illegal Occupation and its Consequences*, 41 Isr. L. Rev. 201, 242 (2008) (Ronen 2008) ("With respect to Israel, there is at least a credible claim that the occupation was a result of lawful action in self-defense"). A notable exception to the foregoing approaches is Azarova (2017), above n31.

It is helpful to divide the occupation into two phases. The first phase covers the existence of a threat giving rise to a legally valid right to self-defense (issue (a)) existing when the occupation commenced in 1967. If not in existence, then the occupation was unlawful *ab initio* because of a legally invalid *casus bellum*.[84] If in existence, this had to justify, as necessary and proportionate, introducing plenary military occupation of the entire West Bank (issue (b)).[85] If the occupation was unnecessary and disproportionate, then (again) it was unlawful *ab initio*. The second phase covers the period after the initial introduction of the occupation to today. For the occupation to be lawful during this second, 50-plus year phase, the original threat, and/ or another threat also falling within the boundaries of that which justifies recourse to force in self-defense (again, issue (a)), has to be in operation.[86] If this is the

---

84    Thus, the UNGA, having defined aggression, explains the types of acts that can qualify for this if they meet the definition, and includes "[t]he invasion or attack by the armed forces of a State of the territory of another State, or any military occupation, however temporary, resulting from such invasion or attack." G.A. Res. 3314 (XXIX), *Definition of Aggression* (Dec. 14, 1974), art. 3(a). This formulation was adopted when aggression was eventually defined for the purposes of the crime of aggression under the Rome Statute for the ICC. *See* Rome Statute art. 8 *bis*, para. 2(a), above n54. The Helsinki Final Act art. 4 proclaimed that "[t]he participating States will refrain from making each other's territory the object of military occupation or other direct or indirect measures of force in contravention of international law.... No such occupation ... will be recognized as legal," Helsinki Final Act, above n75. Eyal Benvenisti characterizes the occupations by the Axis powers before and during so-called World War II as illegal "predicated on the aggression" (*i.e.* illegal use of force) "that led to the occupation," Benvenisti (2012), above n22, at 140. Reviewing the changes in international law on the use of force, Benvenisti observes that "the outlawing of war rendered illegal the occupation that resulted from an act of aggression." *Id.*, at 167–168 (fn omitted referencing the foregoing definition of aggression and proclamation from the Helsinki Final Act),

85    So, for example, in the context of the occupation, writing in 1970 Steven Schwebel observes: "A state acting in lawful exercise of its right of self-defense may seize and occupy foreign territory *as long as such seizure and occupation are necessary to its self-defense*." Schwebel (1970), above n79, at 345 (emphasis added). But see what is covered below when it comes to the test Schwebel articulates in the context of a continued occupation, below n95. As is sometimes evident in analysis on the use of force generally, some commentators miss this second stage of the analysis, focusing only on the legally-permissible "just cause" element. *See e.g.*, Michael Curtis, *International Law and the Territories*, 32 Harvard Int'l L. J. 457, 464 (1991) [*hereinafter* Curtis (1991)].

86    There is a debate as to whether and to what extent Israel has a right of self-defense in relation to threats emanating from the Palestinian territories, bearing in mind the legal status of those territories, and the non-state character (if that is indeed correct) of the actors in them Israel claims poses the threat. This debate came to prominence with the dicta of the ICJ in the *Wall* Advisory Opinion which potentially had implications for it. *See* ICJ Wall Advisory Opinion, above n75, para. 139; *id.*, separate opinions of Judge Buergenthal (para. 6), Judge Higgins (paras. 33–35), and Judge Kooijmans (para. 35). The

case, the plenary occupation has to be a necessary and proportionate response to this threat/these threats. Moreover, both these requirements (the threat, and the necessity of the occupation as a response) need to be evident in a *continuous, unbroken state* for the entire period.

International law experts, and most states, tend to regard as implausible the idea that prolonged occupations, such as those covering the second phase, can ever be justified according to this framework. Including, notably, when it comes to the requirements of necessity and proportionality. Christine Gray, for example, reports that "[n]ecessity and proportionality are ... crucial in the rejection by states of the legality of prolonged occupation of territory in the name of self-defence."[87]

Indeed, it is not credible to regard the occupation as a necessary and proportionate means of ensuring Israel's security, as far as the legitimate imperatives of security are concerned and how they are accounted for in the legal test. These imperatives could be achieved through considerably less extreme measures.[88] Securing them through occupation is excessive, and therefore unnecessary. Thus, the second phase of the occupation, from its introduction to today, has been and is unlawful under the law on the use of force.[89] As such, it meets the definition of aggression.[90] Notably, the UN General Assembly (UNGA) has frequently condemned the continued occupation as a violation of the UN Charter and the principles of international law.[91]

---

issue of whether there is a right of self-defense against non-state actors is of broader relevance and was similarly prominent contemporaneously to the ICJ's pronouncement in the Wall Advisory Opinion in the context of the military action taken by the US against Al Qaeda as part of the "war on terror" following the attacks on the US in 2001. These issues are beyond the scope of the present article (for a discussion of them see the sources in OUP UoF list (2020), above n6). For the sake of addressing all potential justifications Israel might have to maintain the occupation based on the right of self-defense, the present analysis assumes that such a right could arise in the context of threats from non-state actors emanating from occupied territory.

87     Gray (2018), above n71, at 164. *See also* the quotation from S.C. Res. 476, below n101, and the observations by Cassese quoted below, text accompanying n143.

88     On the relevant legal framework, *see* sources contained in the OUP UoF list (2020), above n6. For an application to this situation reaching the same conclusion, *see, e.g.*, Richard Falk & Burns Weston, *The Relevance of International Law to Israeli and Palestinian Rights in the West Bank and Gaza* 32 Harvard Int'l L. J. 129, 148–149 (1991).

89     Quite apart from whether or not the first phase was or was not lawful; on which, *see* the sources cited above n79.

90     On an unlawful occupation in use of force terms constituting aggression, *see* the sources cited above n6, n71 & n84. On the link to the individual crime of aggression, *see* Rome Statute art. 8 *bis*, para. 1, above n54, and below n109.

91     *See* the review and citations in Imseis (2020), above n16, at 1069–1070. Note also quotation from S.C. Res. 476, below n101.

USING THE MASTER'S TOOLS TO DISMANTLE THE MASTER'S HOUSE          27

It is sometimes suggested that an occupation that was initially lawful as a means of self-defense can somehow then remain lawful pending the adoption of peace settlement/agreement.[92] Certain commentators even suggest that the occupation can be maintained until an agreement is adopted which goes beyond the specific defensive needs justifying it originally, encompassing the more general security needs of the occupying state, and/or broader matters that have security and other important implications, such as delimiting disputed borders.[93] These approaches are sometimes linked to a doctrine of justifying the use of force pre-emptively, not to deal with an actual/imminent/ongoing threat but, rather, to prevent such a threat from arising.[94] This doctrine enables Israel to maintain control until an agreement provides an alternative means of preventing future threats.[95]

In his treatment of the oPt, in a section entitled "Is there an obligation to end the occupation?" Eyal Benvenisti asks

> Does the occupant have the right to retain control over the occupied territory until its conditions for a peaceful arrangement are met? Does it have a duty to relinquish control under certain circumstances? Ultimately, the question is, upon whom does the burden of breaking political stalemate lie when negotiations for peace fail?[96]

---

92   Writing in 1970 about the occupation of the Palestinian territories, Rosalyn Higgins states: "there is nothing in either the Charter or general international law which leads one to suppose that military occupation, pending a peace treaty, is illegal. The Allies, it will be recalled, did not claim title to Berlin in 1945; but neither did they withdraw immediately [after] they had entered it." Rosalyn Higgins, *The Place of International Law in the Settlement of Disputes by the Security Council*, 64 Am. J. Int'l L. 8 (1970), reproduced in Rosalyn Higgins, Themes and Theories 181 (2009) (of the reproduced version). Meir Shamgar stated that "pending an alternative political or military solution [occupation] ... could, from a legal point of view, continue indefinitely." Meir Shamgar, *Legal Concepts and Problems of the Israeli Military Government – The Initial Stage*, in Military Government in the Territories Administrated by Israel 1967–1980 43 (Meir Shamgar ed., 1982). *See also* Schwebel (1970), above n79, at 344–346 (discussed further below, n95, n101, & n103).

93   *See, e.g.*, Curtis (1991), above n85, at 464–465.

94   On this issue, *see* the works listed in OUP UoF list (2020), above n6.

95   Following on from his affirmation in 1970, in the context of the Israeli occupation, that self-defense can justify the occupation of territory, quoted above in n85, Steven Schwebel stated that "[a]s a condition of its withdrawal from [occupied] territory, [the occupying] state may require the institution of security measures reasonably designed to ensure that that territory shall not again be used to mount a threat or use of force against it of such a nature as to justify exercise of self-defense." Schwebel (1970), above n79, at 345–346.

96   Benvenisti (2012), above n22, at 244.

The final question implies that, indeed, the right or otherwise to maintain an occupation might be determined by whether or not a peace agreement is reached.[97] Benvenisti takes this view by observing that "[n]either the Hague Regulations nor the [the Fourth Geneva Convention of 1949] limits the duration of the occupation or requires the occupant to restore the territories to the sovereign before a peace treaty is signed" (*id.*).

Given that occupation law (the treaties being referred to) regulates occupations when they happen, rather than addressing their existential legitimacy, this is to be expected. The issue is what the law on the use of force would have to say on the matter. Benvenisti quotes the 1948 Hersch Lauterpacht version of *Oppenheim's International Law*, that

> If a belligerent succeeds in occupying the whole, or even a part, of enemy territory, he has realized a very important aim of warfare. He can now not only use the resources of the enemy country for military purposes, *but can also keep it for the time being as a pledge of his military success, and thereby impress upon the enemy the necessity of submitting to terms of peace ...*[98]

Eyal Benvenisti mentions UNSC Resolution 242 (1967), suggesting that, given that the resolution mentions withdrawal as an element of establishing a "just and lasting peace" in the Middle East, it is therefore in line with this "position."[99] But the resolution doesn't stipulate that the occupation can be maintained until a "just and lasting peace" has been reached in the Middle East, nor does it purport to give Israel the authority to maintain it.[100]

---

97    Elsewhere, Benvenisti states that "because occupation does not amount to sovereignty, the occupation is also limited in time and the occupant has only temporary managerial powers, for the period until a peaceful solution is reached." Benvenisti (2012), above n22, at 6 (emphasis added).

98    Hersch Lauterpacht, Oppenheim's International Law 432 (7th ed. 1948) (emphasis as added by Benvenisti, in *id.*, at 245). Benvenisti's treatment of an earlier version of the same quotation is discussed below, text accompanying n162.

99    *Id.* S.C. Res. 242 (1970), above n75.

100   In the resolution, the UNSC affirms that: "the fulfilment of Charter principles requires the establishment of a just and lasting peace in the Middle East which should include the application of both the following principles: (i) Withdrawal of Israel armed forces from territories occupied in the recent conflict (ii) Termination of all claims or states of belligerency and respect for and acknowledgment of the sovereignty, territorial integrity, and political independence of every State in the area and their right to live in peace within secure and recognized boundaries free from threats or acts of force." S.C. Res. 242 (1970), above n75, para. 1. Here, the UNSC is merely stating that a "just and lasting peace" would require both an end to the occupation and the resolution of all the matters in

# USING THE MASTER'S TOOLS TO DISMANTLE THE MASTER'S HOUSE 29

Appraising the "position" more generally: it would only be lawful if the conditions for lawful self-defense necessitating the occupation are and continue to be met.[101] Understanding the duration of an occupation as contingent on the adoption of a peace agreement is only legally possible if, separately, and in any case, the occupation remains justified according to the *ad bellum* test. A right to use force, including to conduct an occupation, is determined by the nature of the threat only, not also the presence or absence of a peace agreement. To be sure, an agreement can remove the threat. The ending of the threat and the adoption of the agreement can amount to the same thing. But if the threat is no longer present, either at all, or in in a manner that justifies, as necessary and proportionate, a use of force involving an occupation, there is no longer a lawful basis for the occupation, *even if no peace agreement has been reached*. At that point, the occupant has no "right to retain control" and

---

the second sub-paragraph. It does not follow from this that the occupation can therefore continue *until* there is the "just and lasting peace" that also covers the resolution of all the matters in the second sub-paragraph. Or, put differently, that in the absence of any of the elements a "just and lasting peace" it requires as set out in the second sub-paragraph, an absence of the element it sets out in the first sub-paragraph – the end to the occupation – is thereby *justified*. That would be a *non sequitur*. The occupation still has to be justified in self-defense terms, or on the basis of the UNSC lawfully providing authority to Israel to conduct it. The provision of authority to use force only emerged in the practice of the UNSC much later than when Resolution 242 was adopted. And key elements for it – the UNSC acting under Chapter VII, determining the situation to constitute a threat to international peace and security, and calling upon the state to use "all necessary means" – are all absent from this resolution (quite apart from what has already been said about the intended meaning of the relevant provisions). Equally, the practice of the UNSC in purporting to alter the position when it comes to states' rights and obligations in international law, that might in a different fashion from providing authority to use force, somehow render lawful an occupation that would otherwise be illegal, only emerged in the UNSC much later than when 242 was adopted. And again, key necessary elements are missing: the council merely "affirms" a position (less than clearly determinative language); it is not acting under Chapter VII; it does not directly address member states and their behavior and legal position. On the UNSC authorization basis for using force in international law, *see* the relevant sections of the works listed in OUP UoF list (2020), above n6. For a discussion of Resolution 242 and other UN determinations, *see*, *e.g.*, Imseis (2018/2022), above n16, Imseis (2020), above n16. Note also in particular S.C. Res. 476 (1980), above n75, para. 1, where the Security Council "*Reaffirms* the overriding necessity to end the prolonged occupation of Arab territories occupied by Israel since 1967, including Jerusalem" (emphasis in original).

101  So, for example, Steven Schwebel, discussing the situation in 1969, states that "Israel's action in 1967 was defensive ... *since the danger in response to which defensive action was taken remains*, occupation-though not annexation-is justified, pending a peace settlement" (emphasis added). Schwebel (1970), above n79, at 344. However, *see* Schwebel's elaboration of what the "danger" test can justify, above n95.

has a "duty to relinquish control." Moreover, defining the threat for use of force purposes in terms of a potential future threat – the aforementioned doctrine of pre-emptive self-defense – is not a credible position in the law on the use of force.[102] There is no right to maintain the occupation simply as a defensive measure against the territory becoming a source of future attacks.[103]

In any case, Benvenisti states certain UNGA resolutions relating to the oPt "can be seen as an effort to revise" the "position" as he sees it having been set out in UNSC Resolution 242.[104] These resolutions "voiced another message ... that occupation in itself is unlawful or at the very least, that the occupant is not entitled to delay a peaceful solution of the conflict."[105] In the light of this, Benvenisti sets out his view thus:

> It is suggested that an occupation regime that refuses earnestly to contribute to efforts to reach a peaceful solution should be considered illegal. Indeed, the failure to do so should be considered outright annexation. The occupant has a duty under international law to conduct negotiations in good faith for a peaceful solution. It would seem that an occupant which proposes unreasonable conditions, or otherwise obstructs negotiations for peace for the purpose of retaining control over the occupied territory, could be considered a violator of international law.[106]

But quite separately from any considerations arising out of the failure to pursue a settlement in good faith, to be lawful an occupation would still have to meet the *ad bellum* standards, on an ongoing basis. If it does not, which is the case here, then, as mentioned, the occupation is in any case illegal in use of force terms and needs to end immediately for this reason. There is no other "position" to account for that would change this, as a matter of what is operative in international law, whether as articulated by UNSC Resolution 242, Lauterpacht, or Benvenisti.[107]

---

102    The doctrine of a pre-emptive right to use force in self-defense came to prominence in the context of the US response to the attacks on September 11, 2001. It is not supported by the majority of states or most independent international law experts. *See* the general sources in the OUP UoF list (2020), above n6, many of which cover this topic.

103    Thus, the position set out by Schwebel (1970), above n95, is incorrect as a statement of the law on the use of force.

104    Benvenisti (2012), above n22, at 245.

105    *Id.*, at 245. On these resolutions, see Imseis (2018/2022), above n16, Imseis (2020), above n16 (and sources cited therein).

106    Benvenisti (2012), above n22, at 245.

107    Benvenisti returns to the "position" later in his work; this is addressed below, text accompanying n162. UN determinations, including S.C. Res. 242 (1967), have been understood

## USING THE MASTER'S TOOLS TO DISMANTLE THE MASTER'S HOUSE 31

In a separate section of his work, not specifically addressing the oPt, Benvenisti makes a similar point to that set out in the preceding quotation, about the significance of refusing to negotiate. Here, he expressly invokes legality in use of force terms, via the concept of aggression as defined in the Rome Statute for the International Criminal Court:

> While an occupation that results from a defensive attack will obviously not be regarded as a "crime of aggression" because it would not constitute "a manifest violation of the Charter of the United Nations," ... a question will arise whether the occupant, which had seized control in a lawful war of self-defense but refuses to negotiate withdrawal would have criminal responsibility. Arguably, this occupant cannot be considered an "invader" or "attacker;" but to the extent that its presence amounts to a de facto annexation, it might pass the two thresholds of an "act of aggression" and a "crime of aggression."[108]

(In addressing an "occupation that results from a defensive attack" Benvenisti is perhaps using the term "defensive attack" to refer to a use of force in self-defense by the state that goes on to perform the occupation as part of the same overall defensive move [the terminology of "attack" is more commonly used only in the context of an unlawful use of force, as in the reference to "armed attack" in UN Charter article 51]). Again, Benvenisti's question is not the only one that is dispositive of the matter of compliance with the applicable law. Regardless of a refusal to negotiate (and whether or not the presence amounts to *de facto* annexation), if the circumstances that rendered an initial seizure of control lawful in self-defense terms change (the necessary threat and/or proportionality tests are no longer met) then the law has been breached (and, of course, if the initial seizure was unlawful then the occupation has been illegal from the outset).[109]

It is also necessary to account for how certain practices conducted during the occupation have breached IHL in general and occupation law in

---

to justify prolonging the occupation until there is an agreement. This is discussed below, text accompanying n155 *et seq.*

108 Benvenisti (2012), above n22, at 340 (fns omitted).

109 The distinction between an "act of aggression" (the general term denoting state responsibility) and the "crime of aggression" (giving rise to individual criminal responsibility) in the Rome Statute is beyond the scope of this article. For the definitions, *see* Rome Statute art. 8 *bis*, paras. 1 & 2, above n54. Note that Benvenisti discusses his concept relating to the ending of an occupation a third time in his work. This is addressed below, text accompanying n162 *et seq.*

particular.[110] These include the treatment of the Jahalin and their homes, and the plan to forcibly relocate them to near the refuse dump in Abu Dis. Are these *jus in bello* violations significant for *ad bellum* legality? Such violations have been wide-ranging, some falling into the categories of "grave breaches" of the Geneva Conventions, and "other serious violations" of IHL, thereby constituting war crimes.[111] One example, falling into the latter category, is implanting settlements into the oPt, including the settlements next to Khan al-Ahmar.[112] Moreover, more generally, certain practices have constituted unlawful racial discrimination in general and apartheid in particular.[113] These have constituted, in the case of apartheid, an international crime, and, when they have been part of an attack, crimes against humanity.[114] Relatedly, the foregoing norms are classified as peremptory, *jus cogens* norms, which are non-derogable – they cannot be limited by any other areas of international law.[115]

The placing of these violations in an exceptional category, as giving rise, in certain cases, to their classification as international crimes, and having *jus cogens* status, reflects an idea that they can never be justified, including by other rules of international law. For present purposes, this means the law on the

---

110    *See, e.g.*, the treatment of some of these issues in the ICJ Wall Advisory Opinion, above n75, at 114–147. On the Jahalin, *see* the sources cited above n2. For a treatment of initial phase of the occupation, *see, e.g.*, Yahia (1970), above n16, at 163–177.

111    On these types of violations and their classification as war crimes, *see* Rome Statute art. 8, above n54.

112    On the illegality of implanting settlements under occupation law, *see* the sources cited above n31. On the illegality of the Israeli settlements, *see, e.g.*, ICJ Wall Advisory Opinion, above n75, at 115–120.

113    *See* John Dugard & John Reynolds, *Apartheid, International Law, and the Occupied Palestinian Territory*, 24 Eur. J. Int'l L. 867 (2013); Michael Sfard, *Legal Opinion: The Israeli Occupation of the West Bank and the Crime of Apartheid*, Yesh Din (2020); Susan Power, *The Legal Architecture of Apartheid, Against Apartheid and Racial Discrimination*, AARDI/Al-Haq (Apr. 2, 2021), https://aardi.org/2021/04/02/the-legal -architecture-of-apartheid-by-dr-susan-powers-al-haq/; Human Rights Watch, *A Threshold Crossed: Israeli Authorities and the Crimes of Apartheid and Persecution* (Apr. 27, 2021), https://www.hrw.org/report/2021/04/27/threshold-crossed/israeli-authorities-and -crimes-apartheid-and-persecution.

114    *See* Rome Statute art. 7, above n54.

115    On peremptory norms, *see* Vienna Convention on the Law of Treaties art. 53, May 23, 1969, 1155 U.N.T.S. 331; I.L.C., *Articles on Responsibility of States for Internationally Wrongful Acts, with commentaries*, art. 41(2) U.N. Doc. A/56/10 (2001); I.L.C., *Peremptory norms of general international law (jus cogens))*, Text of the draft conclusions and draft annex provisionally adopted by the Drafting Committee on first reading, U.N. Doc. A/CN.4/L.936 (2019) (according to the ILC study, the following constitute *jus cogens* prohibitions (selected list): (c) The prohibition of crimes against humanity; (d) The basic rules of international humanitarian law; (e) The prohibition of racial discrimination and apartheid.).

use of force. Thus, any use of force justification for the occupation associated with them is taken beyond the thresholds of necessity and proportionality.[116] They are regarded to be inherently unnecessary and disproportionate. They cannot be justified through a link back to the just cause of self-defense (assuming it is in operation). Either they cross certain red lines of humane treatment (*e.g.* racial discrimination), or they are of their nature unconnected to that just cause and may, indeed, be linked to another cause that can never serve as a basis for lawful military action (*e.g.* implanting settlements, linked to annexation).[117]

Consequently, the violation of these norms is not only a matter of their "own" internal normative standards, as it were, including the *jus in bello*/IHL/ occupation law. It also has implications for the issue of the legality of the use of force.[118] The *in bello* legal standards are not concerned with the existential legitimacy of the occupation. But the *ad bellum* legal standards which *are* concerned with this matter include within them a test, of necessity and proportionality, which is breached if the former standards are breached. In consequence, a violation of the former standards affects the existential legitimacy of the occupation as a matter of the latter standards. Thus, a state breaching peremptory norms of IHRL and IHL, including occupation law, during an occupation acts beyond what is justified by the law on the use of force. This renders the occupation in and of itself illegitimate as a matter of the latter rules.

That said, such illegitimacy could be remedied by bringing the practice into line with the rules. *Viz.*, a complete reversal of key components of the occupation, including, for example, removing settlements. If this happened, the *ad bellum* requirements of proportionality and necessity would not be breached, insofar as the indirect link to the IHL rules are concerned.

Left to be determined would be whether the requirements of proportionality and necessity are met insofar as the link to the requirements of self-defense are concerned. As mentioned, such a determination leads to a conclusion of illegality. It is only this consideration, then, concerning the occupation's purpose, not its conduct, that is ultimately dispositive of its existential legitimacy in international law. If this test were *not* met, it would not matter whether breaches of the *in bello* standards also rendered the occupation unlawful in *ad bellum* terms because of their significance for the necessity/proportionality test. The occupation is "already" unlawful and thereby existentially

---

116    See, *generally*, the treatment of the interface between the *jus ad bellum* and the *jus in bello* in the sources contained in OUP UoF list (2020), above n6.

117    *Id.*

118    *Id.*

illegitimate – these considerations just aggravate the illegality. If the test *were* met (which is not the case) then the occupation would, as a matter of the law on the use of force, have elements of legality (it has a just cause and is a proportionate means of meeting that cause) and illegality (aspects of its conduct are unjustified).

In addressing the significance of the law on the use of force for the legitimacy of the occupation, it is necessary finally to appreciate a fundamental feature of the legal framework being applied. This concerns the frame of reference adopted by the main component of the legal test: Israel's security needs. The law of self-defense concerns what these security needs are, what Israel should be allowed to do to meet them, etc. The question of the legitimacy of the occupation is assessed according to such considerations. Necessarily, assessing this question as a matter of the position of the Palestinian people is not a direct consideration. The latter position has to accommodate whatever is justified according to the legitimate security needs of Israel insofar as such justification is accommodated by the self-defense test. Put differently, the focus is on the link between the occupation and its effect on the security objective. It is not on the link between the occupation and its effect on the people in the territory affected. In consequence, whether or not the occupation is deemed legitimate has nothing to do directly with the latter effect. Thus, to speak of the "illegal occupation" as a matter of the law on the use of force is to invoke standards that frame the situation as not as oppression and denial of freedom, but as an excess of legitimate administrative authority. The position is different if the term is being used to denote illegality as a matter of the jus *in bello*. Here, the illegality is conceived in part in relation to standards concerning "humane" behavior.

The end result of applying the *ad bellum* standards – that the occupation is existentially illegitimate – might be the same were different standards, concerned directly with the impact on the Palestinian people, in play. But the law's significance is not simply about the position arrived at when it is applied to any given situation, important though that is. It is also about the journey to that position. How is the situation the position relates to portrayed? What factors are regarded as significant or not? To whom are these factors significant? Palestinian people seeking to vindicate their struggle using the terminology of the law on the use of force must do this without referring to the direct impact of the occupation on themselves. Rather, the only direct focus permitted is Israel's defensive security needs. Equally, and in reverse, Israeli people seeking to justify the occupation through this legal framework are able to focus directly only on their own defensive security needs. They are not having to account directly for the effect of the occupation on the Palestinian people. When it

USING THE MASTER'S TOOLS TO DISMANTLE THE MASTER'S HOUSE 35

comes to what is discussed, analyzed, and weighed in the balance, Israel's defensive security needs are in the foreground; the rights of the Palestinian people are in the background. Not only, then, does the occupation exist as a matter of fact, as a practical instantiation of the domination of one people over another. Also, the way this area of international law treats such a situation is to assess things with reference to the needs of the dominant actor directly, and the needs of the subaltern actor indirectly.

So, the international law *ad bellum* and *in bello* frameworks operate as a double bind, offering competing approaches operating dialectically when it comes to their key merits and shortcomings. Palestinian people can invoke their own needs directly but in doing must be silent, when it comes to what these needs cover, on their fundamental aspirations to freedom (*in bello*). Alternatively, they can invoke those aspirations to freedom but must do so through the prism not of their own needs, but, rather, the interests of Israel (*ad bellum*).

## IV Self-Determination as a Legal Right

The other main area of international law addressing the existential legitimacy of the occupation is the law of self-determination.[119] The focus moves away from Israel's security needs (as in the law on the use of force), towards the position of the Palestinian people. Their right of self-determination in international law is universally recognized including, crucially, the right in its "external" manifestation, including an entitlement to choose their international status (*e.g.* statehood).[120]

---

119    The authorities on this topic are voluminous. *See* Thomas Burri & Daniel Thürer, *Self-Determination*, Max Planck Encyc. Pub. Int'l L. (Dec. 2008), https://opil.ouplaw.com/view/10.1093/law:epil/9780199231690/law-9780199231690-e873?prd=EPIL; Oxford University Press, *Oxford Bibliographies – Self-Determination in International Law*, https://www.oxfordbibliographies.com/view/document/obo-9780199796953/obo-9780199 796953-0033.xml; and the sources list in Wilde (2008), above n18, Section 5.4, at 541. *See also*, in particular, International Covenant on Civil and Political Rights art. 1, Dec. 16, 1966, 999 U.N.T.S. 171 [*hereinafter* ICCPR]; International Covenant on Economic, Social, and Cultural Rights art. 1, Dec. 16, 1966, 993 U.N.T.S. 3 [*hereinafter* ICESCR]. On self-determination as a "human right," *see* further below, text accompanying n187 *et seq.*

120    In the words of the ICJ, "[a]s regards the principle of the right of peoples to self-determination, the Court observes that the existence of a 'Palestinian people' is no longer in issue." ICJ Wall Advisory Opinion, above n75, para. 118. *See, e.g.*, Sally Morphet, *The Palestinians and their Right to Self-Determination*, in Foreign Policy and Human Rights: Issues and Responses (R.J. Vincent ed., 2009); Cassesse (1995), above n80, at 230–47 (and sources cited therein); and G.A. Res. 44/48(A-G) (Dec. 8, 1989).

External self-determination was the means through which the international political system, including international law, purported to accommodate the struggle for colonial liberation in the second half of the twentieth century. "Freedom" meant the right of colonial peoples to constitute themselves as states, thereby enjoying formal sovereign "equality" with the states that had been their colonial masters. To attain this, then, colonial peoples were required to accept the state as the primary basis for their collective identity – to adopt the form of association that colonizing societies had adopted for themselves in the metropolis.[121] This echoes Frantz Fanon's observation in the context of colonialism that "it is on that other being, on recognition by that other being, that his own human worth and reality depend."[122] Thus statehood was, in the words of Makau Mutua, "imposed."[123] Forms of collective identity other than statehood or variants that presupposed its validity as the primary model of association (*e.g.* assimilation into another state) were not implemented.[124] Moreover, the particular territorial unit and associated population for each state followed the boundaries adopted by colonial authorities to divide their spheres of influence – the legal concept of *uti possidetis juris* – regardless of any meaningful connection with how societies were collectively constituted.[125] This can be critiqued as, in the words of Makau Mutua writing

---

121  On this process, *see* Mutua (1994), above n12; Anghie (2005), above n12, *passim*.

122  Frantz Fanon, Black Skin, White Masks 216–217 (1967).

123  Mutua 1994, above n12.

124  UNGA Resolution 1541 sets out three scenarios whereby a "Non-Self-Governing Territory can be said to have reached a full measure of self-government": (a) Emergence as a sovereign independent State; (b) Free association with an independent State; or (c) Integration with an independent State. G.A. Res. 1541 (XV) (Dec. 15, 1960), Annex, Principle VI. The later G.A. Res. 2625, the Declaration on Friendly Relations and Co-operation, stipulates the options for external self-determination in the following terms: "[t]he establishment of a sovereign and independent State; the free association or integration with an independent State or the emergence into any other political status freely decided by a people ..." G.A. Res. 2625 (XXV). The terms of the third option might suggest that some non-sovereign-state-based outcome is possible. On these two formulations, *see* ICJ Western Sahara Advisory Opinion, above n75, paras. 57 & 58. The fact that the implementation of the right has in fact always stayed within sovereign-state-based options is perhaps why, in his description of these options, James Crawford follows the approach taken in Resolution 1541 only, without reference also to Resolution 2625. James Crawford, The Creation of States in International Law 621 (2nd ed., 2007) [*hereinafter* Crawford (2007)]. He summarizes the position thus: "[s]elf-determination can result either in the independence of the self-determining unit as a separate State, or in its incorporation into or association with another State on a basis of political equality for the people of the unit." *Id.*, at 128.

125  Mutua (1994), above n12. On the doctrine of *uti possidetis juris, see, e.g.*, Frontier Dispute (Burkina Faso/Republic of Mali), Judgment, 1968 I.C.J. Rep. 554 (Dec. 22), paras. 19–26.

# USING THE MASTER'S TOOLS TO DISMANTLE THE MASTER'S HOUSE

about decolonization in the continent of Africa, a "false" concept of collective identity that constituted a "straight-jacket which continues to deny freedom to millions of Africans."[126] Moreover, "freedom" operated exclusively through a narrow, formal notion of sovereign equality allied to self-rule understood only in terms of the absence of direct colonial administration. This ignored more broad-ranging, complex relations of domination and dependency, notably in the economic sphere, which could continue in the supposedly "post-colonial" period of "liberation."[127]

This is the particular form of "freedom" that the international law of self-determination offers the Palestinian people. Collective identity must be channeled through a link to the territory of the colonial Mandatory Palestine (the League of Nations Mandates were internationally supervised colonies), and via a claim to sovereign statehood. Moreover, within this, the territorial parameters of realizing self-determination through statehood are generally understood to be *not* those of Mandatory Palestine in its entirety. Israel was formed in part of that entity, being recognized by states and the UN as a sovereign state. In consequence, as a matter of international law, the Palestinian people are supposed to settle for that which is "left": the West Bank and Gaza.[128]

---

In that decision, concerning the boundary between two African states, the Court stated that: "At first sight this principle [of uti possidetis juris] conflicts outright with another one, the right of peoples to self-determination. In fact, however, the maintenance of the territorial status quo in Africa is often seen as the wisest course, to preserve what has been achieved by peoples who have struggled for their independence, and to avoid a disruption which would deprive the continent of the gains achieved by much sacrifice. The essential requirement of stability in order to survive, to develop and gradually to consolidate their independence in all fields, has induced African States judiciously to consent to the respecting of colonial frontiers, and to take account of it in the interpretation of the principle of self-determination of peoples." *Id.*, para. 25.

126    Mutua (1994), above n12, at 1175.

127    *See, e.g.*, Anghie (2005), above n12; Chimni (2006), above n12; John Linarelli et al., The Misery of International Law: Confrontations with Injustice in the Global Economy (2018) (and sources cited therein).

128    This position follows from the status of Israel as a state in international law, and its membership as such of the UN. It is advanced by the commentators and authorities cited herein. It should be acknowledged, however, that there nonetheless remains a challenge to this position: that the entirety of the territory and associated population of Mandatory Palestine constitute a single self-determination unit and remain as such, the creation of Israel as a state notwithstanding. In the first place, such a position is based on the treatment of the population of Mandatory Palestine under Article 22 of the League of Nations Covenant, who were, under that instrument, deemed to "have reached a stage of development where their existence as independent nations can be provisionally recognized." Covenant of the League of Nations, Versailles, June 28, 1919. In the second place, either as a supplement or an alternative to this, it is based on an argument that self-determination

So James Crawford observes that "[t]he people of Palestine (*i.e.* of the remaining territories of the Mandate for Palestine) have a right of self-determination."[129] The International Court of Justice (ICJ) ended its Advisory Opinion on the legal consequences of the Wall constructed by Israel in Palestinian territory, in which it affirmed the Palestinian right to self-determination, by drawing the UNGA's attention to the need to achieve "the establishment of a Palestinian State, existing side by side with Israel."[130] Antonio Cassese even suggests that the sole ground for the Palestinian people having a right to self-determination in the first place is the occupation (rather than the occupation being simply a denial of this right).[131] Moreover, because of this, "it follows that only those Palestinians living in the territory occupied by Israel since 1967 are entitled to the exercise of this right."[132]

For people whose primary understanding of collective identity does not fit with sovereign statehood (whether current or future), such as the Jahalin, a Bedouin nomadic people, the foregoing arrangements for self-determination, concerned with issues of sovereignty and statehood, are at odds with this identity. Moreover, these arrangements reinforce the very matters which led to their displacement after the creation of Israel and continue to prevent their return. In a form of international law gaslighting, self-determination is only relevant to the legal status of the territory they were displaced to (West Bank Palestine), while maintaining the legal status of the place they were displaced from (the state of Israel), the establishment of which their displacement, as part of the Nakba, played an integral part in enabling.

Moreover, Cassese bases the existence of the Palestinian people's right to freedom exclusively in being denied the exercise of this right by the occupation. As will be explored further, he posits self-determination as an approach to a legal entitlement rooted in the *perspective of the people*.[133] But the definition of who constitutes that people is not determined by that perspective. Instead, the starting point is the Israeli perspective. What is

---

had become applicable to colonial territories, including Mandatory Palestine, before the UN partition resolution of 1947. In consequence, the entire population and territory of Mandatory Palestine constituted a self-determination unit at that time, and the partition resolution, and Israel's secession from Mandatory Palestine in 1948, did not alter this. A treatment of this challenge to the orthodox position is beyond the scope of the present article.

129   Crawford (2007), above n124, at 444.
130   ICJ Wall Advisory Opinion 2004, above n75, at 162. This statement is discussed further below, text accompanying n206.
131   Cassese (1995), above n80, at 240.
132   *Id.*
133   *See* text accompanying n144 below.

"occupied" *is* the Palestinian people for the purposes of self-determination. And what is "occupied" is legally defined as what is "not-Israel." Moreover, within this concept of collective self-determination arising out of a denial of freedom, only such a denial through the occupation is relevant. The position of Palestinian refugees *as refugees*, whether within the oPt, Israel or internationally, and their inability to return, is excluded. As is the lack of freedom for Palestinian people within Israel.

Overall, the master's tools of the international law of self-determination offer the Palestinian people in general, and the Jahalin in particular, to quote Samera Esmeir again, "itineraries for political life" which drastically diminish "the pursuit of collective freedom adequate to a non-colonial future."[134]

Within this drastically diminished itinerary, the law self-determination purports to provide the following protections. It is because the Palestinian people have the right of self-determination in this way that the oPt are not and have never been for the duration of the occupation *terra nullius* – territory that does not fall under the sovereignty of any international legal person. Rather, sovereignty resides in the Palestinian people. The territory has been and is either a non-state territorial self-determination unit, or the state of Palestine, depending on the view taken on whether or not the assertion of the latter status has been legally effective and, if so, when that happened.[135]

---

134 Esmeir, above n44.

135 The issue of whether Palestine is a state in international law (and when this might have happened) is beyond the scope of this article, and was the subject of much attention and commentary in 2020–21 in the context of the deliberations at the ICC on the question of Palestine's accession to the Rome Statute (above n54), bearing in mind the UNGA decision to upgrade Palestine's status at the UN from non-member entity to non-member state in 2012 (U.N. Doc. A/RES/67/19 (Dec. 4, 2012)). For some commentary on this topic, *see, e.g.,* the relevant parts of the sources cited above n16. A territory that does not fall within the sovereignty of any state and is inhabited by people who have the right of external self-determination is not *terra nullius*. Rather, it has an international legal status where certain rights over the territory are vested in that people. The UNGA stated, in the context of self-determination, that "the territory of a colony or other Non-Self-Governing Territory ... has ... a status separate and distinct from the territory of the State administering it; and such separate and distinct status ... shall exist until the people of the ... territory have exercised their right of self-determination." G.A. Res. 2625 (XXV), above n124. *See also* the ICJ Western Sahara Advisory Opinion, above n19, paras. 80–81; and Crawford (2007), above n124, at 617–619. Writing in 2007, James Crawford took the position that Palestine was not a state, and in this context wrote "[t]he people of Palestine ... have a right of self-determination ... there is thus a non-State legal entity recognized as represented by a national liberation movement. This explains the 'capacity' of the PLO to perform various acts, to enter into treaties, to bear rights and assume obligations ... these are not things which in modern international law only States can do." *Id.,* at 444.

It is because the oPt has this status that the prohibition on annexation through the use of force applies. That prohibition is the modern articulation of a root to title based on "conquest" – taking territory by force from its "owner."[136] For it to apply, there has to be a "sovereign" whose rights would be alienated through force.[137] Given the likely status of the Mandatory Palestine in 1948 and 1967 – as non-state territory – it is only the right to self-determination that introduces an alternative, non-state-based "sovereignty" – vested in the Palestinian people – to trigger the force-enabled-acquisition-prohibition. Without self-determination (or the fanciful notion that the West Bank was somehow part of the territory of Jordan in 1967) the prohibition would not apply.

Another consequence of the oPt not being *terra nullius* is that Israel cannot acquire title on the basis of what is referred to in the law on title to territory as "occupation." This denotes the exercise, for a sustained period, of effective control over *terra nullius*[138] (here, the concept is concerned with the acquisition of title through the conduct of occupation – in the law of occupation it used to define such conduct, which if in existence triggers a regulatory regime). This is related to but distinct from the earlier prohibition on annexation through the use of force. There, the focus of the international legal prohibition is on the forcible means through which sovereignty is alienated, for example by driving out and/or subjugating the existing sovereignty-holder. Here, the focus is on controlling the territory itself. Whereas the force-enabled-annexation prohibition is rooted in the notion of preventing, effectively, violence-enabled-theft, the occupation-enabled-annexation prohibition is rooted in the notion that there is already an "owner" and so acquisition of territory through control is inapplicable.

It is, thus, only because the Palestinian people have a right to self-determination that annexation cannot be effected through either the use of

---

136   *See* the sources cited above n75; and, in particular, *e.g.*, OUP Territorial Title list (2016), above n6; Jennings (1963/2017), above n75, Ch. IV.

137   Hence, Benvenisti defines the prohibition as being based on "the principle of inalienability of *sovereignty* through unilateral action of a foreign power, whether through the actual or threatened use of force ... Effective control by foreign military force can never bring about by itself a valid transfer of *sovereignty*" (emphasis added). Benvenisti (2012), above n22, at 42.

138   On "occupation" as a root of title, *see* the sources cited in the OUP Territorial Title list (2016), above n6; in particular Jennings (1963/2017), above n75, at 33–37. For Robbie Jennings, writing in 1963, "occupation is obsolescent except in relation to the Polar regions." *Id.*, at 33. For Masaharu Yanagihara, occupation is "not usually relevant given the lack of terrae nullius." OUP Territorial Title list (2016), above n6.

force (the "conquest" basis for title) or the exercise of effective control (the "occupation" basis for title).

Furthermore, given that the Palestinian people have not agreed that all or part of the oPt is to be Israeli territory, the default requirement of the law of self-determination is that they should be immediately freed from the impediments to self-rule. This includes freedom from impediments to self-rule realized through independent statehood. If the practical exercise of external self-determination is not happening because a state is exercising control over the territory, whether on the basis of colonial arrangements, or a military occupation, then, according to this logic, that state is obliged to bring the control to a speedy end. The matter of agreement by that state to the ending of its domination is legally irrelevant. The state is already subject to an obligation here. Such consent is legally otiose.

Moreover, crucially, the obligation to bring control to an end does not incorporate a consideration as to whether the people affected are "ready" for self-administration. In the classic formulation of UNGA Resolution 1514 (1960), "inadequacy of political, economic, social or educational preparedness should never serve as a pretext for delaying independence."[139] The requirement that self-determination should be implemented immediately is a general doctrine, not specifically conceived in opposition to "preparedness" as a pretext for delay. In Resolution 1514, the UNGA "Solemnly proclaims the necessity of bringing to a speedy and unconditional end colonialism in all its forms and manifestations."[140] And further states that:

> Immediate steps shall be taken, in Trust and Non-Self-Governing Territories or all other territories which have not yet attained independence, to transfer all powers to the peoples of those territories, without any conditions or reservations, in accordance with their freely expressed will and desire ...[141]

Quoting these provisions, the ICJ in its Advisory Opinion about the Western Sahara described the application of self-determination as being "for the purposes of bringing all colonial situations to a speedy end."[142]

---

139     G.A. Res. 1514 (XV) (Dec. 14, 1960), para. 3.

140     *Id.*, pmbl.

141     *Id.*, para. 5.

142     ICJ Western Sahara Advisory Opinion, above n19, para. 55. *See also* what the ICJ called upon the UK to do in relation to the Chagos Islands in the ICJ Chagos advisory opinion, quoted below, text accompanying n208.

To conclude, the occupation of the Palestinian territories by Israel is a violation of the right of Palestinian self-determination and Israel's concomitant obligation to take the necessary steps to enable this right to be realized. It is, moreover, an egregious violation, given its duration and bearing in mind the foregoing stipulations concerning speedy realization.

That said, such a conclusion can only be drawn *after* one has already adopted the earlier position that Israel's occupation does not meet the test for lawful self-defense as a matter of the *jus ad bellum*. Any occupation of inhabited land meeting the latter test necessarily negatively affects the enjoyment of the self-determination right of the population affected. Yet, it is not regarded as illegal for this reason. Thus, it is necessary, in order to invoke international law to challenge the legitimacy of the occupation, to make a case on the basis of *both* the law on the use of force *and* the law of self-determination. Moreover, the little expert legal analysis that has been done on the intersection between these regimes, by Antonio Cassese, takes the position under the law on the use of force, and reads this into the law of self-determination. Whatever is lawful as a matter of the former is thereby not unlawful as a matter of the latter.[143] Having set this approach out, Cassese observes that

> The right to external self-determination is thus, in a sense, the counterpart of the prohibition on the use of force in international relations. In many cases, the breach of external self-determination is simply an unlawful use of force looked at from the perspective of the victimized *people* rather than from that of the besieged sovereign State or territory.[144]

---

143   For Cassese: "military occupation ... amounts to a grave breach of Article 1(1) [of the ICCPR] (such action is not in conflict with Article 1(1) if it is justified by Article 51 of the UN Charter and, therefore, being restricted to repel an act of aggression, is limited in duration)." Cassese (1995), above n80, at 55. In a later passage in the same work, he elaborates on this theme: "self-determination is violated whenever there is a military invasion or belligerent occupation of a foreign territory, except where the occupation – although unlawful – is of a minimal duration or is solely intended as a means of repelling, under Article 51 of the UN Charter, an armed attack initiated by the vanquished Power and consequently is not protracted." *Id.*, at 99. It is not clear what Cassese means in the second quotation, that the exception to a violation of self-determination he is setting out covers an occupation he still characterizes as "unlawful." In the first quotation, he states that an occupation constituting a lawful use of force "is not in conflict with" the provision on self-determination in the ICCPR. It is submitted that the legal position is as set out in that first quotation.

144   *Id.*, at 99 (emphasis in original).

It is correct that the law of self-determination shifts the focus of the effect of military action justified by the use of force to the population subjected to it (the Palestinian people) in preference to a focus on the collective entity with which they are associated (Palestine). But more fundamentally, the law on the use of force test is not anyway concerned directly with the "perspective" of the object of force, whether a state/non-state territory or a people. The test is an appraisal of the legitimacy of the defensive claims made by the state using force. Thus, setting the boundaries of legality under the law of self-determination according to legality under the law on the use of force flips things back to the "perspective" of the occupying state. The law of self-determination does not, therefore, provide an escape from needing to articulate a case assessing whether Israel's defensive needs legitimize the occupation. This is not a test concerned directly with the "perspective of the victimized people."

## V  Self-Determination Delayed and Potentially Dropped

The common way of understanding the extended duration of the occupation stops at the present stage of analysis: it is a prolonged violation of international law, as has been the case for the people of the Western Sahara since 1975, and as was the case for the people of Timor Leste between 1975 and 1999. However, the link with these examples suggests something more than simply a common practice of lengthy illegality. As this section explores, there are certain trends in the way law is understood that partly explain how its violation has persisted for so long.

It is not unusual for states and the UN to treat situations like the Israeli occupation of the Palestinian territories, where the right of external self-determination applies, as if there is no requirement of immediate termination. The delay in realizing external self-determination is treated as permissible and, even, required. And it can sometimes pave the way for an approach to realizing the right incorporating determinative factors which are incompatible with how the exercise of the right is supposedly understood.

After a quarter of a century of Indonesian occupation the people of Timor Leste, who had a right of external self-determination as the inhabitants of a former Portuguese colony, were permitted to realize this right through independent statehood (after the outcome of a popular consultation). However, Indonesia and Portugal – the occupier and former colonial power – with the blessing of the UNSC, decided that statehood would not be realized immediately. Rather, there would first be a period of administration by the

UN, on the basis that, in the immediate term, the people of Timor Leste were deemed incapable of self-administration.[145] The UNSC created a UN administrative authority – the UN Transitional Administration in East Timor (UNTAET) – to do this.[146]

In Iraq, the US and UK and the UNSC generally conceived the end of the occupation as linked to the question of when the local population would be "ready" to take over control. On this basis, the USNC authorized the CPA to engage in the political, economic, and legal transformation deemed necessary to create the conditions for "readiness," a process that would take place before "sovereignty" would be "transferred" to the Iraqi people's representatives.[147]

In Western Sahara, the idea of linking implementing self-determination to the reaching of an agreement with Morocco has taken hold in UNSC determinations. This has joined the more long-standing, seemingly endlessly deferrable, matter of delaying such implementation until a referendum of the Sahrawi is conducted. A UN peace operation created in 1991 to conduct the referendum, the UN Mission for the Referendum in Western Sahara (MINURSO), has not done this, for 20 years and counting.[148] When MINURSO was created, the UNSC stated its commitment to a "just and lasting solution to the question of Western Sahara."[149] Almost twenty years later, in the most recent resolution on the matter, adopted in 2020, the way the UNSC conceives the "solution" reflects an important shift. It is not to be a "just and lasting" – only solution; it is to be

> a just, lasting, and mutually acceptable political solution, based on compromise, which will provide for the self-determination of the people of Western Sahara in the context of arrangements consistent with the principles and purposes of the Charter of the United Nations.[150]

On the one hand, the solution is to be just, and provide for self-determination. Arrangements have to be consistent with the purposes and principles of the UN Charter, implicating the Charter objectives to "bring about ... in conformity with the principles of justice and international law [the] adjustment or

---

145   *See* the sources cited above n20.

146   *Id.*

147   *See* the sources cited above n22.

148   *See* UN Missions, MINURSO (2021), https://minurso.unmissions.org/.

149   S.C. Res. 690 (Apr. 29, 1991), pmbl.

150   S.C. Res 2548 (Oct. 30, 2020), pmbl. This formulation is repeated in the operative paragraphs (with some important modifications in some places, *see, e.g.,* the extract from para. 2 herein).

USING THE MASTER'S TOOLS TO DISMANTLE THE MASTER'S HOUSE          45

settlement of international disputes" and "to develop friendly relations among nations based on respect for the principle of equal rights and self-determination of peoples."[151] On the other hand, the solution is to mutually-acceptable, *i.e.* acceptable to *both* the Sahrawi and the occupying state, Morocco. And it is to be based on compromise, presumably implying that both sides might have to give certain things up to enable mutual acceptance.

The Sahrawi might, of course, freely choose compromise. And this might enable Moroccan agreement. If validated through a free and fair referendum meeting the relevant standards, this could potentially constitute a valid exercise of self-determination. But what if they freely determine otherwise? Preferring an outcome lacking compromise, which Morocco disagrees with? These stipulations seem to rule out such an outcome. But if the people of the Western Sahara have a right to self-determination, then it is supposed to be their view alone that is determinative of the "solution." And if the solution is to be one that is "just," and "just" means lawful in international law – and so in "conformity with the principles of justice and international law" – then the consent of Morocco cannot be a necessary requirement.[152]

It is unsurprising, therefore, that the referendum has not happened, since holding it would shift the focus onto the Sahrawi position as being potentially exclusively determinative of the solution. Strikingly, in the 2020 UNSC resolution, which is lengthy, there is no reference the holding of the referendum. And the mandate of MINURSO, *which has the word referendum in its name*, is discussed without reference to this task. Indeed, the key operative paragraph relating to that mandate states the following:

> Emphasizes the need to achieve a realistic, practicable and enduring political solution to the question of Western Sahara based on compromise and the importance of aligning the strategic focus of MINURSO and orienting resources of the United Nations to this end.[153]

This does not even attempt, as the preamble does, the uneasy balance between the two contradictory elements. The UN mission created to conduct

---

151     U.N. Charter art. 1, paras. 1 & 2.

152     As James Crawford observes: "where the principle [of self-determination] applies, it does so as a right of the people concerned; it is not a matter simply of rights and obligations as between existing States. Another State may well be interested in the result of an act of self-determination, in that it may stand to gain or regain territory. But to treat self-determination as a right of that State would be to deny the reality of the alternative options open to the people concerned." Crawford (2007), above n124, at 618.

153     S.C. Res. 2548 (2020), above n150, para. 2.

the self-determination referendum that would potentially place the decision exclusively in the hands of the Sahrawi is instructed to adopt a "strategic focus" on a solution rooted only in what is "realistic" and "based on compromise." And to do so without having to account for whether the solution is "just" and provides for self-determination. It is as if the name of the mission, with its reference to a referendum and the implicit link this makes to self-determination, is an unfortunate hangover from, and, as such, an embarrassing reminder of, an earlier position that has been abandoned.

Accordingly, the resolution of the question of Morocco's control of Western Sahara, including if it will end and, if so, when, is something that should depend on Morocco's agreement. Approaching Western Sahara on this basis is especially notable given that it concerns the very situation in relation to which the ICJ made its aforementioned general observation, based on UNGA Resolution 1514, that self-determination requires "bringing all colonial situations to a speedy end." It is one thing for such a situation not to end speedily because the occupying state refuses to comply with this requirement. And because other states fail to address effectively this non-compliance and, even, in the case of the US under President Trump, recognize Moroccan sovereignty over the territory.[154] It is quite another for the UN, the supposed institutional guardian of the international legal order including the law of self-determination (*cf.* those purposes and principles in the UN Charter) to treat the situation as not necessarily to be determined solely according to the wishes of population involved but, rather, also requiring the occupying state's agreement.

The foregoing approaches of linking the end of foreign rule to the meeting of particular conditions – whether normative standards being met (the people of Timor Leste and Iraq being "ready"), or the adoption of an "agreement" involving the foreign ruler's consent (Morocco and Western Sahara) – are at play in relation to the realization of Palestinian self-determination.

As Ardi Imseis argues, the discourse at the UN, and of the self-appointed "Quartet," links ending the occupation to the outcome of peace negotiations and/or the existence of governance in Palestine providing Israel with security guarantees.[155] Thus, the security considerations from the use of force resurface. They are partially incorporated into a standard to be met before people are given freedom. Their significance now is not as a binding, ostensibly "objective"

---

154 On this recognition, *see* Donald J. Trump, *Proclamation on Recognizing The Sovereignty Of The Kingdom Of Morocco Over The Western Sahara*, Trump White House Archives (Dec. 10, 2020) [*hereinafter* Trump White House Archives (2020)], https://trumpwhitehouse.archives.gov/presidential-actions/proclamation-recognizing-sovereignty-kingdom-morocco-western-sahara/.

155 Imseis (2018/2022), above n16; Imseis (2020), above n16.

USING THE MASTER'S TOOLS TO DISMANTLE THE MASTER'S HOUSE        47

test concerning necessity and proportionality to an existential threat. Rather, they constitute a broader standard. And their application is to be determined according to the outcome of negotiations – a political process. And this application only occurs when that outcome happens as a matter of fact. Moreover, as the outcome requires an agreement with Israel, the meeting of the test is not, as in the law on the use of force, determined irrespective of the decision taken on it by the actor to whom it applies. Rather, Israel's decision is an integral part of the test itself. Furthermore, the profoundly unequal negotiating position between Israel and Palestine creates the conditions for this decision to be the predominant determinant. Moreover, security considerations are unlikely to be the exclusive subject of the agreement. Broader matters, such as Israel's annexation aspirations over parts of the West Bank ("land for peace") can and are likely to be included.

The deferred, contingency approach to realizing Palestinian self-determination and/or ending the occupation is also evident in certain academic commentary. James Crawford reported in 2007 that "[t]here is a substantial international consensus that the Palestinian people are entitled to form a State (subject to guarantees as to the security of the other States in the region)."[156] Antonio Cassese stated in 1995 that: "… there is general agreement that the objective of granting Palestinians self-determination should go hand in hand with that of safeguarding the existence, security and independence of Israel as a sovereign State … there is widespread agreement that these two objectives should be achieved through peaceful negotiations."[157] Likewise is Eyal Benvenisti's position from earlier: the occupation can be maintained pending the conclusion of an agreement, if Israel is making good faith efforts to negotiate.[158] Orna Ben-Naftali, Aeyal Gross, and Keren Michaeli offer a complementary proposal, that could presumably be activated if such efforts are absent:

> The international community may wish to entertain the thought that, in cases of occupations lasting longer than a year, and pending a comprehensive political solution, the effective control over the occupied territory be transferred from the occupying power to an appropriate international authority.[159]

---

156   Crawford (2007), above n124, at 438.
157   Cassese (1995), above n80, at 240.
158   *See* above, text accompanying n106 *et seq.*
159   Ben-Naftali, et al. (2005), above n35, at 613 (fn omitted) (citing Orna Ben-Naftali, *A La Recherche du Temps Perdu': Rethinking Article 6 of the Fourth Geneva Convention in the Light of the Legal Consequences of the Construction of a Wall in the Occupied Palestinian*

Nowhere do they suggest that for occupations of a people with a right to self-determination, like the Palestinian people – the very situation addressed in the article where they make the proposal – the law of self-determination requires a transfer of authority automatically and directly *to this people*.[160] Similarly, Benvenisti's answer to his question, when discussing the oPt, "is there an obligation to end the occupation," does not mention self-determination at all, let alone address this aspect of it.[161]

Separately, in the final pages of the conclusion to the same work, Benvenisti returns to the subject of ending occupations, this time as a general matter. Now self-determination is expressly introduced as a consideration. He states that "[a] legal framework that respects human and peoples' rights can no longer support the thesis that the occupant may hold the territory 'as a pledge of his military success, and thereby impress upon the enemy the necessity of submitting to terms of peace.'"[162] Here, then, is a repeat quotation of the same Lauterpacht/Oppenheim "principle" (now termed a "thesis") Benvenisti discussed earlier in the oPt context.[163] In his earlier oPt-specific treatment, Benvenisti discussed potential inroads made to the principle by UNGA resolutions concerning the occupation. This led him to adopt his position nuancing the principle, without referencing Palestinian self-determination as a consideration.[164] Now, when discussing the termination question generically, self-determination *is* expressly referenced, and it is suggested that this renders the principle (now a thesis) unsupportable. It is unclear why Benvenisti did not expressly invoke self-determination when discussing the same issues in the context of the occupation of the Palestinian territories.[165] That said, his articulation of his position on the question generically essentially follows the same lines as the position formulated earlier in the oPt context. As then, it amounts to a qualified version, not outright rejection, of the Lauterpacht/Oppenheim

---

*Territory Advisory Opinion*, 38 Isr. L. Rev. 211 (2005) (where Ben-Naftali makes the same point, at 228–9)).

160   The treatment of the right of the Palestinian people to self-determination in the article is limited to a footnote. Ben-Naftali et al. (2005), above n35, at 554–555 n18.

161   Reviewed above, text accompanying n96 *et seq. N.b.* what is said below, n164, regarding the significance of the UNGA resolutions mentioned in that analysis.

162   Benvenisti (2012), above n22, at 348 (fn omitted) (citing the 1906 version of Oppenheim (2 Lassa Oppenheim, *International Law: War and Neutrality* 167 (1906)).

163   This time the citation for the quote is from an earlier edition of the same source. For the other citation of the later version of Oppenheim, *see* above n98.

164   Clearly, the position adopted by the UNGA in the resolutions on the illegality of the occupation was based in part on the self-determination right of the Palestinian people.

165   Although it is important to acknowledge the motivations that informed the resolutions he does mention, as indicated in the previous footnote.

"principle"/"thesis": the occupation can continue if good faith efforts are made by the occupier to reach an agreement.[166] Considering self-determination does not, then, seem to have made any difference. Certainly, the more fundamental challenge raised by this right to the continuance of the occupation – that it has to end immediately, unless justified in self-defense terms – is not discussed.

Cassese's "hand in hand" approach implicitly eliminates the element of the self-determination entitlement that would require its automatic realization, *regardless* of whether his other objective, concerning safeguards for Israel, is realized. This is remarkable coming from the same commentator who on a generic level articulated the self-determination-use of force interface in a manner that only permitted inroads into the former on the basis of what was justified according to the latter (considerably narrower than the objective of "safeguarding the existence, security and independence of Israel as a sovereign State").[167]

For both Benvenisti and Cassese, then, the coverage of self-determination differs when the occupation of the Palestinian people, rather than occupations generally, is discussed.

These academic approaches, and the more general trend Ardi Imseis identifies at the UN, corresponds to a broader pattern. The end of foreign rule is contingent on factors going beyond the view of the people with the right of external self-determination on the question. At play is a concept in international law and public policy, trusteeship over people, which has its origins in forms of post-Renaissance European colonialism. In previous work, I identified the links between these different forms of "foreign territorial administration," and the overall concept, which was itself often based on a racist distinction, the "standard of civilization," deployed to determine which people were deemed incapable of self-administration and which other "advanced" people were deemed fit to act as trustees.[168] This term covers manifestations of colonialism (*e.g.* under the General Act of the 1899 Berlin Conference). It also covers other forms of colonialism supervised by international organizations – the League

---

166 Benvenisti (2012), above n22, at 348.

167 Cassese's general approach is reviewed above, text accompanying n143 *et seq.* This is assuming that "hand in hand" means there cannot be one without the other, as a matter of legal position. An alternative interpretation of this could be, more loosely, that it would be desirable to have both objectives achieved at the same time, and that, more broadly, both objectives are of merit. But that the realization of one (self-determination) does not depend, legally, on the realization of the other (safeguards for Israel). On this, *see* the discussion above, text accompanying n92 above, *et seq.*, and accompanying n206 below, *et seq.*

168 Wilde (2008), above n18, Ch. 8, *passim.*

of Nations Mandates system, the UN Trusteeship system, and the UN regime for Non-Self-Governing Territories. Thirdly, it covers occupation by states. Fourthly, it covers International Territorial Administration (ITA) (territorial administration by international organizations, like UNTAET in Timor Leste). These practices were linked to international legal arrangements that set up their termination – and so potentially self-rule by the populations affected – in a particular fashion. Termination was to be contingent on certain conditions being met. These conditions concerned standards of governance relating to the populations and territories affected (echoing the security factor raised in this context) and/or the resolution of a dispute (echoing the "outcome of negotiations" factor raised in this context).[169]

However, by the time of the 1967 occupation of the West Bank, this concept of making the end of foreign rule contingent on meeting such conditions had supposedly been repudiated by the external self-determination entitlement, something which was understood in part as a repudiation of the racist civilizational difference between people that underpinned the trusteeship concept itself.[170] The UNGA adopted resolution 1514 in 1960.[171] How is it possible, then, that 60 years after the resolution (regarded as reflective of the position in customary international law at the time) was adopted, the trusteeship basis for ending the occupation, with its racist underpinnings, is still able to predominate within international discussions of the occupation? And be affirmed by the UN, as Ardi Imseis sets out? How can it be that when they address ending the occupation, Orna Ben-Naftali, Aeyal Gross, and Keren Michaeli propose not the immediate transfer of authority to the Palestinian people, but rather a further period of what would presumably be some form of international trusteeship, "pending a comprehensive political solution"? What normative climate has enabled such arguments to remain somehow tenable in mainstream and even ostensibly critical international legal discourse in the supposed "post-colonial," self-determination-era?

## VI      Self-Determination Obscured

This section argues that certain international legal arguments have underpinned the continued legitimation of ideas of trusteeship-over-people in the supposed post-colonial era of self-determination. There is a broad range of

---

169    *Id.*
170    Wilde (2008), above n18, Ch. 8, Section 8.5.
171    G.A. Res. 1514 (XV) (1960), above n139.

USING THE MASTER'S TOOLS TO DISMANTLE THE MASTER'S HOUSE 51

factors at play here, and some are specific to particular situations.[172] As far as the Palestinian people are concerned, one factor is the aforementioned tendency amongst commentators to bypass the significance of the occupation's legality in use of force terms. Commentators bypass this matter either entirely, or insofar as it is relevant to the question of the existential legitimacy of the occupation – the requirement that it end. Both approaches pave the way for being able to view termination as necessarily contingent on an agreement. This section addresses three additional factors: the effect of the exclusive focus on IHL in general and occupation law in particular; the effect of the concept of "trusteeship;" and the conceptualization of self-determination as a "human right."

The first relevant factor is the exclusive focus on IHL in general and occupation law in particular, legal regimes that are not concerned with the existential legitimacy of the occupation. Their concern is only on how "humane" the conduct of the occupation is. Selectivity in choice of law corresponds to selectivity on substantive-issue-focus. The question of the continued existence of the occupation is off the table, to be determined exclusively as a matter of "politics." Whereas law and politics are not divided in this fashion (*e.g.*, political preferences are embedded in the legal rules regulating the occupation), this particular division is significant for the political role it plays in demarcating what should count when the two matters are addressed. Whereas the conduct of the occupation is a matter of rights, the existence of the occupation is not. Instead, the latter is to be resolved exclusively on a different, pragmatic basis of negotiation. There is, therefore, a different power calculus applicable to the existence of the occupation. This then feeds into and reinforces the idea that "humanitarian" agencies, such as the ICRC and Diakonia, are and should be politically neutral and technocratic.[173] They can call upon Israel to behave more "humanely" in how it subjugates the Palestinian people – this is a legal requirement. They cannot tell Israel to end the subjugation itself – such matters are exclusively "political."

The exclusive focus on IHL in general and occupation law in particular is also useful in supporting the "trusteeship" basis for ending the occupation only when people are deemed "ready." Its utility here is based on "trusteeship" being

---

172   For further treatment of different aspects of this general matter, *see* Wilde (2008), above n18, Ch. 8, Section 8.7, & Ch. 9, Section 9.2.2.

173   *See, e.g.*, Denise Plattner, *ICRC neutrality and neutrality in humanitarian assistance*, Int'l Rev. Red Cross 311 (1996), https://www.icrc.org/en/doc/resources/documents/article/other/57jn2z.htm; and, on Diakonia being "committed to upholding the fundamental principles of humanity and impartiality," Diakonia, *Humanitarian Assistance*, https://www.diakonia.se/en/How-we-work/Humanitarian-assistance/.

the underlying rationale for occupation law, because of the power imbalance between occupier and occupied, and lack of sovereignty enjoyed by the former over the territory of the latter.[174] Occupation law is introduced supposedly to guarantee that the occupier acts in the interests of the occupied population only, not also its own interests.

This conception of how the relationship between Israel and the Palestinian people is supposed to operate is compatible with the other forms of international trusteeship. Moreover, in those other forms it is accompanied by the further elements, concerning when the arrangements should end, based on

---

174 In the words of Arnold Wilson: "... enemy territories in the occupation of the armed forces of another country constitute (in the language of Art. 22 of the League of Nations Covenant) a sacred trust, which must be administered as a whole in the interests of both the inhabitants and of the legitimate sovereign or the duly constituted successor in title." Wilson (1932), above n31, at 38. Gerhard von Glahn defines occupation as "... a temporary right of administration on a sort of trusteeship basis ...". Von Glahn (1995), above n31, at 668. Adam Roberts states that, "... the idea of 'trusteeship' is implicit in all occupation law ... all occupants are in some vague and general sense trustees." Roberts (1985), above n31, at 295 (citing Wilson (above) and von Glahn (above, the same quote contained in an earlier edition)). For Roberts, the law of occupation in both the Hague Regulations and the Geneva Conventions "can be interpreted as putting the occupant in a quasi-trustee role." *Id.*, at 295. Perritt describes the occupations of post-Second World War Germany and Japan, and the CPA occupation of Iraq, as instances of the exercise of trust. *See* H. Perritt, *Structures and Standards for Political Trusteeship*, 8 UCLA J. Int'l L. & Aff. 387 (2003), at 410–16, 422 (general discussion of trusteeship and occupation); at 393–395 (on Germany); 395–396 (on Japan); 407–410 (on Iraq). On the link between the lack of sovereignty, and the trusteeship concept, Gerhard von Glahn conceives occupation on a trusteeship basis on the grounds that "the legitimate government of an occupied territory retains its sovereignty" which is only "suspended in the area for the duration of the belligerent occupation;" Von Glahn (1995), above n31, at 668. In the words of Benvenisti, during the "limited period [of an occupation], the occupant administers the territory on behalf of the sovereign. Thus, the occupant's status is conceived to be that of a trustee," Benvenisti (2012), above n22, at 6 (fn omitted which cites the works by Wilson, von Glahn, and Roberts cited herein (in the case of von Glahn, Benvenisti cites the same quote cited above contained in an earlier edition of the same work)). In 1973, Allan Gerson proposed a concept of "trustee occupation" to be applied to Israel's presence in the Palestinian Territories. The idea was that this would enable the situation under evaluation to be *distinguished* from occupation generally and, in consequence, certain obligations in the law of occupation. *See* Gerson (1973), above n31; Gerson (1978), above n76, *passim*, and in particular at 78–82. This notion that "trusteeship occupation" is somehow a distinct category of occupation is not reflected in the generalized notions of trusteeship adopted by the commentators above in the present footnote. Adam Roberts in particular makes the comments reproduced above in the context of dismissing Gerson's notion, and concludes by expressing skepticism that "trusteeship occupation" is a "separate category of occupation;" Roberts (1985), above n31, at 295.

the "ward" people "developing" to the stage when they are "ready" for "self-administration."[175] These additional elements are not part of occupation law, given that it is not concerned with the basis on which occupations end. Nonetheless, the overarching trusteeship link enables approaches echoing those elements, rather than the self-determination approach, to be adopted. Through this, states and the UN can follow the long-standing, wide-ranging adoption of such approaches, running right up to and beyond what happened in Timor Leste at the turn of the 21st century.

According to the normative framework being exclusively followed – occupation law – the Palestinian people are treated as passive beneficiaries of what is supposed to be benevolent rule. Viewing the Palestinian people in this way – lacking agency, needing to be "cared" for, only, an approach with clearly gendered, patriarchal characteristics, as Fionnuala Ní Aoláin points out – necessarily places the viability of Palestinian self-administration into question.[176] This eases the jump to the adoption of the aforementioned trusteeship approaches, independence being rendered dependent on improvements in capacities for self-administration. Put differently, adopting the contrary, self-determination approach of an automatic, immediate right to freedom necessarily requires a sharp rupture from the trusteeship orientation. Indeed, this approach is based on a *repudiation of trusteeship over people in and of itself*. With an occupation lasting over half a century, the embedding effect on the trusteeship approach potentially enabled by an exclusive focus on occupation law is potentially acute. The rupture required to depart from this is, in consequence, correspondingly acute. One can perhaps see the embedding effect of the occupation-trusteeship worldview in Orna Ben-Naftali, Aeyal Gross, and Keren Michaeli's proposal for ending the Israeli occupation.[177] They engage in a prolonged treatment of the illegality of the occupation dominated by a consideration of occupation law, including coverage of the "trusteeship" character of this law. When they then turn, at the end of this analysis, to the

---

175   Wilde (2008), above n18, Ch. 8, *passim*, & in particular Sections 8.3.2 & 8.3.3 (and sources cited therein).

176   Indeed, David Kretzmer has characterized the way the Israeli legal system has conceived the relationship between Israel and the Palestinian people under occupation as that of a "benevolent occupant". See David Kretzmer, The Occupation of Justice: The Supreme Court of Israel and the Occupied Territories (2002) (Ch. 4). On the gendered nature of trusteeship, Fionnuala Ní Aoláin observes that its "masculinity ... derives from the inbuilt assumptions of tutelage, infantilization, and patriarchal ordering". Ní Aoláin (2020), above n31, at 343.

177   *See* above text accompanying n159.

issue of termination, their proposal is not an immediate end to trusteeship via transfer of control to the Palestinian people. Rather, it is the replacement of trusteeship-occupation by Israel with trusteeship-administration by an "appropriate international authority."[178] Ultimately, the only problem seems to be Israel's abusive conduct of the occupation – the breach of trust. Not also trusteeship *itself*. Trusteeship is valid. Moreover, the Palestinian people will still need it even if the abusive trustee in the form of Israel is removed.

This proposal for a (presumably brief) period of trusteeship by an "appropriate international authority" as an alternative to prolonged, abusive state-conducted trusteeship implies a normative distinction between the two, and a consequent legitimation of the former, echoing ideas I have identified in earlier work.[179] Trusteeship conducted by international organizations – ITA – has been treated by commentators as normatively legitimate on the basis that, unlike state-conducted trusteeships, the trustee can be relied upon to be selfless and humanitarian. Consequently, trusteeship will be conducted in good faith, not abusively (in both its conduct, and in its application of the test of when local people are "ready" for self-administration). In this way, trusteeship is revived on a now-supposedly-genuinely-temporary basis. And so, the realization of self-determination is modified.

In a different sense, it can be helpful to *link* state-conducted occupations with ITA and distinguish these practices from state-conducted colonial trusteeship (including under the Mandate and Trusteeship arrangements), to explain another way that the significance of self-determination is obscured when it comes to the former practices. The repudiation of trusteeship-over-people via self-determination in UNGA Resolution 1514 was articulated in general terms ("shall never serve"). However, it was originally affirmed in the colonial context in particular. It is perhaps significant, then, that it is mostly the manifestations of trusteeship-over-people that are not formally designated legally to be "colonial" that have prevailed in the "post-colonial" or, put differently, "post-self-determination-repudiation-of-trusteeship"-era. Describing the state-conducted manifestations of these activities as "occupations" perhaps does the work of obscuring the relevance of self-determination to them.[180] Indeed,

---

178  *Id.*

179  Wilde (2008), above n18, Ch. 8, section 8.7, especially 8.7.2.3.

180  And, indeed, also describing the international-organization-conducted activities (International Territorial Administration-ITA) as such. For scholars describing ITA as a type of occupation. *See, e.g.*, Steven R. Ratner, *Foreign Occupation and International Territorial Administration: The Challenges of Convergence*, 16 Eur. J. Int'l L. 695 (2005); Roberts (2006), above n22; Benvenisti (2012), above n22, Preface, Ch. 10; Richard Caplan, International Governance of War-Torn Territories: Rule and Reconstruction 3–4 (2005);

occupation is commonly defined as something which does not cover colonialism, for example where Adam Roberts states that, "[a]t the heart of treaty provisions, court decisions and legal writings about occupations is the image of the armed forces of a state exercising some kind of domination or authority over inhabited territory outside the accepted international frontiers of their State *and its dependencies*."[181] What might be neo-colonial is treated as something other than colonial, for the purposes of the application of self-determination as an existential challenge. Self-determination is posited as only relevant to hangovers from the colonial era and not also of ongoing significance. Accordingly, the only other ongoing relevant aspect of external self-determination is the highly controversial and contested notion of groups within states engaging in secession.[182] International law regards this type of self-determination to apply only in situations where a group faces an existential threat ("remedial secession") and even here it is of uncertain legal status.[183] In any case, it is concerned only with groups within the state, not the state and its relations to people outside its territory. This focus on a sub-state group exclusively also takes the attention away from the idea that the people of the state as a whole – like the Iraqi people in 2003 – have the right.

Also significant is how the "post-colonial" state-conducted "occupations" have been normatively disassociated from annexation. In some cases, they were not concerned with it (the occupations of Germany, Austria, Japan, and Iraq, all forms of ITA, certain parts of the oPt). Alternatively, if they were associated with it, this was treated as unlawful in international law (certain parts of the oPt including East Jerusalem [if that is what Israel purports to do there], the Golan, Western Sahara, Timor Leste during the period of Indonesian purported annexation, and Crimea).[184] The normative disassociation from annexation may further enable the occupations to be disassociated from colonialism (even though some forms of colonialism did not involve the assertion of

---

      Simon Chesterman, You, The People: The United Nations, Transitional Administration, and State-Building (2004) (at 6–7, 11–12, & 145). For a discussion of how ITA is framed in a way that can obscure the application of self-determination to it, *see* Wilde (2008), above n18, Ch. 8, Section 8.7. This is partly the issue identified earlier, concerning the normative identity of international organizations compared to that of states.

181    Roberts (1985), above n31, at 300 (emphasis added).

182    *See* the sources cited above n119.

183    *Id.*

184    But on the US treatment of some of these purported annexations as potentially lawful, *see* section 7 of this article. On the question of whether Israel has purported to annex East Jerusalem, *see* above n35.

sovereignty-as-title over colonial territories).[185] Thus, labelling a "colony" as an "occupied territory" preserves the colonial concept of trusteeship-over-people, and fends off the application of self-determination. Whereas the designation "occupied territory" brings with it the prohibition of annexation, it does not by itself (in contrast to "colony") involve an obligation that the arrangement be brought speedily to an end through the application of the external self-determination entitlement. Occupiers are supposedly effectively free to end things if and when they see fit, because they are not colonizers, where the rules are different.

The "post-colonial" era, during which certain manifestations of trusteeship-over-people occurred, is significant not only because it is when the seemingly contradictory external self-determination entitlement was adopted. Also, it is when IHRL emerged, and, within this, self-determination was conceptualized as a "human right." This leads to the third way in which international law ideas perpetuated the trusteeship-basis for ending occupations. Here, paradoxically, self-determination has been downgraded in the discourse of the very area of international law – IHRL – within which it was situated.

The humanitarian paradigm shift in the laws of war with the Geneva Conventions can be seen as part of the broader foundation of modern IHRL, starting with the adoption of the UDHR commemorated at the Muwatin conference. The UDHR is part of the so-called "international bill of rights" including the two global human rights covenants. These were followed by a range of instruments dealing with the rights of particular groups and types of rights, many of which Israel and Palestine are parties to.[186]

---

185    On the issue of title over colonial territories, *see, e.g.*, Crawford (2007), above n124, at 282 *et seq*; Anghie (2005), above n12, at 82, stating that "[o]nce colonization took place, the colonizing power assumed sovereignty over the non-European territory ..." *See also, id.*, at 82–3. This is also implicit in Crawford's analysis of the effect of the self-determination entitlement on colonial title. *Id.*, at 613–615. On colonial title generally, *see, e.g.*, W.W. Willoughby & C.G. Fenwick, Types of Restricted Sovereignty and of Colonial Autonomy (1919); M.F. Lindley, The Acquisition and Government of Backward Territory in International Law: Being a Treatise on the Law and Practice Relating to Colonial Expansion (1926); Q. Wright, Mandates Under the League of Nations (1930); D.K. Fieldhouse, Colonialism 1870–1945: An Introduction 16 (1981); Robert Jennings & Arthur Watts, Oppenheim's International Law. Volume I: Peace §§84–85 (9th ed., 1992); O.C. Okafor, Re-Defining Legitimate Statehood: International Law and State Fragmentation in Africa 20–32 (2000); Anghie (2005), above n12 (esp. Chs. 1–4); Anthony Anghie, *Finding the Peripheries: Sovereignty and Colonialism in Nineteenth-Century International Law*, 40 Harvard Int'l L. J. 1 (1999).

186    For the details of which human rights treaties Israel and Palestine have ratified, *see*: https://tbinternet.ohchr.org/_layouts/15/TreatyBodyExternal/Treaty.aspx?CountryID=5& Lang=EN.

USING THE MASTER'S TOOLS TO DISMANTLE THE MASTER'S HOUSE

The UDHR does not contain the right to self-determination. It was only with the covenants, adopted in 1966, that the shift in the global normative treatment of colonialism was reflected in IHRL. The right is included, strikingly, as a common provision at the start of both instruments, in article 1.[187]

> 1. All peoples have the right of self-determination. By virtue of that right they freely determine their political status and freely pursue their economic, social and cultural development.
> [...]
> 3. The States Parties to the present Covenant ... shall promote the realization of the right of self-determination, and shall respect that right, in conformity with the provisions of the Charter of the United Nations.[188]

Through this, self-determination, existing already in international law and, as mentioned, the legal basis for formal sovereign-state-based "independence" for peoples subject to colonial rule, was conceptualized as a "human right."[189] In General Comment 12 on ICCPR article 1, the UN Human Rights Committee stated that:

> Paragraph 3 ... is particularly important in that it imposes specific obligations on States parties, not only in relation to their own peoples but vis-à-vis all peoples which have not been able to exercise or have been deprived of the possibility of exercising their right to self-determination.[190]

---

187    ICCPR art. 1, above n119; ICESCR art. 1, above n119.

188    *Id.*

189    On self-determination as a human right, *see* G.A. Res. 1514 (XV) (1960), above n139, which invokes "fundamental human rights" in its preamble; ICJ Wall Advisory Opinion, above n75, para. 88, which refers to common article 1 of the human rights covenants in its treatment of the law of self-determination; Legal Consequences of the Separation of the Chagos Archipelago from Mauritius in 1965, Advisory Opinion, 2019 I.C.J. Rep. 95 (Feb. 25), para. 144 (which describes self-determination is a "fundamental human right"), and para. 154 (which refers to common article 1 of the human rights covenants in its treatment of the law of self-determination); U.N. C.C.P.R., *General Comment No. 12: Article 1 (Right to Self-determination)*, U.N. Doc. HRI/GEN/1/Rev.1 at 12 (1984) [*hereinafter* General Comment 12]. *See also* the commentary in Wilde (2008), above n18, at 160–1 (and sources cited therein).

190    General Comment 12, above n189, para. 6. Jan Klabbers discusses this general comment, criticizing it for seemingly having an "underlying conception" which "appears to be the rather limited one of a legal norm that can only (or predominantly) be implied domestically" (the word "implied" is perhaps a typo, and should be "applied"). Jan Klabbers, *The Right to Be Taken Seriously: Self-Determination in International Law*, 28 Hum. Rts. Q. 186,

Israel's obligations in this regard apply to the Palestinian people irrespective of whether they are located in a territory forming part of another state also a party to the Covenant, which the Palestinian people in the West Bank and Gaza were not until Palestine ratified the treaty in 2014:[191]

> The obligations exist irrespective of whether a people entitled to self-determination depends on a State party to the Covenant or not. It follows that all States parties to the Covenant should take positive action to facilitate realization of and respect for the right of peoples to self-determination.[192]

The remainder of the covenants, and all the other human rights treaties applicable to both states, cover rights which have implications for the lives of Palestinian people under the occupation only[193] (the Arab Charter on Human Rights, which Palestine is a party to, and Israel is not, contains a right of self-determination with provisions directly relevant to the Palestinian people).[194] Unlike self-determination, these rights do not address the existential legitimacy of the occupation. In this sense, these areas of IHRL operate in the same way as IHL generally/occupation law in particular – as a regulatory system grafted onto the conduct of the occupation.

The UN Human Rights Committee, the body that monitors compliance with and provides authoritative interpretations of the ICCPR, has held that ICCPR article 1 vests a right in only groups, not also individuals. Therefore, an individual cannot claim to be the victim of a violation of the provision for the purposes of bringing an individual complaint (a "communication") to the

---

198. However, Klabbers is focusing only on para. 4 of the General Comment, which might indeed be characterized in this way.

191 On this ratification, *see*: https://tbinternet.ohchr.org/_layouts/15/TreatyBodyExternal/ Treaty.aspx?CountryID=5&Lang=EN. This partly implicates the broader issue, beyond the scope of the present piece, as to whether Palestine is a "state" for the purposes of ratifying the Covenant. On this issue, *see* above n135.

192 General Comment 12, above n189, para. 6.

193 The African Charter of Human and Peoples' Rights, which, obviously, the two states are not a party to, includes a right of self-determination (Art. 20.1). *See* African Charter on Human and Peoples' Rights, O.A.U. Doc. CAB/LEG/67/3 rev. 5 (1981).

194 Arab Charter on Human Rights art. 2 (reprinted in 12 I.H.R.R. 893 (2005) (2004) (*see*, in particular, paras. 3 & 4). On Palestine being a party, *see* Mervat Rishmawi, *The League of Arab States: Human Rights Standards and Mechanisms*, Open Society Foundations, Cairo Institute for Human Rights (2015).

# USING THE MASTER'S TOOLS TO DISMANTLE THE MASTER'S HOUSE

committee.[195] This is not directly relevant to Israel – Israel has not accepted the right of individual complaints to the committee under Optional Protocol 1 to the ICCPR.[196] But the general effect of the committee's position, combined with the absence of the right of self-determination in the American and European regional instruments, is as follows. Most of the generators of jurisprudence on the meaning and scope of human rights treaty law – decisions associated with individual communications or complaints/cases to the committee and the American and European enforcement bodies – has produced what is now a dense field of law in which self-determination is largely absent.[197] When that is considered alongside the body of human rights treaty law, where self-determination is included only in two potentially globally-applicable treaties, the result is a normative mass conceiving IHRL as a regulatory regime grafted onto the conduct of state authority, whether territorially or extraterritorially. And not also a body of law that can, in certain circumstances, place the legitimacy of the existence of that authority into question.

It might have been thought that although the UN Human Rights Committee seems to have excluded considering self-determination through individual communications, it would take the opportunity to address the right through the state reporting system. Indeed, in General Comment 12, the UN Human Rights Committee stated that: "The reports should contain information on the performance of these obligations and the measures taken to that end."[198]

However, for this body, and the other committee operating under the ICESCR, in their concluding observations on Israel, and the related lists of issues they ask that state to take up, the opportunity has been largely missed. When addressing the situation of the Palestinian people in the oPt, the few references to article 1 and the right to self-determination are all made in relation to second-order issues (*e.g.*, the expansion of settlements, freedom of

---

195 In the words of the Committee, "... the Committee observed that the author, as an individual, could not claim to be the victim of a violation of the right of self-determination enshrined in article 1 of the Covenant. Whereas the Optional Protocol provides a recourse procedure for individuals claiming that their rights have been violated, article 1 of the Covenant deals with rights conferred upon peoples, as such." *Ivan Kitok v. Sweden*, U.N. Doc. CCPR/C/33/D/197/1985 (July 27, 1988), para. 6.3.

196 *See* the website cited above n191.

197 *See, e.g.*, the databases of decisions available at: https://juris.ohchr.org/; http://www.oas .org/en/topics/human_rights.asp; http://echr.coe.int/echr/en/hudoc; https://www.achpr .org; http://www1.umn.edu/humanrts/africa/comcases/allcases.html; and the works listed in OUP HR list (2017), above n8; and Robert McCorquodale, *Self-Determination: A Human Rights Approach*, 43 Int'l & Comp. L. Q. 857, 871–872 (1994).

198 General Comment 12, above n189, para. 6.

60                                                                                                                          WILDE

movement etc.).[199] The "external" right to be free of the occupation itself is ignored. Thus, for example, the committees address land expropriation only on an individual level, and only in terms of the impact on the rights of the individuals affected. Yet Israel potentially "expropriates" land also on a collective level, as in the case of the purported annexation of East Jerusalem, which, if the case, involves an effort by the state of Israel to take land from

---

199   C.E.S.C.R., *List of issues to be taken up in connection with the consideration of the second periodic report of Israel*, U.N. Doc. E/C.12/Q/ISR/2 (June 5, 2002), para. 1; *C.E.S.C.R., List of issues to be taken up in connection with the consideration of the third periodic report of Israel*, U.N. Doc E/C.12/ISR/Q/3 (Dec. 9, 2010), para. 3 [*hereinafter* CESCR (2010)]; C.E.S.C.R., *Concluding Observations of the Committee on Economic, Social and Cultural Rights: Israel*, U.N. Doc. E/C.12/1/Add.27 (Dec. 4, 1998), paras. 11 & 16–17 [*hereinafter* CESCR (1998)]; C.C.P.R., *Concluding Observations of the Human Rights Committee: Israel*, U.N. Doc. CCPR/C/ISR/CO/3 (Sep. 3, 2010), paras. 8 & 16 [*hereinafter* CCPR (2010)]; C.C.P.R., *Concluding observations of the Human Rights Committee: Israel*, U.N. Doc. C/ISR/CO/4 (Nov. 21, 2019), paras. 12 & 17 [*hereinafter* CCPR (2019)]; C.C.P.R., *List of issues to be taken up in connection with the consideration of the Third periodic report of Israel*, U.N. Doc. CCPR/C/ISR/Q/3 (Nov. 17, 2009), para. 3 [*hereinafter* CCPR (2009)]; C.C.P.R., *List of issues prior to the submission of the fourth periodic report of Israel*, U.N. Doc. C/ISR/Q/4 (Aug. 31, 2002), paras. 1, 8, & 18–19 [*hereinafter* CCPR (2012)]; C.C.P.R., *List of issues prior to submission of the fifth periodic report of Israel*, U.N. Doc. C/ISR/Q/PR/5 (Sep. 7, 2018), paras. 6, 8, & 18–19 [*hereinafter* CCPR (2018)]. Israel has refuted the applicability of the Covenants to it as far as the oPt are concerned, which has implications for its willingness to report on the situation there to the committees. But both committees have rejected this position on applicability, and have, indeed, addressed the situation of the Palestinian people in the oPt. *See* C.C.P.R., *Concluding observations of the Human Rights Committee: Israel*, U.N. Doc. CCPR/C/79/Add.93 (Aug. 18, 1998), para. 10 [*hereinafter* CCPR (1998)]; C.C.P.R., *Concluding observations of the Human Rights Committee: Israel*, U.N. Doc. CCPR/CO/78/ISR (Aug. 21, 2003), para. 11; CCPR (2010), *id.*, para. 5; CCPR (2019), *id.*, para. 5; CCPR (2012), *id.*, para. 4. On the position under the ICESCR, *see also* CESCR (1998), *id.*, paras. 7–8; C.E.S.C.R., *Concluding Observations of the Committee on Economic, Social and Cultural Rights: Israel*, U.N. Doc. E/C.12/1/Add.69 (Aug. 13–31, 2001), para. 11 [*hereinafter* CESCR (2001)]; C.E.S.C.R., *Concluding Observations of the Committee on Economic, Social and Cultural Rights: Israel*, U.N. Doc. E/C.12/1/Add.90 (June 26, 2003), para. 31 [*hereinafter* CESCR (2003)]; C.E.S.C.R., *Concluding Observations of the Committee on Economic, Social and Cultural Rights: Israel*, U.N. Doc. E/C.12/ISR/CO/3 (Dec. 16, 2011), para. 8 [*hereinafter* CESCR (2011)]; C.E.S.C.R., *Concluding Observations of the Committee on Economic, Social and Cultural Rights: Israel*, U.N. Doc. E/C.12/ISR/CO/4 (Nov. 12, 2019), paras. 9, 11 [*hereinafter* CESCR (2019)]. On this issue, see also Wilde (2018), above n28; and, for the position under the ICESCR, Ralph Wilde, *Pursuing Global Socio-Economic, Colonial and Environmental Justice through Economic Redistribution: The Potential Significance of Human Rights Treaty Obligations*, in Research Handbook on International Law and Social Rights 81–82 (C. Binder, et al. eds., 2020) (and sources cited therein). For two examples of other practice of the committee in relation to Palestinian self-determination in the context of reporting relating to Italy and Jordan, *see* D McGoldrick, The Human Rights Committee 251 (1994); sources cited in n56.

# USING THE MASTER'S TOOLS TO DISMANTLE THE MASTER'S HOUSE

the Palestinian people as a whole.[200] Such purported annexation necessarily constitutes a violation of collective self-determination. Despite this, whether it is happening/has happened, and the legal consequences of this in the law of self-determination, are not addressed. On the one hand, the UN Human Rights Committee refuses to address self-determination on an individual level in individual complaints. On the other hand, when the collective dimension of the right is violated, this is overlooked in favor of an exclusive focus on the individual dimension in country reporting. Either way, then, the more fundamental questions of violations of the collective right of self-determination are not addressed.

The closest things get is when both committees call for the blockade of Gaza to be lifted, the UN Human Rights Committee invoking article 1 (and other articles) in this context.[201] However, these calls are made only in the context of the humanitarian consequences of the blockade. Indeed, when the UN Human Rights Committee makes its call, the call itself is tied to that specific issue. It states that Israel "should lift its military blockade of the Gaza Strip, insofar as it adversely affects the civilian population."[202] The notion that the blockade might also constitute a more fundamental denial of self-sustaining autonomous freedom, which implicates external self-determination, and that this should also be the basis for it to be lifted, is not addressed.

With exception of General Comment 12 of the UN Human Rights Committee, the main contributions to the jurisprudence of self-determination as a "human right," both its meaning and its application to particular situations, have come from a generalist international law court operating outside the human rights-specific system. This is the ICJ in the *Wall* and *Chagos* Advisory Opinions.[203] In the former opinion, the ICJ addressed the legal consequences of the construction of the Wall by Israel in the oPt, holding this to be violation of, *inter alia*, self-determination.[204] It expressly invoked the articulation of self-determination in IHRL.[205] Presumably because of the limitations of the question put to the ICJ by the UNGA, it did not opine on the legitimacy of the occupation *per se*, on any basis, including in self-determination terms. However, at the end of the Opinion, it stated that:

---

200 On Jerusalem, including the issue of purported annexation, *see* the sources cited above n35.

201 CESCR (2011), above n199, para. 8; CESCR (2019), above n199, para. 11. *See also* CCPR (2019), above n199, para. 19; CCPR (2012), above n199, para. 19.

202 CCPR (2010), above n199, para. 8.

203 *See* the quotations and associated citations above n189.

204 *Id.*

205 *Id.*

> The Court considers that it has a duty to draw the attention of the General Assembly ... to the need for ... efforts to be encouraged with a view to achieving as soon as possible, on the basis of international law, a negotiated solution to the outstanding problems and the establishment of a Palestinian State, existing side by side with Israel.[206]

This is notable because it postulates two objectives, an agreement ("negotiated solution to the outstanding problems"), and the need for a Palestinian state to be established (which can be understood as the realization of self-determination), without also, as in some of the other approaches reviewed above, suggesting that the former is a prerequisite for the latter.[207] The requirement that Israel needs to "agree" to the realization of Palestinian statehood is also implicitly ruled out by the ICJ prefacing the achievement of the two objectives as needing to be "on the basis of international law."

When it was asked a broader question encompassing the equivalent matter in the case of the legitimacy of the UK authority over the Chagos Archipelago, the ICJ in the latter Opinion took the step on the question of ending such authority that was absent from the former Opinion. It applied what it now referred to as a "fundamental human right" of self-determination to find that the continued UK administration was unlawful, and the UK had an obligation "to bring an end to its administration as rapidly as possible."[208] There is no mention that such an end should come after an agreement, and/or when the population whose return it might enable are deemed "ready." The requirement is "as rapidly as possible."

That a generalist court could make a greater contribution to the law on self-determination as a human right than human rights bodies is perhaps not just an inevitable consequence of the marginalized treatment of the topic by such bodies.[209] These two related developments may reflect a significant syndrome within each set of actors which operates in a mutually reinforcing fashion.

---

206 ICJ Wall Advisory Opinion, above n75, at 162.

207 For these approaches, *see* above text accompanying n156 *et seq*, & Section 6. For a reading of the meaning of UNSC Resolution 242 consonant with the ICJ approach, *see* above n100. *See also* above n167.

208 ICJ Chagos Advisory Opinion, above n189, paras. 144, 174, & 177–8.

209 For further analysis on the related subject of contribution made by the ICJ to jurisprudence on the extraterritorial application of IHRL generally, *see* Ralph Wilde, *Human Rights Beyond Borders at the World Court: The Significance of the International Court of Justice's Jurisprudence on the Extraterritorial Application of International Human Rights Law Treaties*, 12 Chinese J. Int'l L. 639 (2013).

On the one hand, human rights experts and expert bodies may be uncomfortable straying into a topic requiring them to move outside their specialism to take in general public international law. This may be especially the case on a subject that even by the standards of human rights is contested and controversial. It concerns not simply whether particular state practices are lawful (which they normally consider), but whether the very exercise of state authority in a given territorial area is itself lawful. Moreover, in order to determine the legality of the existence of the occupation, it would be necessary to account for not only the law on self-determination, but also the law on the use of force. The particular area of international law they would have to move into is of the most fundamental character in the field.[210]

On the other hand, and by contrast, ranging across different areas of international law (including the law on the use of force), and addressing such existential questions, is the normal business of the ICJ. The approach taken by human rights experts and expert bodies may also reflect the idea that the relevance of external self-determination in the post-colonial era is exclusively about groups within states, not also when states dominate groups outside their sovereign territories. Since the former category of the concept is regarded to be of somewhat uncertain legal standing (certainly when it comes to its secessionary consequences), the overall topic can itself sometimes appear to be of an extra-legal character: non-justiciable and exclusively political.

Whatever the cause, there is not a rich jurisprudence on external self-determination by human rights bodies that Palestinian people can draw on when seeking to invoke the human right to self-determination to frame their assertion of freedom. And they cannot currently expect the support of international human rights NGOs either. These organizations, such as Amnesty International and Human Rights Watch, have not generally concerned themselves with external self-determination, or called for an end to the occupation on this or any other basis, when it comes to Palestine.[211] It will be recalled that Amnesty International UK asks for support in order to "help end the 50 year oppression of the Palestinians".[212] But it then articulates its objective in this regard "to end the human rights abuses suffered by Palestinians under the

---

210 The potential for this is explored further below, text accompanying n230, *et seq.*

211 *See* Amnesty International, *Israel and the Occupied Palestinian Territories* Amnesty International (2019) [*hereinafter* Amnesty International (2019)], https://www.amnesty.org/en/location/middle-east-and-north-africa/israel-and-occupied-palestinian%20-territories/report-israel-and-occupied-palestinian-territories/; Human Rights Watch, *Israel and Palestine Events of 2019* (2019) [*hereinafter* Human Rights Watch (2019)], https://www.hrw.org/world-report/2020/country-chapters/israel/palestine.

212 Amnesty International UK (2019), above n10.

Israeli occupation," not also to end the occupation itself.[213] In a complementary move, the self-determination-omitting UDHR is posited as the "bedrock of all" Amnesty's campaigning, as "the most concerted effort to date to bring together all fundamental rights, and is used as the basis for all international human rights law."[214] This all fits perfectly for an account of IHRL that focuses exclusively on those areas of this law regulating the treatment of individuals under a state's authority, whilst ignoring the right regulating the legitimacy of the exercise of authority itself. In this way, the "tools" of IHRL are concerned with making conditions for life as part of the master's house better, not dismantling the house – the conditions of oppression – itself. In a gaslighting move, this is placed under the bold, dissimulating banner of efforts to "end" the "oppression of Palestinians".

Here there is symmetry with the aforementioned limited IHL/occupation law focus. For the two human rights committees, and two leading international human rights NGOs, IHRL only means rendering the occupation supposedly more humane, not also ending it. What is striking about adopting the exclusively regulatory approach from IHL in IHRL is that, unlike the former, the latter does actually include a clear existential challenge to the occupation. It was observed earlier that it is necessary to depart from the worldview of IHL and occupation law to challenge the existence of the occupation. It would also seem to be necessary to depart from the worldview of human rights – at least as presently understood by the two human rights committees and two leading international human rights NGOs – to advocate for self-determination, both generally, *and as an entitlement in IHRL.*

IHRL experts, committees and NGOs encourage oppressed people around the world to use the language of IHRL to articulate their demands. But if they do this, and the demand in question is liberation, and the language they use is self-determination, will these experts, and the institutions of IHRL, listen?

The foregoing is predicated on a concept of Palestinian external self-determination within the non-Israeli boundaries of the remainder of Mandatory Palestine, because of the prior acceptance of Israeli statehood as a given. Since Israel's IHRL obligations concerning self-determination apply not only externally, but also internally, there are also implications for Palestinian people within the state.

The UNGA affirmed in 1948 the right of return to Palestinian people displaced from what became Israel in 1948.[215] This has been repeated by that body

---

213   *Id.*

214   Amnesty International UK (2018) above n9.

215   *See, e.g.,* G.A. Res. 194 (III) (Dec. 11, 1948); Kathleen Lawand, *The Right to Return of Palestinians in International Law,* 8 Int'l J. Refugee L. 532 (1996); Yahia (1970), above n16,

numerous times since. Such a right would be the basis for the Jahalin to return to al-Naqab. However, the UN Human Rights Committee has never addressed the right of Palestinian people outside Israel to return there, or, even, the rights of Palestinian people outside the oPt to return to those territories. The only treatment of the return topic, a statement relating to what it calls "the right to return to one's own country," is in the context of the movement of Palestinian people between Gaza, East Jerusalem and the West Bank.[216] This is only "return" in the sense that Palestinian people have to leave Palestine (defined as the oPt) and "return" to it to get between the West Bank and Gaza. And even this doesn't happen when Palestinian people move between East Jerusalem and the rest of the West Bank – it is "returning" to a different location within, not returning to from outside, the "country" (unless Israel is regarded as having lawfully annexed East Jerusalem ...). Thus, the UN Human Rights Committee invokes a "right to return," only to define it in a manner that is distorted for its own purposes and excludes entirely the issue the term is usually invoked to address. Under this approach, the right to so-called "return" of the Jahalin is a right to move between the place they were displaced to in East Jerusalem, and Gaza, if they happen to wish to visit Gaza, and back again. There is no right to return *to the place they were displaced from*.

The UN Committee on Economic, Social and Cultural Rights (CESCR) has addressed the issue of return to Israel thus:

> The Committee notes with concern that the [Israeli] Law of Return, which allows any Jew from anywhere in the world to immigrate and thereby virtually automatically enjoy residence and obtain citizenship in Israel, discriminates against Palestinians in the diaspora upon whom the Government of Israel has imposed restrictive requirements which make it almost impossible to return to their land of birth.[217]

Thus, concerns about "return" are limited to restrictions on migration to Israel that are discriminatory as between Jewish and Palestinian people. Presumably, if Israel halted further inward migration, the concerns would fall away. As would any Palestinian right to return. The statement also implicitly treats the issue of the return of Palestinian people who were displaced from the place they would return to, as equivalent to the ability of all Jewish

---

at 106–115; Albanese & Takkenberg (2020), above n38, at 342–375 (and sources cited therein); Terry Rempel, *The Right to Return: Drafting Paragraph 11 of General Assembly Resolution 194 (III), December 11, 1948*, 21 Palestine Y.B. Int'l L. 78 (2020).

216   CCPR (1998), above n199, para. 22.

217   CESCR (1998), above n199, para. 13. *See also* CESCR (2001), above n199, para. 14; and CESCR (2003), above n199, para. 18.

people from anywhere in the world to perform Aliyah, regardless of any prior similar direct past personal experience of displacement from the territory which has since 1948 been Israel. For the committee, the merit of Amran Reshaq's wish to return to the land of his birth has no significance by itself. It is only to be appraised *when compared to* the possibilities that exist for Jewish people generally, regardless of an equivalent place-of-birth-connection, to migrate to Israel.

Otherwise, the only focus has been on return within Israel, *i.e.* of Palestinian citizens of Israel who were internally-displaced (irrelevant to the Jahalin and to many other Palestinian refugees). Only the CESCR has addressed this.[218] The UN Human Rights Committee has been silent, just as it has been on return to Israel. The CESCR has partially conceptualized its focus on internal return under article 1. This reflects the position both committees, and also Amnesty International, took in invoking Palestinian self-determination in the context of the enjoyment of this right *as citizens of Israel* when considering the 2018 Israeli nation-state law. That law defines Israel as the "Nation State of the Jewish People." In this context, they expressed concerns about (the CESCR), asked questions about (the UN Human Rights Committee), criticized (Amnesty) the law for its (potentially, for the committees) discriminatory effect on non-Jewish people in Israel when it comes to their enjoyment of, *inter alia*, their right to self-determination.[219] For the committees, this comes in the context of the aforementioned exclusive focus on second-order aspects of self-determination for the Palestinian people. For Amnesty, this is the only instance where any form of self-determination is referenced at all.[220] Seemingly, this right is only relevant to the human rights situation across Israel and the oPt insofar as Israeli citizens within the Israeli state are concerned. The only issue of Palestinian self-determination Amnesty is concerned with is the status of Palestinian citizens of Israel.

Moreover, the pejorative description of the nation state law as (potentially) discriminatory with respect to the enjoyment of self-determination implies that the self-determination unit of the people of Israel, in which equal

---

218    CESCR (1998), above n199, para. 25; CESCR (2010), above n199, para. 3.

219    CESCR (2019), above n199, paras. 16–17 & 68; CCPR (2012), above n199, para. 1; C.E.S.C.R., *List of issues in relation to the fourth periodic report of Israel*, U.N. Doc. E/C.12/ISR/Q/4 (Apr. 3, 2019), paras. 11–12 & 25 [*hereinafter* CESCR (2019)b]; CCPR (2018), above n199, para. 6. *See also* the determinations on prior iterations of the Basic Law, in CCPR (2010), above n199, para. 6; C.C.P.R., *Concluding observations of the Human Rights Committee: Israel*, U.N. Doc. CCPR/C/ISR/CO/4 (Nov. 21, 2014), para. 7 [*hereinafter* CCPR (2014)]; CCPR (2009), above n199, para. 2; CCPR (2012), above n199, para. 5.

220    Amnesty International (2019), above n211.

USING THE MASTER'S TOOLS TO DISMANTLE THE MASTER'S HOUSE  67

participation is being (potentially) denied, is legitimate. Otherwise, the denial would not be problematic. Implicitly, the right of self-determination of the people of the state of Israel is affirmed as legitimate. Thus, an approach which is ostensibly not concerned with such existential matters as whether or not a particular group has a right of self-determination – hence the absence of any concern for (Amnesty) or very partial treatment of (the two UN committees) Palestinian self-determination – ends up in such terrain, but only as far as Israeli self-determination is concerned. What is supposedly about Palestinian rights – not to be discriminated against – ends up being doubly objectionable. First, it ignores the right of Palestinian collective self-determination, whether entirely (Amnesty) or for the most part (the committees). Second, this neglect occurs in the context of an affirmation of the right of self-determination of the people *of the very state* whose actions in a different (but related) context are preventing Palestinian self-determination from being realized. Put differently, an effort to combat discrimination against Palestinian people relative to treatment of Jewish people within Israel actually discriminates *against* them relative to the treatment of Jewish people. And it does so on the more relevant matter of their right to self-determination as part of a collective Palestinian identity rather than as citizens of Israel. Invoking discrimination in this context is particularly, ironically egregious given how racism underpins the concept of trusteeship that operates as the alibi for denying self-determination to the Palestinian people. An ostensibly 'anti-discrimination' critique thus serves racist ends.

## VII    Erosion of Legal Standards?

The analysis in sections 3 and 4 indicates how the application of the international law on the use of force, and self-determination, leads to the position that the occupation should end, and Israel's purported annexation of Palestinian territory, whether existent (*e.g.*, potentially, East Jerusalem) or prospective, is/would be without legal effect. Sections 5 and 6 illustrate how, despite this, occupations have sometimes been prolonged, and *de facto* annexations are not subjected to much effective criticism, in part because the significance of self-determination has been downgraded and even overlooked entirely.

All of this presupposes that the legal framework is as sections 3 and 4 describe. And it assumes, in consequence, that the practice under evaluation and the reactions to it by other states indicates a situation of prolonged legal violation and a failure by other states to stop this. But there is a different possibility: that this practice and the responses to it by states might somehow have effected, or might be in the process of effecting, a normative shift. Are the rules being altered to accommodate that which had previously been prohibited?[221]

Writing in 1963 about the prohibition on annexation through the use of force, Robbie Jennings suggested that in a situation where the law on the use of force has not been enforced, in the sense that a state controlling territory unlawfully has not been made by the "international community" to withdraw,

> it may eventually come about that a title by consolidation is acquired through recognitions or other forms of the position expressive of the will of the international community. On the other hand the general reaction of third states may be to adopt an attitude of non-recognition; and in these circumstances it seems illogical to suppose that any form of prescription even by adverse possession could begin to run.[222]

Jennings made the foregoing remark in the context of a situation where a state has "successfully seized possession of territory by illegal force and seems likely to stay."[223] It would apply *a fortiori* if, as here, the "stay" has been prolonged and sustained through an unlawful use of force. According to this possibility, whereas an unlawful occupation could not by itself found valid title, the taint caused by being based on the use of force could be remedied through recognition by other states.

Jennings speculates about this possibility, presumably, on the basis of an orthodox, positivist approach to international law. Rules are made by states, and states can change these rules through practice ("expressive of the will of the international community"). The very existence, or at least the application in particular instances, of the international legal protections against force-enabled annexation are, therefore, potentially precariously linked to the position states take. One might also ask whether this idea could also operate to encompass the law on self-determination and *its* significance to the prohibition on annexation. And also how this law, and the law on the use of force, prohibit the prolonged occupation.

States individually and through the UN have mostly taken the position that the Palestinian territories, including East Jerusalem, are "occupied." This presupposes non-recognition of any annexation, whether generally or specifically

---

221  For a discussion of this general topic when it comes to Israeli and US policy, with a predominant focus on IHL rules, *see* George Bisharat, *Violence's Law Israel's Campaign to Transform International Legal Norms*, 43 J. Palestine Stud. 68 (2013).

222  Jennings (1963/2017), above n76, 2017 reprint version, at 84. *See also id.*, at 78–82.

223  *Id.*, at 84.

# USING THE MASTER'S TOOLS TO DISMANTLE THE MASTER'S HOUSE 69

as far as East Jerusalem is concerned (if relevant).[224] But it seems the US position has shifted, both in relation to Jerusalem, potentially, with the relocation of the US embassy there from Tel Aviv in 2019, and other parts of the West Bank covered by President Trump's "deal of the century" in 2020.[225] Furthermore, the Trump administration recognized Israeli sovereignty over the Golan heights, and Morocco's sovereignty over Western Sahara.[226] The Golan recognition defies the prohibition of annexation through the use of force. The two recognitions defy the invalidity of claims to title over territory when another state is sovereign over that territory (Syria in the Golan) or the territory is a non-state self-determination unit where "sovereignty" resides in the people (Western Sahara). The US position on the non-East-Jerusalem parts of the West Bank covered by the "deal of the century" may shift in the post-Trump era. But when it comes to the embassy in Jerusalem, the Biden Administration stated it would not move back to Tel Aviv, and the new US Senate in 2021 voted to affirm funding for the embassy in its Jerusalem location.[227] At the time of writing, President Biden had not shifted the US position on sovereignty over the Golan or Western Sahara (although on the former, his Secretary of State seemed to indicate the matter was to be reviewed).[228]

---

224  *See, e.g.*, Roberts (1990), above n31, at 69 (and sources cited therein). On the question of whether Israel has purported to annex East Jerusalem, *see* above n35.

225  A treatment of the nature of the US position on Jerusalem, both prior to and with the relocation of the embassy in 2019, and the prospects of Israeli annexations based on the "deal of the century," are beyond the scope of the present piece.

226  On the recognition re the Golan heights, *see* Donald J. Trump, *Proclamation on Recognizing the Golan Heights as Part of the State of Israel*, Trump White House Archives (Mar. 25, 2019), https://trumpwhitehouse.archives.gov/presidential-actions/proclamation-recogni zing-golan-heights-part-state-israel/; Hoffman (2020), above n19, para. 33; *United States Recognizes Israeli Sovereignty Over the Golan Heights*, 113 Am. J. Int'l L. 613 (2019). On the recognition re Western Sahara, *see* Trump White House Archives (2020), above n154.

227  *See Biden says he'd leave US embassy in Jerusalem if elected*, Al Jazeera (Apr. 29, 2020), https://www.aljazeera.com/news/2020/4/29/biden-says-hed-leave-us-embassy-in-jeru salem-if-elected; *Roll Call Vote 117th Congress – 1st Session: To establish a deficit-neutral reserve fund relating to maintaining the United States Embassy in Jerusalem, Israel*, United States Senate (Feb. 4, 2021), https://www.senate.gov/legislative/LIS/roll_call_lists/roll_call _vote_cfm.cfm?congress=117&session=1&vote=00030; *US to keep embassy in Jerusalem: Biden's top diplomat*, Al Jazeera (Jan. 20, 2021), https://www.aljazeera.com/news/2021/1/ 20/us-secretary-of-state-blinken-us-embassy-to-remain-in-jerusalem.

228  On US Secretary of State position on the Golan, *see, e.g.*, Jacob Magid, *Blinken supports Israel holding Golan, but backs off recognizing sovereignty*, Times of Israel (Feb. 9, 2021), https://www.timesofisrael.com/blinken-supports-israel-holding-golan-but-backs-off -recognizing-sovereignty/. On the Western Sahara, 27 US Senators wrote to President Biden in January 2021 calling on him to reverse the recognition of Moroccan sovereignty

This practice suggests that the possibilities outlined by Jennings have to be considered seriously. Whether the substantive rules of international law can be and are in the process of being altered is beyond the scope of this article. Jennings wrote in 1963 and does not account for the law of external self-determination, which was still in the process of being widely acknowledged to exist at that time. Further developments, to treat prohibitions on the use of force, and obligations to respect self-determination, as having *jus cogens* status (mentioned above in relation to other obligations), and the latter as having *erga omnes* status, were also yet to happen.[229] These developments implicate whether and on what basis state practice could water down the prohibitions (*jus cogens*) and also, relatedly, the legal consequences of any state practice incompatible with these prohibitions (*erga omnes*). Moreover, the US is an outlier in its position on the Golan, East Jerusalem, and Western Sahara.

Nonetheless, it is not a huge leap from the position adopted by the two UN human rights committees and leading human rights NGOs, which fails to characterize the continued occupation as a violation of self-determination, to a position that positively affirms the occupation as not such a violation (indeed, as not an occupation at all). Creating a bigger space between their position and the latter position might negatively impact the prospects of the latter position taking hold. Those seeking to hold the line on the current legal standpoint on the right of Palestinian self-determination, when this is under threat, need to consider the normative consequences of their silence on the question of the significance of this right to ending the occupation.

In General Comment 36 of 2018, on the right to life under article 6 of the ICCPR, the UN Human Rights Committee made the remarkable statement that "states parties engaged in acts of aggression as defined in international law, resulting in deprivation of life, violate ipso facto article 6."[230] This potentially constitutes an expression of willingness to address the implications of the law on the use of force for one of the rights under the covenant. The committee seemingly crossing this Rubicon when it comes to the right to life sets a precedent for it and the CESCR to assess the legality of the continued

---

by President Trump; *see*: https://www.inhofe.senate.gov/newsroom/press-releases/inhofe-leahy-lead-25-colleagues-to-urge-biden-to-reverse-misguided-western-sahara-decision.

229    On *jus cogens, see* the sources cited above n115. The prohibition of aggression, and the right of self-determination, are included as further examples ((a) and (h)) on the ILC list cited above in that note. On self-determination as having *erga omnes* status, *see* the sources cited in n119 above.

230    C.C.P.R., *General comment No. 36 (2018) on article 6 of the International Covenant on Civil and Political Rights, on the right to life*, U.N. Doc. CCPR/C/GC/36 (Oct. 30, 2018), para. 70.

occupation according to the right to self-determination and the law on the use of force. Whether they, and human rights NGOs, step up to this challenge and thereby begin to engage with Palestinian claims to end the occupation remains to be seen.

## VIII   Conclusion

> What does it mean when the tools of a racist patriarchy are used to examine the fruits of that same patriarchy? It means that only the most narrow parameters of change are possible and allowable.
>
> AUDRE LORDE[231]

When general areas of international law are invoked to address the needs of the Palestinian people, this is typically done in an uncritical fashion. The present article has attempted to complicate the picture, suggesting some of the downsides to these legal frameworks in how they relate to the existential question of Palestinian liberation.

In certain important respects, the starting point for international law on this subject is to accept Israeli statehood as a given. In consequence, Palestinian freedom must fit around and/or be articulated in relation to Israel's needs. The territory covered by the right of self-determination is that which is "left" of the territory of the Palestine Mandate once Israel is taken into account.[232] Occupation law, the international legal framework commonly invoked, is concerned not with ending the occupation, but with merely "humanizing" it within an overall framework of domination. Even to invoke these standards, it is necessary to recognize Israel's statehood. And this has to be done when it is statehood that is the very thing that the occupation prevents the Palestinian people from realizing effectively. And, moreover, it has to be done despite the fact that it is this statehood on the part of Israel that was created through and continues to operate on the basis of the Nakba, with the consequent position

---

231   Lorde (1984), above n5. On the links between trusteeship and racism, and patriarchy, see above, text accompanying n168 & n170 (racism) and n176 (patriarchy). On the problematic invocation of discrimination by certain human rights bodies, see above, the final paragraph of Section 6. On gender and occupation more generally, see Ní Aoláin (2020), above n31.

232   This reflects the establishment view held by international law experts. But see earlier for the challenge that can be made to it, above n128. Moreover, in any case the position on Jerusalem is more complicated, and, certainly, East Jerusalem is not "Israel" for the purpose of this analysis.

of many Palestinian people as refugees, and the treatment of Palestinian people within Israel as second-class citizens.

Taken together, the law on the use of force and the law of self-determination offer a basis for challenging the legitimacy of the continued existence of the occupation. This can pave the way for the limited version of freedom international law offers to the Palestinian people: statehood in a territory outside the green-line-defined borders of Israel. It also renders unlawful Israeli annexation of that territory, including (if this is what Israel has purported to do) East Jerusalem. But sometimes commentators are fixated on the prohibition of annexation only, without also addressing the ending of the occupation. To make the argument on the latter point requires a move beyond the exclusive annexation-prohibition-fixation, and its partner, the occupation-law fixation. Moreover, Palestinian people are required to counter a further *idée fixe*: the commentariat's predominant approach, and also significant practice within the UN, that Palestinian self-determination should only be realized once there is a peace agreement with Israel. One can challenge this approach, making the case for an immediate end to the occupation by applying the law on the use of force, which is the only basis on which Israel can lawfully maintain the occupation. This leads to the conclusion that the occupation is illegal and constitutes aggression. However, most experts fail to address this area of law, thus making it more difficult to appreciate the significance of it, let alone to invoke and apply it. This enables the "wait for an agreement" alternative to have purchase as an operative norm. Moreover, making the challenge requires an assessment through a framework exclusively concerned with the question of Israel's security needs. Using the law's "tools," therefore, requires Palestinian people to frame their case for liberation not in terms of their perspective at all, but rather in terms of the illegitimacy of Israel's position.

Furthermore, it is difficult to make the self-determination element of the challenge. This is in part because of the way IHRL jurisprudence downgrades and sometimes even completely ignores the significance of the right's external dimension. Such an approach is evident in the practice and statements of the two main international expert committees charged with monitoring the implementation of IHRL, and two leading international human rights NGOs. Just as with the exclusive occupation law-focus, these bodies address second-order issues only without also considering whether the occupation is, in and of itself, a violation of self-determination. It is as if the Palestinian right to external self-determination does not exist. Moreover, paradoxically, when these bodies have addressed the rights of Palestinian citizens of Israel, this has partly included coverage of their right to participate in the collective self-determination unit of that state. Thus, Palestinian self-determination gains attention, but only indirectly, via participation in and as part of the collective self-determination unit of the Israeli people. This brings things full circle, back to the starting point: Israeli statehood and the legal consequences that follow from its recognition (in this case, Israeli statehood as the external instantiation of the collective self-determination right of the people of that state.)

Finally, even these remarkably limited approaches are themselves based on legal concepts – external self-determination and the prohibition on annexation through the use of force – which have been placed under strain by the Trump administration's recognitions in relation to Israel and the Golan, Morocco and Western Sahara, and the moving of the US embassy in Israel to Jerusalem (maintained by the Biden administration). There has been a degree of handwringing by international lawyers about this, notably when it comes to the Golan recognition.[233] But critics need to appreciate how close these policies are to the much more widespread position of ignoring or downplaying the significance of Palestinian external self-determination. It is also necessary to appreciate the relevance of the law on the use of force to the questioning of the existence of the occupation itself, as opposed to merely the implications it has for annexation. More fundamentally, it is necessary to appreciate the risk that framing such criticism by affirming the legal *status quo* might operate as a further distraction technique from the limitations of the current normative order.

The common critique made of international law, including the areas of law this article reviews, is that it may be all well and good, but it is not enforced, because of power imbalances and politics.[234] The present article foregrounds the existence of such imbalances and political preferences *in* the law, and the law's role in enabling them. It is for the Palestinian people to decide what is in their best interests in general, and as regards the deployment of international legal arguments and recourse to international legal mechanisms. What the present article has aimed to do is identify some of the issues at stake with the general features of the legal system that might be relevant when such decisions are made.[235]

---

233    Annexation Letter (2020), above n75.

234    *See, e.g.*, the reported remarks of Mudar Kassis in 2014 Birzeit Conference, above n16, at 152: "Palestinians have seen little enforcement of international law for ... [political/ power] reasons, and [therefore] international law is of limited use for the Palestinian struggle against Israeli colonialism." *See also* the remarks of John Dugard, *id.*, at 154 "the main problem is not the law but those who do not act upon the legal rules."

235    For further discussion of different aspects, *see, e.g.*, the works cited above n16.

## Acknowledgments

Warm thanks are due to Nabila Roukhamieh-McKinna, doctoral student at the UCL Faculty of Laws, for excellent research assistance, and to Ata Hindi of this Journal, for his meticulous editing, and to the participants at the two conferences mentioned in this article, and panels at the Law and Society Association conference, where some of the ideas contained herein were presented, and to the anonymous peer reviewers both at this Journal and in my faculty peer-review college, and to the Editor-in-Chief of this Journal, for their valuable feedback. Warm thanks also to Aseel Albajeh, Ata Hindi, Eitan Diamond, Ellen Saliba, Gëzim Visoka, Marco Longobardo, and Susan Power for kindly sourcing, copying and sending me texts I was unable to obtain through other means. And to Samera Esmeir for kindly giving me the text of her presentation at one of the conferences mentioned in this article, enabling me to cite it herein. My warm thanks also to the following people, with whom I have discussed various aspects of my ideas that have ended up in this article, and have benefited from their insights on them: Laith Abu Zeyad, Matilda Arvidsson, Valentina Azarova, Clive Baldwin, Aslı Bâli, Antal Berkes, Reem Al-Botmeh, James Crawford, Eitan Diamond, Cordula Droege, Noura Erakat, Orna Ben-Naftali, Smadar Ben Natan, Dana Farraj, Rotem Giladi, Daphna Golan, Shahd Hammouri, Ata Hindi, Ardi Imseis, Shawan Jabarin, Mudar Kassis, Asem Khalil, David Kretzmer, Anne Lagerwall, Eliav Lieblich, Karin Loevy, Itamar Mann, Anna Mykytenko, Fionnuala Ní Aoláin, Munir Nusseibeih, Helena van Roosbroeck, Tom Ruys, Charles Shamas, Diala Shamas, Omar Shakir, Nadera Shalhoub-Kevorkian, Raja Shehadeh, Hala Shoaibi, Janique Thoele, Pål Wrange, and the brilliant students at Birzeit University, Al-Quds University and on my "decolonizing law" LLM course at UCL. This article is dedicated to the memories of James Crawford, Vera Gowlland-Debbas and Chandra Lekha Sriram.

# Fact and Fiction: The Nation-State, Colonialism, and International Minority Law

*Sally Shammas*

### Contents

I  Introduction
II  Creating Majorities and Minorities
   A  *Searching for Adequate Definitions*
   B  *Legitimate Power, the Nation-State, and Popular Sovereignty*
III  Minority Rights in International Law
   A  *International Law, Imperialism, and Minorities*
   B  *Friends or Foes? Human Rights Framework and Minority Populations*
IV  The Iraqi Nation-state, Sectarian Politics, and the Question of Minorities
   A  *The Ottomans, the Empire, and the Millet*
   B  *Imperialism, the Mandate, and the Iraqi Nation-State*
   C  *The Post-Conflict Iraqi State and the Minority Question*
V  Conclusions

## I  Introduction

It may sound counter-intuitive to challenge the recognition of minority rights in international law. Why shouldn't the rights of "minority" communities be protected under the umbrella of international human rights law (IHRL)? Why shouldn't communities who possess cultural, linguistic, ethnic, and religious characteristics that differ from those endorsed by the nation-state in which they live be granted protection and autonomy from state interference? Indeed, minority rights are considered as a part of the human rights protection regime because they protect what are deemed as fundamental factors of the human experience – the right to individuality and the right to be able to express that individuality, both as individuals and as part of a larger community.[1] With

---

[1]  See Patrick Macklem, *Minority Rights in International Law*, 6 Int'l J. Const. L. 531, 532 (2008) [hereinafter Macklem].

the rise of "sectarian" conflicts in the Middle East and elsewhere, the need to protect minority communities has become imperative. The rise of extremist identity groups like the Islamic State of Iraq and the Levant (ISIL) and the "genocides" they committed against Christian and non-Sunni communities in Iraq and Syria, illustrates this need.[2]

This article explores the complex relationship between colonialism and international minority rights with special attention to the status of minorities in the current Iraqi governance structure. The article focuses on the extent to which the construction of the nation-state creates such political categories, how international law legitimizes those categories, and how the power-sharing agreements that sanction these categories magnify and politicize human reality. There has been little analysis of the relationship between minority rights as reflected in international conventions and minority rights as translated into power-sharing arrangements. The question thus is whether minority protections in international law are able to provide efficient protection for vulnerable groups or whether they amplify differences and exacerbate violence. In other words, whether international minority law is the solution to the problem or part of the problem.

Minority rights have long been an integral part of international law, dating back to early state treaties in Europe. The League of Nations and primary international legal instruments, such as the minority treaties, made minority status a central concern. It thus can be said that minority rights "[served] as a precursor of human rights protection under international law."[3] Today, many conventions, declarations, and treaties include protections for minorities, particularly in terms of the right to their identity and culture. However, despite their early manifestations within the international legal field, developing a comprehensive understanding of the "minority" category has been challenging because international law overlooks the conditions which create such a category in the first instance. This failure to offer a comprehensive account creates consequences for which particular non-dominant groups are officially recognized as a "minority." In addition, international law is ambiguous surrounding the actual substantive measures that states must take to guarantee the rights of their "minorities." This ambiguity is coupled with an obvious lack of enforcement mechanisms when a given state violate these rights. Moreover, minority rights have a tenuous relationship with the universal human rights regime, because the latter is applicable to individuals only whereas the former's application contains individual as well as communal elements.

---

2   Resolution on 4 February 2016 on the systematic mass murder of religious minorities by the so-called 'ISIS/Daesh,' Eur. Parl. Doc. 2016/2529 (RSP).

3   Wade Mansell & Karen Openshaw, International Law: A Critical Introduction 10 (2013).

FACT AND FICTION                                                                    77

These issues become particularly pressing in situations of conflict, particularly "ethno-sectarian" conflicts where identity plays a central role in the outbreak of violence. More often than not, these types of conflict are not resolved through military victory, but rather through peace-building negotiations, resulting in peace arrangements that seek to conclude fighting and disarm combatants. These peace agreements include power-sharing arrangements between different communal groups involved in a conflict. This governance model has greatly "influenced international policy prescription for conflict zones."[4] Power-sharing arrangements seek to fragment state power between the major stakeholders to decrease majoritarian domination, increase political participation across major national groups, and promote peace and cooperation through democratic means.[5]

If international minority rights provisions inform post-conflict rehabilitation processes, then their incompleteness is unsurprising. The only legally binding provision in international law[6] that covers minority protection focuses exclusively on the exercise of cultural rights while simultaneously creating a tenuous relationship between the state and its citizens by organizing human realities into legally sanctioned categories. Minority rights overlook the existence of intersectional issues, such as poverty, ethnicity, access to governmental resources, and employability. Power-sharing arrangements, on the other hand, specifically legislate in order to guarantee minority representation and political participation. What happens instead is power-sharing arrangements usually harden ethnic divisions by allowing political parties to adopt an identitarian political discourse by affiliating themselves with one ethnic group. Parties that represent majority groups therefore mobilize voters through ethnic incentives, all while excluding non-dominant communities from any substantial decision-making power.

The approaches of both international minority rights and minority rights in power-sharing arrangements overlook the way in which the existence of categories like "majorities" and "minorities" contribute to the outbreak of conflict in the first instance or how they may aggravate conflict through their mobilization. Equally problematic is the assumption that terms like "minority" and "majority" are self-evident, apolitical, and objective categories. Yet these classifications were inseparable from prevailing political conditions, notably

---

4  Allison McCulloch, *Consociational Settlements in Deeply Divided Societies: The Liberal-Corporate Distinction*, 21 Democratization 501 (2014).

5  *See* Sadiki Koko, *The Challenges of Power-sharing and Transitional Justice in Post-Civil War African Countries: Comparing Burundi, Mozambique and Sierra Leone*, 19 Afr. J. Conflict Resol. 81, 84 (2019).

6  *See* International Covenant on Civil and Political Rights art. 27, Dec. 16, 1966, 999 U.N.T.S. 171 [*hereinafter* ICCPR]. *See* section III below.

the exportation of the nation-state form onto countries carved out by imperial rulers in London and Paris.[7] International law sanctified the nation-state which in itself necessitated the creation of minority rights because of the cultural majoritarianism that the nation-state model legitimizes.

In the context of former colonies in the Middle East, the imposition of an arbitrary identity in an arbitrarily defined territory combined with the provision of special treatment for some, but not all, groups has prevented the establishment of a common and inclusive civic identity, regardless of cultural affiliation. In scholarship and practice in the Middle East, the minority/majority dichotomy and other identity categorizations are often used to explain violent conflict. However, such explanations overlook the way in which authoritarian regimes mobilize such categories as "strategies of survival."[8] Authoritarian elites often manipulate popular political demands because they "draw life from ethnic or religious intolerance as a way of justifying the degree of violence required to maintain [and perpetuate] power."[9] In Syria, what started in 2011 as protests against an authoritarian and corrupt regime became a violent ethno-sectarian conflict that has neglected the original demands of reform, equality, and freedom. In Iraq, the power-sharing model has not resulted in political stability or peace. Instead, elites have monopolized it to maintain their hold on political power by increasing sectarian division through the institutionalization of identity politics. This dynamic has resulted in the almost complete eradication of non-Muslim Iraqi communities.

Syria and Iraq share a similar colonial history, as well as a history of authoritarian regimes that proclaimed to be Arab nationalist and were headed by leaders belonging to "minority" groups. The Assad family, members of the small Alawite community, led the Ba'athists in Syria, while Saddam Hussein, a member of the Sunni minority in a majority-Shi'a country, led the Ba'athist regime in Iraq. While the conflict in Syria is far from over, it is likely that its conclusion will come through negotiations and painful concessions by the different warring parties. In Iraq, the instalment of a post-conflict governance model has theoretically concluded the conflict, yet the governance structure has arguably failed to encourage significant political, social, or economic development

---

7  *See* Benjamin White, The Emergence of Minorities in the Middle East: The Politics of Community in French Mandate Syria 22 (2011) [*hereinafter* White (2011)].

8  Joel S. Migdal, Strong Societies and Weak States: State-Society Relations and State Capabilities in the Third World 206–235 (1988).

9  Nader Hashemi & Danny Postel, *Introduction: the Sectarianization Thesis*, in Sectarianization: Mapping the New Politics of the Middle East 9 (Nader Hashemi & Danny Postel eds., 2017) [*hereinafter* Hashemi & Postel].

FACT AND FICTION

for the majority of the population. By taking Iraq as the main case study, this article contends that there are many lessons that can be learned and different strategies of implementation that can be sought when designing a transitional constitution and institutional reform in other cases like Syria.

The remainder of the article is organized as follows. Section II examines international law's contribution to the creation of the majority/minority dichotomy and ties their emergence with the onset of the nation-state form, legitimate governance, and popular sovereignty. Section III then considers the role of minority rights in contemporary international law and assesses the major legal instruments that stipulate these rights, namely the International Convention on Civil and Political Rights (ICCPR) and other United Nations (UN) declarations. It also examines the enduring tension within international law itself, between the individuality of human rights law and the communitarianism underpinning the law on minorities. Section IV considers the case study of Iraq, the way in which Ottoman rule and European imperialism compounded cultural categories and introduced the "number games" from which claims to political power were articulated. It also assesses the ways in which the post-conflict governance restructuring of Iraq continuously fails to adopt an Iraqi identity that is civic, inclusive, and based on equality and human rights. The article maintains that the incompletion and lack of commitment to find a comprehensive minority protection regime has real world consequences when articulating modes of governance in colonially created nations where the state is a by-product of European intervention. It further argues that the international legal regime fails to provide an adequate mechanism for minority protection and has actually led to the further vilification of groups that exist on the margins.

## II    Creating Majorities and Minorities

In the context of governance, the term "minority" indicates a special kind of relationship vis-à-vis the state. This category is not apolitical, objective, or self-evident. Instead, it is contingent on the circumstances in which it emerges and on the power that distributes and institutionalizes its particular understanding. This section explores how notions of "minorities" and "majorities" emerge, their political nature, and their intertwinement with the development of the nation-state form and ensuing ideas of legitimate governance. The enquiry enables an understanding of the general process of creating citizenship as an activity of inclusion and exclusion that creates different tiers of citizenship.

It also considers the legal sanctioning of these categories within the international legal regime of the 20th century.

## A    *Searching for Adequate Definitions*

Etymologically, "minority" connotes a small part of a larger group or item. It indicates a numerical value that is inferior in relation to the larger category, depending on the variable being quantified. However, in socio-political and legal discourse, "minority" takes on an entirely different meaning and can induce far-reaching consequences for those who are designated as members of a minority, as well as for those who are not. Contrary to the perceived self-evident nature of the term "minority," there is no universal consensus of what constitutes a community as a minority. Its definition remains ambiguous, even though the term is widely circulated in international law and acts as a framework for many human rights instruments. It should not be taken for granted that general categories such as "minority," "ethnicity," and "nationalism" are naturally occurring and self-informing because they do not exist outside the context that humans assign to them. Benedict Anderson describes such categories as "cultural artefacts of a particular kind" with the nation itself as an "imagined political community ... imagined as both inherently limited and sovereign."[10] It is this imagined political community that, when "willing itself into existence" by an act of fictive constitution,[11] imagines for itself a culture, religion, or a language by virtue of which it is united for the common good. Only then, in the instance where a relationship develops between the "state" and the "polity," does the concept of minority as a "numerically inferior, culturally defined groups [become] politically meaningful."[12]

Defining who belongs to the "minority" category, by virtue of certain cultural characteristics and by reference to the central state is by no means a clear, simple exercise. Rather than fruitlessly pondering an objective understanding, universally applicable to any given group in any given context, one should consider the relationship between minorities and majorities, and the modern nation-state. The common theme in the different approaches (ranging from political theory to anthropology to sociology) is that minorities are groups, who by virtue of some cultural characteristic, are different from the dominant social group. In some accounts, the term "minority" has developed a

---

10      Benedict Anderson, Imagined Communities: Reflections on the Origin and Spread of Nationalism 37 (2016).

11      Jean-Jacques Rousseau, The Social Contract and Other Later Political Writings 44 (Victor Gourevitch ed., 1997).

12      Benjamin White, *The Nation-State Form and the Emergence of "Minorities" in Syria*, 7 Stud. Ethnicity & Nationalism 64, 65 (2007) [*hereinafter* White (2007)].

FACT AND FICTION 81

narrow political meaning where minorities are understood as "political outsiders whose identities do not fit the criteria defining political membership in the sovereign jurisdiction on whose territory they reside."[13] This definition takes the notion of "identity" as a definitive indicator of political belonging. Thus, for example, because group members speak a different language from that spoken by most citizens, they are considered a permanent political anomaly vis-à-vis the state. As such, the definition does not necessarily explain *why* said group is considered as a *political* anomaly. On the other hand, John Packer, who discusses ethnic and linguistic minorities in Europe, maintains that defining the word "minority" is "too complex" and proposes that freedom of association should form the basis of the concept of minorities.[14] Others refer to cultural characteristics such as ethnicity, religion, and language, that put their members at a social, political, and legal disadvantage as a result.[15] The reference to cultural characteristics is what informs international law and the human rights framework which seek to correct this perceived disadvantage that it has itself created. Other than collective belonging to a cultural group, "minority" has often been used to refer to "various groups sharing some kind of subordinate status on the assumed basis of their belonging to that group,"[16] such as women, non-heterosexuals, the disabled, and the legal restrictions that follow from that subordination. Benjamin White ponders the centrality of "subordination" to the definition of minority groups by posing valuable questions regarding the appropriateness of the term when, for example, the oppressed group is a numerical majority and the numerical minority has monopolized state power.[17] He finds that the assumption of disadvantaged status takes for granted the existence of a unified and "uniformly privileged majority thus obscuring the realities of power distribution within a society, especially within the majority."[18] This is not to say that minorities do not suffer some type of

---

13 Jennifer Jackson Preece, *Minority Rights in Europe: From Westphalia to Helsinki*, 23 Rev. Int'l Stud. 75 (1997) [*hereinafter* Preece].

14 John Packer, *On the Definition of Minorities*, in The Protection of Ethnic and Linguistic Minorities in Europe 24 (John Packer & Kristian Myntti eds., 1st ed., 1993).

15 *See* White, at 34. *See also* Francesco Capotorti, *Study on the Rights of Persons Belonging to Ethnic, Religious and Linguistic Minorities, U.N. Sub-Commission on Prevention of Discrimination and Protection of Minorities*, U.N. Doc. E/CN.4/Sub.2/384/Rev.1 (1979), at para. 242.

16 *See Minorities*, in International Encyclopedia of the Social Sciences, Vol. 10 (1968) [defines "Minorities" as "a minority's position involves exclusion or assignment to a lower status in one or more of four areas of life: the economic, the political, the legal, and the social-associational."].

17 *See* White (2011), at 26.

18 *Id.*, at 25–26.

subjugation as a result of their cultural affiliation, but it does point to ideological motivations through the politics of "othering," especially by regimes whose legitimacy lies in their ability to either claim they are an expression of majoritarian will, or that they are the protectors of minority groups.[19]

While previously cleavages between different communities living within the same spatial territory were recognized, these fissures were not contingent on numerical inferiority nor were they as salient in determining the treatment of that community. White develops a compelling analysis of the term, particularly when tracking its emergence in international public discourse as well as international law.[20] Unlike those who assume that the majority/minority dichotomy is self-explanatory, White rightly argues that the concept of minority "makes little sense without the context of the state."[21] As the following illustrates, the emergence of representative government changed the relationship between the ruler and the ruled, where categorizations like majority/minority, numerical membership to a community, and ethnicity acquired political currency.

### B    *Legitimate Power, the Nation-State, and Popular Sovereignty*

Legitimacy is a highly contested but highly coveted feature in political governance. As an elusive concept with varying understandings and approaches, perfect legitimacy is virtually unachievable. Its assessment is a subjective practice that consists of deciding what kind of social, political, or economic organization is sufficient enough to be considered acceptable or justifiable.[22] Determining a state's legitimacy entails more than just assessing the origins of political authority – it requires looking at the totality of state behavior across all policies, procedures, and institutional organizations. Whether normatively or descriptively defined, legitimacy in this context is understood as both "a set of norms and values relating to politics that are sufficiently shared to make a political system possible" and "the extent to which the relevant population perceives the regime is behaving according to [those norms]."[23]

Vincent Depagine describes a legal paradox that the notion of legitimacy must confront, whereby "someone entitled to make laws needs to be authorized

---

19    *See id.*, at 53. For an idea of "othering," *see* Allan Laine Kagedan, The Politics of Othering in the United States and Canada 11–26 (2020).

20    *See* White (2011), at 43.

21    *Id.*

22    *See, generally,* Nimer Sultany, Law and Revolution: Legitimacy and Constitutionalism After the Arab Spring (2017).

23    G. Hossein Razi, *Legitimacy, Religion, and Nationalism in the Middle East*, 48 Am. Pol. Sci. Rev. 69, 70 (1990).

FACT AND FICTION

by a prior law ... a rule of recognition."[24] Prior to the establishment of states in the modern sense, that is, representative entities derived from and answerable to their constituents, the rule of recognition referred to the divine right of kings.[25] At that time, the relationship between those in power and those who were subjects relied on an entirely different foundation. Religion was the primary vehicle of legitimation, and a reference to God was enough to answer any questions regarding the hold on power, the exercise of coercive power, and the use of legislative power.[26] For that reason, hugely diverse dynastic empires such as the Ottoman Empire and the Austro-Hungarian Empire were able to rule over populations who spoke different languages, practiced different religions, and had different cultures.[27] There was no need to justify rule on the basis of representation because divine legitimation secured and maintained monarchical power. This type of legitimation reserved a secondary, often subjugated, place for those whose faiths and/or ethnicities differed from those of the monarch. These groups were not secondary and subjugated because they were "minorities" per se, but rather because they were non-Muslim in the case of the Ottoman Empire or non-Catholic in Austria-Hungary.[28]

The change in the foundation of the state, usually attributed to the Treaty of Westphalia, demonstrated "an inversion of the respective institutional powers of religion and state ... the rise of the state power in religious matters,"[29] and linked spatial space and religious identity together under the ambit of state sovereignty and the rule of law.[30] While this did not automatically entail a decline in religious legitimation, it meant that the state, or the King, had control over religious institutions as well as monopoly over religious law. In other words, "the sovereignty of God [became] the sovereignty of the king (before becoming later the sovereignty of the people)."[31] The transformation of the holders of sovereignty points to the transformation of the relationship between religion

---

24   Vincent Depaigne, Legitimacy Gap: Secularism, Religion, and Culture in Comparative Constitutional Law 29 (2017) [*hereinafter* Depaigne].

25   *See id.*, at 23.

26   *See id.*, at 4.

27   *See* Ussama Makdisi, Age of Coexistence: the Ecumenical Framework and the Making of the Modern Arab World 19 (2019) [*hereinafter* Makdisi (2019)].

28   *See* H. Müller-Sommerfeld, *The League of Nations, A-Mandates and Minority Rights during the Mandate Period in Iraq (1920–1932)*, in Modernity, Minority, and the Public Sphere: Jews and Christians in the Middle East 264 (S.R. Goldstein-Sabbah & H.L. Murre-van den Berg eds., 2016) [*hereinafter* Müller-Sommerfeld].

29   Depaigne, at 24.

30   *See* Mario Silva, State Legitimacy and Failure in International Law 11 (2014) [*hereinafter* Silva].

31   Depaigne, at 25.

and state and, more importantly, between king (who transforms into the state) and subjects (who transform into citizens). European Enlightenment, characterized by the rise of modernism and prominence of individualism in legal, social, and philosophical discourse, resulted in the desire to "distinguish exactly the business of civil government from that of religion."[32] This type of "secularism" meant that the source of moral political authority had to be reformulated. References to divine forces as justification for governance could no longer be considered a sufficient answer to the question of legitimacy. Even though, at the time, secularism did not advocate for the complete elimination of religion within society, it entailed redefining the role which religion occupies within the social order.[33] The meaning of secularism, much like that of legitimacy, is broad and indicates different relationships in different contexts. Generally speaking, secularism involves the relationship between the state and religion and is more than just about separating state institutions from the religious order. Simply put, it requires reimagining the entire social organization in such a way that the state is considered "politically neutral."[34] Religion, at most, plays a politically marginal role while its individual practice is privatized as a guaranteed right.[35]

The source of legitimate political power thus needs to be relocated when religious legitimation and divine rights are no longer powerful tools in a ruler's repertoire. Obedience to the sovereign is questioned when God is no longer the source of his rule.[36] The decline of divine legitimation meant that sovereignty was dislocated from its holder. Modern states have therefore come to be formulated on the basis of two distinct but inter-connected ideals: self-governance which understands "freedom as the rule of law among a community of equals who are citizens of the polis and who have a right to rule and be ruled," and a territorially circumscribed nation-state which "conceives of the citizen first and foremost ... as the subject of rights and entitlements."[37] The idea of citizens, people, and constituents really came into play upon emergence of that gap in political legitimacy.[38] The question that naturally follows is therefore

---

32  John Locke, *A Letter Concerning Toleration* (1689).

33  *See, generally*, Viet Bader, Secularism or Democracy? Associational Governance of Religious Diversity (2007).

34  Talal Asad, Secular Translations: Nation-State, Modern Self, and Calculative Reason 17 (2018).

35  *See* Viet Bader, *Secularism or Liberal Democratic Constitutionalism*, in The Oxford Handbook of Secularism (Phil Zuckerman & John R. Shook eds., 2017).

36  *See* Silva, at 10.

37  Selya Benhabib, *Borders, Boundaries, Citizenship* 38 Pol. Sci. & Pol. 673, 673 (2005).

38  Depaigne, at 77.

FACT AND FICTION

*who* are the citizens of the polis that are able to rule and be ruled, and also possess rights and entitlements?

Bernard Yack accurately puts it as "wherever popular sovereignty leads, nationalism seems to follow."[39] This is not to say that processes of democratization and self-governance enable national identities to assert themselves. Indeed, even the most authoritarian regimes use the language of popular sovereignty and nationalism to pass off their own agendas as policies by the people, and for the nation. Rather, popular sovereignty interacts with nationalism by "introducing a new image of political community, an image that tends to nationalise political loyalties and politicise national loyalties."[40] Ascribing political legitimacy to the idea of popular sovereignty meant that there had to be stronger links between representative government and society itself, which could justify the dimensions of this new relationship.[41]

In order to defend the erection of the institutional, constitutional, and permanent state structures, that relationship necessitated a type of link that would go deeper than politics. That link, in the nation-state, is found through the "identification of political with cultural community" by looking at the "prepolitical and cultural roots that bind people into a community."[42] Popular sovereignty necessitates the endorsement of historical, cultural, linguistic, or ethnic identities to substantiate the chains that bind citizens to political authority. This exercise becomes increasingly tenuous when there is an attempt to establish the pre-political and cultural ties of a heterogeneous population that finds itself in a territorially fixed space. It is at this point that the number games begin to gain political and social currency. States begin to assume "a cultural identity that is acceptable to the majority of their population."[43] Minorities only come into existence when a "majority" has been designated and a state has been formulated on the basis of the "majority's" identity. Where there are communities who fall out of the cultural ambit associated with the "majority," then they are "minorities." Only by this way can one understand both the emergence of politically charged categories such as "minorities" and the consequences of having "minority" groups. Furthermore, the requirement that states have clearly delineated, fixed boundaries subordinates minority groups to the majority-culture nationhood which ensues because "the people is imagined *both* as existing

---

39    Bernard Yack, *Popular Sovereignty and Nationalism*, 19 Pol. Theory 517 (2001) [*hereinafter* Yack].

40    *Id.*, at 523.

41    *See* White (2007), at 66.

42    Yack, at 525–526.

43    White (2007), at 67.

prior to the state and as defined by the borders of an already constituted state ... [thus] raising the prospect of a prepolitical community on which the legitimacy of the state rests."[44] It is understandable therefore, that international law, which affirms popular sovereignty and self-determination, creates tiers of national belonging that it must then rectify through regulating the protection of cultural anomalies that it has itself created.[45]

## III Minority Rights in International Law

These ideas of popular sovereignty and legitimacy directly inform the development of minority rights under international law. The assumption that minorities objectively form a permanent political anomaly for the state by virtue of certain cultural characteristics requires a mobilization of extra-legal protections that go beyond those already provided for under the general human rights framework. In reality, the sheer presence of minority rights, communitarian in nature, presents a dilemma for human rights law, which privileges liberal individualism. There is also an inherent colonial dimension to the prevalence of minority rights in the international legal regime because "minority guarantees" were both a conditional factor for the independence of certain states,[46] and an excuse for external intervention in a state's affairs.[47] This section explores the origins, dimensions, and influence of international minority rights.

### A *International Law, Imperialism, and Minorities*
A Eurocentric analysis of international law considers the Treaty of Westphalia, and the establishment of a global political order "based on the plurality of independent states, recognising no superior authority above them," as the defining point of the transformation of inter-state relations.[48] The transforma-

---

44 Yack, at 522–523.

45 *See* Macklem, at 532.

46 *See* The London Protocols 1830 [a condition of Greek independence was to guarantee the rights of Muslims within its territory]; *see* Preece, at 80. *See also* League of Nations minority treaties such as the Treaty of Versailles 1919 and the League of Nations' Mandate Treaties and other similar legal documents that emerged during the Paris Peace Conference relating to the existence and status of minorities.

47 The imposition of minority rights by Britain and France on the Ottoman Empire to guarantee the rights of its non-Muslim, particularly Christian communities; Tanzimat reforms were the result of pressure by the European powers on the Ottomans; *see* Makdisi (2019), at 51–54. *See also* the Capitulations Regime of the Ottoman Empire.

48 Antonio Cassesse, International Law 37 (2nd ed., 2004).

FACT AND FICTION

tion of international relations occurred gradually and over time. Westphalia's importance lies not in the territorial redistribution that took place between parties to the Thirty-Year War, but in the changes to the conception of sovereignty.[49] First, the principle of *cuius regio, eius religio* granted the sovereign the right to decide the religion of the realm over which he presided.[50] Second was the emergence of the first inklings of minority rights under the ambit of the "special relationship between a prince and his co-religionists,"[51] whereby the monarch granted concessions to certain Christian communities whose denomination, as a result of the spatial redistribution, differed from that of the sovereign. These communities were thus allowed to maintain and practice their faith, in public and private, on the basis of the sovereign's "moral responsibility for the survival of these transferred co-religious communities."[52] What happened at Westphalia is often designated as the first emergence of the right to religious freedom.[53] However, the provisions relating to the question of non-dominant Christian communities were far from a universal guarantee of religious freedom for all and every religious group. Rather, Westphalia set a precedent regarding the use of religious guarantees in international law as a condition for establishing peace between sovereign states.[54]

Minorities featured briefly in the two other major congresses concerning inter-state relationships,[55] but their systematic prescription did not occur until the aftermath of the First World War. Generally, imperial dynasties dealt with internal diversity, or "outsiders," through "tolerance, persecution, assimilation, and expulsion."[56] The subsequent rise of nationalism, the nation-state, and popular sovereignty changed the understanding of minorities. Popular sovereignty became the new legitimizing principle, based on a type of majoritarian and cultural nationalism. This change gave credence to the majority/minority dichotomy because it placed the "people" (their constitution and identity) at the center of the governance model. This is not to say that in the 19th century states were organized around the democratic majoritarianism that is familiar today, but that the structure on which sovereign power was formulated had changed: the new nationalism became more inclined to justify power on

---

49    *See* Preece, at 79.
50    *See* Francois Venter, Constitutionalism and Religion 21 (2015) [*hereinafter* Venter].
51    Preece, at 77.
52    *Id.*
53    *See* Venter, at 21.
54    *See* Treaty of Paris (1763); Treaty of Warsaw (1772); and Treaty of Hubertusburg (1763).
55    *See* Congress of Vienna (1814); and the Congress of Berlin (1878).
56    Karen Barkey, Empire of Difference: The Ottomans in Comparative Perspective 18 (2008).

the basis of majoritarian representation.[57] This transformation in statehood meant that "religious minorities" became "national minorities" because religion ceased to be the sole vehicle of legitimation for the state.

The use of minority protection language had featured in international relations before the systematic prescription of minority rights into international law in the early 20th century. In fact, European powers had used the protection of "national minorities" by "[giving] them the opportunity to interfere in the internal constitution of other states."[58] Notably, the guise of protecting Christians in Ottoman territory was instrumental in pressuring Ottoman officials to modernize their governance regime to the extent that "it became impossible to separate the emancipation of Christians [in the Ottoman Empire] from Western imperialism."[59] Indeed, hegemonic European powers intervened in the Ottoman Empire as "Christian Powers" who existed to liberate other fellow Christians from the Muslim Sultan. The entrenchment of identity cleavages in the Ottoman Empire's legal framework is discussed below in greater detail, but it is important to note here the general politicization of "minorities" and that imperial powers used minority legal guarantees as evidence of "civilization," and a condition for sovereignty recognition.[60]

Therefore, it is unsurprising that minority protection clauses were a central feature of the then-newly proclaimed League of Nations. The end of the Great War saw the disintegration of the massive multi-ethnic, multi-religious dynastic empires. In their wake, emerged the various nation-states predicated on political and cultural characteristics of numerical majorities as a variant of popular representation. In order to join the League of Nations and become part of the family of nations, the independence of these new states was contingent on their acceptance and commitment to make special provisions for their minorities, those who require "racial, religious, and linguistic protection."[61] Herein lies the contradiction of international law at the time: it institutionalized the nation-state form as the civilized, modern, and only acceptable form of

---

57  *See* Depaigne, at 193–194.

58  Müller-Sommerfeld, at 264.

59  Ussama Makdisi, *The Problem of Sectarianism in the Middle East in an Age of Western Hegemony*, in Sectarianization: Mapping the New Politics of the Middle East 28 (Nader Hashemi & Danny Postel eds., 2017) [*hereinafter* Makdisi (2017)].

60  For an explanation of the standard of the civilization in international law, *see* Antony Anghie, *The Evolution of International Law: Colonial and Postcolonial Realities*, 27 Third World Q. 739 (2006).

61  League of Nations, *Protection of Linguistic, Racial or Religious Minorities by the League of Nations. Resolutions and Extracts from the Minutes of the Council, Resolutions and Reports adopted by the Assembly, relating to the Procedure to be followed in questions Concerning the Protection of Minorities*, C.8.M.5.1831.I, Geneva (1832).

FACT AND FICTION

governance, but it also understood the tensions that such a form can create; and so it sought to correct those tensions through the protection of minority rights. It was quickly understood that creating homogenous nation-states was an impossible task, and forcible population transfers were not a sustainable option.[62] The League, therefore, developed the first international legal framework of substantive protection of minorities without actually defining what a minority is. The lack of definition, as the discussion below shows, makes it harder to legislate for a group in the absence of agreement on what constitutes the group as such. Nevertheless, the reasoning behind this was expressed in the language of equality before the law, participation, representation, and self-determination.[63]

Specifically, the League promulgated important mechanisms that were intended to ensure these rights and protections. First, the protection of minorities was transferred from the imperial powers and placed "under the guarantee of the League of Nations."[64] This meant that states were unable to modify the protections granted to minority groups and were answerable to the Council of the League should they breach the content of the guarantees. Second, was the establishment of a petition system whereby minority groups could directly petition to the Council in the case of a state infraction. While these mechanisms may have been developed on the goodwill of the Great Powers, they failed in guaranteeing any nominal protection. Petitions were largely ignored by the Council, "particularly Great Britain and France, who were reluctant to become involved when their national interests were not concerned."[65] Furthermore, the goodwill of member states was insufficient to prevent them from engaging in assimilatory as well as discriminatory practices.[66]

The prevalence of minority rights in the post-war period only worked to further entrench social categorizations such as the minority/majority dichotomy.[67] Serious questions relating to the equality and representation of non-dominant groups became highly politicized matters, embedded with issues of nationalism and self-determination.[68] States that were obligated to sign and accept such provisions expressed resentment, and new neighboring states competed

---

62    *See* Preece, at 81.

63    *See* Müller-Sommerfeld, at 264.

64    Treaty of Poland 1919 art. 12 (available at: http://www.forost.ungarisches-institut.de/pdf/19190628-3.pdf).

65    Preece, at 83.

66    *See id.*, at 81.

67    *See* Joshua Castellino & Kathleen Cavanaugh, Minority Rights in the Middle East 185, 285–289 (2013) [*hereinafter* Castellino & Cavanaugh].

68    *See* Ivor Jennings, The Approach to Self-Government 55–56 (1956).

over territorial acquisition through the language of "minorities." Consequently, the "League of Nations System of Minority Guarantees ... ultimately became an instrument for fomenting international rivalry and discontent."[69] Identity mobilization emerged as a popular way of challenging the imposed territorial boundaries, and minorities themselves were often perpetrators of violence.[70] The categorization began to take on a life of its own, and identity distinctions were rigidified in ways that would become increasingly difficult to overcome.[71] Furthermore, when the Second World War erupted, as with other aspects of international law, minority guarantees became entirely and completely ineffective. The minority question was side-lined until after the atrocities of the 1940s, the bulk of which, ironically, were aimed at exterminating certain "minority" groups.

## B Friends or Foes? Human Rights Framework and Minority Populations

The aftermath of World War II changed many normative conceptions about law, rights, and nationalism. The human devastation that occurred throughout the course of the war envisioned a universal human rights framework that would cover the "fundamental" characteristics of the human experience, namely those found in Western political and liberal philosophy.[72] The development of a universal, liberal, and individualistic human rights regime overshadowed the previous minority protection structure, rendering it obsolete.[73] Yet, it remained so that minority rights discourse was still prevalent in mainstream legal thought, particularly in the aftermath of the Cold War.[74] IHRL still sought to protect certain localized groups from intrusion by the central state, regardless of the protection offered to all individuals, from all backgrounds and all characteristics, under the adopted human rights framework.[75] While undoubtedly the rights of non-dominant groups are more fragile than of those belonging to the majority, minority rights "possess the capacity to divide

---

69    Preece, at 83.

70    See Hashemi & Postel, at 4–8.

71    See Eskandar Sadeghi-Boroujerdi, Strategic Depth, Counterinsurgency, and the Logic of Sectarianization: The Islamic Republic of Iran's Security Doctrine and its Regional Implications, in Sectarianization: Mapping the New Politics of the Middle East 184 (Nader Hashemi & Danny Postel eds., 2017).

72    See Vincent Depaigne, Individualism, Human Rights and Identity, Semantic Scholar (2005), at 1.

73    See Jelena Pejic, Minority Rights in International Law 19 Hum. Rts. Q. 665 (1997) [hereinafter Pejic].

74    See id., at 666–667.

75    See Macklem, at 553.

FACT AND FICTION

people into different communities, create insiders and outsiders, pit ethnicity against ethnicity, and threaten the universal aspirations that inform the dominant understanding of the mission of the field."[76] Minority rights as they exist in international law do not attempt to reconcile majoritarianism with the particularities of history but, rather, they seek to shield specific groups from the state's assimilation attempts.[77]

This need to shield from assimilation is a result of a specific understanding of the central state, as an entity with a particular agenda, culture, and language which seeks to subsume difference by manufacturing a uniformity that would justify its hold on coercive power.[78] This is the nature of the nation-state and this is how it has been understood in international law.[79] The fact is that, with this type of governance structure, "minority groups may not be accommodated in modern states."[80] International law, then, attempts to correct its own errors by "participating in the creation of national, cultural, religious, and linguistic minority communities"[81] through the imposition of a legal order based on a notion of popular sovereignty, understood as a corollary of nationalism. International law seeks to protect what it understands as endemic features of mankind from the nation-state while simultaneously avoiding issues relating to nation-state reformulation. Arguably, human rights do the same thing because they protect what are considered fundamental features of humankind. There is, therefore, a tension between minority rights and human rights: while the latter seek to regulate individual freedom, the former reference elements of communitarianism.[82] This tenuous relationship also raises important questions about the nature and distribution of state sovereignty and self-determination, in other words, the grounds upon which a given state is formulated and the criteria for determining its membership.

---

76    *Id.*, at 532.

77    *See* Alywn Peter Jones, *Minority Rights in International Law: Minority Rights and Identity Conscious Decision-Making* (2006) (PhD Dissertation, University of Leicester), at 119. *See also* Draft Protocol on the Rights of National Minorities for the European Convention of Human Rights art. 3 (1993).

78    *See* Max Weber, Politics as Vocation (1919).

79    *See* Michael von der Schulenberg, *Rethinking Peacebuilding: Transforming the UN Approach*, International Peace Institute (2014), at 2, 7–8 [*hereinafter* von der Schulenberg].

80    Joshua Castellino, *No Room at the International Table: The Importance of Designing Effective Litmus Tests for Minority Protection at Home*, 35 Hum. Rts. Q. 201, 205 (2013) [*hereinafter* Castellino].

81    Macklem, at 533.

82    *See* Adeno Addis, *Individualism, Communitarianism, and the Rights of Ethnic Minorities*, 67 Notre Dame L. Rev. 615, 640–645 (1993).

The UN Charter makes no mention of minorities. The Universal Declaration of Human Rights (UDHR) explicitly left out minority protections because the drafters considered it "difficult to adopt a uniform solution to this complex and delicate question, which has special aspects in each state in which it arises."[83] Too much political disagreement made it impossible to reach a consensus on either the definition or the normative framework to be adopted. Those present at the negotiations at the time felt that the inclusion of minority rights could perpetuate some sort of state fragmentation "if the myriads of 'peoples' or 'nations' seek to constitute their own homogenous states."[84] Additionally, the drafters understood that the general human rights framework would be enough to maintain some sort of minority protection.[85] Yet, the UN General Assembly (UNGA) stated that there still needed to be a "thorough study of the problem of minorities, in order that the [UN] may be able to take effective measures for the protection of racial, national, religious or linguistic minorities."[86] The UNGA therefore transferred the issue to the UN Commission of Human Rights and the subsequent Sub-Commission on Prevention of Discrimination and Protection of Minorities, which was instructed to study the matter further in order to inform the actions needed to be taken.[87] This accurately sums up the general attitude of the UN towards minority groups: a "no-indifference-but-no-preparedness-to-take-steps" approach that arguably continues to characterize the UN's position today.[88] Both the UN Charter and UN peace-building practices adopt the nation-state and the idea of majoritarian popular sovereignty as the go-to governance model, which, in turn, unwillingly creates national "minorities,"[89] an action which international minority rights then seek to mitigate.

It is therefore unsurprising that there are few legally binding provisions regarding minority rights – those that do exist generate disagreement regarding their interpretation and application. While the most comprehensive document on minority rights is the UN Declaration on the Rights of Persons Belonging

---

83    G.A. Res. 217 (III) C, *Preparation of a Draft Covenant on Human Rights and Draft Measures of Implementation* (Dec. 10, 1948), at 77.

84    Castellino, at 206.

85    *See* Macklem, at 531–532.

86    G.A. Res. 217(III) C, U.N. GAOR, 3d Sess., 1st plen. Mtg., U.N. Doc. A/810 (Dec. 12, 1948), at 77.

87    *See* Pejic, at 668–669.

88    *See* Peter Hilpold, *UN Standard-Setting in the Field of Minority Rights* 14 Intl. J. Minority & Grp. Rts. 181, 182 (2007).

89    *See* UN Charter art. 1(2), para. 1; ICCPR art. 1 [right to self-determination]. *See also* von der Schulenberg.

FACT AND FICTION 93

to National or Ethnic, Religious or Linguistic Minorities,[90] it only provides a set of recommendations rather than any binding provisions. Particularly problematic is the lack of definition afforded to such groups, making it difficult to adjudicate adequate protections. At the instruction of the Sub-Commission, the ICCPR makes an explicit mention of minorities. In fact, the only legally binding provision on minority rights is ICCPR article 27. The article reads,

> In those States in which ethnic, religious or linguistic minorities exist, persons belonging to such minorities shall not be denied the right, in community with the other members of their group, to enjoy their own culture, to profess and practice their own religion, or to use their own language.[91]

There are several limitations that can be discerned from the wording, the application and interpretation of the article. The wording works only to increase the ambiguity regarding both the recognition of non-dominant groups as well as the requirements that states have to take. In terms of the substantive content, there are multiple things to note.

First, the article leaves room for states to declare that they have no minorities, thereby negating the applicability of the obligation,[92] as France has done previously.[93] Even though the UN Human Rights Committee has indicated the recognition of a minority should be assessed by objective criteria, states are still able to enter reservations to the clause.[94] This objective criteria, in its practical application, has made the *de jure* existence of a minority group contingent on the recognition of that group's culture, religion, or language being different from that of the majority population. Even though the UN Human Rights Committee has held that "State Parties cannot constrict the definition

---

90    *See* G.A. Res. No. 47/135 (Dec. 18, 1992).

91    ICCPR art. 27.

92    *See* Pejic, at 670.

93    *See* Tove H. Malloy, *Dialogue with the Unwilling: Addressing Minority Rights in So-Called Denial States*, ECMI Working Paper No. 77 (2014), https://www.files.ethz.ch/isn/183486/ECMI_WP_77.pdf. *See also* "Proposition de loi tendant à la suppression du mot « race » de notre legislation," passed by l'Assemblée Nationale on Apr. 24, 2013 (Fr.).

94    *See* U.N. Hum. Rts. Comm., *General Comment 23, Article 27* (50th session, 1994), Compilation of General Comments and General Recommendations Adopted by the Human Rights Treaty Bodies, U.N. Doc. HRI/GEN/1/REV 1, at 38 [*hereinafter* CCPR General Comment 23]. *See also* U.N. Hum. Rts. Comm., Communication No. 220/1987, *TK v France*, U.N. Doc. CCPR/C/37/D/220/1987 (Jan. 12, 1987).

of particular 'minorities', nor can they define the membership of a minority,"[95] enforcing UN Human Rights Committee decisions remains optional.

Second, the obligation is negatively phrased, meaning that states can only refrain from interfering with those cultural, religious, and linguistic attributes – they are not textually required to guarantee the exercise of said rights. There is no clear indication either, of what states must do in order to legally guarantee the cultural independence of minorities, nor to ensure their participation and representation in political life. There is no specific procedure to make a claim should there be a potential breach of obligation. Additionally, there is no attempt at delineating the individuals, or the groups, that fall under the ambit of the article – meaning that the practice of this right is contingent on states' definition of "majority." The text of the article indicates that "minority rights are individual rights to engage in particular activities in community with others" and "not collective rights of a minority population to a measure of autonomy from the broader society in which it is situated."[96] Article 27 was designed to protect individual claims of a violation rather than a systemic breach of the rights of a group of individuals.[97] The idea of collective rights falls under ICCPR article 1, which covers the right of "a people" to self-determination – a right the HRC held as "not cognisable under the Optional Protocol,"[98] meaning that claims relating to a violation of self-determination could not be actionable before the Committee. This further confuses the very place of minority rights in international law: if these are individualistic rights then those rights are already covered in the general human rights regime. The idea behind IHRL, particularly the UDHR, is that those provisions are applicable to all, and exclusively, private individuals. While it is true that "the civil and political freedom of minority members is more likely to be interfered with than those of the majority,"[99] the UDHR includes rights that are directly related to both minority and majority groups (such as the right to non-discrimination, the right to freedom of religion and consciousness, the right to freedom of expression, and the right to nationality).[100]

---

95     Sarah Joseph & Melissa Castan, The International Covenant on Civil and Political Rights – Cases, Materials, and Commentary 24.2 (3rd ed., 2014) [*hereinafter* Joseph & Castan]. *See also* U.N. Hum. Rts. Comm., Communication No. 24/1997, *Lovelace v Canada*, U.N. Doc. CCPR/C/13/D/24/1997 (Dec. 29, 1977) [*hereinafter* Lovelace].

96     Macklem, at 535.

97     *See* Joseph & Castan. CCPR General Comment 3, paras. 2–5.

98     CCPR General Comment 23, para. 3.1.

99     Macklem, at 533.

100    *See* Universal Declaration of Human Rights arts. 7, 18, 19, & 15, respectively.

FACT AND FICTION

Considering the practical and theoretical issues presented above, Joshua Castellino posits three reasons as to why minority rights present a real obstacle on an international scale. He postulates that, primarily, the question of minority rights, and minorities in general, is uncomfortable for states to answer not just because it relates to a matter of internal sovereignty, but also because the "average postcolonial state is about fifty years old, and a large number of constituents within these states have not successfully consolidated their national identity."[101] Secondly, is the somewhat exclusive concentration on civil and political rights. This is a truism of the (Western) human rights regime in general, as it almost exclusively provides civil and political rights which, "with many of the world's minorities mired in poverty ... the creation of [such] remedies only partially addresses their situation" making it so that the "failure to develop adequate standards for socioeconomic and cultural rights directly determines the choices they are forced to make."[102] Lastly, Castellino argues that the inability to develop an adequate minority protection regime relates to the "complex issue of how to generate systems of group rights protection that nonetheless provide room for the individual to opt out."[103] In addition to these reasons, one may add a fourth reason as to why there is a conceptual confusion regarding the place of minorities in international law as well as the subsequent legal mechanisms regulating their protection. It relates to the inability to adequately define such groups, pointing to the inherent *political* nature of such categorizations – categorizations that do not exist outside certain *political* perspectives. It is also an inability of translating into law facts of the human experience. Indeed, "the law is always deficient, not because it is imperfect in itself but because human reality is necessarily imperfect in comparison to the ordered world of law."[104]

The ambiguity surrounding the status of minority rights in international law has tangible consequences in state practice, particularly in scenarios of post-conflict governance reconstruction. In cases of conflict that take on an identarian aspect, international minority law becomes important because it supposedly "mitigates dangers of violence, cruelty, and political humiliation [that] so often accompany ethnic politics."[105] The cyclical approach of formulating, and reformulating, citizenship and governance structures on the basis of group identity, notably in ways that make it impossible to opt out from one's

---

101    Castellino, at 209.

102    *Id.*

103    *Id.*

104    Hans-Georg Gadamer, Truth and Method 316 (Joel Weinsheimer & Donald G. Marshall trans., 2nd ed., 1989).

105    Jacob Levy, The Multiculturalism of Fear 12 (2000).

allocated communal identity, only works in favor of those who are willing to use ethnic and identity politics to gain political power. Otherwise, it prevents the development, reconciliation, and reconstruction of a more inclusive, less divisive, political and constitutional formula.

## IV    The Iraqi Nation-State, Sectarian Politics, and the Question of Minorities

Particularly in the aftermath of intrastate conflict, the question of minorities and their status in a given society is heightened, demanding to be answered. When conflict develops an identity dimension, minorities are specifically persecuted because of their perceived identity, one which is understood to bring certain political and nationalist aspirations. Simultaneously, a minority group could become a militant force as a result of historical violence and exclusion it has suffered because it has been perceived as a "minority." On both occasions, when a conflict reaches a negotiated closure, the post-conflict governance reconstruction often takes on these perpetuated identity cleavages and institutionalizes them into the constitutional structure. Previous peace-building literature and practice have taken this method as a way to manage what are understood as unmanageable sectarian feuds, of which minorities are a primary victim.[106] This assumption falls into a common error found in academia and state practice – the belief that the conflicts in places such as Iraq and Syria can be answered by a simple-but-complicated reference to "sectarianism." Assuming that the Syrian civil war or the renewed calls for freedom in Iraq can be downplayed to historic inter-group tension or a matter of religious intolerance are rooted in Orientalist understandings of the Middle East that overlook the nature of power, legitimacy, and authoritarianism in the region. They forgo the fact that armed conflict is more often a matter of power, resources and their distribution within society.[107] These approaches also do not consider the way in which identity cleavages can be manipulated as a means of maintaining and/or gaining power – to the point that "identity mobilization is rooted in the project of power acquisition by state factors."[108]

---

106    *See* Martin Wählisch, Peace-Making, Power-Sharing and International Law: Imperfect Peace (2019).

107    *See* Chris Chapman, *Why a Minority Rights Approach to Conflict? The Case of Southern Sudan*, Minority Rights Group International, (2008), at 5.

108    Vali Nasr, *International Politics, Domestic Imperatives, and Identity Mobilisation: Sectarianism in Pakistan 1979–1998*, in Sectarianization: Mapping the New Politics of the Middle East 81 (Nader Hashemi & Danny Postel eds., 2017).

FACT AND FICTION                                                                    97

   This section examines the crucial impact those Orientalist understandings of Iraq's social composition had on the Iraqi nation-state. It starts with the Ottoman *millet* system and the different socio-legal categories that existed within the Empire. It also considers the impact of the Mandate system and European colonialism on the status of minority groups, particularly through the creation of the nation-state. It then discusses the status of minorities in Iraq through a constitutional analysis from the Ba'ath period to the current constitutional arrangement. The section then concludes by arguing that, while "minority" protection is often necessary during political transitions, the entrenchment of identarian political representation in post-conflict constitutions effectively serves the agendas of those who have mobilized around group identity in the first place. Such a system prevents the adoption of equal citizenship, equal access, and equal opportunity for all members of society regardless of ethnicity or religion, of minority or majority status. Rather, it overemphasizes, vilifies, and victimizes difference and the historic diversity of this ancient region.

## A      *The Ottomans, the Empire, and the Millet*

The Ottoman Empire was a massive, dynastic empire that ruled over a vast and diverse collection of territories, reaching at its height from the Balkans in Eastern Europe, encompassing the Fertile Crescent and large parts of West Asia, all the way down to North Africa. Described as the "empire of difference,"[109] Ottoman subjects were composed of a multi-ethnic, multi-religious, as well as multi-lingual group of communities that had all been, at some point, conquered by Ottoman forces. Its sultans, much like other religious and dynastic empires, legitimated their rule by "[their] supposed upholding of Islam, [their] defense of the realm against infidels, and [their] stamping out of heresy within it."[110] The rulers made no attempt to claim that they were representatives of this diverse population, nor that their legitimacy was contingent on the population's acceptance of their rule – as Makdisi points out, "religion legitimated empires before secularism."[111] Furthermore, the fact that, numerically, Muslims made up the largest bloc of the Ottoman subjects was largely irrelevant prior to the 19th century. Rather, the Sultan was divinely appointed through his own god, and thus had the right to rule over everyone in the realm as a protector of his god against

---

109    *See, generally*, Karen Barkey, Empire of Difference: The Ottomans in Comparative Perspective (2008).
110    Makdisi (2017), at 26.
111    Makdisi (2019), at 28.

perceived infidels, regardless of whether everyone subscribed to the same religious ideology.

Subordination during the period prior to the expansion of European imperialism was not based on a numerical evaluation of the population, nor was it determined by ethnic or linguistic belonging. Because of the way in which religious legitimation works,[112] the dichotomy that we understand as majority/minority was formulated on the premise of Muslim and non-Muslim. The latter group were not subordinate because they were numerically inferior or because they were not Ottoman or did not speak Turkish – they were subordinate by virtue of the fact that they were not Muslim. While Islamic law does provide a place in the social and political order for non-Muslims, that place (according to orthodox interpretations) is inherently and structurally inferior to their Muslim counterparts.[113] As a foundational imperial policy, the subjects of the Ottoman Empire were divided and organized on that basis, and "the discrimination between Muslim and non-Muslim was a defining paradigm of Ottoman rule."[114]

The Ottoman state's approach to regulating and managing those religious differences in order to maintain social order in the realm has been a point of interest for scholars from a wide range of academic fields. The oft-cited Ottoman *millet* system provided a certain brand of group autonomy for the "people of the book," the Christian and Jewish populations of the Empire, while simultaneously adopting a general category of "Muslim." This system allowed for an autonomy over internal group management and ecclesial jurisdiction over matters relating to "personal status," namely issues such as marriage, divorce, and inheritance. Legal matters of personal status were "dominated by the ecclesiastical leadership,"[115] and were decided upon with reference to the respective canonical authority of each religious bloc. Even prior to the 19th century reforms, this brand of autonomy was available to these communities despite the fact that "Ottoman Muslim supremacy was deeply imbued within the ideological, political, and legal terrain."[116] For example, Boogert points out that while Muslim rulers did not interfere with liturgical or theological matters, "the Islamic environment encroached on any other aspect that took place in public" such as the restoration of churches and synagogues, public

---

112    *See* discussion above in Section II.

113    *See* White (2011), at 66.

114    Makdisi (2019), at 28.

115    Maurits H. van der Boogert, *Millets: Past and Present*, in Religious Minorities in the Middle East: Domination, Self-Empowerment, Accommodation 32 (Anne Sofie Roald & Anh Nga Longva eds., 2011).

116    Makdisi (2017), at 26.

FACT AND FICTION

religious symbols of faith, the importation of wine and kosher bread "must have been a constant reminder of the balance of power."[117] This balance of power, or tolerance for non-Muslim groups, could be withdrawn at any time should the Sultan be persuaded to do so. There was also the *jizya* tax, a poll-tax was imposed on all non-Muslim males, "as the most symbolically charged example of such a communal levy."[118] This is not to demonstrate that the Ottomans exercised a specific flavor of intolerance or that they were particularly brutal towards non-Muslim communities. Rather, it points out the existence of a religious order that was *accepted* across the different communities via the ecclesiastical leadership, where even Christian and Jewish religious leaders, accepting their secondary status, "constantly exploited, legitimated, and drew strength from a world without citizenship, secularism, or equality."[119] This facilitated the fact that all these different groups were bound to live together side by side.[120]

In Iraq, what is often described as an inherent hatred between Shi'ites and Sunnis is better understood as a political struggle for political power, even during Ottoman times. At the outset, the struggle for Iraq was between the Ottoman Empire, a Sunni hegemon, and the Safawid Empire, a Persian Shi'a force. The divide between Sunni and Shi'a was therefore used "entrepreneurially, with each entity claiming that it had the support of its respective sect,"[121] regardless of politics or policy. Still, Ottomans managed to maintain a generally stable as well as effective form of governance that only at times resulted in inter-sectarian violence. The question is about why sectarian violence emerges as particularly salient at certain times and is substituted with intergroup cooperation at others.[122] The delicate balance of power transformed on various occasions, when the British established the Iraqi nation-state during Saddam Hussein's rule, and once again during the Anglo-American invasion and occupation of Iraq.

## B    *Imperialism, the Mandate, and the Iraqi Nation-State*
The change in modes of political legitimation dismantled the balance of power. As previously mentioned, numbers, ethnicity, and religion only become politically relevant when the state is conceived as a representative entity. This is not to say that the state is transformed into a democratic body once it established

---

117    *Id.*, at 31.
118    *Id.*
119    Makdisi (2019), at 41.
120    *See* Makdisi (2017), at 26.
121    Castellino & Cavanaugh, at 185.
122    *See id.*

itself as representative. Rather, the state plants its legitimacy in the people over whom it is to rule over – a "prepolitical community"[123] – legitimating the chains that bind humans when they are born. This exercise works to create circles of inclusion and exclusion: who is to be represented and what are the conditions for seeking representation. It points to the identarian root of representative government from which nationalism often emerges.

In the context of the Middle East, Ussama Makdisi points to three factors that changed Middle Eastern politics, and which have contributed to the rise of identity nationalism and decisive sectarian discourse. First, the rise of ethno-religious nationalism challenged the nature of Muslim supremacy of the Ottoman Empire on geographical, political, and ideological levels. Second, is the rise of Western and so-called "humanitarian" imperialism, resulting in the third change, that the Ottoman Empire went from "being an empire of difference [to paradoxically], an empire of citizens."[124] The European powers put enormous pressure on the Empire to engage in reforms that would emphasize non-discrimination between its citizens, rather than its subjects, while simultaneously guaranteeing a special relationship between the empire, the imperial power, and the non-Muslim. These reforms, known as the *Tanzimat*, were had "as [their] core mantra the declaration of non-discrimination between Muslim and non-Muslim subjects of the Empire,"[125] thus reformulating the very imperial ideology on which the Ottoman Empire rested. This is not to say that all subjects of the Empire became politically sovereign, equal citizens, but rather that all subjects were equally unequal.[126] The reasoning of the Europeans insisting on such measures was based on an orientalist understanding of Middle Eastern society as one that is overtly religious in nature, requiring a "sectarian political framework to resolve what were taken to be endemic sectarian hatreds,"[127] even though the European powers themselves ruled over empires as diverse as that of the Ottomans. While sectarian relations in the region cannot all be chalked up to a "divide-and-rule" imperial policy, European involvement in shaping a sectarian state structure must be succinctly acknowledged.[128]

It is therefore unsurprising that "the protection of racial, religious, and linguistic minorities under international law was also central to A-Mandates."[129]

---

123   Yack, at 519.

124   Makdisi (2017), at 27.

125   Makdisi (2019), at 46.

126   *See id.*, at 53.

127   *Id.*, at 29.

128   *See* Makdisi (2019), at 32–33.

129   Müller-Sommerfeld, at 264.

FACT AND FICTION

Yet the European understandings of both the *millet* system and the social structure in the Levantine territories – perhaps because European involvement was justified on the basis of protecting their co-religionists – concentrated almost exclusively on religious difference.[130] Rather than differentiating by language or ethnic group, the religious marker continued to be the way in which people were categorized vis-à-vis their relationship with the new state. It was also accepted that Islam itself is a monolithic, uniform practice across all different segments that could be thought of as "Muslim" – so much so that the Alawites in Syria, a historically persecuted minority of Islam, were not eligible for minority status. The Sunnis in Iraq were not considered to be a minority either, even though they were numerically inferior to their Shi'a counterparts. The Kurds in both new nations were also not deemed a minority – they were Muslim, after all.[131] Nevertheless, the nationalism that had swept the region during the Great Arab Revolt showed that non-Muslim communities, such as certain Christian communities in Syria as well as the Jewish community in Iraq, rejected their special status outright because they considered themselves wholeheartedly "Arab" and an integral part of the new, secular, and modern state.[132]

This is not to say that during the mandates a new socio-legal formula was introduced. Instead, the *millet* legal system of the previous Ottoman Empire was entrenched in the new representative state structure. However, the establishment of a state structure on the basis of institutionalized identities meant that "patterns and mechanisms were set in motion with far-reaching consequences for Iraq [and Syria's] political development and national cohesion."[133] The post-colonial state was organized on the logic that "a citizen of an Arab state is first and foremost a member of his or her immediate ethnic [religious] community."[134] This remained true even when those states adopted a nationalist, secular Arab ideology after independence; those identity cleavages still made their way into the new state formulation, becoming both constitutionally guaranteed and internationally sanctioned.

Even though British rule in Iraq was somewhat brief, they were able to transform Iraqi society in a way that would facilitate their rule as mandate holder

---

130   *See* White (2007), at 73.

131   *See* White (2011), at 57.

132   *See* Müller-Sommerfeld, at 265.

133   Fanar Haddad, *Sectarian Relations Before "Sectarianization" in Pre-2003 Iraq*, in Sectarianization: Mapping the New Politics of the Middle East 111 (Nader Hashemi & Danny Postel eds., 2017) [*hereinafter* Haddad].

134   Elham Manea, The Arab State and Women's Rights: The Trap of Authoritarian Governance 3 (2012).

and colonial administrator. Their time in Iraq also changed the course of Iraqi politics for the long-term. Iraq moved from mandate to treaty quite quickly, becoming the first newly established Middle Eastern nation to join the League of Nations. The British had previously signed a treaty with Iraq in 1922 in anticipation for its independence,[135] and was the result of 2 considerations: an increasing Iraqi nationalist movement; and a state-building process that took less time than previously anticipated.[136] It did not mean, however, that Iraq was *de facto* independent, free from British mandatory rule. While the British present the treaty as evidence of a relationship between two sovereign states, it was far from an agreement of equal partnership. Scholarship described the treaty as one with "the goal [of facilitating] a change from Britain's position [as] League of Nation's mandate holder for Iraq to its colonial ruler."[137] The British were able to maintain the privileges they had under the mandate system as well as the Ottoman capitulations regime while Iraqi leadership was largely coerced into agreeing to the terms of the treaty. From this came the Organic Law of 1924, the first constitutional-type law in the new nation-state of Iraq. This law contained a number of invocations from the new body of international minority law, as transformed by the League of Nations, such as the protection of linguistic and religious rights, equality before the law, and the guarantee of civil and political rights for Iraq's recognized minority groups.[138] Recognized religious minorities were also allowed to maintain their own jurisdiction over matters of personal status,[139] a continuation of the *millet* system.

Furthermore, Iraqi independence was contingent upon the acceptance of these constitutional protections by the Iraqi government. However, one must critically consider why minority guarantees were so important to the Mandate power, as well as why groups were selectively granted their application. Castellino and Cavanaugh present an interesting account of the ways in which minority rights were used to "serve the British colonial power via the strategic privileging of groups calculated to facilitate Britain's interest in the region."[140] The concern for situation of certain minorities was only important to the extent that it benefited the colonial power's interests. Even though the Assyrians and the Kurds, for example, petitioned to form their own homogenous state away from the Arabs, their wishes fell on deaf ears. Their demands

---

135    *See* Treaty Alliance between Britain and Iraq (Oct. 10, 1922).
136    *See* Castellino & Cavanaugh, at 190.
137    *Id.*
138    *See id. See also Review of Legislation,* 15 J. Comp. Legis. & Int'l L. 172 (1933).
139    *See* Ordinance 24 of 1930, http://archive.spectator.co.uk/article/5th-july-1930/6/the-anglo -iraq-treaty.
140    Castellino & Cavanaugh, at 193.

FACT AND FICTION

did not fit with the British plan for the territorially defined, resource-rich Iraq, nor did they help its colonial interests of "[establishing] Sunni hegemony within."[141] Similar to the French policy towards the Alawites in Syria,[142] the British adopted "political and administrative measures" that would "eventually lead to a new system of allegiances and loyalties" with the "institutionalisation of Sunni dominance over various ethnic, sectarian and linguistic groups."[143] This decision was taken largely based by Britain for two motivations: to maintain a safe passage through from India, and to gain access to the oil fields located near Mosul.[144] Consequently, the Iraqi nation and national identity adopted were more about guaranteeing colonial objectives than they were about "minority" protection.

European colonial policies would cement themselves in a way that would allow future despotic regimes to use those politically malleable identity cleavages to maintain and perpetuate power. Rather than attempt to encourage a truly civic state identity that would be inclusive to all who lived on the land, the codification of minority rights in international law and subsequently into domestic law meant that differences were highlighted and even weaponized, rather than overcome.[145] While minority rights may have offered certain communities protection *de jure*, particularly in terms of their right to self-organization, they also created a platform from which "otherness" could be used, manipulated and vilified. This "otherness" became an indispensable tool for authoritarianism, increasing the reach of the central state and intensifying the division between insider and outsider.

Perhaps with the exception of the Kurds, religious and ethnic identities were largely absent from the Iraqi political scene prior to the arrival of the Ba'athist regime. Saddam Hussein capitalized on those ethnic divisions that became politically significant with the formation of the nation-state. Like its Syrian counterpart, the Ba'athists in Iraq adopted systems of exclusive patronage – ones that privileged certain communal identities over others.[146] Authoritarian

---

141  *Id.*
142  *See* Aslam Farouk Ali, *Sectarianism in Alawite Syria: Exploring the Paradoxes of Politics and Religion* 34 J. Muslim Minority Aff. 207, 214 (2014) [*hereinafter* Farouk Ali].
143  Liora Lukitz, Iraq: The Search for National Identity 14 (1995).
144  *See* Castellino & Cavanaugh, at 189.
145  *See* Stephen May, Tariq Modood & Judith Squires, *Ethnicity, Nationalism and Minority Rights: Charting the Disciplinary Debates,* in Ethnicity, Nationalism and Minority Rights 1 (Stephen May, Tariq Modood & Judith Squires eds., 2004).
146  For an account of sectarianism in Syria, *see* Raymond Hinnebusch, *Syria's Alawis and the Ba'ath Party,* in The Alawis of Syria: War, Faith and Politics in the Levant 107 (Michael Kurr & Craig Larkin eds., 2015). For Iraq, *see* Haddad. Comparatively, *see* the British sectarian policy in Bahrain in: Omar Hesham AlShehabi, *Contested Modernity: Divided Rule and the*

regimes in the Middle East often use this tactic as a mode of furthering their own legitimacy within their own specific traditional base of power; so much so that the "anti-democratic context is essential for understanding sectarian conflict in Muslim societies."[147] Saddam Hussein, a Sunni, staffed the party structure, civil office, lawyers, the intelligence services, and the upper echelons of the military with members from his community.[148] Sectarianism became part of state policy during this time, as Saddam Hussein's policy "for creating a centralised and controlled power base internally and in the region was constructed around the promotion of sectarian identities."[149] The numerical significance of the Shi'a community did not prevent it from forming a political minority in the Iraqi state, or from facing minority-like persecution.[150] It is from this base that the Shi'a elites sought to politically mobilize – their existence as the numerical majority within the Iraqi territory, encouraged by their co-religionists in Iran – rather than as disenfranchised Iraqis in general.

C    *The Post-conflict Iraqi State and the Minority Question*

In the aftermath of the fall of Saddam and the US occupation of Iraq, the reforms to the Iraqi government attempted to transform the state into a "market-embedded democracy within a federal decentralised and consociational order ... and a full-fledged rentier economy with strong command features."[151] This order sought to constitutionally fragment state power between what the occupying forces understood to be the main interest groups in Iraq namely, Shia, Sunni, and Kurd. Special provisions were proposed in the Transitional Administrative Law, the interim constitution adopted without popular participation, for the remaining groups, the "minorities" of Iraq: the various Christian denominations and ethnicities, Yezidis, Mandeans, Turkmen and other minority groups.[152]

---

      *Birth of Sectarianism, Nationalism, and Absolutism in Bahrain*, 44 Brit. J. Middle Eastern Stud. 333 (2016).

147    Hashemi, at 5.

148    *See* Miranda Sissons & Abdul Razzaq al Saidi, *A Bitter Legacy: Lessons of De-Ba'athification in Iraq*, International Centre for Transitional Justice (2013), at 1 [*hereinafter* Sissons & al Saidi].

149    Castellino & Cavanaugh, at 198.

150    *See* Mokhtar Lamani, *Minorities in Iraq: The Other Victims*, Centre for International Governance Innovation (2009), at 4 [*hereinafter* Lamani].

151    Renad Mansour & Faleh Jabar, *Inter- and Intra-Ethnic Relations and Power Sharing in Post-Conflict Iraq* 11 Y.B. Minority Issues 187 (2012) [*hereinafter* Mansour & Jabbar].

152    *See* Andrew Arato, Constitution Making Under Occupation: The Politics of Imposed Revolution in Iraq 86 (2009).

FACT AND FICTION

The adopted constitutional and institutional organization in the aftermath of 2003 meant that, "religion and tribe emerged and transformed Iraqi society into identity/group politics."[153] In particular, two elements of such an organization stand out. First, the weaponization of sectarian identity as a mode of political organization by those who opposed Saddam Hussein's rule sought to accede to state power through majoritarian discourse and minoritarian vilification. Second is the Coalition Provisional Authority's (CPA) disastrous mismanagement and its deployment of Orientalist understandings of Iraqi society. The CPA, an extension of the United States (US) Department of Defense adopted in a UN Security Council resolution,[154] had a responsibility of transitioning Iraq from authoritarianism to democracy. One of the CPA's most notable, as well as infamous, decision was that of "de-ba'athification."[155] This policy banned those who had been previously, even if indirectly, affiliated with the Ba'ath regime from holding any type of position public office. Similar to the de-Nazificiation process that took place in post-war Germany, de-ba'athification sought to eliminate the Ba'athist state structure while simultaneously preventing the resurgence of Ba'athist elements in leadership positions.[156] In practice, this decision had drastic effects on Sunni members of society, as they were the primary patrons of Saddam's regime because they were members of his sect. Those Sunni members found themselves out of a job and disenfranchised by the new government as punishment for the offences of an authoritarian dictator.[157] Moreover, the external removal of the previous regime and the disbandment of the national army, created not only a security vacuum but also an "ideological and political void."[158] That void was to become a site of feverous contestation between different identity groups seeking to define what the new Iraq is, and who the Iraqis were to become.

At the request of the CPA, the Iraqi Governing Council, albeit the most diverse representative body Iraq had ever had, was formed on the basis of ethnic and religious quotas: 13 seats went to Shi'a members (as the numerical majority within Iraq), 5 seats were given to Sunni members, 5 to the Kurds,

---

153    Mansour & Jabar, at 188.

154    *See* S.C. Res. 1483 (May 22, 2003).

155    *See* Coalition Provisional Authority Order Number 1: De-Ba'athification of Iraqi Society (May 16, 2003).

156    *See* Omar Abdel-Razzak & Miriam Puttick, *Majorities and Minorities in Post-Isis Iraq*, 9 Contemp. Arab Aff. 565, 568 (2016) [*hereinafter* Abdel-Razzak & Puttick].

157    *See id.*, at 570. *See also* Sissons & al Saidi, at 15–18.

158    Ranj Alaaldin, *Sectarianism, Governance, and Iraq's Future*, Brookings Doha Center Analysis Paper (2018), at 7 [*hereinafter* Alaaldin].

and one seat each for a Christian and a Turkmen.[159] The preference given to the Shi'a community in the post-conflict reconstruction was symbolic of their deliverance as a majority and an end to their marginalization. For the Kurds, their equivalence with the previously powerful Sunni Arabs was not without its significance. It pointed to, firstly, the important concessions and recognition of the Kurds as a politically important group. Secondly, it served to further agitate the Arab Sunnis, whose political engagement prior was necessarily linked to Saddam and his party – as "all politically active members were forced to be part of Saddam's regime, and were now deemed unacceptable in the new Iraq."[160] Nevertheless, it meant that there were now two foundational identities in Iraq: being Kurdish or being Arab (Sunni and/or Shi'a). The form of governance established also took place over 3 levels: a devolved central administration, an autonomous and regionally concentrated Kurdistan, and locally decentralized governance in the remaining provinces.[161]

Overall, the decentralized system was supposed to be, in theory, based on regional representation. However, the animosities that had incurred over time between the different segments of society, compounded by US occupation and maladministration of the post-conflict reconstruction, meant instead that the decentralized system was now based on "communal factors."[162] The US pushed for a "constitutional framework [where] ... religion serves as the foundation on which political communities are constituted."[163] Identity politics became the only possible mobilizing factor in the Iraqi political scene, and identities became primary instruments "for securing the largest share possible of political and ... economic resources, laying the grounds for interethnic and intercommunal splits."[164] In practice, the articulation of identity politics was almost exclusively established with reference to the three main communal groups of Sunni, Kurd, and Shi'a; the smaller minority communities were collateral damage in the rush for power, influence and resources.[165] The constitutional drafting process provided for very limited minority participation.

---

159   *See* Toby Dodge & Renad Mansour, *Sectarianisation and De-Sectarianisation in the Struggle for Iraq's Political Field*, 18 Rev. Faith & Int'l Aff. 58, 61 (2020) [*hereinafter* Dodge & Mansour].

160   Mansour & Jabar, at 191.

161   *See id.*

162   *See id.*, at 189.

163   Larry Catá Backer, *God(s) over Constitutions: International and Religious Transnational Constitutionalism in the 21st Century*, 11 Miss. C. L. Rev. 145, 145 (2008).

164   *Id.*, at 145.

165   *See* Abdel-Razzak & Puttick, at 565.

FACT AND FICTION

Additionally, since the ethno-sectarian power-sharing agreement is not constitutionally subscribed, the prevalence of religiously or identity based political parties are derived from elite negotiated pacts that reinforce notions of sectarian politics – "communities mobilised around political objectives based on their ethnicity or sect, which came at the expense of a common national identity and the pluralistic politics of coexistence."[166]

The Iraqi Constitution includes provisions that relate to the rights of minorities and other vulnerable groups by providing for strong equality rights that should be applicable across all constitutional provisions and other laws as such.[167] The Preamble of the 2005 Constitution invokes the religious and ethnic diversity of Iraq, however, "several key provisions are yet to be implemented, leaving minorities and other vulnerable groups without protection from harm."[168] There is a non-discrimination clause, encapsulated in article 14, which states that Iraqis are equal before the law without distinction based on sect, religion, ethnicity, gender and so on. However, the reference in article 2,[169] which establishes Islam as the official religion of the state and prohibits the promulgation of any laws that may be contrary to Islamic law, works to cement the social hierarchy by casting non-Muslims as secondary citizens. Furthermore, the allocation of parliamentary seats proportionally and by sect puts minorities at a disadvantage because they are numerically inferior while solidifying identarian discourse as the primary vehicle for political participation.[170]

What does all this mean for the minority communities that exist outside the Shi'a-Sunni-Kurd paradigm? Long periods of oppression and violence mean that all Iraqis, regardless of ethnic or religious background, were victims of the central state as well as the occupying force. However, minorities were impacted specifically because the post-conflict reconstruction did not have their concerns at heart. Minorities make up only 5% of the overall population but 20% of the current displaced population.[171] With the onset of overtly sectarian politics and regional representation, the previously mixed areas of Iraq have become enclaves for either Sunni or Shi'a communities. Minorities

---

166 Alaaldin, at 9.
167 *See* Iraqi Constitution art. 14 (2005).
168 Institute for International Law and Human Rights, *Iraq's Minorities and Other Vulnerable Groups: Legal Framework, Documentation and Human Rights* (2013), at 54.
169 Iraqi Constitution art. 2(1)(a).
170 *See id.*, art. 16.
171 *See* Kathryn Westcott, *Iraq's Rich Mosaic of People*, BBC News (Feb. 27, 2003), http://news .bbc.co.uk/2/hi/middle_east/2783989.stm.

in previously mixed neighborhoods, namely the various Christian ethnicities, Yezidis, Turkmen, Mandeans, and others, became targets of ethnic cleansing in order to create ethnically homogenous localities for electoral purposes.[172] Some of these minorities have sought refuge in Iraqi Kurdistan where "religious identity is less of a determining factor in security."[173] However, the Kurdistan region, as well as other neighboring countries to which these groups have fled, dispose of limited resources to house, feed, and educate these communities to an acceptable and dignified standard.

The situation of these minorities has several implications for international law. First, UDHR article 18 provides the right to freedom of thought, conscience and religion as well as the right to non-discrimination. The ICCPR also grants minorities the right to practice their religion, culture and language free from interference. In terms of political representation, ICCPR article 25 guarantees the right to participate in public affairs, voting rights, and the right of equal access to public service regardless of race, sex, religion, language, and other differentiating factors. The political situation in Iraq is inconsistent with these articles and impacts all members of society, regardless of sect.

As one scholar rightly argues, these problems, that relate not just to the question of minorities but to the violent competition over state power and resources, "have at their root the lack of a common Iraqi identity."[174] The use of patronage, cooptation, and clientelism have only served to diminish the possibility of adopting an Iraqi identity based on equal citizenship with a neutral political formula. With major parties formulated on religious/sectarian identities, largely concentrated on consolidating their traditional bases of power, they are forgoing any real process of national reconciliation.[175] The current governing body has been so preoccupied with maintaining its hold on power through the articulation of ethnic politics that it has allowed the almost complete eradication of the diverse mosaic of people that have made up the demographic of Iraq since the beginning of time.[176] Political competition should not be encapsulated through the nation-state formulation based on the majority/minority dichotomy, nor should it be formulated on the basis of sectarian affiliation. The only way forward is to strive for a citizenship that would embrace the long-standing Iraqi diversity, rather than seek to undermine it.

---

172    *See* Lamani, at 10.
173    *Id.*, at 4.
174    *Id.*
175    *See* Lamani, at 13.
176    *See* Dodge & Mansour, at 61.

# FACT AND FICTION

## V    Conclusions

Minorities, in general, pose a political problem for the nation-state and a legal problem for international and human rights law. In terms of the former, the transformation of empire to state, and subject to citizen, meant that the source of legitimate political power had to be relocated. It took root in the idea of popular sovereignty where the people themselves are the highest authority from whom political power is legitimately derived and thus consensually binding. However, the process of tying power to people raises important questions about who the people are and how they are to be defined. The nation-state answers these questions with reference to specific factors that existed in the pre-political community, such as a common history, a religion, and a language – an inherently exclusionary process. In order to decide who is included one must necessarily decide who is excluded on the periphery of acceptance.

International law was the first to diffuse the idea of minorities as groups who may pose some type of defiance for the ruler or the state, and so they must be shielded from assimilation by the authorities. We are also able to discern the political nature of minority rights through the colonial rationale after the Great War, then by the League of Nations, and subsequently in modern international law. When the nation-state form was exported through imperialism, "international minority rights speak to wrongs that international law itself produces by organising global political realities into a legal order."[177] Those international minority rights, nevertheless, sit uncomfortably with the human rights regime in general, primarily because the category of minority is inherently political, making it highly contextual and politically malleable. Additionally, the UN Human Rights Committee interpreted ICCPR article 27 as "individual rights, [that] depend in turn on the ability of the minority group to maintain its culture, language or religion."[178] The fact that it is individually exercisable, and protected, only with reference to a larger community makes it increasingly complicated to prove breach of systemic abuse.[179]

The events that took place in Iraq in the aftermath of the occupation and civil war demonstrate that the adoption of a political paradigm which encourages, and even sanctions, ethnic and identity mobilization has left non-dominant numerical groups vulnerable to the whims of politicians

---

177    Macklem, at 532.

178    U.N. Doc. HRI/GEN/1/REV 1, at para. 6.2.

179    *See* Hum. Rts. Comm., Communication No 197/1985, *Kitok v Sweden*, U.N. Doc. CCPR/C/33/D/197/1985. *See also* Lovelace.

who seek to perpetuate power through the articulation of those ethnic and sect-based identities. The fact that regional representation became dependent on local ethnic quotas meant that minority communities were being forced out of their homes in order for other numerically significant groups to create homogenous political districts.[180] Rather than engage in a process of national reconciliation, education, and acceptance, the strategy adopted in Iraq prevented the development of a national and civic Iraqi identity of which all groups, regardless of numerical presence, religion or ethnicity, can become a part of. The result has been the near-complete eradication of groups who have formed part of Iraqi and Mesopotamian society for centuries.[181] It has led to the forceful migration and in some cases, the ethnic cleansing of communities who do not fit with the political and legal discourse being used by elites. International minority rights, their rationale, as well as their incompletion, have highlighted the precarious relationship between different communities in the nation-state, and have also failed to protect cultural difference when it was needed the most.

Therefore, when the time comes to adopt a reconstruction and rehabilitation strategy in other cases like Syria, things must be done differently. Otherwise, the same consequences are likely to be replicated. The authoritarian regime in Syria has been led by a disenfranchised community, the Alawites. As the Syrian revolution descended into the Syrian civil war, calls for the eradication of the entire group have been nascent, which have only helped the Syrian president use the language of minority protection against the rise of "Sunni extremism."[182] Indeed, the fact that Sunnis constitute a numerical majority has been a primary tool in the opposition's repertoire for the acquisition of power, using discourse of sectarian victimhood by fighting against the minoritarian "Alawite" regime, rather than framing the battle of power against an authoritarian regime that has oppressed all sects and ethnicities in Syria for over 40 years now.[183] Adopting a power-sharing arrangement in Syria, one that is similar to that of Iraq and Lebanon, is likely to result in the same violence perpetrated against the various minority communities, and will not address the root causes of the conflict, namely the presence of a violent, corrupt, and kleptocratic authoritarian dictatorship.

---

180  *See* Lamani, at 10.

181  *See id.,* at 3.

182  *See* Paulo Gabriel Hilu Pinto, *The Shattered Nation: The Sectarianisation of the Syrian Conflict,* in Sectarianization: Mapping the New Politics of the Middle East 124 (Nader Hashemi & Danny Postel eds., 2017).

183  *See id.,* at 132.

FACT AND FICTION

The only hope that Syria has for a non-violent future where all Syrians of all faiths, ethnicities, languages, and cultures can live side-by-side is through "the entrenchment of a strong Syrian national identity within the framework of equal citizenship, pluralistic democracy, and the [temporary] protection of minority rights."[184] As paradoxical as it may sound, the only way to protect minorities over the long-term is to forgo their "minority" status and begin the process of their acceptance as members of the community, equal to all and subordinate to none.

### Acknowledgments

I am grateful for the guidance and comments of Dr. Nimer Sultany.

---

184    Farouk Ali, at 207.

# Systemic Economic Harm in Occupied Palestine and the Social Connections Model

*Shahd Hammouri*

## Contents

I   Introduction
II  Identifying Systemic Economic Harm in Occupied Palestine
    A   Empirically Identifying Systemic Economic Harm in Occupied Palestine
    B   Normatively Identifying Systemic Economic Harm
III Alternative Paths of Redress for Systemic Economic Harm under Occupation
    A   Systemic Economic Harm and the Business and Human Rights Framework
    B   Third States and Systemic Harm in Occupation
IV  Concluding Remarks

## I   Introduction

Legal imagination is predisposed to think of the world in terms of physicality. If one's property is stolen, a lawyer does not need creativity to write up the claim; but what of the rights of someone whose business has been damaged as a result of discriminatory economic policies? The effect of such impediments can be described under the notion of "systemic economic harm." In theory, all humans have the right to pursue their economic development.[1] In practice, one's economic positioning is shaped by a set of predetermined conditions, prompted by a host of discourses,[2] and affected by a number of

---

[1] See International Covenant on Economic, Social and Cultural Rights, Dec. 16, 1966, 993 U.N.T.S. 3.
[2] See Iris Marion Young, Responsibility for Justice 56–59 (2011) [hereinafter Young (2011)].

SYSTEMIC ECONOMIC HARM IN OCCUPIED PALESTINE

actors including states and corporations.[3] Herein, one's capacity to pursue such development can be indirectly impeded by structural injustice engraved within a given normative system. In this respect, the international legal imagination, limited by needs of legality and coherence, cannot fully integrate all structural and contextual considerations. Yet, it is in contexts of heightened precarity caused by direct acts of domination such as a prolonged occupation, where the disparities caused by the absence of structural thought call for a more nuanced approach.[4]

This present article tackles the context of the Israeli occupation of Palestine to ask whether the existing framework of international law applied in situations of occupation captures and adequately addresses situations of systemic economic harm. Acknowledging the limitations of international law, it ventures to explore the remedial potentialities of different frameworks which escape traditional limitations of national legal systems. How is responsibility for systemic economic harm imagined? What are the avenues of redress available to address systemic economic harm in situations of occupation? Part one attempts to empirically and normatively identify such systemic economic harm. The second part investigates possible remedial paths for such systemic economic harm via international responsibility mechanisms for corporate actors involved in the occupation's economic apparatus, as well as states interacting with it.

This article is premised on the theoretical claim that remedying such injustice requires a holistic perception of causality to trace the connections sustaining dire economic conditions. In effect, it argues that the rare presence of such structural thinking in international law renders it inadequate to address systemic economic harm impeding on the right of the occupied population to pursue economic development. In one respect, the call for the integration of structural perspectives within the optic of international law bears the risk of increased indeterminacy.[5] In another respect, accepting this absence sets low expectations for international law and deepens the insecurities caused by its

---

3   According to Iris Marion Young, structural injustice entails a duty on different actors to remedy the systems that sustain such structural harm, including legal persons such as corporate actors and states. *See id.*, at 144–150.

4   Structural injustice exists, according to Iris Marion Young, when "social processes put large categories of persons under a systematic threat of domination or deprivation of the means to develop and exercise their capacities." *Id.*, at 143.

5   "As soon as the law tries to make an assessment about the larger interest, and evaluate the relevant contextual data, it will move on to an area of indeterminacy and political conflict." Martti Koskenniemi, *Between Impunity and Show Trials*, 6 Max Planck Y.B. U.N. L. 1, 29 (2002).

claim for some form of international prosperity. Furthermore, as shown below, the absence of structural thinking serves to deepen the disadvantages of international law's "others." This appeal to structural thinking has gained further prominence in international legal literature over the past few years, with works of authors such as Zinaida Miller,[6] Larissa van den Herik,[7] John Linarelli, Margot E. Salomon, Muthucumaraswamy Sornarajah,[8] among others.

To evaluate the capacity of international law to address systemic economic harm, this paper relies on Young's account of the "social connections model." This model provides a critical account geared towards capturing indirect causality in globalized systems.[9] To introduce this perspective, prior reference to John Glatung's work is warranted. Glatung gives a broad understanding of violence, as the cause of difference between a potential state of affairs and the actual state of affairs.[10] For example, if $A$ had the potential and initial capacity to go to school, but the occupation forces built a settlement on the road leading to the school, then $A$'s access to school is limited.[11] The difference between his initial potential, and the actuality of limited access, is a form a violence from Galtung's perspective. Such violence comes in many different forms: direct

---

6    Despite her focus on transnational justice, the work of Zinaida Miller provides crucial insights for the general cohort of international law. "The literature, institutions and international enterprise of transnational justice have historically failed to recognize the full importance of structural violence, inequality and economic distribution in conflict..." Zinaida Miller, *Effects of Invisibility: In Search of the "Economic" in Transitional Justice*, 2 Int' J. Trans. J. 266, 267 (2008).

7    "The current justice processes offer only a one-dimensional narrative that is focused on physical violence, and in which economic structural root causes remain invisible." Larissa van den Herik, *Economic, Social, and Cultural Rights – International Criminal Law's Blind Spot?* in Economic, Social, and Cultural Rights in International Law 343, 365 (Eibe Riedel, Gilles Giacca, and Christophe Golay eds., 2014).

8    *See, e.g.*, discussion of structural vulnerabilities in: John Linarelli, Margot E. Saloman, and Muthucumaraswamy Sornarajah, The Misery of International Law: Confrontations with Injustice in the Global Economy 60–63 (1st ed., 2018).

9    *See, e.g.*, Catherine Larrère, *Responsibility in a Global Context: Climate Change, Complexity, and the "Social Connection Model of Responsibility"*, 49 J. Soc. Phil. 426 (2018); Harry J. Van Buren, Judith Schrempf-Stirling, & Michelle Westermann-Behaylo, *Business and Human Trafficking: A Social Connection and Political Responsibility Model*, 60 Bus. & Soc'y 341–375 (2021).

10   *See* Johan Galtung, *Violence, Peace, and Peace Research*, 6 J. Peace Res. 167, 168 (2016) [*hereinafter* Galtung].

11   This example relies on real events, under which access is schools is impeded by the policies of the Israeli occupation. *See* Commission of the Churches on International Affairs, World Council of Churches, *Education under Occupation: Access to Education in the occupied Palestinian territory* (2013) [report no longer available on UNICEF website; see: https://eappi.org/en/resources/publications/education-under-occupation-2013].

and indirect, physical and psychological, intended and unintended.[12] Some forms of violence are not traceable to a specific person. Rather, they are the effect of structures that sustain uneven the distribution of resources.[13] As this paper will show, in the occupation context, such structures are often the result of international law violations. The harm inflicted by such structures is less apparent given that they manifest over an extended period of time.[14] This article applies this general understanding of violence to a specific form of it: the indirect violence of occupation policies that cause systemic economic harm.

The proliferation of indirect forms of violence among members of a given community often indicates structural injustice. Structural injustice is often experienced on a collective level. Such a collective group can include, for example, economically less privileged classes in a given state, indigenous people, or people under the occupation. To this end, Young finds that structural injustice "exists when social processes put large groups of persons under systemic threat of domination or deprivation of the means to develop and exercise their capacities – at the same time that these processes enable others to dominate or have a wide range of opportunities for developing and exercising capacities available to them."[15] Therefore, domination and deprivation are constitutive elements in the processes sustaining structural injustice. In this light, Young finds that the Palestinian peoples' right of self-determination can be conceptualized as the right of non-domination.[16]

In response to structural injustice, the social connections model suggests that all actors who contribute to the structural processes that produce injustice have a responsibility to work to remedy these injustices.[17] Responsibility in this context is understood expansively as a duty to evaluate one's positioning towards the collective. Accordingly, all agents who take part in the connections establishing structural injustice have to take a critical stance to assess their position and take action to redress such harm within their capacities.

Young's formula identifies the elements which shape an agent's responsibility towards a given structural injustice, which include: (1) the agent's positioning of power towards the given injustice, that is often accompanied by a level of privilege that indicates a capacity to undertake action against such structural

---

12    *See* Galtung, at 169–173.

13    *See id.,* at 170, 175.

14    *See id.,* at 174.

15    Young (2011), at 52.

16    *See* Iris Marion Young, *Self-determination as non-domination: Ideals applied to Palestine/ Israel,* 5 Ethnicities 139, 140 (2005).

17    *See* Iris Marion Young, *Responsibility and Global Justice: A Social Connections Model,* 23 Soc. Phil. & Pol'y 102, 103 (2006).

causes;[18] (2) the agent's interest in eradicating a given structural injustice, such interest is often that of the subject affected by the structural injustice (with this element, Young's perspective endows an obligation on those affected by the injustice to contest the structure);[19] and, lastly, (3) "collective ability" to undertake action.[20]

Indeed, in practice such elements entrap the subjugated in a paradoxical situation, as those with power and privilege often lack any interest in changing the structure, and those whose are interested in change it rarely have the capacity to do so.[21] Thus far, Israel has not exhibited any will to change the structure sustaining systemic economic harm inflicted upon Palestinians. Consequently, Palestinians are left in a space where their legal and political capacity to contest the structure is stripped to the bare minimum. While Young's model is not intended to be legal, her thinking can serve to guide alternative approaches to harnessing remedies for systemic harm caused by the Israeli occupation.

The context of occupation is apt for such an investigation into structural justice as the infliction of indirect harm is somewhat spatially defined within the parameters where the policies of the occupation apply (this is especially true in the case of settlements). More so, such indirect violence is also inflicted on account of one's legal status as a Palestinian. These parameters limit the scope of assessment for structural injustice paving the way for legal scrutiny. Secondly, international law has a role to play in the normalization of the general apparatus of occupation as an exceptional act of domination under the 1907 Hague Regulations.[22] Thirdly, the prolongation of the occupation has allowed for the normalization of systems designed in the spirit of occupation.

Concurrently, the context of occupation is ripe for the proliferation of systemic harm as it facilitates the possibility of exploitation and depravation in a defined temporal and spatial framework. It is for this reason that its temporary nature has been repeatedly stressed,[23] especially with relevance to the context of the Israeli occupation of Palestine.[24] These factors come together to shape the precariousness of the Palestinian population to severe economic impoverishment under a direct act of domination discussed in the following part.

---

18    *See* Young (2011), at 144–145.

19    *See id.*, 145–146.

20    *See id.*, at 147.

21    *See id.*, at 148.

22    *See* Chris af Jochnick & Roger Normand, *The Legitimation of Violence: A Critical History of the Laws of War*, 35 Harv. Int'l. L. J. 49 (1994).

23    *See* Commentary on the Geneva Conventions of 12 August 1949: IV Geneva Convention relative to the Protection of Civilian Persons in Time of War 275 (Jean S. Pictet ed., 1958); Iain Scobbie, *International Law and the Prolonged Occupation of Palestine* (2015), https://papers.ssrn.com/abstract=2611130.

24    Omar M. Dajani, *Israel's Creeping Annexation*, 111 AJIL Unbound 51–56 (2017).

## II Identifying Systemic Economic Harm in Occupied Palestine

This part substantively identifies systemic harm and its causality in the context of occupation. To do so, it is divided into two sections. The first section sets out to empirically identify forms of systemic harm in occupied Palestine in relation to international law violations, whereas the second section addresses the theoretical legal issues which arise when we attempt to imagine systemic harm through the international law lens.

### A *Empirically Identifying Systemic Economic Harm in Occupied Palestine*

Systematic and repeated international law violations generate domination and deprivation causing structural injustice. In this respect, the Israeli occupation is accompanied by a number of blanket violations which breed systemic economic harm – such as the violation of the Palestinian right to self-determination,[25] and the installment of a discriminatory regime of governance that many deem as a form of apartheid.[26] That is in addition to a host of blanket violations which are more spatially defined such as the settlements,[27] and the blockade on Gaza.[28] This section illustrates the interrelation between the accumulation of international humanitarian law violations, including the law of occupation, and the dire conditions of the Palestinian economy.

In 2016, the United Nations (UN) Conference for Trade and Development (UNCTAD) submitted a report to the UN General Assembly, drawing a link

---

25 *See* Legal Consequences of the Construction of a Wall in the Occupied Palestinian Territory, Advisory Opinion, 2004 I.C.J. Rep. 136 (July 9), paras. 115, 118, 122; Susan Hattis Rolef, *The Palestinians' Right to Self-Determination*, 16 J. Palestine Stud. 17 (1987).

26 *See* John Dugard, *Implementation of General Assembly Resolution 60/251 of March 2006 entitled 'Human Rights Council', Report of the Special Rapporteur on the situation of human rights in the Palestinian territories occupied since 1967, John Dugard,* U.N. Doc. A/HRC/4/17 (Jan. 29, 2007), paras. 49–50. *See also* Ilan Pappé, Israel and South Africa: The Many Faces of Apartheid (2015); Uri Davis, Israel: An Apartheid State (1987); Michael Sfard, *The Israeli Occupation of the West Bank and the Crime of Apartheid: Legal Opinion,* Yesh Din (June 2020), https://s3-eu-west-1.amazonaws.com/files.yesh-din.org/Apartheid+2020/Apartheid+ENG.pdf; B'Tselem, *A regime of Jewish supremacy from the Jordan River to the Mediterranean Sea: This is apartheid* (Jan. 2021), https://www.btselem.org/publications/fulltext/202101_this_is_apartheid; Nathan Thrall, *The Separate Regimes Delusion,* 43 London Rev. Books (Ja. 21, 2021), https://www.lrb.co.uk/the-paper/v43/no2/nathan-thrall/the-separate-regimes-delusion.

27 *See, generally,* Simon McKenzie, Disputed Territories and International Criminal Law: Israeli Settlements and the International Criminal Court (2019).

28 *See, generally,* Marty Gitlin, The Blockade of the Gaza Strip (2019) [*hereinafter* Gitlin].

between the institutional policies of the Israeli occupation and the deterioration of the Palestinian economy.[29] It also drew a link between such economic deterioration and systemic forms of suffering imposed upon the Palestinian people.[30] Overall, the report illustrates how the policies of the Israeli occupation have been a main factor in the economic impoverishment of the Palestinian people. This claim is exemplified in the following observations: had the trends of growth observed prior to the occupation in 1967 continued, the real Gross Domestic Product in Palestine would have been 88% higher.[31] Thus, the occupation has drastically stymied Palestinian economic growth. Likewise, it is also estimated that the Palestinian economy suffered a $48 billion revenue loss between 2000–2017 as a result of the occupation.[32] As such, the general context of prolonged occupation causes systemic harm to the Palestinian economy on a macro-level. This comes in tandem to the micro-level economic harm that different Israeli institutional structures and policies cause, especially in the agricultural and industrial sectors where the policies of land confiscation result in a systemic loss of grazing and agricultural land.[33]

Overall, the occupation has obstructed the development of the Palestinian economy. In one respect, Israeli policies impede Palestinians' productive and commercial capacities and make competition on global markets for goods and services nearly impossible.[34] In another respect, Israeli control over the regulation of investment creates uncertainty and thus deters foreign investment in Palestine.[35]

---

29    *See* Raja Khalidi & Sahar Taghdisi-Rad, *The economic dimensions of prolonged occupation: Continuity and change in Israeli policy towards the Palestinian economy: A special report commemorating twenty-five years of UNCTAD's programme of assistance to the Palestinian people*, UNCTAD (Aug. 2008), https://unctad.org/system/files/official-document/gds20092_en.pdf.

30    UNCTAD, *Economic costs of the Israeli occupation for the Palestinian people*, U.N. Doc. A/71/174 (July 21, 2016), para. 18 [*hereinafter* UNCTAD (2016)].

31    *Id.*, para. 17.

32    *$48 billion is the estimated revenue loss by Palestine from 2000–2017 due to occupation*, UNCTAD (Dec. 2, 2019), https://unctad.org/news/48-billion-estimated-revenue-loss-palestine-2000-2017-due-occupation.

33    *See id.*, para. 16. *See also* Yehezkel Lein, *Land Grab: Israel's Settlement Policy in the West Bank*, B'Tselem (May 2002), https://www.btselem.org/publications/summaries/200205_land_grab; Nir Shalev, *Under the Guise of Legality: Israel's Declarations of state land in the West Bank*, B'Tselem (Mar. 2012), https://www.btselem.org/publications/summaries/201203_under_the_guise_of_legality.

34    *See* Peter Lagerquist, *Privatizing the Occupation: The Political Economy of an Oslo Development Project*, 32 J. Palestine Stud. 5 (2003) [*hereinafter* Lagerquist]; UNCTAD (2016), n26.

35    *See, generally*, Lagerquist; UNCTAD (2016).

SYSTEMIC ECONOMIC HARM IN OCCUPIED PALESTINE 119

In the interim, economic agreements such as the Oslo Accords and the Paris Protocol (which were devised to organize economic relations between Israel and Palestine) are deeply defined by the asymmetrical and dominating reality of the occupation.[36] As Mohammad Samhouri illustrates, such agreements provide very minimal support for the Palestinian economy, which requires independence as a primary precondition for growth.[37]

The spill over of the asymmetrical nature of this economic relationship is also evidenced in how projects undertaken under the banner of "development" often lack good faith in operation. Peter Lagerquist illustrates this point in his study of one of the Oslo-affiliated development projects in the 1990s. This project included the construction of a series of industrial zones in the West Bank and the Gaza border with Israel and received funding from multiple international financial institutions. Lagerquist showcases how the project's design alienated Palestinian investors and worked as a space to direct excess foreign investment from Israel in pursuit of cheap operation costs.[38] Eventually, programs designed under the banner of development often supplement Israeli exploitation.[39]

This exploitation is also evident in the context of rules of usufruct.[40] As an occupying power, Israel has a duty to administer the resources of the occupied territories within the rules of usufruct under the Hague Regulations (which are distinct in their reference to private property and discussion of economic considerations, not found elsewhere in the body of the laws of war). There are different interpretations as to the rules governing the boundaries of the standard of usufruct. Yet, as a general rule of thumb, Jessup notes, the occupant's actions ought to have a solid basis in law, and its acts ought to be "in good faith for the management of the community under war conditions and not for his [i.e. the occupant's] own enrichment."[41]

---

36 *See* Raja Khalidi, *The Structural Transformation of the Palestinian Economy after Oslo*, in From the River to the Sea: Palestine and Israel in the Shadow of Peace 95 (Mandy Turner ed., 2019).

37 *See* Mohammed Samhouri, *Revisiting the Paris Protocol: Israeli-Palestinian Economic Relations, 1994–2014*, 70 Middle East J. 579 (2016).

38 *See* Lagerquist.

39 *See id.*

40 Usufruct is defined as: "The right of reaping the fruits (fructus) of things belonging to others, without destroying or wasting the subject over which such rights extend." Jonathan Law, *Usufruct, Oxford Dictionary of Law* (9th ed., 2018). Hague Convention IV – Laws and Customs of War on Land art. 55, Oct. 18, 1907, 3 Martens Nouveau Recueil (ser. 3) 461 [*hereinafter* Hague Regulations].

41 Philip C. Jessup, *A Belligerent Occupant's Power over Property*, 38 Am. J. Int'l L. 457, 458 (1944).

Against the backdrop of this standard, one should assess Israeli policies for administering water resources and quarries. UNCTAD notes that "By 2004, more than 85 per cent of Palestinian water from West Bank aquifers had been taken by Israel, covering 25.3 per cent of Israel's water needs."[42] Such policies contravene Appendix I and Annex III of the Israeli-Palestinian Interim Agreement on the West Bank and the Gaza Strip (1995).[43] This policy exemplifies systemic depravation, which eventually leads Palestinians to depend on Israeli water imports, or resorting to unsafe water resources.[44] Such policies effectively violate the right to safe and clean water.[45] Mark Zeitoun describes Israeli water extraction policies under the term hydro-hegemony.[46] Zeitoun finds that "Israeli control over transboundary fresh water is complete at many levels,"[47] and that water deprivation in Palestine "is the result of extremely varied but systematic endeavours by one of the parties to perpetuate and extended their superiority over the other."[48]

The violation of the rules of usufruct is also evident in the case of quarries. Israeli and multinational corporations have been actively investing in the quarrying business in the West Bank for the benefit of Israel since the 1970s.[49] Quarrying in the West Bank requires cheap Palestinian labor, and the externalization of the environmental effects of quarrying to Palestinian territories. From an economic perspective, such activities provide minimal economic gain for Palestinians in return for the exploitation of their natural resources. Ultimately, the exploitation of the occupied population's natural resources

---

42  UNCTAD, *The Economic Costs of the Israeli Occupation for the Palestinian People: The Unrealized Oil and Natural Gas Potential*, UNCTAD/GDS/APP/2019/1 (2019), at 8 [*hereinafter* UNCTAD (2019)].

43  *See* H.R.C., *Israeli settlements in the Occupied Palestinian Territory, including East Jerusalem, and in the occupied Syrian Golan*, U.N. Doc. A/HRC/34/39 (Apr. 13, 2017), para. 11; UNCTAD (2019), at 8–12.

44  U.N. Doc. A/HRC/34/39 (2017), para. 16 (which notes that Palestinians have lost 82% of their water resources due to the occupation).

45  *See The human right to water and sanitation*, U.N. Doc. A/RES/64/292 (July 28, 2010).

46  *See* Mark Zeitoun, Power and Water in the Middle East: The Hidden Politics of the Palestinian-Israeli Water Conflict 145–155 (2012).

47  *See id.*, at 49.

48  *Id.*, at 146–147.

49  *See* Maha Abdallah & Lydia De Leeuw, *Violations Set in Stone: HeidelbergCement in the Occupied Palestinian Territory*, Al-Haq & SOMO (Feb. 2020), http://www.alhaq.org/publications/16408.html; B'Tselem, *High Court sanctions looting: Israeli quarries in the West Bank* (Jan. 2012), https://www.btselem.org/settlements/20120116_hcj_ruling_on_quarries_in_wb.

SYSTEMIC ECONOMIC HARM IN OCCUPIED PALESTINE

is undertaken for the sole enrichment of Israel, in contravention the rules of usufruct.[50]

Taxation policies further exemplify the systemic harm that the Israeli occupation inflicts on Palestinians under its control. Hague Regulations article 48 stipulates that the occupier ought to abide as far as possible with existing taxation regimes when it regulates tax in an occupied territory, and that tax proceeds are to be paid to facilitate the administration of the occupied territory. Article 49 prohibits the collection of further levies unless justified for military purposes or required for the administration of the occupied area. In reality, the occupying power imposes differential tax regimes that place a heavier burden on Palestinians engaged in economic activities, whether in Palestine or in Israel, and that mark a deep asymmetry in the economic relations between the two parties.[51] Selective taxing policies deepen the market disadvantage of Palestinian goods and services competing with Israeli products.[52] Similarly, the occupation's tax regime incites systemic transfer of resources that is not supplemented by investment in the Palestinian public sector. For example, the taxes that Palestinian workers in Israel pay go directly to Israel, but Israel does not dispense expenditures on public services to Palestinians.[53] Overall, "the total of these resource transfers is large and, according to some estimates, exceeds in any given year 15 per cent of the Palestinian GDP."[54]

---

50 *See* Yesh Din, *The Great Drain: Israeli quarries in the West Bank: High Court Sanctioned Institutionalized Theft* (Sep. 2017), https://www.yesh-din.org/en/great-drain-israeli-quarries-west-bank-high-court-sanctioned-institutionalized-theft/; Valentina Azarova, *Exploiting A 'Dynamic' Interpretation? The Israeli High Court of Justice Accepts the Legality of Israel's Quarrying Activities in the Occupied Palestinian Territory*, EJIL: Talk! (Feb. 7, 2012), https://www.ejiltalk.org/exploiting-a-dynamic-interpretation-the-israeli-high-court-of-justice-accepts-the-legality-of-israels-quarrying-activities-in-the-occupied-palestinian-territory/.

51 In agriculture, systems of land tax as derived from the commutation of the old Ottoman tithe and imposed on Palestinian farmers have placed a disproportional tax burden on them. In manufacture, Palestinian manufactures pay 35–40% more tax than their Israeli counterparts, eventually leading to the reality where almost no capital market exists in the occupied territories as cash flows are drained by higher taxes or invested back in the building of family dwellings or placed in liquid funds in Jordanian dinars. *See* The Palestinian Economy: Studies in Development under Prolonged Occupation 68 (George T. Abed ed., 1988) [*hereinafter* Abed]; Roger Owen, *Economic Development in Mandatory Palestine: 1918–1948*, in Abed; Raja Khalidi, *The Economy of Palestinian Arabs in Israel*, in Abed.

52 *Id.*

53 *See* UNCTAD (2016), at 10.

54 *See* UNCTAD (2019), at 10.

Likewise, the establishment and maintenance of settlements is a spatially limited form of a violation that breeds systemic economic harm on a given collective of people. In the settlements, the spatial context of the economic activity itself is illegal, as the establishment of settlements violates the prohibition against displacing the civilian population,[55] and the prohibition against confiscating land in occupied territories (except in specific circumstances).[56] The continuation of this illegality fosters a host of systematic human right violations,[57] the effect of which proliferates with the occupation's exploitative and discriminatory economic policies. For example, Israeli settlements disproportionally drain the water resources shared with Palestinians.[58] Likewise, the infrastructure networks which were built to serve settlements cross through Palestinian lands, denying Palestinians proper access to roads.[59] Moreover, the geographical choices of settlement building hinder existing commercial communication lines contributing to the segmentation of Palestinian economies.[60]

The act of displacement in and of itself impacts the population's economic capacity. It displaces their sources of livelihoods,[61] denies their property rights, impedes their access to natural resources, and eventually forces Palestinians to accept low wage, low-skill manual labor. This results in a labor flow that redistributes the economic yield of such productive capacities from the Palestinian economy to the Israeli economy. It thus provides a considerable source of financing for imports on the Israeli side.[62]

---

55   Geneva Convention (IV) Relative to the Protection of Civilian Persons in Time of War art. 49(6), Aug. 12, 1949, 75 U.N.T.S. 287 [*hereinafter* Fourth Geneva Convention]; Protocol Additional to the Geneva Conventions of 12 August 1949, and relating to the Protection of Victims of International Armed Conflicts art. 85(4)(a), June 8, 1977, 1125 U.N.T.S. 3.

56   *See* ICRC, *Rule 51. Public and Private Property in Occupied Territory*, IHL Database: Customary IHL, https://ihl-databases.icrc.org/customary-ihl/eng/docs/v1_rul_rule51; Ghazi Falah, *Dynamics and patterns of the shrinking of Arab lands in Palestine*, 22 Pol. Geography 179 (2003); *Land Confiscation* 6 J. Palestine Stud. 153 (1976).

57   *See* Human Rights Watch, *Occupation, Inc: How Settlement Businesses Contribute to Israel's Violations of Palestinian Rights* (Jan. 2016), https://www.hrw.org/news/2016/01/19/occupation-inc-how-settlement-businesses-contribute-israels-violations-palestinian.

58   *See, generally,* Abed.

59   *Id. See also* Samira Shah, *On the road to apartheid: the bypass road network in the West Bank*, 29 Columbia Hum. Rts. L. Rev. 221 (1997); B'Tselem, *Forbidden Roads Israel's Discriminatory Road Regime in the West Bank* (Aug. 2004), https://www.btselem.org/publications/summaries/200408_forbidden_roads.

60   *See, generally,* Abed.

61   Alex Pollock *Society and Change in the Northern Jordan Valley*, in Abed.

62   UNCTAD (2016), para. 13.

SYSTEMIC ECONOMIC HARM IN OCCUPIED PALESTINE

Finally, acute forms of systemic economic harm have manifested in Gaza, in part as consequence of the siege. Israel has imposed considerable restrictions on movement in the Gaza Strip since the 1990s citing security concerns. Following Hamas' victory in the internationally monitored elections for the Palestinian authority in 2007, Israel imposed a more severe form of blockade on land, air, and sea unto the territory of the Gaza Strip.[63] The practice of blockade is itself illegal,[64] and a form of collective punishment,[65] that "is being imposed to apply pressure to the de facto authorities, and in response to acts committed by various groups in Gaza."[66] Such a form of punishment is prohibited under Fourth Geneva Convention article 33 and Hague Regulations article 50.[67]

The effects of such collective punishment are crippling. Gaza has one of the highest rates of unemployment worldwide due to the limitations on the growth of its economy.[68] Movement restrictions impede its capacity to undertake commercial activities with the rest of the world, especially given the Israeli imposition of quotas on imports and limitations on fishing activities.[69]

---

63   *See* Gitlin; U.N. OCHA, Occupied Palestinian Territory, *Glaza Blockade*, see: https://web
.archive.org/web/20210615053559/https://www.ochaopt.org/theme/gaza-blockade.

64   *See* Russell Buchan, *II. The Palmer Report and the Legality of Israel's Naval Blockade of
Gaza*, 61 Int'l & Comp. L. Q. 264 (2012).

65   *See* H.R.C., *Implementation of Human Rights Council Resolutions S-9/1 and S-12/1*, U.N.
Doc. A/HRC/34/36 (Jan. 25, 2017), para. 36.

66   H.R.C., *Human rights situation in the Occupied Palestinian Territory, including East
Jerusalem*, U.N. Doc. A/HRC/24/30 (Aug. 22, 2013), para. 22.

67   "No protected person may be punished for any offense he or she has not personally committed. Collective penalties and likewise all measures of intimidation or of terrorism are prohibited." Fourth Geneva Convention art. 33. "No general penalty, pecuniary or otherwise, shall be inflicted upon the population on account of the acts of individuals for which they cannot be regarded as jointly and severally responsible" Hague Regulations art. 50. *See also* Amnesty International UK, *Gaza Blockade: 'collective punishment' condemned*, Press Release (Jan. 21, 2008), https://www.amnesty.org.uk/press-releases/gaza-blockade-collective-punishment-condemned; ICRC, *Gaza closure: Not another year!*, Press Release (June 14, 2010), https://www.icrc.org/en/doc/resources/documents/update/palestine-update-140610.htm ("The whole of Gaza's civilian population is being punished for acts for which they bear no responsibility. The closure therefore constitutes a collective punishment imposed in clear violation of Israel's obligations under international humanitarian law.").

68   At the time of the research unemployment rates in Gaza stood at 49.1%. Relief Web, *Gaza unemployment rate in the second quarter of 2020: 49.1%*, Press Release (Sep. 21, 2020) https://reliefweb.int/report/occupied-palestinian-territory/gaza-unemployment-rate-second-quarter-2020-491.

69   *See, generally*, UNCTAD (2016).

The Gazans suffer from these restrictions on a daily basis, as they manifest in wide-range limitations including on housing,[70] healthcare,[71] food security,[72] basic needs (such as water and electricity),[73] and education.[74] Consequently, they feed into the de-development of Gaza.[75]

To sum up, the accumulation of international law violations in the context of occupation has resulted in an overall apparatus of domination that creates a gross asymmetry in economic relations between the two sides. Overtime, such relations have resulted in systemic economic harm for the Palestinian people. The relation between such harm and violations of international law is apparent, and yet it seems difficult to articulate such harm from the lens of international law.

## B      *Normatively Identifying Systemic Economic Harm*

In theory, the aforementioned violations are "wrongful acts" which give rise to Israeli responsibility for the harms they cause. According to the International Law Commission's draft articles on Responsibility of States for Internationally Wrongful Acts (ARISWA), "every internationally wrongful act of a state entails the international responsibility of that state."[76] An internationally wrongful act is identified as "a breach of an international obligation of the state,"[77] especially "an obligation arising under a preemptory norm of general international law,"[78] that is attributable to the state. A breach of peremptory norms is identified as a "serious breach" which substantively includes the prohibition

---

70      *See* Norwegian Refugee Council, *Overview of the Housing Situation in the Gaza Strip* (Mar. 2013), at 45, 51–52.

71      *See* U.N. OHCHR, *UN experts say Gaza health care at "breaking point"* (June 21, 2018), https://www.ohchr.org/en/NewsEvents/Pages/DisplayNews.aspx?NewsID=23236 &LangID=E.

72      *See* U.N. OCHA, Occupied Palestinian Territory, *Food insecurity in the oPt: 1.3 million Palestinians in the Gaza strip are food insecure* (Dec. 14, 2018), https://www.ochaopt.org/content/food-insecurity-opt-13-million-palestinians-gaza-strip-are-food-insecure.

73      *See* U.N. Doc. A/HRC/24/30, paras. 10–23.

74      *See* U.N. OCHA, Occupied Palestinian Territory, *Education*, see: https://web.archive.org/web/20210506153606/https://www.ochaopt.org/theme/education.

75      *See* Sara M. Roy, The Gaza Strip: The Political Economy of De-development 135 (1995). Such policies have also be described as "institutionalized impoverishment;" *see* Trude Strand, *Tightening the Noose: The Institutionalized Impoverishment of Gaza*, 2005–2010, 43 J. Palestine Stud. 6, 17 (2014) 17.

76      U.N. Int'l L. Comm'n, *Draft Articles on Responsibility of States for Internationally Wrongful Acts, with commentaries*, in Report of the International Law Commission on the Work of Its Fifty-third Session, U.N. Doc. A/56/10 (2001), art. 1 [*hereinafter* ARSIWA, with commentaries].

77      *Id.*, art. 2(b).

78      *Id.*, art. 40.

SYSTEMIC ECONOMIC HARM IN OCCUPIED PALESTINE 125

against apartheid and violations of the peoples' right to self-determination.[79] Meanwhile, such seriousness is further escalated if it is "a gross or systematic failure by the responsible state to fulfil the obligation in question."[80] As such, Israel would be responsible for wrongful acts committed by its representatives in terms of administration in contravention of the rules of usufruct, prohibition against the forceful transfer of civilians, prohibition against collective punishment, and violation of bilateral economic agreements (among others).

However, the question remains as to how one should understand the harm such violations cause for the purpose of providing for a legal remedy. The attempts to articulate systemic economic harm in international law faces two sets of hurdles ingrained within normative structures for international responsibility.

Firstly, traditional liability models are focused on conduct rather than on effect.[81] Accordingly, ARISWA is concerned with the violation rather than the harm caused.[82] In addition, the substantive body of international law does not explicitly find occupation as a violation of the state's responsibility under international law.[83] Therein, international law invites an assessment of the violation in a separate light from the harm caused. This approach entails accepting the risk of underrepresenting the systemic nature of the harm resulting from wrongdoing in occupation. Secondly, even if we are to assess the harm that the occupation causes outside of the ARISWA, structural economic harm is often hard to capture under a traditional liability model, as the causality is often seen as too indirect. There are three theoretical premises that underpin this shortcoming that originate in liberal political thought and foreground international legal thinking about responsibility:

- (1) The prominence of methodological individualism in contemporary legal thought.[84] Captured in the work of Weber, this methodological choice calls for the conceptualization of causality and responsibility in terms of direct

---

79  *See id.*, art. 40, at 112–113.

80  *Id.*, at 113.

81  *See* Andrew Nollkaemper & Dov Jacobs, *Shared Responsibility in International Law: A Conceptual Framework,* 34 Mich. J. Int'l L. 359, 396 (2013).

82  *See* James D. Fry, *Attribution of Responsibility,* in Principles of Shared Responsibility, in International Law: An Appraisal of the State of the Art 98, 101–2 (André Nollkaemper & Ilias Plakokefalos eds., 2014).

83  Hague Regulations art. 43 refers to the authority of the occupying power as legitimate. In this sense, a legitimate by-product of armed conflict. *See* Eyal Benvenisti, The International Law of Occupation 39–40 (2nd ed., 2012).

84  "The Liberal vision of law and economics idealizes individual independent agency as the essence of responsible power." Martha T. McCluskey, *Personal Responsibility for Systemic Inequality,* in Research Handbook on Political Economy and the Law 228, 238 (Ugo Mattei & John D. Haskell eds., 2015). Galtung also notes that traditional thinking is focused

relations among the actions of agents.[85] Accordingly, legal liability systems consider injustice to arise in the course of relations among individuals, with minimal reference to how social structures shape a given outcome.[86] As such, traditional thinking about accountability rests on facts primarily relevant to direct interpersonal relations. This thinking reflects what Kutz terms an "evaluative solipsism" that inadequately assesses collective and systemic forms of harm.[87]

– (2) Methodological nationalism, which is the tendency to frame societal issues within the national-territorial confines of the nation-state.[88] It thus overlooks the interconnected and cross-border nature of the causality chains in the assessment of wrong-doing; particularly in relation to the indirect role of other states and private actors.

– (3) The private-public distinction, found in the theoretical premises of international law, renders economic considerations outside public international law's assessment.[89] As a result, economic realities resulting from economic competition and free enterprise are discussed only with reference to regimes of economic law, alienating relevant public international considerations.[90] For example, there are ongoing scholarly disputes on international investment law's lack of appreciation for human rights considerations.[91]

---

on personal violence, as it is more apparent; this perception is rooted in the Judaeo, Christian, Roman traditions. *See* Galtung, at 173.

85    *See* Christopher Kutz, Complicity: Ethics and Law for a Collective Age 188 (2000) [*hereinafter* Kutz]; John Elster, *Marxism, functionalism, and game theory: The case for methodological individualism*, 11 Theory & Soc'y 453 (1982).

86    In her discussion of the dynamics governing social structural processes, Young contrasts methodological individualism's understanding of direct relations to the view that social structural processes exist and are produced only in action. *See* Young (2011), at 59–62.

87    *See* Kutz, at 3–6.

88    *See* Ulrich Beck & Elisabeth Beck-Gernsheim, Individualization: Institutionalized Individualism and its Social and Political Consequences xxi (2001); Susan Marks, *State-Centrism, International Law, and the Anxieties of Influence*, 19 Leiden J. Int'l L. 339 (2006). International Law upholds the liberal statist position whereby states are subject and sources of international law. *See* A. Claire Cutler, Private Power and Global Authority: Transnational Merchant Law in the Global Political Economy 21 (2003) [*hereinafter* Cutler]. *See also, generally*, Andreas Wimmer & Nina Glick Schiller, *Methodological Nationalism, the Social Sciences, and the Study of Migration: An Essay in Historical Epistemology*, 37 Int'l Migration Rev. 576 (2003); Young, at 135.

89    *See* Cutler, at 26–27.

90    *See id.*, at 57–58.

91    *See* Barnali Choudhury, *International Investment Law and Non-Economic Issues*, 50 Vanderbilt J. Transnat'l L. 1 (2020); Monica Feria-Tinta, *Like Oil and Water? Human Rights in Investment Arbitration in the Wake of Philip Morris v. Uruguay*, 34 J. Int'l Arb. 601 (2017).

SYSTEMIC ECONOMIC HARM IN OCCUPIED PALESTINE                    127

In this context, ARISWA's focus on "violations" instead of "harm" goes hand in hand with a juridical mindset that conceptualizes responsibility as one arising out of direct interpersonal relations and within the confines of national borders and separated from economic considerations. The joint effect of these three elements undermines the ability of international law to capture and remedy systemic economic harm. Nonetheless, there exists a number of frameworks (especially those not transposed from national law) which escape such theoretical limitations, perhaps offering unusual remedial paths. Such frameworks are discussed in the following part.

## III    Alternative Paths of Redress for Systemic Economic Harm under Occupation

At this juncture, the paper will refocus the attention from the general question of responsibility for systemic economic harm, to investigating alternative forms of redress for systemic economic harm, as imagined in relation to the social connections model. In this respect, the *Basic Principles and Guidelines on the Right to a Remedy and Reparation for Victims of Gross Violations of International Human Rights Law and Serious Violations of International Humanitarian Law* define victims as: "persons who individually or collectively suffered harm, including physical or mental injury ... *economic loss* ... through acts or omissions that constitute gross violations of international human rights law, or serious violations of international humanitarian law."[92] Once identified as such, the victim has the right to: equal and effective access to justice; adequate, effective and prompt reparation for harm suffered; and access to relevant information concerning violations and reparation mechanisms.[93]

Under this definition, we can say that people suffering from economic loss prompted by blanket violations of international law are victims who deserve redress. Once again, the traditional framework of responsibility provides little aid as, international law lacks the procedural and substantive capacity to juridically offer redress for a systemic harm prompted by a given state.[94] This absence calls for the pursuit of alternative paths. This section investigates such paths. To do so, it looks at frameworks that invite some forms of redress from two other agents with the power and privilege to affect the structure causing the systemic harm: the corporate actor and third states.

---

92    U.N. Doc. A/RES/60/147 (Mar. 21, 2006), at V (emphasis added).

93    *Id.*, at VII.

94    *See* Dinah Shelton, Remedies in International Human Rights Law 7 (3rd ed., 2015).

A    *Systemic Economic Harm and the Business and Human Rights Framework*

Corporations, as the main engine of capital accumulation,[95] have considerable power and privilege in local economies.[96] In light of this positioning, the social connections model would impose social duties on the corporate actor. Nevertheless, traditional corporate governance frameworks do not often account for such a duty. This absence creates a "governance gap" in relation to transnational human rights.[97] This gap means that few legal constraints exist to contain the risk of the involvement of business enterprises in exploitative relations which generate systemic economic harm in conflict areas.[98] Consequently, little use was made of the power of corporations to influence systems sustaining structural injustice.

This gap is rooted in the fact that corporations are not formally subjects of international law.[99] Formal legal mechanisms of accountability such as the Rome Statute of the International Criminal Court do not reference corporations, despite the fact that the drafters considered such inclusion.[100] Exceptionally, some human rights instruments leave a space for interpretation, under which some obligations can be extended to corporations.[101] There are also mechanisms of accountability which reference corporate accountability such as the work of the International Law Commission on the liability of legal

---

95    *See* Bastiaan Van Apeldoorn & Nana de Graaff, *The Corporation in Political Science*, in The Corporation: A Critical Multi-disciplinary handbook 134, 135 (Grietje Baars & Andrew Spicer eds., 2017).

96    *See* Ulrich Beck, Power in the Global Age: A New Global Political Economy 52–55 (2014).

97    *See* Beate Sjåfjell & Mark B. Taylor, *Clash of Norms: Shareholder Primacy vs. Sustainable Corporate Purpose* (2019) [*hereinafter* Sjåfjell & Taylor], https://papers.ssrn.com/sol3/papers.cfm?abstract_id=3444050.

98    *See* Hugo Slim, *Business actors in armed conflict: towards a new humanitarian agenda*, 94 Int'l Rev. Red. Cross 903 (2012).

99    "They – Corporations-remain entities created by the national law of their place of incorporation." Brief of Amicus Curiae Professor James Crawford in Support of Conditional Cross-Petitioner, Presbyterian Church of Sudan et al. v. Talisman Energy Inc., No. 09-1418 (Jun. 23, 2010), at 11.

100   In the course of drafting the Rome Statute, suggestions to include reference to corporate personality in the ethos of the case law of the industrialists' trials in Nuremberg were overruled. *See, generally,* Michael J. Kelly, Prosecuting Corporations for Genocide (2016).

101   An explicit account of such extended obligations is found in: David Weissbrodt & Muria Kruger, *Norms on the Responsibilities of Transnational Corporations and Other Business Enterprises with Regard to Human Rights*, 97 Am. J. Int'l L. 901 (2003).

SYSTEMIC ECONOMIC HARM IN OCCUPIED PALESTINE 129

persons for crimes against humanity,[102] the Special Tribunal for Lebanon,[103] and the Malabo Protocol.[104]

Different attempts to draft international legal instruments that consider the corporate actor a responsible social actor, who can support the interests of the local community, failed to gain sufficient support. One notable attempt in the 1970s sought to address Global South states' dismay with transnational corporations' negative impact on their local economies.[105] A draft proposed a code of conduct for transnational corporations as a binding international instrument that would impose on corporations a social role.[106] The drafts of the proposed code (the last version of which was published by the UN Centre for Transnational Corporations in 1988), can be read as a counter-narrative to the traditional understanding of causality entrenched in methodological individualism and nationalism.

Adopting a developmental rhetoric, enshrined in an appeal to the interdependent nature of the global economy, the proposed code imposed direct international obligations on corporations to respect public considerations like responsible engagement with the local economy in a manner that would avoid

---

102   "There are several treaties that address the liability of legal persons for criminal offences, notably: the 1973 International Convention on the Suppression and Punishment of the Crime of Apartheid; the 1989 Basel Convention on the Control of Transboundary Movements of Hazardous Wastes and Their Disposal; the 1999 International Convention for the Suppression of the Financing of Terrorism; the 2000 United Nations Convention against Transnational Organized Crime; the 2000 Optional Protocol to the Convention on the Rights of the Child on the sale of children, child prostitution and child pornography; the 2003 United Nations Convention against Corruption; the Protocol of 2005 to the Protocol for the Suppression of Unlawful Acts Against the Safety of Fixed Platforms Located on the Continental Shelf; and a series of treaties concluded within the Council of Europe. Other regional instruments address the issue as well, mostly in the context of corruption." U.N. Int'l L. Comm'n, *Report of the International Law Commission*, 71st session (29 April–7 June and 8 July–9 August 2019), U.N. Doc. A/74/10 (2019), at 82–83.

103   In the cases of New TV S.A.L. and Akhbar Beirut S.A.L., the Special Tribunal for Lebanon decided to hold corporate legal persons liable for the crime of contempt. *See* Nadia Bernaz, *Corporate Criminal Liability under International Law: The New TV S.A.L. and Akhbar Beirut S.A.L. Cases at the Special Tribunal for Lebanon*, 13 J. Int'l Crim. Just. 313 (2015).

104   Protocol on Amendments to the Protocol on the Statute of the African Court of Justice and Human Rights, June 27, 2014. Annex article 1 (3).

105   *See* Center for Transnational Corporations, *Transnational Corporations: Issues Involved in the Formulation of a Code of Conduct*, U.N. Doc. E/C.10/17 (July 20, 1976) [*hereinafter* CTC Code of Conduct]. *See also* Karl P. Sauvant, *The Negotiations of the United Nations Code of Conduct on Transnational Corporations: Experience and Lessons Learned*, 16 J. World Inv. & Trade 11 (2015).

106   *See* CTC Code of Conduct.

direct and systemic harm.[107] The code also took account of the asymmetrical relation between Global South states and foreign investors from developed states, by instating clauses about technology transfers and the renegotiation of investment agreements in good faith.[108]

Had party members accepted the proposed UN Code of Conduct, a corporation operating in the occupied Palestinian territories would have had a positive obligation to adhere to the local community's economic goals, development objectives, and socio-cultural objectives.[109] In addition, it would have required the corporation to contribute to the Palestinian economy's well-being by, for instance, making investment decisions which support the diversification of Palestinian exports.[110] The proposed code would have empowered the relevant national courts to enforce these obligations, and would have established an international institutional mechanism to monitor this enforcement.[111]

Other attempts followed the 1988 proposed code.[112] The most recent and successful of these is the United Nations Guiding Principles on Business and Human Rights (UNGPs), endorsed unanimously by the UN Human Rights Council in 2011.[113] The UNGPs put forth a framework rooted in: (1) the corporation's duty to respect human rights; (2) the state's duty to protect from human rights infringement; and (3) the victim's right to remedy. UNGP Principle 7 addresses the situation of "conflict affected areas" placing a higher level of responsibility on the home state and neighboring states.[114] This stance presumes that the host state, in which corporate activity takes place, lacks effective control over its own territories at the time of war. This is the case of Palestine, which considerably lacks control over foreign corporations operating within its territories. In this context, the UNGPs require home states

---

107    See *United* Nations Centre for Transnational Corporations, *The United Nations Code of Conduct on Transnational Corporations* U.N. Doc. ST/CTC/SER.A/4 (1988) paras. 9–16 [*hereinafter* CTC Code of Conduct].

108    CTC Code of Conduct, paras. 11, 28–29, 36.

109    *Id.*, at paras. 9, 12.

110    *Id.*, at 14.

111    *Id.*, at 22–26.

112    U.N. ECOSOC, *Norms on the responsibilities of transnational corporations and other business enterprises with regard to human rights*, U.N. Doc. E/CN.4/Sub.2/2003/12/Rev.2 (Aug. 26, 2003), pmbl.

113    See H.R.C., *Guiding Principles on Business and Human Rights: Implementing the United Nations "Protect, Respect and Remedy" Framework*, A/HRC/17/31 (2011); U.N. OHCHR, *Guiding Principles on Business and Human Rights: Implementing the 'Protect, Respect and Remedy framework,'* HR/PUB/11/04 (2011) [*hereinafter* UNGPs].

114    "Because the risk of gross human rights abuses is heightened in conflict affected areas, States should help ensure that business enterprises operating in those contexts are not involved with such abuses, including by: ... etc." UNGPs, Principle 7.

SYSTEMIC ECONOMIC HARM IN OCCUPIED PALESTINE 131

where the corporation is incorporated to help corporations "identify, prevent and mitigate the human rights-related risks of their activities and business relationships."[115]

This identification of risk is relevant to an important mechanism that the UNGPs endorse, and that is the conjuring of due diligence reports within the context of corporations' responsibility to protect.[116] This mechanism is originally found in legal tools that states have already been using to ensure corporations' responsible behavior with respect to other topics, including situations of war.[117]

Due diligence reporting in the realm of business and human rights denotes, among other things: an obligation to identify, mitigate, and prevent the human rights risks that are related to corporate activities. The obligation is general to all situations,[118] and is heightened in the context of war.[119] This heightened duty can be understood to widen the scope of consideration to include an assessment of systemic forms of harm. Despite the framework's exclusive focus on the language of human rights, its postulation of due diligence as a preventive

---

115 UNGPs, Principle 7(a).
116 *See* the Human Rights Due Diligence (HRDD) Project, which was launched by the International Corporate Accountability Roundtable (ICAR), the European Coalition for Corporate Justice (ECCJ), and the Canadian Network on Corporate Accountability (CNCA): Human Rights Due Diligence Project, *Coalition for Human Rights in Development*, https://rightsindevelopment.org/human-rights-due-diligence-project/.
117 *See, e.g.*, Section 1502 of the Dodd-Frank Wall Street Reform and Consumer Protection Act which requires companies with securities registered with the Securities and Exchange Commission to report on their due diligence with respect to conflict minerals to address corporate complicity in resource war of the DRC; later endorsed by the OECD's "Due Diligence Guidance for Responsible Supply Chains of Minerals from Conflict-Affected and High-Risk Areas." Olivier De Schutter, Anita Ramasastry, Mark B. Taylor, Robert C. Thompson, *Human Rights Due Diligence: The Role of States* (Dec. 2012), at 46, 84, https://en.frankbold.org/sites/default/files/publikace/human_rights_due_diligence-the_role _of_states.pdf.
118 According to the UNGPs Reporting Framework, human rights due diligence is: "An ongoing risk management process … in order to identify, prevent, mitigate and account for how [a company] addresses its adverse human rights impacts. It includes four key steps: assessing actual and potential human rights impacts; integrating and acting on the findings; tracking responses; and communicating about how impacts are addressed." *See*: https://www.ungpreporting.org/wp-content/uploads/UNGPReportingFramework_2017 .pdf.
119 UNGPs, Principle 7, commentary ("States should warn business enterprises of the heightened risk of being involved with gross abuses of human rights in conflict-affected areas. They should review whether their policies, legislation, regulations and enforcement measures effectively address this heightened risk, including through provisions for human rights due diligence by business".).

mechanism necessitates stretching the analysis over a wider temporal and spatial frame of consideration. Such frame can capture the indirect harms that daily economic activities generate, such as utilizing water resources extracted in contravention to the rules of usufruct.

Once identified, such risks become ingrained within the corporate duty of care and it has a duty to mitigate such adverse effects.[120] If such risks were to occur, victims ought to have recourse to national tort adjudication, or non-judicial grievance mechanisms that the state or the corporation provides.[121] Setting this standard for transnational businesses indirectly encourages states to ensure that their legal systems and economic policies do not permit indirect involvement in human rights violations for corporations.

As suggested by their title, adherence to the UNGPs is voluntary.[122] Voluntarism denotes that a given standard is favorable but not obligatory. For some scholars, voluntarism allows for the application of incentivizing tools which promote responsible corporate behavior in a dynamic fashion.[123] Meanwhile, others argue that the absence of stringent legal standards,[124] promotes a culture where corporations are allowed to do minimal efforts while avoiding structural changes in their behavior towards communities.[125] Yet such voluntarism does not concretely break away with the entrapment in a paradoxical situation that Young identified. This is because it is not in the interest of the corporation to cut profits for the sake of local communities. Such a hurdle might be overcome through the recently proposed mandatory due diligence framework in the European Union, or if the initiative of a binding treaty on business and human rights were to succeed.[126]

---

120    UNGPs, Principle 13(b).

121    UNGPs, part 3.

122    *See* Steven Bittle & Laureen Snider, *Examining the Ruggie Report: Can Voluntary Guidelines Tame Global Capitalism?* 21 Critical Criminology 177 (2013); Beate Sjåfjell, *Why Law Matters: Corporate Social Irresponsibility and the Futility of Voluntary Climate Change Mitigation* (2011), https://papers.ssrn.com/sol3/papers.cfm?abstract_id=1774759.

123    *See* John J. Kirton & M. J. Trebilcock, Hard Choices, Soft Law: Voluntary Standards in Global Trade, Environment, and Social Governance (2004).

124    *See* Sjåfjell & Taylor; Björn Fasterling & Geert Demuijnck, *Human Rights in the Void? Due Diligence in the UN Guiding Principles on Business and Human Rights*, 116 J. Bus. Ethics 799 (2013).

125    *See* Upendra Baxi, *Towards socially sustainable globalization: reflections on responsible contracting and the UN guiding principles on business and human rights*, 57 Indian J. Int'l L. 163 (2017).

126    *See* European Coalition for Corporate Justice, *Commissioner Reynders announces EU corporate due diligence legislation* (Apr. 30, 2020), https://corporatejustice.org/news/commissioner-reynders-announces-eu-corporate-due-diligence-legislation/.

## SYSTEMIC ECONOMIC HARM IN OCCUPIED PALESTINE

In 2014, the UN Human Rights Council initiated another attempt to draft a binding treaty through the establishment of an open-ended intergovernmental working group on transnational corporations and other business enterprises with respect to human rights.[127] The group's main mandate is to oversee the drafting of a binding treaty "to regulate, in international human rights law, the activities of transnational corporations and other business enterprises."[128] Thus far, the working group has presented a number of drafts for a binding treaty. The most recent (at the time of writing) focuses predominantly on access to justice for victims,[129] criminal and civil liability with reference to crimes under the Rome Statute,[130] and prevention mechanisms solidifying the duty of corporate human rights due diligence.[131] The draft also requires that such human rights considerations are taken into account in future business relations and that current contracts are interpreted in line with the obligation to respect human rights.[132]

While restrictive in scope, keeping a distance from economic considerations,[133] the treaty would nonetheless crystallize the notion of corporate due diligence allowing for wider consideration of systemic forms of harms. This would indirectly shift corporate attitude towards becoming a more active actor in reforming policies which incite systemic economic harm. Despite upholding a state-centric perspective, the draft stresses internal civil and criminal accountability mechanisms reliant on the scope of duty of care set in the due diligence framework opening new remedial pathways that focus on non-state actors with power and privilege and collective ability. It further sets a juridical basis for extraterritorial jurisdiction, under which victims can prosecute corporations in their home states. The absence of such jurisdiction, linked

---

127    *See* Pierre Thielbörger & Tobias Ackermann, *A Treaty on Enforcing Human Rights Against Business: Closing the Loophole or Getting Stuck in a Loop?*, 24 Ind. J. Glob Leg. Stud. 43 (2017).

128    H.R.C., *Elaboration of an international legally binding instrument on transnational corporations and other business enterprises with respect to human rights*, U.N. Doc. A/HRC/RES/26/9 (July 14, 2014), para. 1.

129    OEIGWG Chairmanship, *Legally binding instrument to regulate, international human rights law, the activities of transnational corporations and other business enterprises* (Rev. draft, July 16, 2019), art. 4 [*hereinafter* OEIGWG Revised Draft], https://www.ohchr.org/Documents/HRBodies/HRCouncil/WGTransCorp/OEIGWG_RevisedDraft_LBI.pdf.

130    *Id.*, art. 6.

131    *Id.*, art. 5.

132    *Id.*, art. 12.

133    The discussion over the draft had included requests to include references to corporate capture and development. *See* H.R.C., *Report on the fifth session of the open-ended intergovernmental working group on transnational corporations and other business enterprises with respect to human rights*, U.N. Doc. A/HRC/43/55 (Jan. 9, 2020), paras. 13, 67.

with an appeal to methodological nationalism which denies the trans-border nature of corporate activity, has been one of the dominant reasons for the impunity of corporate actors.[134] Such mechanisms can indirectly function to change state-investor dynamics. States wishing to attract investment will have to provide a better environment for investment where the corporate actor will not easily find themselves connected to human rights and humanitarian violations. It thus would indirectly pressure states to address some forms of structural injustice.

In the context of the Israeli occupation, the ethos of the UNGPs paid particular attention to the role of corporations as active actors with power and privilege. The UN Human Rights Council initiated this discussion in the aftermath of UN Security Council Resolution 31/36, which condemned Israeli settlements built in occupied Palestine.[135] The Resolution requested the UN Office of the High Commissioner for Human Rights (OHCHR) to prepare a report on the implications of the issue.[136] Eventually, this led to the creation of the UN database on business enterprises involved in Israeli settlements. The database is seen as a transparency tool to guide later assessments.[137]

In the preliminary report on the UN database,[138] the OHCHR determined that economic actors investing in the settlements are benefitting from policies that produce systemic economic harm. For example, corporations benefit from access to surplus cheap labor that the systematic illegality of the settlements breeds, exploitation of contested resources, and from Israeli investment policies.[139] Hence, corporations' involvement indirectly enables the deterioration of the Palestinian economy.[140] Additionally, the report points out that corpora-

---

134 *See* Nadia Bernaz, *Enhancing Corporate Accountability for Human Rights Violations: Is Extraterritoriality the Magic Potion?* 117 J. Bus. Ethics 493 (2013).

135 H.R.C., *Israeli settlements in the Occupied Palestinian Territory, including East Jerusalem, and in the occupied Syrian Golan*, U.N. Doc. A/HRC/RES/31/36 (Mar. 24, 2016), para. 17.

136 The issue had been presented in a prior report. H.R.C., *Report of the independent international fact finding mission to investigate the implications of the Israeli settlements on the civil, political, economic, social and cultural rights of the Palestinian people throughout the Occupied Palestinian Territory, including East Jerusalem*, U.N. Doc. A/HRC/22/63 (Feb. 7, 2013).

137 *See* H.R.C., *Database of all business enterprises involved in the activities detailed in paragraph 96 of the report of the independent international fact-finding mission to investigate the implications of the Israeli settlements on the civil, political, economic, social and cultural rights of the Palestinian people throughout the Occupied Palestinian Territory, including East Jerusalem – Report of the United Nations High Commissioner for Human Rights*, U.N. Doc. A/HRC/37/39 (Feb. 1, 2018), para. 9.

138 *See id.*

139 *Id.*, paras. 43–45.

140 *Id.*, paras. 47, 54.

tions benefit from filling the space that Israeli policies create and which render Palestinians incapable of exploiting their own oil and gas among other natural resources.[141] The importance of the database and its novelty lie in the fact that it relies on the business and human rights framework in its assessment. Thus, the database is able to capture different forms of systemic economic harms. This is achieved by linking between, on the one hand, the deterioration of the Palestinian economy and, on the other hand, Israeli policies and business enterprises.

The discussion of these previous attempts (the 1988 proposed code, UNGPs, 2014 attempt to draft a treaty, and the UN database) showcases the availability of alternative frameworks that can provide some form of redress for different forms of structural injustice through imposing obligations on the corporate actor. If adopted and enforced, such mechanisms are likely to directly impact the corporation's participation in economic systems, and to indirectly encourage states to deter policies that may induce systemic economic harm.

In this respect, human rights due diligence frameworks offer a window of hope where indirect causality can be imagined and further integrated in responsibility frameworks, opening new remedial paths for victims. In such frameworks, corporations that benefit from or contribute to structural forms of injustice that originate in violations of international law can be held accountable. They can be incentivized to use their leverage to demand a fairer economic environment. However, voluntarism and the marginalization of economic considerations limit the capacities of these new mechanisms to lead to profound changes in an occupation's policies. Nonetheless, this framework can be complemented with another framework designed to call upon the leverage of third states discussed in the next section.

## B    *Third States and Systemic Harm in Occupation*

Third states are connected to the occupation's apparatus by virtue of global economic and political interdependence. Like other actors, their role in the connections upholding a given structural injustice varies according to their own power, leverage, interest, and collective ability. To begin with, as states theoretically have leverage over corporations incorporated under their own jurisdiction, they can practice their influence to deter corporations from undertaking activities which contribute to or benefit from an apparatus sustaining systemic economic harm. To this end, the UNGPs place a responsibility on states "where they fail to take appropriate steps to prevent, investigate,

---

141    *Id.*, paras. 43–45.

punish and redress private actors' abuse,"[142] and the proposed draft aims to solidify this obligation.[143] Likewise, under the ARISWA framework, there are limited cases where states can be held responsible for the conduct of business enterprises acting in governmental authority.[144]

For the purpose of remedying systemic harm, one particular duty set out in ARISWA, provides an interesting perspective which speaks to the thinking behind the social connections model, and that is the third state's positive duty to cooperate and its negative duty of non-recognition in the face of a given serious violation of international law.[145] The term "serious breach" denotes breaches of the peremptory norms of international law, in particular the prohibition against apartheid and violations of the peoples' right to self-determination.[146] Such seriousness is also assessed in terms of "a gross or systematic failure by the responsible state to fulfil the obligation in question."[147] The UN repeatedly stressed such duties of third states in relation to occupied Palestine, specifically in the context of Israeli settlements, as in UN Security Council Resolution 465.[148] Similarly, Resolution 2334 establishes a duty on third states "not to provide assistance" to activities undertaken to sustain or build settlements.[149]

This duty articulates how the interconnected positioning of the economy of other states to the Israeli economy grants third states power and privilege with regards to the dynamics sustaining systemic economic harm. It thus requires non-recognition of the effects born out Israeli violations of international law, and consequently imposes responsibility on third states to withhold different forms of cooperation which can sustain or contribute to ongoing violations of international law.

The implementation of these principles of third states' responsibility in relation to the context settlement activity generates a lively scholarly debate. At one end, there is Moernhout's intervention, which is premised on the illegality settlement activity.[150] His assessment adopts a systematic view that

---

142     "States may breach their international human rights law obligations where such abuse can be attributed to them, or where they fail to take appropriate steps to prevent, investigate, punish, and redress private actors' abuse." *See* UNGPs, Principle 1, commentary.

143     *See* OEIGWG Revised Draft.

144     *See, generally,* ARSIWA.

145     *See* ARSIWA Commentaries, at 31, 112–116, art. 41.

146     *See id.,* art. 40, at 112–113.

147     *See id.*

148     S.C. Res. 465 (Mar. 1, 1980).

149     S.C. Res. 2334 (Dec. 23, 2016).

150     Tom Moerenhout, *The Obligation to Withhold from Trading in Order Not to Recognize and Assist Settlements and Their Economic Activity in Occupied Territories,* 3 J. Int'l Human. Legal. Stud. 344 (2012) [*hereinafter* Moerenhout].

looks at the effects of the spatial and temporal stretch of the settlements and determines that the illegal nature of the context deems economic activities by third states in the settlements altogether illegal. He concludes that this illegality imposes an obligation on third states to withhold trade with the settlements in adherence to the duty of non-recognition, as well as an obligation to prohibit multi-national corporations under their jurisdiction from undertaking such activities.[151]

In reply to Moernhout's position, it can be argued that this determination of state responsibility contradicts non-discrimination clauses in the General Agreement on Tariffs and Trade (GATT) under the regime of the World Trade Organization (WTO). This is because the act of halting economic activities can be portrayed as a disruption of the flow of free trade. Such a position would presume that the GATT is applicable in occupied Palestine. However, Palestine is a not a member of the WTO. Application of the GATT to its territory can only be understood as an extension of Israeli jurisdiction by virtue of its occupation. Such an extension can only be possible if one relies on an interpretation that deems occupied territories a part of the occupying state's territory. Under this interpretation, the occupying power would have the authority to decide whether or not to include the occupied territories under the regime of the GATT. Nonetheless, the only evidence to support this interpretation is weak. It is found in the travaux préparatoires of the GATT in 1957, where the suggestion to include an exclusion of occupied territories was dismissed, which could arguably insinuate that they are included under the jurisdiction of the occupying power.[152]

In response to this interpretation, Moerenhout argues that even if the GATT were to apply to the Palestinian territories, a harmonized reading of international law as a self-contained system would consider the duty of non-recognition as possessing a humanitarian appeal which warrants an exception to the non-discrimination rule.[153] Several scholars advocate for this

---

151    *Id.*, at 354–361.

152    This argument is based on interpretive notes to Article XXVI: 5(b) of the GATT "Until the Review Session amendments agreed in 1954–55, an interpretative note to Article XXVI provided that 'Territories for which the contracting parties have international responsibility do not include areas under military occupation.'" A Final Note provided that "The applicability of the General Agreement on Tariffs and Trade to the trade of contracting parties with the areas under military occupation has not been dealt with and is reserved for further study at an early date. Meanwhile, nothing in this Agreement shall be taken to prejudge the issues involved. This, of course, does not affect the applicability of the provisions of Articles XXII and XXIII to matters arising from such trade". These provisions were deleted effective October 7, 1957. *See* W.T.O. *Analytical Index of the GATT* (1994), https://www.wto.org/english/res_e/publications_e/ai17_e/gatt1994_art26_gatt47.pdf.

153    *See* Moerenhout, at 376–377.

harmonized reading because they maintain that the absence of unity in reading international law emits inconsistencies and collisions in practice.[154]

Advocates for a harmonized reading of international law argue that harmony is an essential element for coherence and legitimacy. Among those advocating for a harmonized reading of international law is the former president of the International Court of Justice Stephen Shewebel, who expresses his dissatisfaction with fragmentation of international law, when he argues that it fosters further confusion and threatens the legitimacy of international law. As a remedy, he proposes a unification scheme that starts with allowing all courts to refer cases to the International Court of Justice.[155] In contrast, the International Law Commission's draft articles on the fragmentation of international law provide a formalistic middle way that promotes acceptance of the current fragmented state but pushes for some elements of harmonization.[156]

From the perspective of Young's connections model, which this article adopts, a fragmented reading of international law further distorts the law's perception, as it deepens the exclusion of economic considerations from the public sphere and obstructs a proper understanding of causality. In the case of third states' obligation not to recognize serious breaches of international law, prioritizing the free trade rhetoric insinuates a disregard of serious breaches by the international community. Additionally, this fragmentation encourages a multiplicity in legal analyses of global issues, each time under the language of a different code without an effort to establish a more holistic understanding that bears the fruit of addressing structural injustice.

Another mechanism, reliant on the will of third states, which captures connections that affect a given dominating apparatus, is that of multilateral or unilateral economic sanctions. Economic sanctions utilize economic privilege of third states to pressure a given state into abiding by international law. With relation to affecting the apparatus upholding systemic economic harm in occupation, national jurisdictions and international instruments are reluctant to criminalize or prohibit economic dealings with occupying states and occupied territories, even in cases of systematic breach of international law as is the case with the settlements.

---

154   "Contemporary international law is torn between opposing dichotomies, competing languages, and uncovered subjectivities." Sahib Singh, *The Potential of International Law: Fragmentation and Ethics*, 24 Leiden J. Int'l L. 23 (2011).

155   *See* Address to the Plenary Session of the General Assembly of the United Nations by Judge Stephen M. Schwebel, President of the International Court of Justice (Oct. 26, 1999).

156   *See, generally,* U.N. Int'l L. Comm., *Conclusions of the work of the Study Group on the Fragmentation of International Law: Difficulties arising from the Diversification and Expansion of International Law*, in U.N. Doc. A/61/10 (2006).

Lastly, other softer mechanisms put forth by third states with the aim of deterring trade to affect Israeli policies include anti-normalization laws against Israeli occupation that used to exist in the Arab region but heavy US diplomacy thwarted such measures (similar to those legislated against the South African apartheid regime),[157] the European Commission's "Interpretative Notice on the Indication of Origin of Goods from the Territories Occupied by Israel since June 1967,"[158] and the European Court of Justice's judgement on the labelling of products coming from Israeli settlements.[159]

## IV   Concluding Remarks

Applying the perspective of the social connections model to the reality of occupation, it is apparent that the effects of Israeli policies as an occupying power have a structural effect on the individual and collective capacity of Palestinians to pursue economic development. Many of these policies, which are intertwined with blanket violations of international law, eventually deepen the dependence and fragility of the Palestinian economy and cripple its capacity to develop and to undertake competitive economic activities globally. Israeli policies, therefore, cause systemic economic harm.

It is difficult to conceptualize legal redress for such forms of systemic harm in legal systems that understand and frame responsibility with relevance to direct relationships within nation states, rather than networked relations of a transnational nature. This difficulty is exacerbated in relation to economic harm as it is harder to conceptualize and is historically marginalized under the premise of the private-public distinction. Thus, even if blanket violations committed by the occupation were to be condemned, current responsibility frameworks are still inadequate because they do not account for casual links between systemic economic harm and the violations committed. Ways around this substantive shortcoming are found in alternative paths which focus on the responsibility of other actors with power, privilege, and collective ability such as corporations and third states.

The argument in support of providing a remedy for structural injustice through engraining a social role for corporate actors has been present in the

---

157  These laws are an in enactment of the Arab league's boycott of Israel, however most of its clauses are dormant. Andre M. Saltoun, *Regulation of Foreign Boycotts*, 33 Business Lawyer 559–603 (1978).

158  Interpretative Notice on Indication of Origin of Goods from the Territories Occupied by Israel Since June 1967, 2015 O.J. (C 375).

159  C-363/18, Vignoble Psagot Ltd v. Ministre de L'Economie et des Finances, 2019 E.C.R. 954.

halls of the UN since early seventies. Nonetheless, attempts to assign direct responsibility to corporations have met little success thus far. One positive development has been the establishment of a discourse around a duty of human rights due diligence for corporate actors, and which is considered a heightened duty in conflict-affected areas. Such due diligence requirement allows the assessor to stretch their gaze over a longer temporal and spatial span. This in turn paves the way for an appreciation of systemic harm that corporate activity induces, whether directly or through apparatuses from which it benefits, or to which it contributes. Although the voluntary nature of this duty remains its biggest weakness, it nevertheless had considerable political value in triggering the publication of the UN database on corporations involved in Israeli settlements. Despite being in its early stages, the database has already steered the discussion towards a more inclusive understanding of causality, particularly with respect to the context of settlements.

Finally, another route to provide for redress for systemic economic harm is through the enactment of third states' duty not to recognize serious breaches of international law. The application of this duty would foreground a more egalitarian economic footing between the Palestinians and Israel. Yet, in order to enable the application of this duty one needs to overcome a fragmented reading of international law whereby the practice of such non-recognition would contravene the duty of non-discrimination under the GATT, according to a conservative reading of the text Such a fragmented reading further deepens international law's substantive shortcoming in relation to systemic harm and diminishes the right of the occupied population to seek economic development.

### Acknowledgments

The author would like to thank Dr. Nimer Sultany for his vigilant revision, discussion, support, and commentary, and Dr. Ralph Wilde whose support and courage inspired this paper.

# Restrictions on Freedom of Movement in the West Bank: A Policy of Apartheid

*Costanza Ferrando*

## Contents

I  Introduction
II  A Legal Analysis of Restrictions on Freedom of Movement in the West Bank: The Blind Spot in the Occupation Paradigm
   A  *Freedom of Movement in International Human Rights and Humanitarian Law*
   B  *Behind Proportionality: The Paradox of Security*
   C  *Behind Discrimination: The Systematic Dimension of Racial Exclusion*
   D  *Towards a New Understanding*
III  Movement Restrictions Reframed: Embracing the Apartheid Paradigm
   A  *The Legal Framework of the Apartheid Paradigm: An Unambiguous Definition*
   B  *Movement Restrictions as a Policy of Apartheid: A Tool for Segregation*
   C  *Movement Restrictions as a Policy of Apartheid: A Tool for Exclusion*
IV  Purposes Unveiled: The Ultimate Goals of Inhuman Acts of Apartheid
   A  *Elements of Surveillance and Arbitrariness: The Purpose of Domination*
   B  *Elements of Harassment and Humiliation: The Purpose of Oppression*
V  Conclusion

## I  Introduction

Freedom of movement is a protected fundamental right under international law. In the West Bank, the Israeli authorities impose obstacles and restrictions that severely constrain the enjoyment of this right. Physical barriers and bureaucratic impediments dramatically impact the living standards of the population and paralyze meaningful aspects of the social, civil and political life of Palestinians. In consideration of the disproportionate and discriminatory nature of the restrictions, a multitude of human rights reports, academic commentaries, United Nations (UN) resolutions, and even an advisory opinion by the International Court of Justice (ICJ) have denounced Israeli violations of international human rights law (IHRL) and international humanitarian law (IHL). None of these efforts have proved effective in impacting the events on the ground, and the situation worsens constantly.

In response to the past futility of attempts to address the issue, this article argues that the system of restrictions on Palestinian freedom of movement should be analyzed from a different angle. Building on the paradigm shift proposed by notable scholars, this work reframes the Israeli practices of movement constraint as manifestations of systematic inhuman acts designed to strengthen Israeli domination. This study discards the claim that restrictions are enacted for security objectives; a claim that burdens the current paradigm. Instead, it examines the merits of a new and potentially more appropriate approach that analyzes the restrictive policies of denial of free movement as a form of oppressive domination based on racial discrimination. Once verified, such a claim unveils different features of the Israeli occupation, revealing the existence of an underlying regime of apartheid. Consequently, this article seeks to offer a holistic approach that offers a systematic analysis of the root cause, rather than a legal analysis, that responds to the symptoms.

This article undertakes a legal analysis of the policies of movement restriction and delineates the violations of Palestinian rights with regards to IHRL and IHL. It draws upon scholarly articles and reports to reinforce the academic arguments. Section II presents the traditional legal framework concerning the unlawfulness of the restrictions imposed on the West Bank. It identifies and discusses the analytical gaps and the failure of IHL in grasping the motives and implications of the system of restrictions. Section III suggests the adoption of a new paradigm. After introducing the legal definition of apartheid, it responds to objections to the application of the apartheid paradigm and argues that Israeli restrictive policies amount to inhumane acts and constitute a strategic tool for the implementation of an apartheid regime. Section IV focuses on domination and oppression as core elements of apartheid and main features of the inhumane acts inflicted on the Palestinian people.

## II A Legal Analysis of Restrictions on Freedom of Movement in the West Bank: The Blind Spot in the Occupation Paradigm

Over the past few decades, the measures of movement constraints that Israel imposes on Palestinians never ceased to attract the attention of human rights organizations, scholars, and international institutions. Activists, experts, and researchers have unveiled the complex system of physical, legal, and administrative obstacles preventing Palestinians from exercising their right to freedom of movement in the West Bank. The Separation Wall carves deeply beyond the "Green Line," encircling and effectively annexing most of the settlements and the land surrounding them, while cutting off Jerusalem and some ten percent of the West Bank.[1] The Wall condemns inhabitants of the vicinity to the capricious openings of the gates – which are largely there for the sake of appearances – and the bureaucratically impenetrable granting process of the permit system.[2] The network of roads connecting Israeli settlements to each other and to Israel results in a constantly expanding maze of segregated roads that bypass Palestinian centers for the ease and supposed safety of the settlers. A variety of measures further sterilize the separation: lack, or obstruction, of entry and exit points for Palestinian communities; permanent and "flying" checkpoints; gates; concrete roadblocks; and deterrent enforcement penalties such as fines and confiscation of vehicles.[3] In addition, the Israeli military deploys road obstacles to funnel Palestinian traffic towards junctions controlled by checkpoints where searches are carried out on drivers and vehicles.[4] The repercussions of such measures go far beyond their effects on travel habits and deprivation of the right to freedom of movement. Not only do they condemn the Palestinian population to long and costly detours, but they block access to services and livelihoods for entire communities, impeding the fulfillment of basic human needs and paralyzing meaningful aspects of social, civil, and political life. In fact, the disruptive impact of these restrictions affects the ability of West Bank residents to exercise economic, social, and cultural rights, such as the right to health, work, education, family life, and freedom of religion.[5]

The legal analysis of the phenomenon is generally grounded on the standards of IHRL and IHL, based on the assumption that the relation between Israel and Palestine constitutes a situation of belligerent occupation. Despite the multiple notable efforts, denunciation of Israeli conduct based on these

---

1 See U.N. OCHA, Occupied Palestinian Territory, *The Humanitarian Impact on Palestinians of Israeli Settlements and Other Infrastructure in the West Bank* (July 2007), https://www .ochaopt.org/sites/default/files/ocharpt_update30july2007.pdf.

2 See, *generally*, Yael Berda, The bureaucracy of the Occupation: the permit regime in the West Bank (2012).

3 See U.N. OCHA, Occupied Palestinian Territory, *Over 700 road obstacles control Palestinian movement within the West Bank* (Sep. 2018), https://www.ochaopt.org/content/over-700-road -obstacles-control-palestinian-movement-within-west-bank.

4 See *id*. In July 2018, OCHA recorded 705 permanent obstacles across the West Bank, including 140 fully or occasionally staffed checkpoints.

5 See U.N. OHCHR, *Human rights situation in the Occupied Palestinian Territory, including East Jerusalem. Report of the Secretary-General to the United Nations Human Rights Council*, U.N. Doc. A/HRC/31/44 (Jan. 20, 2016).

tools has failed to effectively impact the policies on the ground, while Israel maintains that the restrictions are justified by security concerns and are therefore legitimate under IHL. The expedience of security has served to successfully divert the attention of scholars from other possible scopes of analysis and has generated a legal debate predominantly focused on the legitimacy of the constraints adopted under the pretext of security. Far from grasping the full depths and implications of what is in fact an articulated system of discriminatory practices, this approach produces an analytical gap. Although occupation is an undeniable reality, the conceptual tools that the IHL paradigm provides are inadequate to engage with the true logic of movement constraint and to explore the many dimensions of an apparatus of restrictions. This apparatus is so pervasive and structural that it turns a human right into an exception, rendering civil life practically impossible. This article argues that the adoption of a different analytical framework – namely, the apartheid paradigm – can explain and ultimately overcome the gaps and paradoxes unresolved by the occupation paradigm. These gaps and paradoxes are briefly examined in what follows.

A       *Freedom of Movement in International Human Rights*
        *and Humanitarian Law*

Freedom of movement is a human rights concept provided and protected by norms of international law and most notably enshrined in article 13 of the Universal Declaration of Human Rights and article 12 of the International Covenant on Civil and Political Rights (ICCPR), ratified by Israel.[6] Despite its reluctance to acknowledge its human rights obligations, Israel bears responsibility for the application of IHRL in the occupied Palestinian territories (oPt). Contrary to Israel's argument for the mutual exclusivity of IHRL and IHL, scholars observed that "[t]he conventional division between the law of war and the law of peace is no longer tenable [and that] [t]he application of the law of war no longer automatically excludes the application of the law of peace."[7] In addition, the UN General Assembly (UNGA) has affirmed that "fundamental human rights, as accepted in international law and laid down in international

---

6  Israel is a signatory to the Universal Declaration of Human Rights, which prominently features on the website of the Israeli Parliament (https://knesset.gov.il/docs/eng/un_dec_eng .htm), and ratified the ICCPR on Oct. 3, 1991 (*see:* https://tbinternet.ohchr.org/_layouts/15/ TreatyBodyExternal/Treaty.aspx?CountryID=84&Lang=en).

7  Dietrich Schindler, *Human Rights and Humanitarian Law: Interrelationship of the Laws*, 31 Am. U. L. Rev. 935, 941–942 (1982). *See also* Cordula Drogege, *The Interplay between International Humanitarian Law and International Human Rights Law in Situations of Armed Conflict*, 40 Israel L. Rev. 310 (2007); Oona A. Hathaway et al., *Which Law Governs During Armed Conflict? The Relationship Between International Humanitarian Law and Human Rights Law*, 96 Minn. L. Rev. 1883 (2012).

RESTRICTIONS ON FREEDOM OF MOVEMENT IN THE WEST BANK

instruments, continue to apply fully in situations of armed conflict."[8] The ICJ confirms this view, stating that:

> The protection offered by human rights conventions does not cease in case of armed conflict ... As regards the relationship between international humanitarian law and human rights law, there are three possible situations: some rights may be exclusively matters of international humanitarian law; others may be exclusively matters of human rights law; yet others may be matters of both these branches of international law. In order to answer the question put to it, the Court will have to take into consideration both these branches of international law.[9]

Israel has also argued that it has no human rights responsibilities in territories that are not under its sovereignty.[10] In response to this assertion, the ICJ observed that the applicability of international human rights conventions to which Israel is party in the oPt derives from its territorial jurisdiction.[11] It is a basic principle of IHRL that treaties are applicable in all areas in which state parties exercise effective control, regardless of the actual sovereignty.[12]

---

8    G.A. Res. 2675, *Basic principles for the protection of civilian populations in armed conflicts*, U.N. GAOR, 25th Sess., Supp. No. 28, U.N. Doc. A/8028 (Dec. 9, 1970), para. 1.

9    Legal Consequences of the Construction of a Wall in the Occupied Palestinian Territory, Advisory Opinion, 2004 I.C.J. Rep. 131 (July 9), para. 106 [*hereinafter* ICJ Wall Advisory Opinion].

10   Israel's position is illustrated in the second periodic report on its compliance with the ICCPR, presented to the UN Human Rights Committee on July 24, 2003. *See* U.N. Doc. CCPR/C/ISR/2001/2 (Dec. 4, 2001).

11   "The Court [affirmed] that the territories occupied by Israel have for over 37 years been subject to its territorial jurisdiction as the occupying power, thus making the international human rights conventions to which Israel is party applicable to the Occupied Palestinian Territory." U.N. Secretary-General, *Report on the Israeli practice affecting the human rights of the Palestinian people in the Occupied Palestinian Territory, including East Jerusalem*, U.N. Doc. A/69/347 (Aug. 25, 2014), para. 12.

12   *See* Mara'abe v. Prime Minister of Isr., HCJ 7957/04 [2005] (Isr.), translated in 45 I.L.M. 202, 27 (2006) (stating that the Israeli High Court of Justice "shall assume ... that the international conventions on human rights apply in the area"). The European Court of Human Rights upheld the obligation of the contracting parties to secure the rights and freedoms laid down in the Convention even in the circumstances deriving from military action: when a Party exercises effective control on an area outside its national territory, the obligation arises from such control, regardless whether it be exercised directly, through its armed forces, or through a subordinate local administration. The same principle could be brought in response to Israel's claim that, because the Oslo Accords transferred civil responsibilities, the Palestinian Authority is directly responsible and accountable *vis-à-vis* the entire Palestinian population with regard to the implementation of international human rights law.

The extraterritoriality of IHRL has been confirmed by the UN Human Rights Committee, both in general terms,[13] and with specific respect to Israel's human rights obligations in the oPt.[14] The determinations of treaty bodies and of the ICJ validate the positions of academic advocates with respect to the applicability of IHRL during situations of occupation.[15]

Without prejudice to the applicability of IHRL, it is IHL – namely, the Hague Regulations, the Fourth Geneva Convention, and Second Additional Protocol to the four Geneva Conventions – that, as *lex specialis*, provides the primary legal framework for setting the rules in the relations between an occupying power and the inhabitants of the occupied territory under its authority. In the text of the Fourth Geneva Convention, the protection of the right to freedom of movement is not specifically mentioned. Article 27 lays down a general principle of respect for fundamental rights, which authoritative interpretations understand as respect for the person in its widest sense, so as to cover all the rights of the individual, freedom of movement included. Although Israel has never accepted it, the UNGA,[16] the UN Security Council,[17] the High

---

13    *See* U.N. Hum. Rts. Comm., *General Comment 31: Nature of the General Legal Obligation Imposed on States Parties to the Covenant*, U.N. Doc. CCPR/C/21/Rev.1/Add.13 (May 26, 2004), para. 10 ("... a State party must respect and ensure the rights laid down in the Covenant to anyone within the power or effective control of that State Party, even if not situated within the territory of the State Party.").

14    *See* U.N. Hum. Rts. Comm., *Concluding Observations of the Human Rights Committee: Israel*, U.N. Doc. CCPR/CO/78/ISR (Aug. 21, 2003).

15    *See, generally,* Esther Rosalind Cohen, Human Rights in the Israeli-Occupied Territories (1985); Adam Roberts, *Prolonged Military Occupation: The Israeli-Occupied Territories Since 1967*, 84 Am. J. Int'l L. 44 (1990); Eyal Benvenisti, *The Applicability of Human Rights Conventions to Israel and to the Occupied Territories*, 26 Israel L. Rev. 24 (1992); Michael J. Dennis, *Application of Human Rights Treaties Extraterritoriality in Times of Armed Conflict and Military Occupation*, 99 Am. J. Int'l L. 119 (2005).

16    The UNGA affirmed that: "the Geneva Convention relative to the Protection of Civilian Persons in Time of War, of 12 August 1949, is applicable to the Occupied Palestinian Territory, including Jerusalem, and other Arab territories occupied by Israel since 1967." It also demanded that: "Israel accept the *de jure* applicability of the Convention ... and that it comply scrupulously with the provisions of the Convention." *Applicability of the Geneva Convention relative to the Protection of Civilian Persons in Time of War, of 12 August 1949, to the Occupied Palestinian Territory, including Jerusalem, and the other occupied Arab territories*, U.N. Doc. A/RES/56/60 (Dec. 10, 2001), paras. 1–2. Similar statements were reiterated in: *Applicability of the Geneva Convention relative to the Protection of Civilian Persons in Time of War, of 12 August 1949, to the Occupied Palestinian Territory, including Jerusalem, and the other occupied Arab territories*, U.N. Doc. A/RES/58/97 (Dec. 9, 2003), paras. 1–2.

17    The UNSC recommended "the scrupulous respect of the humanitarian principles governing ... the protection of civilian persons in time of war contained in the Geneva Conventions of 12 August 1949." U.N. Doc. S/RES/237 (June 14, 1967), para. 2. It also called "upon Israel scrupulously to observe the provisions of the Geneva Conventions." U.N. Doc. S/RES/271 (Sep. 15, 1969), para. 4. It again affirmed "once more that the Geneva

RESTRICTIONS ON FREEDOM OF MOVEMENT IN THE WEST BANK    147

Contracting Parties to the Fourth Geneva Convention,[18] the ICJ,[19] and the International Committee of the Red Cross (ICRC)[20] – unanimously maintain the applicability of the Fourth Geneva Convention in the occupied territories. As evident, the current direction of international law aligns with the trajectory of what Theodor Meron described as a process of convergence of IHRL and IHL.[21] Although this "entangled relationship ... is intended to maximize the protection,"[22] the combination of the two laws might result in harmful effects. Contrary to the assumption that the application of human rights treaties in occupied territories is beneficial to the interests of the civilians, Aeyal Gross notes that "righting" the occupation rather undermines the protection of the occupied community.[23] As a consequence of the merger, Israel's conduct in relation to freedom of movement must be measured against both international human rights conventions and the Fourth Geneva Convention. Both instruments dictate the standards for derogation, thus providing, according to Gross, more, rather than less, justifications for limiting rights: "the rights of people living under occupation ... can now be limited both for 'public interest' or the rights of others *and* for military necessity."[24]

IHL mandates that considerations for military exigencies must not affect the fundamental rights of the population. Fourth Geneva Convention article 27, paragraph 4 lays down the general provision that the parties to the conflict may implement "measures of control and security," but does not further specify the nature or extent of such measures. According to ICRC commentary, the

---

Convention ... is applicable to the Arab territories occupied by Israel since 1967, including Jerusalem." U.N. Doc. S/RES/446 (Mar. 22, 1979).

18  In 2001, the High Contracting Parties reaffirmed "the applicability of the Convention to the Occupied Palestinian Territory," reiterated "the need for full respect for the provisions of the said Convention in that Territory" and recalled the obligations of Israel as the occupying power. Conference of High Contracting Parties to the Fourth Geneva Convention, *Final Declaration*, Geneva, Switz. (Dec. 5, 2001), para. 3.

19  In the Wall Advisory Opinion, the ICJ reaffirmed the applicability of the Fourth Geneva Convention to the Geneva Conventions to the oPt.

20  *See* Peter Maurer, *Challenges to international humanitarian law: Israel's occupation policy*, 94 Int'l Rev. Red Cross 888 (2012).

21  *See, generally*, Theodor Meron, Human Rights in Internal Strife: their International Protection (1987). In the controversy on the applicability of human rights in occupied territories, Ben-Naftali and Shany reject Israel's arguments and posit that IHRL and IHL apply in parallel and not to the exclusion of one another. *See* Orna Ben-Naftali & Yuval Shany, *Living in Denial: The Application of Human Rights in the Occupied Territories*, 37 Israel L. Rev. 17 (2003).

22  Mais A.M. Qandeel, Enforcing Human Rights of Palestinians in the Occupied Territory 67 (2018).

23  *See* Aeyal M. Gross, *Human Proportions: Are Human Rights the Emperor's New Clothes of the International Law of Occupation?* 18 Eur. J. Int'l L. 1 (2007) [*hereinafter* Gross].

24  *Id.*, at 9 (emphasis in the original).

restriction of freedom of movement can be justified under this clause[25] and enacted with wide discretion of the parties as regards the choice of means, with the only limitation that they "should not affect the fundamental rights of the persons concerned."[26] By the terms of ICCPR article 12, paragraph 3, restrictions to freedom of movement must qualify as exceptions and are only legitimate when they satisfy three requirements: they must be directed to the authorized ends, they must be strictly necessary for the achievement of those ends and – once again – they must not prevent the enjoyment of other fundamental rights. The UN Human Rights Committee rephrased the concept, affirming that restrictions "must conform to the principle of proportionality" and "must be the least intrusive instrument amongst those which might achieve the desired result."[27]

For decades, human rights reports, academic commentaries, UN resolutions, and even an ICJ advisory opinion have criticized Israeli restrictive policies on grounds of violation of the aforementioned provisions. In particular, they have pointed out the disproportionate and discriminatory nature of the measures implemented. Although technically correct, these analyses tend to overlook critical indications of a much more serious condition. Instead of trying to address the symptoms in isolation, one should instead observe them holistically in order to reach a thorough diagnosis.

## B  *Behind Proportionality: The Paradox of Security*

In order for military action to be deemed proportional, it must pursue a legitimate objective, it must cause the least possible danger to civilians, and it must conform to the principle of "true" proportionality.[28] The principle of propor-

---

25    *See* Commentary on the Geneva Conventions of 12 August 1949: IV Geneva Convention relative to the Protection of Civilian Persons in Time of War 201–202 (Jean S. Pictet ed., 1958).

26    *Id.* ("The right to personal liberty, and in particular the right to move about freely, can naturally be made subject in war time to certain restrictions made necessary by circumstances. So far as the local population is concerned, the freedom of movement of civilians of enemy nationality may certainly be restricted, or even temporarily suppressed, if circumstances so require ... but that in no way means that it is suspended in a general manner. Quite the contrary: the regulations concerning occupation and those concerning civilian aliens in the territory of a Party to the conflict are based on the idea of the personal freedom of civilians remaining in general unimpaired.").

27    U.N. Hum. Rts. Comm., *CCPR General Comment No. 27: Article 12 (Freedom of Movement)*, U.N. Doc. CCPR/C/21/Rev.I/Add.9 (Nov. 2, 1999), para. 14.

28    *See* Bernard L. Brown, *The Proportionality Principle in the Humanitarian Law of Warfare: Recent Efforts at Codification*, 10 Cornell Int'l L. J. 134 (1976); Duncan Kennedy, *Proportionality and 'Deference' in Contemporary Constitutional Thought*, in The Transformation of Reconstitution of Europe: The Critical Legal Perspective on the Role of

tionality requires that a balance be reached between an action's anticipated military advantage and the means used to obtain it.[29] While accommodating military needs, a state should avoid unnecessary harm to the civilian population.[30] When observing the restrictive measures that Israel imposes in the West Bank, failure to satisfy the harm-and-benefit test is evidenced by the disproportionately negative impact on other fundamental rights. According to the UN Human Rights Council:

> It is difficult to adequately express the wide scope of human rights violations that these extreme restrictions impose on the Palestinian population. These severe restrictions themselves amount not only to a violation of the right to freedom of movement, but also result in situations where Palestinians are effectively prevented from exercising other rights, including the right to work (art. 6 of ICESCR), the right to an adequate standard of living (art. 11), the right to health (art. 12), and the right to education (art. 13). Though comprehensive data do not exist, thousands of people are effectively prevented on a daily basis from accessing workplaces, schools and health-care facilities, from purchasing necessary goods and from visiting family.[31]

When weighed against the stated goals and the benefits gained in terms of security, the restrictions appear to disproportionately harm the Palestinian population in spite of less harmful alternatives being available.[32] With regards to the Wall and its associated regime of checkpoints and permits, the ICJ found that conditions of necessity, least-intrusiveness, and proportionality

---

Courts in the European Union 29 (Tamara Perišin & Siniša Rodin eds., 2018). Both authors express their criticism with regards to the limits of proportionality as a workable principle of effective civilian protection.

29    For a thorough breakdown of the concept of military necessity and advantage, *see* Nobuo Hayashi, *Requirements of Military Necessity in International Humanitarian Law and International Criminal Law*, 28 Boston Univ. Int'l L. J. 39 (2010).

30    *See* Michael N. Schmitt, *Military Necessity and Humanity in International Humanitarian Law: Preserving the Delicate Balance*, in Essays on Law and War at the Fault Lines 89 (2012).

31    H.R.C., *Human rights situation in Palestine and other Occupied Arab Territories. Report of the United Nations High Commissioner for Human Rights on the implementation of Human Rights Council resolution S-9/1*, U.N. Doc. A/HRC/12/37 (Aug. 19, 2009), para. 76.

32    In fact, "had the State of Israel wanted to fulfill ... its obligation to protect the lives of every settler living in the West Bank, it clearly could have done so by pinpoint means causing much less harm to Palestinian movement than the means it has chosen." B'Tselem, *Ground to a Halt: Denial of Palestinians' Freedom of Movement in the West Bank* (Aug. 2007), at 93, https://www.btselem.org/download/200708_ground_to_a_halt_eng.pdf.

were being disregarded, and further observed that the extent of the restrictions enacted is so vast that it subverts the relationship between rule and exception.[33] The argument can be extended to the web of roads reserved for Israeli use. While the Israeli army maintains that the purpose of separate roads is to ensure the settlers' security, the military necessity and legitimacy of such a network is questionable. Further, since settlements contravene Fourth Geneva Convention article 49, paragraph 6, "any measures undertaken to protect settlers must also be considered unlawful."[34]

Moreover, according to Samira Shah, the efficacy of the measures in protecting the beneficiaries is equally questionable. In fact, as she notes, the incidence of Israeli settler killings on the bypass roads attests that the network of separate roads fails to ensure security, and actually places settlers at risk. Some of them refuse to use the roads because they feel more exposed to the eventuality of attacks when travelling on roads used only by Israelis. The roads, Shah concludes, "actually decrease the security of the settlers by rendering anyone on the road an easy target, and they have already resulted in the deaths of several settlers."[35] Analogous conclusions were reached by researchers exploring the relationship between impediments to mobility and support for militancy: "there is little question that checkpoints are an impediment in the lives of Palestinians, but it is ... noteworthy finding that they might be a detriment to Israeli and regional security as well by making Palestinians more likely to support violence and radicalism."[36]

John Dugard, former special rapporteur for the (former) UN Commission on Human Rights, extended the reasoning to all other measures applied to restrain Palestinian movement in the West Bank. In his 2008 report, he stated that "restrictions on freedom of movement of the kind applied by Israel do

---

33 ICJ Wall Advisory Opinion, para. 136 ("The Court would observe that the restrictions provided for under Article 12, paragraph 3, of the International Covenant on Civil and Political Rights are, by the very terms of that provision, exceptions to the right of freedom of movement contained in paragraph 1. In addition, it is not sufficient that such restrictions be directed to the ends authorized; they must also be necessary for the attainment of those ends ... they must conform to the principle of proportionality and must be the least intrusive instrument amongst those which might achieve the desired result ... On the basis of the information available to it, the Court finds that these conditions are not met in the present instance.").

34 Victor Kattan, *The Legality of the West Bank Wall: Israel's High Court of Justice v. the International Court of Justice*, 40 Vanderbilt J. Transnat'l L. 1425, 1435 (2007) [*hereinafter* Kattan].

35 Samira Shah, *On the Road to Apartheid: The Bypass Road Network in the West Bank*, 29 Columbia Hum. Rts. L. Rev. 221, 262 (1997).

36 Matthew Longo, Daphna Canetti & Nancy Hite-Rubin, *A Checkpoint Effect? Evidence from a Natural Experiment on Travel Restrictions in the West Bank*, 58 Am. J. Pol. Sci. 1006, 1018 (2014) [*hereinafter* Longo et al.].

more to create insecurity than to achieve security,"[37] and ventured the hypothesis that the numerous prohibitions on travel respond more to the need "to impress upon the Palestinian people the power and presence of the occupier"[38] than to a security imperative. The tools provided by the wording of applicable legal instruments, however, do not allow for suitable and exhaustive analysis of the motives highlighted by Dugard. While acknowledging the legitimacy of the measures dictated by Israel's security exigencies, the IHL approach can at best detect discrepancy with the requirement of proportionality. However, it cannot explain the paradox that Israel's alleged security measures – with their excessive burden on the Palestinian population – produce, overall, no significant gain in terms of security for Israeli citizens. Although a claim that the alleged security measures are ultimately counterproductive may not be universally accepted, it is nevertheless reasonable to state that "security concerns do not justify Israel's extensive and excessive imposition of obstacles to Palestinian freedom of movement."[39] Hence the need for further investigation.

## C  *Behind Discrimination: The Systematic Dimension of Racial Exclusion*

The obligation that Israel bears to facilitate the movement of Palestinians in the oPt allows for exceptions in case of imperative reasons of security and only in response to specific security threats. In order to minimize the impact on innocent Palestinian civilians, whose protection forms the goal of the Fourth Geneva Convention, the measures implemented by Israel to pursue its alleged security objectives should only target those individuals who might endanger Israel's security. However, the restrictions on movement in the West Bank, supposedly aimed at mitigating the risk of attacks, are imposed broadly and indiscriminately on the whole population, not targeting particular individuals who are believed to pose a threat.

---

37    H.R.C., *Human rights situation in Palestine and other occupied Arab territories, Report of the Special Rapporteur on the situation of human rights in the Palestinian territories occupied since 1967, John Dugard*, U.N. Doc. A/HRC/7/17 (Jan. 21, 2008), para. 35.

38    *Id.*

39    Al-Haq, *Submission to the Human Rights Committee on the occasion of Israel's fourth periodic review, Alternative Report to the UN Human Rights Committee regarding Israel's violation and failed implementation of Art. 1, 2, 6, 7, 9, 12, 14 of the International Covenant on Civil and Political Rights* (Sep. 2014), https://tbinternet.ohchr.org/Treaties/CCPR/Shared%20 Documents/ISR/INT_CCPR_CSS_ISR_18198_E.pdf. Israeli officials "claim there is an alleged need to protect Israeli security interests, attempting to promote the argument that the Palestinians are primarily to blame for the continued control over them ... Security concerns, however, have little to do with Israel's policy." B'Tselem, *The Occupation in its 51st Year* (2018), at 9, https://www.btselem.org/sites/default/files/publications/51st_year_ of_occupation_eng.pdf.

This generalized condition of constraint dates back to the very beginning of the occupation. Although in the early years a general exit permit allowed residents of the oPt to travel into East Jerusalem and Israel during daylight hours with few limitations, it was still through a military concession that Palestinians were able to enjoy relatively free movement. Despite the wide scope of the permit, the ability to travel was entirely dependent on the will of the occupying forces and could be easily revoked at any time by military orders.[40] As of 1991, the general exit permit was withdrawn and replaced with a system of personal permits, which gradually became harder and harder to obtain.[41] The new policy unveiled the nature of a reality of containment – unchanged until now – in which freedom of movement was turned into an exception, while restrictions were the rule. Ever since then (and especially during the two *intifadas*), Israel resorted to more and more disruptive strategies of constraint. Some of them were soon identified as unlawful by human rights activists and legal observers. This was the case for curfews and closures, used as means of collective punishment against entire communities,[42] and for the Wall, found to violate multiple principles of international law and to ultimately reverse (as the ICJ has stressed),[43] the relationship between the ability to exercise the right, which constitutes the rule, and the restriction, which constitutes the exception.

What generally does not emerge from legal analyses of the movement situation in the West Bank is that the different restrictive measures, considered as a whole, create a sophisticated apparatus that, by altering the relation between rule and exception, operates a systematic mechanism of exclusion that severely impairs the lives of millions of Palestinians who did not commit any offence.

---

40    *See, generally*, Makan, *Freedom of Movement* (Jan. 2018), https://www.makan.org.uk/wp-content/uploads/2018/02/FreedomOfMovement.pdf; Nadia Abu Zahra, *IDs and Territory. Population control for Resource Expropriation*, in War, Citizenship, Territory (D. Cowen & E. Gilbert eds., 2008); Ron J. Smith, Freedom Is a Place: the Struggle for Sovereignty in Palestine (2020).

41    *See* B'Tselem, *Restrictions on movement* (Nov. 11, 2017), https://www.btselem.org/freedom_of_movement.

42    *See* B'Tselem, *Civilians under Siege: Restrictions on Freedom of Movement as Collective Punishment* (Jan. 2001), https://www.btselem.org/publications/summaries/200101_civilians_under_siege. The closure of entire villages is a means of frequent resort for the military, to the point that it "has long since become a routine method of oppression that Israel uses against Palestinian residents of the West Bank". B'Tselem, *Jan.–Feb. 2020: Military blocks five West Bank villages as collective punishment* (Apr. 9, 2020), https://www.btselem.org/freedom_of_movement/20200409_military_blocks_five_west_bank_villages_as_collective_punishment_in_jan_feb_2020.

43    ICJ Wall Advisory Opinion, para. 136.

# RESTRICTIONS ON FREEDOM OF MOVEMENT IN THE WEST BANK 153

Moreover, at the risk of stating the obvious, Israeli settlers are not affected by the restrictions. They pass completely unhindered through all checkpoints and circulate freely in special lanes with no impediments or obstructions.

The logical conclusion would be that obstacles are imposed on all Palestinians because they are Palestinians,[44] therefore belying the argument that there is no racial discrimination. Contrary to the basic principle of non-discrimination, the measures adopted to restrict movement in the West Bank create unfavorable conditions for Palestinians only, based on the tenet that every Palestinian represents a security threat. Meanwhile, favored treatment is given to the settlers, who live in the occupied territory in violation of international law.[45] The unequal application of restrictions violates ICCPR article 4, since the discrimination is based on distinctions of race and national origin (the hardships deriving from the Wall, checkpoints, restricted roads and permit system exclusively target Palestinians and their ability to enjoy other human rights, while serving the settlements and benefitting Israeli citizens in the West Bank).

Scholars of the occupation paradigm have pointed out the discriminatory nature and the consequent unlawfulness of such restrictions.[46] However, what this kind of approach fails to fully appreciate is that the discrimination under analysis is not unfortunate, incidental, or collateral, but rather systemic and endemic. Additionally, as it is practiced by the state, it constitutes an institutionalized regime of systematic racial discrimination, whose gravity deserves dedicated attention and investigation.

## D    *Towards a New Understanding*
Having highlighted the unlawfulness dictated by the international law framework, further consideration of the scope and implications of such violations is

---

44    *See* Amnesty International, *Israel and the Occupied Territories: Surviving under Siege: The Impact of Movement Restrictions on the Right to Work* (Sep. 2003), at 11 [*hereinafter* Amnesty International (2003)], https://www.amnesty.org/en/documents/mde15/001/2003/en/.

45    *See* The Association for Civil Rights in Israel (ACRI), *One Rule, Two Legal Systems: Israel's Regime of Laws in the West Bank* (Oct. 2014), https://law.acri.org.il/en/wp-content/uploads/2015/02/Two-Systems-of-Law-English-FINAL.pdf ("[T]he movement of Palestinians throughout the West Bank is ... significantly restricted compared to that of Israelis ... By contrast, the movement of Israelis is permitted almost without any restrictions in most of the West Bank area.").

46    *See, Ronit Sela, *Freedom of Movement v. Restrictions on Movement under the Two Legal Systems*, 21 Palestine-Israel J. Pol. Econ. & Cult. 31 (2016); Carol Bisharat, *Palestine and Humanitarian Law: Israeli Practice in the West Bank and Gaza*, 12 Hastings Int'l & Comp. L. Rev. 325 (1989).

necessary. Although provisions of IHRL and IHL allow the occupying power to limit the right to freedom of movement in the occupied territories under certain circumstances, the analysis developed above clarifies that the nature of the restrictions imposed by Israel in the West Bank is somewhat anomalous. While Israel claims that the reasons behind the strict measures of constraint are solely related to security needs, their discriminatory and disproportionate nature can hardly be justified, even under the broad terms of IHL which acknowledge the legitimacy of pursuing security purposes. Despite the availability of more adequate instruments, Israel never loosened its restrictive policies in compliance with the concerns expressed by international authorities. Instead, it used security as a fig leaf to cover persistent violations, stretching the legal categories provided by the law of belligerent occupation beyond recognition in order to forcibly fit in the limitations imposed on the Palestinians. As highlighted by Hani Sayed,

> the conceptual and doctrinal tools available to international lawyers to engage the legal status ... [of the occupied territories] have a blind spot that, in the long run, legitimized Israel's control ... International lawyers have had difficulties in capturing and incorporating in their analysis the systemic aspects of the occupation, and were immersed in quarrels on the legality of certain actions taken within it.[47]

In order not to reduce the debate to a cycle of futile disquisitions, we must overcome the analytical gap that reduces studies on restriction of freedom of movement to a catalogue of violations of IHL, and focus, instead, on a crucial aspect of the phenomenon: the institutionalized aspect of the discriminatory system of restrictions. What the occupation paradigm tends to disregard is the intensely hierarchical and State-sustained dimension of an apparatus that functions as "a whole whose purpose is to keep the Palestinian Arabs in a subordinate status."[48] Because the examined approach fails to grasp the logic of

---

47 Hani Sayed, *The Fictions of the "Illegal" Occupation in the West Bank and Gaza*, 16 Or. Rev. Int'l L. 79, 82 (2014). The author echoes the argument of the "emperor's new clothes," whereby the convergence of international human rights and humanitarian law ultimately allows to "maintain the existing (im)balance of security, whereby the rights of settlers, conceived as security, usually trump the rights of the local population. The new framing of those conflicts in human rights terms may turn IHRL into the emperor's new clothes of the law of occupation." Gross, at 26.

48 John Quigley, *Apartheid Outside Africa: The Case of Israel*, 1 Ind. Intl & Comp. L. Rev. 221, 250 (1991).

such an apparatus, a different prism of analysis needs to be adopted to unveil new patterns.

Although occupation is an undeniable legal fact, the assumption that the relevant legal framework is primarily IHL has so far precluded exploring the possibility of grounding a legal analysis on different legal instruments. As noted by Ben-Naftali, Gross and Michaeli, "the reason [for the application of the international laws of occupation] lies in the perception of occupation as a factual, rather than a normative, phenomenon,"[49] which has conferred the regime virtual immunity from inquiries about its legality. The authors argue that, while denying the applicability of the Fourth Geneva Convention to the oPt, Israel consistently exercised the powers of a belligerent occupant, restricted the rights of Palestinians on the basis of the law of occupation, and enjoyed both the powers of an occupant and a sovereign in the oPt, while disenfranchising Palestinians of both the rights of citizens and the rights of occupied people. Their conclusion is that this continuous interplay of occupation/non-occupation has enabled the Israeli regime to don a mantle of legitimacy that obfuscates its intrinsic illegality.[50]

According to Virginia Tilley, the unproductive debate on the applicability of IHL and the detailed documentation of Israel's violations of humanitarian provisions "introduced a debilitating analytical error by obscuring recognition that Israel's occupation also involves a crime against humanity,"[51] namely, apartheid. Therefore, the contours of the legal discourse on Israeli occupation need to be redefined accordingly. Rethinking the question from the apartheid perspective creates space for new and unexplored levels of analysis. Once the gaps produced by the reductive analytical scope of the occupation paradigm are overcome, it is finally possible to achieve a deeper understanding of the violations perpetrated for decades against Palestinians' freedom of movement.

---

49   Orna Ben-Naftali, Aeyal M. Gross, & Keren Michaeli, *Illegal Occupation: Framing the Occupied Palestinian Territory*, 25 Berkley J. Int'l L. 551, 552 (2005).

50   Ben-Naftali further develops this argument and insists on the normative implications. She suggests that, because of its contribution in the shaping of such a regime, the law itself becomes "infected," and is likely to operate in a manner that will defy its normative purpose. The result is that the law advances the interests of the occupying power at the expense of the occupied people and facilitates the consolidation of an environment of tolerance of human rights violations that reflects systemic state policies. *See* Orna Ben-Naftali, *PathoLAWgical Occupation: Normalizing the Exceptional Case of the Occupied Palestinian Territory and Other Legal Pathologies*, in International Humanitarian Law and International Human Rights Law 8 (Orna Ben-Naftali ed., 2011).

51   Virginia Tilley, Beyond Occupation: Apartheid, Colonialism and International Law in the Occupied Palestinian Territories xii (2012).

## III Movement Restrictions Reframed: Embracing the Apartheid Paradigm

Over the past years, it has been suggested that comparison to the South African apartheid is the best means of portraying the elements of the system of restrictions that impede Palestinian movement in the oPt (*e.g.* "Apartheid Wall"; "Apartheid Roads"; the analogy between Area A and the Bantustans; between the permit regime and the South African passbook system).[52] Because they powerfully evoke loaded historical memories, these expressions have often been appropriated by activist circles to shake public opinion and arouse outrage. As suggested by Raef Zreik, "[t]hat the apartheid model has relevance to the Palestinians is clear, given the basic similarities between the Israeli and South African cases."[53] However, to shift from the occupation paradigm to the apartheid paradigm is not a mere matter of labels; it requires cautious reconsideration of old phenomena in the light of new schemes of thinking. This new analytical framework is outlined by those provisions of international law that define and prohibit apartheid, enabling a disentanglement of the Palestinian experience from the South African model and to appreciate it in its peculiar features. Such a framework provides new tools to describe, comprehend, and explain the unlawful violations of human rights in the West Bank.

The applicability of this analysis has obviously been strongly opposed, and not exclusively by advocates of Israel.[54] Before advancing further, it may therefore be helpful to briefly dispel the preliminary objections to the validity of the apartheid paradigm. The first issue is non-annexation or, in other words, the argument that Israel should not be held accountable for apartheid in the

---

52  *See,* most notably, Jimmy Carter, Palestine: Peace Not Apartheid (2006); Desmond Tutu, *Apartheid in the Holy Land,* Guardian (Apr. 29, 2002), https://www.theguardian.com/world/2002/apr/29/comment. *See also* Ian Urbina, *The Analogy to Apartheid,* 223 Middle East Rep. 58 (2002); Gabriela Becker, *'Final Borders' and 'Security Zones' in Palestine: Israeli Plans for a Bantustan 'State,'* 41 Econ. & Pol. Wkly. 1237 (2006); Ma'an Development Center, *Apartheid roads. Promoting settlements, punishing Palestinians* (Dec. 2008), https://www.maan-ctr.org/old/pdfs/Apartheid%20Roads.pdf; Leila Farsakh, *Independence, Cantons, or Bantustans: Whither the Palestinian State?,* 59 Middle East J. 230 (2005) [*hereinafter* Farsakh]; Julie Peteet, *Beyond Compare,* 253 Middle East Rep. 16 (2009) [*hereinafter* Peteet (2009)].

53  Raef Zreik, *Palestine, Apartheid and the Rights Discourse,* 34 J. Palest. Stud. 68, 71 (2004).

54  *See* Ran Greenstein, *Israel–Palestine and the Apartheid Analogy: Critics, Apologists and Strategic Lessons,* in Israel and South Africa: the many faces of Apartheid 279 (Ilan Pappé ed., 2015).

West Bank, because it has no formal sovereignty over the oPt.[55] However, as Virginia Tilley argues, "the presumption that a state can be held culpable of apartheid only regarding the population within its formal sovereign territory is simply incorrect."[56] Official annexation is but a legal formality, the lack of which is abundantly counterbalanced by the actual practices on the ground and, first and foremost, by the irreversible incorporation resulting from Israel's prolonged hold over the West Bank.[57] Sfard argues that, let alone the "explicit, direct proclamations by the government of Israel and its leadership regarding plans to annex part or all of the occupied territories," the abovementioned practices on the ground and the "slow but steady trickle of legislative changes" cumulatively result in a creeping annexation of the West Bank.[58] So, the pretense that no *de jure* annexation has occurred cannot disguise the fact that Israel exerts *de facto* sovereignty in the oPt.[59] In fact, Israel is "deceptively abjuring an open claim of sovereignty in order to avoid the legal obligations or consequences that would pertain to that sovereignty."[60] Israel attentively

---

55    *See, e.g.,* Yaffa Zilbershats, *Apartheid, International Law, and the Occupied Palestinian Territory: A Reply to John Dugard and John Reynolds,* 24 Eur. J. Int'l L. 915 (2013).

56    Virginia Tilley, *Redefining the Conflict in Israel-Palestine: The tricky Question of Sovereignty,* in Israel and South Africa: The Many Faces of Apartheid 255, 256 (Ilan Pappé ed., 2015) [*hereinafter* Tilley]. In these regards, Tilley stresses the analogy with Apartheid South Africa's governance of Namibia.

57    In the 1980s, Meron Benvenisti argued that it was nonsensical to refer to the occupation as temporary and introduced the concept of "creeping annexation." *See* Meron Benvenisti, The West Bank Data Project: A Survey of Israel's Policies (American Enterprise Institute for Public Policy Research, 1984).

58    Yesh Din, *The Israeli Occupation of the West Bank and the Crime of Apartheid: Legal Opinion by Adv. Michael Sfard* (June 2020), at 31 [*hereinafter* Sfard], https://s3-eu-west-1 .amazonaws.com/files.yesh-din.org/Apartheid+2020/Apartheid+ENG.pdf. Not only the *de facto* situation invalidates the argument of non-annexation: even more so does the consideration that East Jerusalem – an integral part of the West Bank – has been annexed to Israel, in defiance of international law. The unlawful annexation was first established *de facto* by an amendment to the 1948 Law and Administrative Ordinance, passed on June 27, 1967. It was then constitutionally formalized by the Basic Law: Jerusalem, Capital of Israel, July 30, 1980, S.H. No. 980, p. 186 (Isr.).

59    The focus of the present article is on the West Bank. However, it is worth highlighting that, in spite of the so-called "Disengagement Plan," Israel's withdrawal from the Gaza Strip was only apparent. In fact, Israel still maintains effective control over Gaza as well. *See* Iain Scobbie, *An Intimate Disengagement: Israel's withdrawal from Gaza, the Law of Occupation and Self-determination,* 11 Y.B. Islamic & Middle Eastern L. 3 (2004); Gisha: Legal Center for Freedom of Movement, *Disengaged Occupiers: The Legal Status of Gaza* (Jan. 2007), https://www.gisha.org/UserFiles/File/publications_english/Publications_and _Reports_English/Disengaged_Occupiers_en.pdf.

60    Tilley, at 258. Besides, despite the different levels of "disenfranchisement" [*see* Mark Marshall, *Rethinking the Palestine Question: The Apartheid Paradigm,* 25 J. Palestine Stud.

pursues and takes advantage of this legal indeterminacy as a form of control to maintain its status quo and pursue the project of Greater Israel,[61] while avoiding accountability in the international community.

Another preliminary question concerns the identification of Jews and Palestinians as racial groups. One key argument against the application of the apartheid paradigm to Israel is that apartheid applies only to racial groups, and neither Jews nor Palestinians are today qualified as races.[62] In this respect, a legal definition of racial group becomes of paramount importance but, as Carola Lingaas observes, "international criminal law seemingly tries to avoid any confrontation with race and racial groups."[63] In the Apartheid Convention, the notion of race is not clearly defined. However, by invoking the International Convention for the Elimination of All Forms of Racial Discrimination (ICERD) in its preamble, the Apartheid Convention appears to allude and refer to ICERD's definition of racial discrimination, which embraces a whole range of group identities: race, color, descent, and national or ethnic origin.[64] These labels identify social identities shaping groups relations as a result of mutual and self-ascription of attributes and qualities perceived by the subjects as essential and immutable.[65] As Dugard and Reynolds opine, the question of racial groups is a sociological rather than a biological one:

---

15 (1995); Oren Yiftachel, *"Creeping Apartheid" in Israel-Palestine*, 253 Middle East Rep. 7 (2009)], it needs to be highlighted that the Palestinian population must be here considered as a whole precisely because the distinct geographic and juridical circumstances imposed by Israel aim to create splintered conditions that serve to befog the regime's very existence. In this regard, *see also* Nathan Thrall, *The Separate Regimes Delusion* (Jan. 21, 2021), https://www.lrb.co.uk/the-paper/v43/no2/nathan-thrall/the-separate-regimes-delusion; Daryl Glaser, *Zionism and Apartheid: a moral comparison*, 26 Ethnic & Racial Stud. 403 (2006).

61 *See* Ardi Imseis, *Zionism, Racism and the Palestine People: Fifty Years of Human Rights Violations in Israel and the Occupied Territories*, 8 Dalhousie J. Legal Stud. 1 (1999).

62 *See* Oren Kroll-Zeldin, *Does Israel Function as an Apartheid State? Critically Engaging the Complexities of the Apartheid Debate in Palestine/Israel*, in Social Justice and Israel/Palestine: Foundational and Contemporary Debates 175 (Aaron J. Hahn Tapper & Mira Sucharov eds., 2019).

63 Carola Lingaas, *The Crime against Humanity of Apartheid in a Post-Apartheid World*, 86 Oslo L. Rev. 86, 101 (2015) [*hereinafter* Lingaas].

64 *See* International Convention for the Elimination of All Forms of Racial Discrimination art. 1, Dec. 21, 1965, 660 U.N.T.S. 195 [*hereinafter* ICERD].

65 *See* Karine Mac Allister, *Applicability of the Crime of Apartheid to Israel*, BADIL (Summer 2008), https://www.badil.org/publications/al-majdal/issues/items/225.html.

the interpretation of racial groups as developed in international law appears sufficiently broad to understand Jewish Israelis and Palestinian Arabs as distinct groups. Jewish and Palestinian identities, while not typically seen as 'races' in the old (discredited) sense of biological or skin colour categories, are constructed as groups distinguished by ancestry or descent as well as ethnicity, nationality, and religion. As such they are distinguished from each other in a number of forms within the parameters of racial discrimination under international human rights law.[66]

In this sense, the concept of race can be understood as a synonym of *people* or, better, of *ethnic group*, and leads to a broad definition of race as a socially constructed identity.[67] Therefore, the main determining element of race is perception of differentness and, eventually, inferiority – in the meaning of the crime of apartheid, a racial group qualifies as such if it is perceived and treated as a distinct social group.[68]

A deep analysis of the full complexity of Jewish and Palestinian identity goes beyond the scope of this article. What matters for our purposes is whether relations between Jews and Palestinians correspond to the racial dynamics described above. Because of their distinct identities, the two groups perceive themselves[69] and each other as such, generating relations of discrimination and exclusion. This suffices to justify the concern for racial discrimination expressed in ICERD and, by means of shared definition, of the Apartheid Convention.

---

66  John Dugard & John Reynolds, *Apartheid, International Law, and the Occupied Palestinian Territory*, 24 Eur. J. Int'l L. 867, 889 (2013) [*hereinafter* Dugard & Reynolds]. The authors further strengthen their argument through reference to the body of jurisprudence on the Rwandan genocide. Similarly, Hussein Adem highlights that the understanding of the concept of race as socially constructed instead of scientific reality is also endorsed by the jurisprudence of the International Criminal Tribunal for the former Yugoslavia. *See* Seada Hussein Adem, Palestine and the International Criminal Court 158 (2019).

67  *See* Steven Kaplan, *If there are no 'Races', how can Jews be a 'Race'?* 2 J. Modern Jewish Stud. 79 (2003).

68  *See* Lingaas; David Davis, *Constructing Race: A Reflection*, 54 William & Mary Q. 7 (1997).

69  The Committee on the Elimination of Racial Discrimination has stressed that group identities emerge from the members' self-identification. In its General Recommendation No. 8, *Identification with a particular racial or ethnic group* of August 22, 1990, the CERD explains that: "the ways in which individuals are identified as being members of a particular racial or ethnic group ... shall, if no justification exists to the contrary, be based upon self-identification by the individual concerned." U.N. Doc. A/45/18 (1991), part 7, para. 1.

## A  The Legal Framework of the Apartheid Paradigm: An Unambiguous Definition

When the ICERD was adopted in 1965, the state parties, driven and "alarmed by manifestations of racial discrimination still in evidence in some areas of the world and by governmental policies based on racial superiority or hatred, such as policies of apartheid, segregation or separation,"[70] committed to eradicating all forms and manifestations of racial discrimination. ICERD article 3 condemns all practices of racial segregation and apartheid. While not providing an exact definition of the latter, the drafters chose to mention it specifically, as an exception to the practice of not referring to specific forms of discrimination in the treaty.[71] The need for an international instrument that would make it possible "to take more effective measures at the international and national levels with a view to the suppression and punishment of the crime of apartheid"[72] was only satisfied in 1973, with the adoption of the International Convention on the Suppression and Punishment of the Crime of Apartheid, more commonly known as the Apartheid Convention. Apartheid Convention article 2 provides a definition of the crime as "inhuman acts committed for the purpose of establishing and maintaining domination by one racial group of persons over any other racial group of persons and systematically oppressing them," and lists examples of practices amounting to apartheid when committed with the purpose of domination and oppression. Because of the gravity of the inhumane acts identified in article 2, state parties to the Apartheid Convention declared the crime of apartheid a crime against humanity, that violates "the principles of international law, in particular the purposes and principles of the [UN Charter], and [constitutes] a serious threat to international peace and security."[73]

The Rome Statute of the International Criminal Court includes apartheid in the list of crimes against humanity,[74] and formulates a definition that echoes the one given by the Apartheid Convention: "inhumane acts ... committed in the context of an institutionalized regime of systematic oppression and domination by one racial group over any other racial group or groups and

---

70  ICERD pmbl.

71  Human Sciences Research Council, *Occupation, Colonialism, Apartheid? A re-assessment of Israel's practices in the Occupied Palestinian Territories under international law* (2009), at 49 [*hereinafter* HSRC Report].

72  International Convention on the Suppression and Punishment of the Crime of Apartheid *chapeau*, Nov. 30, 1973, 1015 U.N.T.S. 243 [*hereinafter* Apartheid Convention].

73  Apartheid Convention art. 1.

74  Rome Statute of the International Criminal Court art. 7, para. 1(j), July 17, 1998, 2187 U.N.T.S. 90.

# RESTRICTIONS ON FREEDOM OF MOVEMENT IN THE WEST BANK 161

committed with the intention of maintaining that regime."[75] Both the Rome Statute and the Apartheid Convention recognize and emphasize the particularly systematic, institutionalized, and oppressive character of the discrimination that apartheid entails, which justifies its inclusion in ICERD as a distinct and special form of racial discrimination. While a majority of States including Israel have ratified ICERD, fewer are part to the Apartheid Convention. Nevertheless, the prohibition of apartheid is "considered today as a rule of customary law and a norm of *jus cogens* creating obligations *erga omnes*"[76] – that is, obligations owed by all states towards the international community as a whole.

In 2007, the UN Committee on the Elimination of Racial Discrimination expressed its deep concern over the "severe restrictions on the freedom of movement in the [oPt], targeting a particular national or ethnic group."[77] At the same time the UN special rapporteur on the human rights situation in the Palestinian territories drew attention to the analogy with the crime of apartheid, noting that "the [Apartheid Convention] appears to be violated by many practices, particularly those denying freedom of movement to Palestinians."[78] Determination of whether the imposed restrictions represent an instance of apartheid depends on the correspondence of these practices to one of the six categories of inhuman acts illustratively listed in Apartheid Convention article 2. Positive ascription to one of these acts would be sufficient to determine the existence of apartheid.

## B    *Movement Restrictions as a Policy of Apartheid: A Tool for Segregation*

One of the main effects obtained through the imposition of movement restrictions on the Palestinian people in the West Bank is a geographic fragmentation of the territory. This allows for the allocation of some areas and facilities to the exclusive use of Jews and for the creation of spaces where Palestinians are ultimately confined. However, this is hardly surprising, considering that "the fragmentation of the Palestinian people is the core method through which Israel

---

75    *Id.*, art. 7, para. 2(h).

76    HSRC Report, at 51.

77    C.E.R.D., *Consideration of reports submitted by States parties under Article 9 of the Convention. Concluding observations: Israel,* U.N. Doc. ICERD/C/ISR/CO/13 (June 14, 2007), para. 34.

78    H.R.C., *Human rights situation in Palestine and other occupied Arab territories, Report of the Special Rapporteur on the situation of human rights in the Palestinian territories occupied since 1967, John Dugard,* U.N. Doc. A/HRC/4/17 (Jan. 29, 2007), at 2.

enforces apartheid."[79] This fragmentation has many faces and is achieved through different tools. Geographical fragmentation in the West Bank is undoubtedly constructed to a significant extent through the system of prohibitions, impediments, and obstacles that obstruct the movement of Palestinians.

By way of comparison, segregation of the population was one of the pillars of the South African apartheid, where different geographic areas were assigned to different racial groups and passage into a certain area by members of an alien group was restricted.[80] In this model of spatial confinement, contact between groups was severely limited.[81] Segregation of a similar kind is pursued in the West Bank. Access to East Jerusalem is restricted and the territorial space available to Palestinians is shrinking,[82] turning the West Bank into an archipelago of besieged and non-contiguous Palestinian cantons, divided by an intricate network of well-connected Jewish settlements and infrastructures.[83] This process, often referred to as "bantustanization," transforms the oPt into "*de facto* population reserves out of which Palestinians cannot exit without the possession of a permit issued by Israeli military authorities."[84]

---

79    *See* Richard Falk & Virginia Tilley, *Israeli Practices Towards the Palestinian People and the Question of Apartheid*, U.N. Doc. E/ESCWA/ECRI/2017/1 (2017), at 37 [this report was censored by the UN but published by the Palestine Yearbook of International Law. *See* 20 Palestine Y. Int'l L. 201 (2019)].

80    *See* Julie Peteet, *The work of comparison: Israel/Palestine and Apartheid*, 89 Anthropological Q. 247 (2016).

81    *See, generally*, Barbara Rogers, Divide and Rule: South Africa's Bantustans (International Defence & Aid Fund for Southern Africa, 1980); Christopher Hills, Bantustans: The Fragmentation of South Africa (Institute of Race Relations, 1964).

82    *See* HSRC Report, at 21. For accurate and detailed information on the restrictions affecting East Jerusalem, *see* U.N. OCHA, Occupied Palestinian Territory, *East Jerusalem: Key Humanitarian Concerns* (Mar. 2011), https://www.ochaopt.org/sites/default/files/ocha _opt_jerusalem_report_2011_03_23_web_english.pdf. *See also* Hanna Bauman, *Enclaves, borders, and everyday movements: Palestinian marginal mobility in East Jerusalem*, 173 Cities 59 (2016). OCHA also provides a detailed map of the obstacles in East Jerusalem area, available at: https://www.ochaopt.org/content/new-movement-restrictions-east -jerusalem-october-2015.

83    BADIL Resource Center for Palestinian Residency & Refugee Rights, *Working Paper No. 23: Forced Population Transfer: Segregation, Fragmentation, Isolation* (Feb. 2020), at 99 ("[Israel's] policies reduce Palestinian communities to strangled and isolated Bantustans, surrounded by Israeli colonies, with no continuity and lacking the organic connections that once unified them.").

84    Farsakh, at 231. Alina Korn argues that the Palestinian enclaves resemble the classic ghetto more than the South African Bantustans: "[The Palestinian ghettoes] are smaller, splintered, and they serve as containers for storing unnecessary population. Their inhabitants are trapped behind barbed wire, fences, ditches and walls. [These ghettoes] are designed

The Oslo II agreement facilitated this "grand apartheid" strategy by establishing borders for the Palestinian autonomous enclaves,[85] and paved the way for Israeli authorities to restrain and confine the Palestinian people in residential areas in the middle of West Bank. As a result, the map of the West Bank appears like a region of Israeli Jewish domination, dotted with Palestinian autonomous zones, outside which Palestinian presence is unwelcome. Settlements and all the main roads are located in Area C all around Palestinian villages and cities and are used by Israel to keep the Palestinian communities effectively isolated in small areas and completely disconnected from one another.[86]

Road 55 is one of the so-called apartheid roads that Israel designates in order to support the settlement infrastructure.[87] Indeed, the infamous epithet is well deserved for a number of reasons. First of all, although they are built on lands confiscated from Palestinians, Palestinians are banned from travelling on them. Secondly, bypassing Palestinian villages and cities, these roads effectively contribute to marking the boundaries of the Palestinian cantons.[88] Finally, thanks to a system of tunnels, bridges and interchanges, the separation of high-speed Israeli roads from Palestinian "fabric of life" roads is achieved. In this way, settlers can virtually travel around the West Bank without crossing

---

to preserve the Territories under Israeli control without providing for the existence of the non-Jewish population ... The ghetto ... is a double-edged socio-spatial formation: it operates as an instrument of exclusion and ethno-racial discrimination from the standpoint of the dominant group." Alina Korn, *The Ghettoization of the Palestinians*, in Thinking Palestine 116, 122 (Ronit Lentin ed., 2008).

85    On how the "peace process" contributed to the advancement of apartheid in Palestine, *see* Marwan Bishara, Palestine/Israel, Peace or Apartheid: Occupation, Terrorism and the Future (2002).

86    *See* Breaking the Silence, *Highway to Annexation. Israeli Road and Transportation Infrastructure Development in the West Bank* (Dec. 2020), https://www.breakingthe silence.org.il/inside/wp-content/uploads/2020/12/Highway-to-Annexation-Final.pdf; Ariel Handel, *Gated/gating community: The settlement complex in the West Bank*, 504 Transactions Inst. Br. Geographers 39 (2013); David Delaney, *Parsing Palisraelestine*, in Territory: a short introduction 102 (2008).

87    *See* Jacob Magid, *Netanyahu inaugurates West Bank bypass road, vows more projects to come*, Times of Israel (Jan. 3, 2010), https://www.timesofisrael.com/netanyahu-inaugurates -west-bank-bypass-road-vows-more-projects/; B'Tselem, *West Bank roads on which Israel forbids Palestinian vehicles* (Jan. 31, 2017), https://www.btselem.org/freedom_of_move ment/forbidden_roads.

88    As pointed out by the former special rapporteur Richard Falk, "[the Apartheid Roads] continue to reinforce the exclusion of Palestinians from the primary road network and undermine the territorial contiguity between different areas." H.R.C., *Human rights situation in Palestine and other occupied Arab territories, Report of the Special Rapporteur on the situation of human rights in the Palestinian territories occupied since 1967, Richard Falk*, U.N. Doc. A/HRC/16/72 (Jan. 10, 2011), para. 21.

paths with Palestinians.[89] The Israeli-only roads run beside Palestinian towns but do not serve them. The roadside landscape is dotted with Israeli settlements and Palestinian villages, but only Jewish localities are signposted on the road signs. Another example of this kind is Road 443. In late 2001, citing security concerns, the Israeli Defense Forces (IDF) banned Palestinians from using the roadway and placed roadblocks to obstruct access to Route 443 from Palestinian villages. Although a ruling of the Israeli High Court of Justice clarified in 2009 that a road that caters solely to Israeli drivers discriminates against local Palestinians and ordered the military forces to put an end to the unlawful closure, the blockage to Palestinian traffic continues thanks to the addition of new checkpoints, which render the alleged opening of the road quite meaningless.[90] Security concerns still represent the main justification to disproportionate measures of segregation, as in the case of brand new Route 4370, North-East of Jerusalem, which separates Israelis and Palestinians, running side by side but divided by an eight-meter wall.[91] At the end of the Israeli side of the road, cars pass straight into Jerusalem city, without having to queue at a checkpoint, while Palestinians continue driving on a diverted road to the southern West Bank. As well as effectively easing traffic congestion to the benefit of the settlers, Route 4370 supports Israel's separation policy and strengthens the creation of Israeli-only enclaves.[92]

Altogether, these measures "are intended to segregate the population along racial lines"[93] and "combine to ensure that Palestinians remain confined to

---

89      With regards to the apartheid roads system, other authors stressed how this infrastructure system stemmed from the settlers' urge not to see Palestinians. "It was the desire [of the colonists] to live without seeing Palestinians ... that forced Palestinians into small spaces." Nadia Abu Zahra & Adah Kay, Unfree in Palestine: Registration, Documentation and Movement Restrictions 116 (2013).

90      The decision of the High Court (HC 2150/07 Ali Hussein Mahmud Abu Saffiyah v. Minister of Defence et al., Dec. 29, 2009 (Isr.)) followed a petition filed by the Association for Civil Rights in Israel in March 2007, when residents of six of the villages along Route 443 turned to the judiciary for the removal of the obstructions that had been placed to prevent access from the villages to the road, and the cancelation of the ban on Palestinian travel on the road. The Association for Civil Rights in Israel (ACRI), *The illusion of the rule of law on route 443* (May 25, 2010), https://law.acri.org.il/en/2010/05/25/the-lllusion-of-rule-of-law-on-route-443/.

91      *See* Ian Lee, *A wall runs through it: New road divides Israelis and Palestinians*, CNN (Jan. 11, 2019), https://edition.cnn.com/2019/01/11/middleeast/israel-apartheid-road-west-bank-intl/index.html.

92      *See* Lisa Gleeson, *Erasing Palestine*, 1211 Green Left Wkly 16 (2019).

93      HSRC Report, at 21. Similarly, Falk claimed that: "it seems incontestable that Israeli measures do divide the population of the Occupied Palestinian Territory along racial lines [and] create separate reserves for Palestinians." H.R.C., *Human rights situation in*

RESTRICTIONS ON FREEDOM OF MOVEMENT IN THE WEST BANK        165

the reserves designated for them while Israeli Jews ... enjoy freedom of movement throughout the rest of the Palestinian territory."[94] When analyzed from this perspective, the measures enforcing segregation of Palestinian and Jewish populations seem to pertain to the category of inhuman acts outlined under Apartheid Convention article 2(d): "any measures, including legislative measures, designed to divide the population along racial lines by the creation of separate reserves and ghettos for the members of a racial group or groups." This analysis is also supported by the final conclusions of the Russell Tribunal on Palestine, which confirmed:

> Israel has through its laws and practices divided the Israeli Jewish and Palestinian populations and allocated them different physical spaces ... The end result is wholesale territorial fragmentation and a series of separate reserves and enclaves, with the two groups largely segregated ... Such a policy is formally described in Israel as *hafrada*, Hebrew for separation.[95]

C       *Movement Restrictions as a Policy of Apartheid: A Tool for Exclusion*
Among the categories of inhuman acts listed by the Apartheid Convention, under article 2(c), we find:

> any legislative measures and other measures calculated to prevent a racial group or groups from participation in the political, social, economic and cultural life of the country and the deliberate creation of conditions preventing the full development of such a group or groups, in particular by

---

  *Palestine and other occupied Arab territories, Report of the Special Rapporteur on the situation of human rights in the Palestinian territories occupied since 1967, Richard Falk*, U.N. Doc. A/HRC/25/67 (Jan. 13, 2014), para. 71.

94 HSRC Report, at 21. The Committee on the Elimination of Racial Discrimination recently reiterated its concern with regards to this reality: "the Committee is appalled at the hermetic character of the separation of the two groups, who live on the same territory but do not enjoy either equal use of roads and infrastructure or equal access to basic services, lands and water resources. Such separation is materialized by the implementation of a complex combination of movement restrictions consisting of the Wall, the settlements, roadblocks, military checkpoints, the obligation to use separate roads and a permit regime that impacts the Palestinian population negatively (art. 3)." C.E.R.D., *Concluding observations on the combined seventeenth to nineteenth reports of Israel*, U.N. Doc. CERD/C/ISR/CO/17-19 (Jan. 27, 2020), para. 22.

95 Russell Tribunal on Palestine, *Are Israel's practices against the Palestinian People in breach of the prohibition of Apartheid under International law*, para. 5.39, Cape Town, Nov. 5–7, 2011.

denying to members of a racial group or groups basic human rights and freedoms, including ... the right to freedom of movement ...

It is no mystery that, as previously highlighted, Israeli measures of movement constraint in the occupied territories impede Palestinian participation in political, social, economic, and cultural life and create conditions that prevent the population from the enjoyment of further basic human rights, impeding Palestinians' full fulfillment as a group. Numerous reports of reputable human rights organizations provide evidence of the devastating effects of movement restrictions, and denounce the consequent disruption of access to everything that depends on movement: school, shopping, health, education, work, fun, and so on.[96]

The multiple restrictions on the right to freedom of movement combine to form an all-encompassing system of racial discrimination that effectively paralyzes Palestinians' lives, satisfying article 2(c) on all accounts.

## IV     Purposes Unveiled: The Ultimate Goals of Inhuman Acts of Apartheid

Identifying discrete policies and practices as corresponding to those listed in the Apartheid Convention does not *per se* allow for a positive determination on the apartheid test. As required by the wording of article 2, policies and practices must be found to ultimately serve the goal of imposing and maintaining racial domination and systematic oppression on the subordinated racial group. In other words, the human rights violations that were found to match the categories of inhuman acts should not be isolated events or contingencies that prevent Palestinians from travelling, but rather systematic and discriminatory policies and practices of institutionalized domination and oppression. Based on an asymmetry of power, racial domination exists when a given ethnic or racial group is able to exert unconstrained and unjust control over another

---

96    To name but a few: BADIL Resource Center for Palestinian Residency & Refugee Rights, *Forced Population Transfer: The Case of Palestine. Installment of a permit regime* (Dec. 2015), https://www.badil.org/phocadownloadpap/badil-new/publications/research/working -papers/wp18-FPT-Israeli-permit-system.pdf; Human Rights Watch, *Separate and Unequal. Israel's Discriminatory Treatment of Palestinians in the Occupied Palestinian Territories* (Dec. 2010), https://www.hrw.org/sites/default/files/reports/iopt1210webw cover_0.pdf; Amnesty International (2003); B'Tselem, *Arrested Development. The Long Term Impact of Israel's Separation Barrier in the West Bank* (Oct. 2012), https://www.btse lem.org/sites/default/files/sites/default/files2/201210_arrested_development_eng.pdf.

RESTRICTIONS ON FREEDOM OF MOVEMENT IN THE WEST BANK 167

group, which is thereby deprived of the ability to dictate their own terms: the dominator gets to choose when and how to use the power, with no consideration for the interests of the subjugated.[97] When the abuse of power results in acts of social, psychological or physical violence perpetrated systematically by institutional actors, domination gives way to oppression, leaving the targeted group in a condition of extreme vulnerability and exposure to further violations in their rights and dignity. The existence of these features can be determined through consideration of the methods and techniques deployed to implement the restrictions. The following sections highlight the primary features of the Israeli system of domination in the West Bank: surveillance, arbitrariness, harassment, and humiliation.

A    *Elements of Surveillance and Arbitrariness: The Purpose of Domination*

In an article published in Haaretz in 2005, Amira Hass wrote: "Israel's control of ... the Palestinians' freedom of movement is not reflected merely in Israel's presence in roadblocks and checkpoints. It derives first and foremost from controlling the Palestinian population registration."[98] Indeed, identification is central to the system of governance implemented by Israel in the West Bank. The lesser status Palestinians are condemned to, also in terms of freedom of movement, is implemented through the bureaucracy of mobility. A sophisticated and computerized identification system,[99] ID cards and different types of permits combine to determine a match between the cardholders and a map of the zones they are allowed into or banned from.[100] Because identification leads to an automation of deprivation and exclusion, it was argued that

> the quintessential Palestinian experience ... takes place ... at any one of those many modern barriers where identities are checked and verified ... for it is at these borders and barriers that the Palestinians are singled out

---

97    *See* Antony Anghie, *Domination*, in Concepts for International Law 222 (Jean D'Aspremont & Sahib Singh eds., 2019).

98    Amira Hass, *You exist if the Israeli computer says so*, Haaretz (Sep. 28, 2005), https://www.haaretz.com/1.4876118.

99    "Personal details, including name, age, date and place of birth, political affiliation and security record, are held in a central database accessed by Israeli officials at checkpoints and borders." David Lyon, *Identification, colonialism, and control. Surveillant sorting in Israel/Palestine*, in Surveillance and Control in Israel/Palestine, Population, Territory and Power 49, 53 (Elia Zureik et al. eds., 2011).

100   See Jennifer Loewenstein, *Identity and Movement Control in the OPT*, 26 Forced Migration Rev. 24 (2006).

for 'special treatment' and are forcefully reminded of their identity: of who they are, and of why they are different from others.[101]

Following the 1982 Identity Card Carrying and Displaying Act, all residents over sixteen years old had to carry their cards at all times and display it on demand to Israeli officers. The ID cards, fixing identities on pieces of paper and on their holders, function as a means of social sorting. Palestinian residents of the West Bank are issued green cards, while Jewish-Israelis are issued blue cards no matter where they reside.[102] By virtue of this differentiation, the settlers are entitled to enjoy unfettered mobility, while Palestinians are contained within specific boundaries and "dependent on the Israeli state apparatus for the authorization to move across certain spaces inside and between the OPTs."[103] Moreover, when a card is issued, the identity of the holder is matched by the Israeli Ministry of Interior to an identification number. This code allows access to the holder's personal details and information (down to political affiliation and security record) held in a central database easily accessible to the officers stationed at the checkpoints.[104] Through these identification numbers, Israeli authorities render Palestinians more legible. They function as a point of contact where the Israeli regime of population control meets the Palestinian individuals, transforming them into an underprivileged and motionless group. The ID cards with their identification numbers embody the symbol of a widespread surveillance mechanism,[105] and contribute significantly to the nexus of power that enables Israel to create fragmented and controlled spatial conditions and to manage Palestinians' activities.

---

101    Rashid Khalidi, Palestinian Identity: The Construction of Modern National Consciousness 1 (1997).

102    See Helga Tawil-Souri, *Orange, green and blue, Color-coded paperwork for Palestinian population control*, in Surveillance and Control in Israel/Palestine, Population, Territory and Power 219 (Elia Zureik et al. eds., 2011).

103    Helga Tawil-Souri, *Uneven border, coloured (im)mobilities: ID cards in Palestine/Israel*, 17 Geopolitics 153, 164 (2012).

104    See Andrew Stevens, *Surveillance Policies, Practices and Technologies in Israel and the Occupied Palestinian Territories: Assessing the Security State* (Social Sciences and Humanities Research Council of Canada, 2010), https://www.sscqueens.org/sites/ssc queens.org/files/2011-11-Stevens-WPIV_0.pdf.

105    The entanglement of the ID system with a politics of control, coercion and fear is further analyzed in: Nadia Abu Zahra, *Identity cards and coercion in Palestine*, in Fear: Critical Geopolitics and Everyday Life (Rachel Pain and Susan Smith eds., 2008); Nigel Parsons & Mark B. Salter, *Israeli Biopolitics: Closure, Territorialisation and Governmentality in the Occupied Palestinian Territories*, 13 Geopolitics 701 (2008).

# RESTRICTIONS ON FREEDOM OF MOVEMENT IN THE WEST BANK 169

The system is enforced to effectively restrict freedom of movement and access, but also (and above all) to give the Palestinian population the feeling that they are being constantly watched, as if in some kind of panopticon. This is the exact purpose of checkpoints (especially flying checkpoints), where identities are verified, documents checked, vehicles searched, people stopped, questioned, delayed, and sometimes harassed and sent back for no apparent reason. Despite the declared purpose of security,[106] testimonies of former Israeli soldiers reveal that checkpoints actually pursue a different intent:

> the goal is that as many people as possible are aware that there could be a checkpoint when they leave home ... As a Palestinian, you should always have the feeling that the IDF can catch you somewhere along the way ... The goal of this is ... causing a feeling that the IDF controls the area. That your ability to reach point Y from point X depends on the IDF.[107]

Every Palestinian has experienced being stopped unexpectedly along their way and knows perfectly well that it can happen anytime. Checkpoints serve as a warning and constant reminder that the military forces are keeping watch, like a Big Brother. These dynamics reveal a dimension of ruling for the sake of governance, where security is a mere pretext for displaying power. Besides, the control is carried out with such a scantily disguised neglect and ill-concealed arbitrariness that it is more than evident that the logic of checkpoints is not related to security, but rather to demonstrating presence and displaying supremacy while disrupting the normal daily life of a subdued population that has no effective means of disputing even the most unreasonable of commands.

Further subjugation of Palestinian civilians comes from the unpredictable and capricious behavior of soldiers on duty.[108] The military have the power

---

106 As highlighted by Victor Kattan, "not all ... checkpoints ... separate Israelis from Palestinians. Some of them separate Palestinians from each other, and in these cases, it is difficult to see what the security rationale for their existence is." Kattan, at 1509.

107 Breaking the Silence, *Causing a feeling that the IDF controls the area*, Testimony of a First Sergeant of Nahal Unit, 50th Battalion, Nablus area (2013), https://www.breakingthe silence.org.il/testimonies/database/140630.

108 "The level and type of enforcement of checkpoints shifted from day to day and hour to hour. Sometimes only women were let through, and sometimes nobody. Occasionally the checkpoint was open all day, and at other times closed in the afternoon. Often no cars would be allowed through and people would have to pass on foot. At other times the soldiers would not let people pass through the checkpoint at all but would allow them to walk over the hill in full view. These constant shifts meant that when approaching a checkpoint, it was never entirely clear whether a person, even one with normally 'valid' identity papers, would be allowed through, turned back, or detained at the side of the

of not letting people through checkpoints, and they use it in the most creative and arbitrary declinations, even when all the paperwork is in order and there is no hint of a security threat.[109] Such arbitrariness is a key feature in the implementation of restrictions. It does not amount to randomness. In fact, it is a systematic, routinized, and generalized form of arbitrariness. Likewise, the consequent extensive production of uncertainty and confusion is not a collateral effect, but rather an anticipated component whose effect is to transform nearly every movement into a lottery. The result is that the surveilled clearly perceive that their rights are at the mercy of the military, and that the military hold full control and decision-making power.

A certain degree of arbitrariness pertains to almost all instruments designed to manage Palestinian movement. Although the Wall's massive and imposing structure leaves no doubt about the presence of a permanent barrier,[110] the opening times of its gates are not only limited but also extremely arbitrary.[111] The process of permit granting and the grounds for permit denial are arbitrary. The placement and the types of inspections at the flying checkpoints are arbitrary. They all depend on the will of the Israeli authorities and express the supremacy of Israeli power. In this sense, it was argued that "Israeli controls on Palestinian mobility are arguably worse than the passbook system, because they are capricious and random."[112] Unlike the highly regulated and predictable apartheid in South Africa, the Israeli regime of discriminatory and arbitrary restrictions is realized through a "web of relatively obscure and inaccessible military orders and regulations,"[113] combined with bureaucratic procedures and practices that are most often racialized in implementation rather than in wording. The result – meticulously pursued – is that Palestinians are unable to anticipate what kind of unexpected event will hinder their travel. Such unpredictability can be best observed in relation to the permit regime.

---

road. Much depended on the individual soldier." Tobias Kelly, *Documented Lives: Fear and the Uncertainties of Law during the Second Palestinian Intifada*, 12 J. Royal Anthropology Soc'y 89, 100 (2006).

109     Observers on shift from MachsomWatch report an example that verges on the absurd: "five or six people were sent home [from A'anin Checkpoint] because they were dressed too nicely. Why? Because people who have permits to cross at an agricultural checkpoint should not be dressed in clean clothes. They must be headed for some coffee house or to blow up Tel Aviv." MachsomWatch, *Northern checkpoint: Why have I been going to the checkpoints for 17 years?* (May 15, 2019), https://machsomwatch.org/en/reports/checkpoints/15052019/morning/65647.

110     ICJ Wall Advisory Opinion, para. 121.

111     *See* U.N. Doc. A/HRC/12/37 (Aug. 19, 2009).

112     Peteet (2009), at 24.

113     Dugard & Reynolds, at 897.

RESTRICTIONS ON FREEDOM OF MOVEMENT IN THE WEST BANK 171

As previously noted, the permit system through which the Israeli authorities selectively authorize Palestinian movement in restricted areas and on
restricted roads can give the misleading impression that Israel is showing
concern and consideration for the needs of the civilians.[114] However, the true
rationale of the policy lies behind the opacity of the procedures of permit
granting. The complete lack of transparency creates space for discretionary
responses and ultimately makes approvals exceptional.[115] Different types of
permits of different durations exist. According to the nature of the needs to
be satisfied, the applicants are requested to fill out forms and submit documentation to certify their needs. On top of the complexity and duration of the
procedure, what matters is that, in the end, "in most cases the decision is based
on the discretion of the DCL staff,"[116] and rejections are often vaguely justified
by unspecified security reasons.[117] The fact that the procedures are so obscure
that the granting of a permit seems more of a random exception than a matter
of paperwork, and the absence of recourse against denials leaves Palestinians
once again exposed to the authority and whims of those in power.

The many elements of the system of restrictions combine to form Israel's
"matrix of control,"[118] a grid of obstacles that paralyzes Palestinians and
cements Israel's supremacy. In short, movement restrictions are part of a system of control that Israel uses to dominate over the Palestinian territory and
people, to maintain the supremacy, and to deepen the occupation. Overall,
it has been argued that the efforts Israel puts into tightening its grip on the
area and weakening Palestinians through restrictive measures and impediment of movement is "so intense, that the evidence ... of Israel's intent to

---

114    See B'Tselem, *Forbidden Roads. Israel's Discriminatory Road Regime in the West Bank*
(Aug. 2004), [*hereinafter* B'tselem Forbidden Roads] https://www.btselem.org/publica
tions/summaries/200408_forbidden_roads.

115    OCHA reported a dramatic decline in the approval rate over the past years: from
76% of successful applications in 2014 to 28% in 2018. *See* U.N. OCHA, *Fewer permits
granted to access land behind Barrier* (Feb. 2019), https://www.ochaopt.org/content/
fewer-permits-granted-access-land-behind-barrier.

116    B'Tselem, Forbidden Roads, at 37. Established in 1995 in the framework of the Oslo II
agreement, the District Civil Liaison office was meant to foster coordination between
Israel's governmental systems and the Palestinian Authority. Among its functions, there is
the handling of permit applications.

117    "This regime has no clear rules. Decisions are made arbitrarily and without explanation,
and Israel views every permit it issues as an act of charity on its part, a favor it bestows."
B'Tselem, *The Occupation in its 51st Year* (2018), at 5, https://www.btselem.org/sites/
default/files/publications/51st_year_of_occupation_eng.pdf.

118    See Jeff Halper, *The 94 Percent Solution: A Matrix of Control*, 216 Middle East Res. & Info.
Project 14 (2000).

172                                                                    FERRANDO

maintain control over the area permanently is ... unequivocal, manifest and conclusive."[119]

## B        *Elements of Harassment and Humiliation: The Purpose of Oppression*

Together with domination, the purpose of oppression constitutes a structural element of the inhuman acts as defined by the Apartheid Convention and the Rome Statute. Oppression subsists in cases of systemic and institutional abuse of power resulting in acts of social, psychological, and sometimes physical violence against a group that is considered and consequently treated as inferior. According to the former UN Special Rapporteur Richard Falk, in the West Bank

> Israeli policies have ... institutionalized just how lightly a civilian Palestinian life may be weighed, when placed on the scales against claims of overarching security concerns ... The combined effect of the measures designed to ensure security for Israeli citizens ... is *hafrada*, discrimination and systematic oppression of ... the Palestinian people.[120]

This is because the enforcement of such measures is accompanied by humiliating procedures, practices of harassment, and – perhaps to a lesser extent nowadays than before – excessive use of force, which reflect and preserve the unjust relations between groups and the monopoly of privilege and power to the detriment of Palestinians. Once again, the checkpoints prove to be the stage where these dynamics are most evident. Checkpoints – where Israeli authorities and Palestinians most frequently interact and where roles and identities are continuously reaffirmed – unveil the relation of subjugation that forces many Palestinians to perform rituals of obedience and submission to gratuitous and deliberate persecution. As indicated by John Dugard, "one quarter of all IDF soldiers who have served at roadblocks in the West Bank reported having witnessed or taken part in an act of abuse against a Palestinian civilian."[121] He claims that the checkpoints serve to harass and humiliate Palestinians, and his assertion rests on countless testimonies of civilians, human rights defenders and former members of the armed forces. Military testimonies describe the operative intent of checkpoints as "to torment"[122] the Palestinian population. In the way the soldiers perform their duty, a great deal has to do with

---

119    Sfard, at 32.
120    U.N. Doc. A/HRC/16/72 (Jan. 10, 2011), para. 77.
121    U.N. Doc. A/HRC/7/17 (Jan. 21, 2008), para. 35.
122    Breaking the Silence, *We're going up now to mess up the everyday routines*, Testimony of a First Sergeant of Nachshon Battalion Unit, Tulkarem area (2008), https://www.breaking thesilence.org.il/testimonies/database/217805.

RESTRICTIONS ON FREEDOM OF MOVEMENT IN THE WEST BANK          173

the awareness of their superior status, which they continuously express and
reaffirm by means of arbitrarily castigating and punishing civilians with the
sole intention of displaying power and causing subjection. Willful vexation is
pursued through the invasiveness of controls, the mortification of privacy and
dignity and the soldiers' aggressive and humiliating demeanor. In some – for-
tunately exceptional – cases, episodes of ordinary and daily harassment can
escalate and result in violence and casualties.[123]

However, even without pointing out episodes of particularly extreme and
cruel initiatives of the military, the very existence of checkpoints and the routine security procedures that lots of Palestinians undergo daily are enough to
show how unbearable and oppressive the mechanisms of movement restrictions are designed to be. The misery of the checkpoint experience is encapsulated in the words of Abu Hashhash – field officer for the human rights
organization B'Tselem – who confirmed that the essential logic of checkpoints

> is humiliation. It is to harden your life, to make your life hell ... Humiliation
> can be as simple as being made to stand – to stand, just looking, knowing
> nothing about when you will be released ... You are not under arrest. But
> they can do whatever they want. They can forbid you from smoking, or
> from talking to your friend next to you ... you have to hold things on your
> shoulder, waiting for gates to be open, in the sun or sometimes in the
> rain. This is humiliation.[124]

It is clear then that security is at best a secondary justification for the intricate and capricious system of movement restrictions in the West Bank. A
careful analysis of the measures as implemented and experienced by the subjects involved reveals features of intended domination and oppression over
the Palestinian population. From the above examination of the inhuman acts
of denial of freedom of movement perpetrated by Israel in the West Bank,
it is clear that such acts do not occur in a random and isolated manner but
rather contribute to the implementation of a widespread, institutionalized,
and oppressive regime, founded on discriminatory practices which result in

---

123    *See* Yoav Zitun, *Humiliation and sloppy security checks at IDF checkpoints*, Ynet News
        (July 27, 2015) https://www.ynetnews.com/articles/0,7340,L-4682202,00.html. In addi-
        tion, evidence of this kind of incidents is provided by several human rights organizations.
        Wide collections of testimonies are available on their websites. *See* Breaking the Silence
        (https://www.breakingthesilence.org.il/testimonies/database/?ci=141); MachsomWatch
        (https://machsomwatch.org/en/daily-reports/checkpoints); Al-Haq (*see* Al Haq, *Death
        Traps: Israel's Use of Force at Checkpoints in the West Bank* (July 2011), https://www.alhaq
        .org/publications/8154.html).
124    Longo, at 1018.

the oppressive domination of the Palestinian people. Consequently, the commission of such practices satisfies the definition of inhuman acts of apartheid provided by international law.

## V    Conclusion

Taking as its springboard that approaching the restrictions on freedom of movement imposed by Israel in the West Bank as violations of IHL provides a limited understanding of the phenomenon, this article argues that applying the apartheid paradigm for the assessment of movement restrictions leads to a more precise comprehension of Israeli practices. As demonstrated in this article, such practices do not respond to concerns for a security threatened by the risk of Palestinian attacks. They are designed and implemented with the goal of maintaining absolute domination over the Palestinian population. The restrictions on freedom of movement as enacted by Israel in the West Bank are part of a widespread and systematic regime of subjugation of the Palestinian population, and not only constitute discrete violations of IHL, but also represent a strategic tool in pursuing forcible segregation of the population, discriminatory access to resources, differentiated enjoyment of rights, and consequent dynamics of power and domination. In other words, Israel has established a system of apartheid.[125]

---

125    It must be noted that Israeli policies and practices amount to apartheid in all four domains identified by the ESCWA report: Palestinian citizens of Israel, Palestinian residents of Jerusalem, Palestinians of the oPt, and Palestinian refugees or exiles. This article focused exclusively on the West Bank as part of the third domain. However, the prolonged illegal closure of the Gaza Strip constitutes an integral part of Israel's fragmentation of the Palestinian people of the Occupied Territories, as it is "committed with the intention of maintaining its institutionalized regime of systematic racial domination, oppression, and persecution of the Palestinian people." Al Mezan Center for Human Rights, *Human rights organizations welcome Concluding Observations of the UN Committee on the Elimination of Racial Discrimination on racial segregation and apartheid on both sides of the Green Line*, Press Release (Dec. 20, 2019). For a thorough focus on the Gaza Strip in the apartheid perspective, *see* Adel Manna, *Deconstructing the Israeli Socio-political Apartheid System*, 18 Theory & Event (Jan. 2015). For a holistic and comprehensive analysis of the apartheid system in historic Palestine, *see* Al-Haq, BADIL, The Palestinian Center for Human Rights, Al Mezan, Addameer, The Civic Coalition for Palestinian Rights in Jerusalem, The Cairo Institute for Human Rights Studies, and Habitat International Coalition, *Joint Parallel Report to the United Nations Committee on the Elimination of Racial Discrimination on Israel's Seventeenth to Nineteenth Periodic Reports* (Nov. 10, 2019), https://tbinternet .ohchr.org/Treaties/CERD/Shared%20Documents/ISR/INT_CERD_NGO_ISR_39700_E.pdf.

RESTRICTIONS ON FREEDOM OF MOVEMENT IN THE WEST BANK          175

This conclusion is not just a subtle formality nor a mere matter of labels. Israel's system of imposed restrictions constitutes a breach of the prohibition of apartheid. Such an absolute prohibition stands in contrast to the grey area left by doctrines of international humanitarian law such as "military necessity" and "security needs," that Israel easily manipulates and distorts in its narratives in order to justify its practices. As the prohibition of apartheid entails international legal responsibility for the perpetrator, in the event of these findings being confirmed by an authoritative advisory opinion of the ICJ, there would be far-reaching legal consequences.[126] Notwithstanding the undiminished responsibilities Israel bears as the occupying power under IHL, new responsibilities arise for the international community from the finding that Israel is breaching the international legal prohibition on apartheid. Since the unlawful regime of apartheid is contrary to peremptory norms of *jus cogens*, all states must oppose its perpetration.

While Israel bears an obligation to cease its acts of apartheid and make reparation for its wrongful practices, third states must comply with the legitimate common interest in such violations not occurring and not being excused or justified. All states – whether or not they are individually affected by the gross violations – bear a duty to cooperate to bring Israeli inhuman acts of apartheid to an end, and a duty to abstain from rendering aid or assistance to Israel and from recognizing the illegal situations arising from such acts.[127] Likewise, the intergovernmental organizations are bound by the peremptory prohibition on apartheid, with consequent responsibility for failure in acting to end unlawful regimes.[128]

---

126    The State of Palestine acceded to the Apartheid Convention on Apr. 2, 2014; *see*: https:// treaties.un.org/Pages/ViewDetails.aspx?src=IND&mtdsg_no=IV-7&chapter=4&clang=_ en). As soon as Dec. 2014, the Government of Palestine also lodged a declaration under Rome Statute article 12(3), accepting the ICC's jurisdiction and subsequently acceding to the Rome Statute. *See* President Mahmoud Abbas, *Declaration Accepting the Jurisdiction of the International Criminal Court*, International Criminal Court Press Release (Dec. 31, 2014), http://www.icc-cpi.int/iccdocs/PIDS/press/Palestine_A_12-3.pdf; ICC, *Palestine declares acceptance of ICC jurisdiction since 13 June 2014*, ICC Press Release (Jan. 5, 2015), https://www.icc-cpi.int/Pages/item.aspx?name=pr1080&ln=en.

127    *See* Sean D. Murphy, *Peremptory Norms of General International Law (Jus Cogens) and Other Topics: The Seventy-First Session of the International Law Commission*, 68 Am. J. Int'l L. 114 (2020); Diakonia International Humanitarian Law Resource Centre, *Everyone's Business: Third Party Responsibility and the Enforcement of International Law in the oPt* (Oct. 2016), https://www.diakonia.se/ihl/publications/israeli-palestinian-conflict/third -party-responsibility-enforcement-international-law-palestine/.

128    *See* Magali Thill, EU obligations and duty to end Israeli policies of Forced Transfer, Colonialism and Apartheid in Occupied East Jerusalem (European Coordination of

The significance of the above conclusions on apartheid does not only lie in the different applicable international law or in the legal consequences entailed: it calls into question the very nature of the conflict and opens new prospects for its resolution. The core feature of the regime perpetrated by Israel was never effectively addressed by past attempts to resolve the conflict, which always focused on peace talks and definition of borders. Instead, identification of the underlying logic of racial domination and oppression should be the starting point for the successful defeat and elimination of the doctrine and practice of domination of which the inhuman acts of apartheid committed by Israel are a manifestation.

Committees and Associations for Palestine, 2014); Cezary Mik, *Jus Cogens in Contemporary International Law*, 27 Polish Y.B. Int'l L. 33 (2014); Ramses Wessel, *The UN, the EU and Jus Cogens*, 1 Int'l Org. L. Rev. 3 (Jan. 2006).

# PART 2

*Case Commentaries*

∴

# Will the German Judiciary Protect the Right to Boycott, Divestment, and Sanctions?

*Nadija Samour and Ahmed Abed*

### Contents

I    Case Overview and Implications
II   Access to Venues
    A   *Access to Public Venues*
    B   *Access to Private Venues*
III  Visa Withdrawal and Ban of Political Activities
    A   *The Case of Rasmea Odeh*
    B   *The Case of Khaled Barakat*
    C   *International Reactions to the Bundestag Motion*
IV  Outlook: The Defamation of BDS as a Matter of Constitutional Rights

---

In recent years, Germany has become one of the fiercest battlegrounds for the Israeli Ministry of Strategic Affairs. Besides orchestrated public smear campaigns against individuals[1] and organizations – not only because of their support for

---

1   For example, the resignation of Professor Schäfer from his post as Director of the Jewish Museum Berlin following a retweet of the statement of 240 Jewish and Israeli intellectuals opposing the anti-BDS motion and asking for maintaining the liberal notion of freedom of speech which they see threatened. *See* Jewish Museum Berlin Foundation, *Professor Schäfer resigns from his post as Director of the Jewish Museum Berlin Foundation*, Press Release (June 14, 2019), https://www.jmberlin.de/en/press-release-june-14-2019. *See also* the statement of Jewish scholars defending Mr. Schäfer: *Jewish Studies and Other Scholars in Support of Prof. Peter Schäfer*, https://docs.google.com/document/d/1VxNVOk2n3UESYMbfeSovM4mpSLPKgj1nyWhsDBOIWPo/edit. Another attempt at a "social death" following an accusation of being anti-Semitic concerns Dr. Anna Younes, contributor to the Islamophobia Report 2015, 2017, and 2018. She was disinvited from a panel on anti-Muslim racism organized by the party DIE LINKE because of her "proximity to BDS" – which is a typical phrasing describing guilt by association. *See* Academia for Equality, https://www.facebook.com/academiaforequality/posts/a-letter-we-sent-to-die-linke-the-german-left-party-protesting-its-conduct-towar/2433957430193575/. In the course of the events, it has become clear that the panel organizers were provided with data on Dr. Younes (possibly collected unlawfully) by RIAS, a publicly funded organization combatting anti-Semitism.

Palestinian rights, but also due to their deviance from the official German official line[2,3] – the Ministry has intensified its "lawfare." This involves the strategic deployment of legal means to achieve political ends, namely, to undermine the campaign for Boycott, Divestment, and Sanctions (BDS) that seeks to hold Israel accountable for violating its obligations under international law. This lawfare's most crucial achievement in 2019 was the push for the German Bundestag's motion titled "Firmly opposing the BDS movement – fighting anti-Semitism," which was passed on May 17, 2019. The motion, which compares the BDS campaign to anti-Semitic Nazi practices, contained 6 resolutions:

> The German Bundestag resolves
> 1. to once again resolutely oppose any form of anti-Semitism as it arises and to condemn the BDS campaign and the call to boycott Israeli goods or companies as well as Israeli scientists, artists or sportsmen and women;
> 2. not to offer access to premises and facilities under the administration of the Bundestag available to any organizations that make anti-Semitic statements or question Israel's right to exist. The German Bundestag calls on the Federal Government not to support any events by the BDS movement or by groups actively pursuing its goals;
> 3. to continue its support for the Federal Government and the Commissioner for Jewish Life in Germany and the fight against anti-Semitism both in the prevention and in the determined fight against anti-Semitism and any form of extremism;
> 4. not to financially support organizations that question Israel's right to exist;
> 5. not to financially support projects that call for a boycott of Israel or that actively support the BDS movement;
> 6. to call on the federal states, cities and municipalities and all public actors to adopt this position.

---

2  For example, the German section of Jewish Voice for Peace has been smeared as anti-Semitic for defending the right to BDS. In 2019, the organization was awarded the Göttinger Peace Award, which came along a vile smear-campaign but also countless acts of solidarity. For a documentation of the events, *see* Jüdische Stimme, *Stellungnahme des Vorsitzender der Jury zu Kritik an dem Preisträger*, die Jüdische Stimme (Feb. 15 2019), https://www.juedische-stimme.de/2019/02/15/stellungnahme-des-vorsitzender-der-jury-zu-kritik-an-dem-preis traeger-die-juedische-stimme/.

3  *See* Speech of Chancellor Dr. Angela Merkel in front of the Israeli Knesset on Mar. 18, 2008, https://www.bundesregierung.de/breg-de/service/bulletin/rede-von-bundeskanzlerin -dr-angela-merkel-796170.

The motion generated an intense debate within and outside of the Bundestag.[4] Members of parliament (MPs) expressed their concerns with regards to an "atmosphere of intimidation" targeting critics of Israeli occupation.[5] Policy experts criticized the motion as stigmatizing and as a violation of the constitutional right of holding and expressing an opinion.[6] Activists in Germany[7] and outside it[8] mobilized against the motion. Even 32 leading cultural institutions have founded the "Initiative GG 5.3 Weltoffenheit" to request the redemption of the motion.[9] An investigative report by the German magazine Der Spiegel shed light on dubious lobby activities and unprecedent influence exerted on members of parliament that led to the passing of the motion.[10] The "Werteinitiative," an association dedicated to promote "German-Jewish positions," which was founded only in 2018, pushed behind the scenes for the stigmatization of BDS as anti-Semitic. According to Der Spiegel, some MPs described the association's activities as "systematic interference" with parliamentary affairs, for example by pre-formulating and presenting the draft that later became the anti-BDS motion.

However, the content and goal of the Bundestag motion is nothing new to the informed observer. Parliaments of German federal states and communes such as Bonn, North Rhine-Westphalia, Munich, and others have already adopted similar motions to further the defamation and stigmatization of the

---

4   See Friedrich-Ebert-Stiftung Palestine, *Bundestag's Resolution on BDS Sparks Widespread Outrage* (May 24, 2019), https://palestine.fes.de/de/e/bundestags-resolution-on-bds -sparks-widespread-outrage.

5   See Interview with MP and former minister for environmental affairs Jürgen Trittin, *Ein Klima der Einschüchterung*, TAZ (May 16, 2019), https://taz.de/Juergen-Trittin-zur -Boykottbewegung-BDS/!5592992/.

6   See *Im Kampf gegen Antisemitismus hilft das nicht*, Die Zeit (June 4, 2019), https://www .zeit.de/politik/deutschland/2019-06/israel-boykott-bds-antisemitismus-meinungsfrei heit-bundesregierung/komplettansicht; *A Call to German Parties not to equate BDS with anti-Semitism*, statement by more than 240 Jewish and Israeli scholars, May 2019, available at: https://www.haaretz.com/embeds/pdf_upload/2019/20190516-185634.pdf.

7   See, e.g., Palästina Spricht, the coalition for Palestinian rights and against racism, that organized a protest in front of the Bundestag on June 28, 2019, https://www.facebook .com/events/891718771177610/.

8   See Palestinian National BDS Committee, *Palestinians unanimously condemn German Parliament's attack on the right to boycott Israel's apartheid and colonization* (May 24 2019), https://bdsmovement.net/news/palestinians-unanimously-condemn-german -parliament's-attack-right-boycott-israel's-apartheid.

9   See Plädoyer der „Initiative GG 5.3 Weltoffenheit" (Dec. 2020), https://www.hebbel-am -ufer.de/fileadmin/Hau/website_material/pdfs/201210_PlaedoyerFuerWeltoffenheit.pdf.

10  See *Wie zwei Vereine die deutsche Nahostpolitik beeinflussen wollen*, Der Spiegel (July 12, 2019), https://www.spiegel.de/politik/lobbyismus-im-bundestag-wie-zwei-vereine-die -deutsche-nahostpolitik-beeinflussen-wollen-a-00000000-0002-0001-0000-000164871539.

BDS movement. Even before the passing of motions became popular, individuals and organizations affiliated with BDS had already faced a backlash in German media outlets. In the past, public and private rooms for events on Palestine were cancelled,[11] individuals lost their jobs or were withheld job and funding opportunities,[12] and cultural projects and events were threatened with losing funding,[13] all because of actual or seeming BDS affiliation.

What is the effect of the Bundestag motion? What is certain is that there is no legal foundation for how the motion is being used in the battle against Palestinian rights. The entire (legal) backlash is unfolding even though the motion of the Bundestag claims to be non-binding. This means that BDS activists are not confronted with a law that clarifies in which legal space they are supposed to navigate. What is worse is that BDS activists in Germany are facing a legal grey-zone whose undefined limits have chilling effects on political speech and protest.

Some commentators refer to the motion as "criminalizing" BDS,[14] but it is important to stress that it technically has not done so. The campaign for Palestinian rights is not and cannot be criminalized in a legal sense; neither can the publicly expressed position of supporting BDS be banned according to criminal law. Lawyers agree that this would be a clear violation of the constitutional right to hold and express an opinion. Furthermore, BDS in Germany is not organized as a registered association but rather as a loose network, which makes it practically and legally impossible to ban it. Still, it is no wonder that the term "criminalization" is used because, in fact, the exclusion and defamation that activists faced have developed into something that now appears to be state-sanctioned. In contrast, in the past, such backlash had been an often inconvenient but tolerable factor in the public battle of opinions. Whereas in

---

11    A list of cancelled or disrupted events on Palestine between 2005 and 2018 counts almost 100 such incidents in Germany; *see*: https://senderfreiespalaestina.de/pdfs/liste-absage -veranstaltungen-01.12.18-2.pdf. The list has been updated but has not been uploaded yet. As of Jan. 2020, more than 150 cancelled or disrupted events have been counted.

12    Among many, *see* the following examples: "political scientist Roldán Mendivíl loses teaching contract at the Freie University Berlin because of BDS-affiliation": *Peinliche Posse bei den Politologen*, TAZ (Jan. 18, 2018), https://taz.de/Meinungsfreiheit-an-Berliner -Universitaet/!5372052/.

13    An Iranian refugee NGO in Berlin was threatened by the Berlin municipality with financial cuts if they allowed a BDS event to happen in their center. *See* Benjamin Weinthal, *Berlin-financed NGO cancels talk with 'antisemitic' activist Manal Tamimi*, Jerusalem Post (Sep. 12, 2018), https://www.jpost.com/BDS-THREAT/Berlin-financed-NGO-cancels-talk -with-antisemitic-activist-Manal-Tamimi-567063. See also the repeated threats of cutting state funding against Theater X, a migrant youth self-organized theatre in Berlin: *Staatlich geförderter Antisemitismus*, Die Welt (June 2, 2019), https://www.welt.de/politik/ deutschland/article194562691/BDS-Bewegung-Staatlich-gefoerderter-Antisemitismus.html.

14    *See Bundestag verurteilt BDS-Bewegung*, Zeit Online (May 17, 2019), https://www.zeit.de/ politik/deutschland/2019-05/israel-boykott-bds-bundestag-foerderung-entzug.

WILL THE GERMAN JUDICIARY PROTECT THE RIGHT TO BDS? 183

the past, public smear campaigns by pro-Zionist outlets or organizations were a necessary component in banning anything BDS related, today, following the anti-BDS motion of the Bundestag, state authority itself is mobilized. This is the case for example in extremely repressive acts such as visa withdrawals, bans of political activities, or the recent announcement of the Berlin minister for domestic affairs that the intelligence service ought to begin observing BDS activists.[15] Just recently, in July 2020, the federal intelligence service mentioned BDS in a special report on anti-Semitism under the category "secular Palestinians," neglecting the systematic discrimination of Palestinians, and mentioning the motion of the Deutsche Bundestag.[16]

While it is fair to say that the Israeli Ministry for Strategic Affairs has intensified its lawfare, BDS activists and Palestinians in Germany have come together to protect freedom of speech and the right of assembly. They have done so with a clear analysis of the political context in which these developments have been taking place, namely, that all of this is happening in the context of a wider shift to the political right throughout Europe.

This commentary will present an overview of the legal achievements and setbacks and focus on the question: will the German judiciary be able to protect the right to BDS? As shall be illustrated below, the Bundestag motion had significant effects despite its non-binding legal status, because officials and judges across Germany cited it to justify encroachments upon political speech of pro-Palestine activists in cases ranging from access to public and private venues to granting visa to speakers.

## I    Case Overview and Implications

The violation of fundamental rights of BDS activists or those who have been rightly or wrongly associated with BDS is reflected in various ways. This section focuses on cases that have been litigated in court, either because of their high topicality or because of their severity. However, it must be noted that the backlash against BDS is broader than what can be reflected by analyzing court cases. Yet, these cases are worth mentioning. For example, we are aware of dozens of cases in which individuals applied for jobs or public funding for their projects and were rejected. In some cases, the rejections have officially been based on general considerations, but it has become clear in private

---

15    See *Sie stellen das Existenzrecht Israels in Frage*, Zeit Online (Sep. 25, 2019), https://www.zeit.de/politik/deutschland/2019-09/andreas-geisel-innensenator-berlin-bds-bewegung-verfassungsschutz.

16    See Bundesamt für Verfassungsschutz, *Lagebild Antisemitismus* (July 2020), at 77, https://www.verfassungsschutz.de/SharedDocs/publikationen/DE/2020/lagebild-antisemitismus.html;jsessionid=6AEA7003503560BA9A45B28E2A26F4B9.intranet241.

conversations that in fact these rejections were decided based on the applicants' pro-BDS positions.

In other cases, rejections were explicitly justified because of the applicants' pro-BDS positions. For instance, a renowned anti-discrimination organization in Berlin first accepted, then declined, employing an individual to offer anti-discrimination training to civil servants. The anti-discrimination training would not have touched any issues related to BDS or Palestine. Yet, the organization wrote: "Dear [XY], we cannot continue to work with you due to your positions with regards to the BDS campaign." In another case, a cultural worker received a termination for a project to sensitize pupils for racism and discrimination. The organizers took her suggestion to discuss their own Palestinian refugee history as a hint to check if she ever supported BDS and justified their cancellation of contract with her support of an open letter in support of author Kamila Shamsie.[17]

It is also worth mentioning the backlash in the cultural and art scene that the Bundestag motion gave cover for. Some cases have gained international attention, such as the principled stance of United States (US) rap artist Talib Kweli not to sign an agreement to distance himself from BDS.[18] Also, the case of Kamila Shamsie, renowned British-Pakistani author, drew international attention when the jury of the Nelly-Sachs prize reversed its decision to honor her work with an award, citing her support for BDS.[19] Moreover, the international arts festival "Ruhrtriennale" drew attention when postcolonial scholar Achille Mbembe was disinvited from giving a speech because of his support for the academic boycott call against Israel.[20] In all three cases, the Bundestag motion was cited to justify the backlash against the artists. On the other side, the case of US-American/Lebanese artist Walid Raad should be mentioned: the city of Aachen tried to prevent the award ceremony, but the jury was principled enough to withstand the pressure.[21]

---

17    Letter dated 22 October 2019 and 15 October 2020 (on file with authors). Claims for damages are being asserted, the cases are still pending.

18    PACBI, *Palestinians call for boycott of Open Source Festival in Germany over its censorship of Talib Kweli*, Statement (June 17, 2019), https://bdsmovement.net/news/boycott-open-source.

19    Alison Flood, *Kamila Shamsie's book award withdrawn over her part in Israel boycott*, Guardian (Sep. 19, 2019), https://www.theguardian.com/books/2019/sep/19/kamila-shamsies-book-award-withdrawn-over-her-part-in-israel-boycott.

20    *See* the resolution: *Opposing Political Litmus Tests – Scholars and cultural figures stand against silencing of advocates for Palestinian rights in Germany*, https://nopoliticallitmus tests.wordpress.com.

21    Patrick Bahners, *Preview einer Ausstellung, die vielleicht verboten wird*, Frankfurter Allgemeine Zeitung (Oct. 15, 2019), https://www.faz.net/aktuell/feuilleton/kunst-und-archi tektur/verleihung-des-aachener-kunstpreises-an-walid-raad-16432860.html.

Furthermore, the academic world is struggling with anti-BDS smears. In its unsettling statement on November 19, 2019, the German Rectors' Conference gave in to pro-Zionist encroachment upon academic freedom.[22] The consequences of this statement and of the Bundestag resolution were reflected by the withdrawal of any support by the Kunsthochschule Weißensee for the art lectures of the "The School for Unlearning Zionism" in October 2020, that included several Jewish and Palestinian scholars and artists.[23] Even the event website was put down after pressure of the German Federal Ministry for Education and Research (BMBF) and an antisemitism-smearing campaign by the prominent anti-Palestinian activist Volker Beck. Other reactions have yet to be seen. Even before this step, actual or seeming BDS support has been used to attack academic freedom, with only few examples that have gone public.[24]

## II    Access to Venues

The Bundestag motion explicitly demands that access to premises and facilities should be denied to BDS events and activists. This form of exclusion has indeed been applied multiple times. Yet, the majority of court decisions rejected such acts as unlawful. While contract law regulates privately-owned rooms (including properties of churches, civil society associations), publicly-owned rooms are subject to administrative law.

---

22    Hochschulrektorenkonferenz *Entschließung der 27. Mitgliederversammlung der HRK am 19. November 2019 in Hamburg, Kein Platz für Antisemitismus*, https://www.hrk.de/fileadmin/redaktion/hrk/02-Dokumente/02-01-Beschluesse/HRK_MV_Entschliessung _Antisemitismus_19112019.pdf. An open petition has been initiated against this motion; *Objection against language rules for universities*, https://www.openpetition.de/petition/online/objection-against-language-rules-for-universities.

23    Weißensee kunsthochschule berlin, *Stellungnahme zur Veranstaltung (School for Unlearning Zionism)* (Oct. 13, 2020), https://www.kh-berlin.de/projekt-detail/Project/detail/stellungnahme-zur-veranstaltung-school-for-unlearning-zionism-3239.html; Stefan Reinecke, *Zoff um Antisemitismus-Vorwurf*, TAZ (Oct. 14, 2020), https://taz.de/Zionismus kritik-an-Kunsthochschule-in-Berlin/!5717567/.

24    For example, a course on "The social situation of youth in Palestine" was cancelled at the University of Hildesheim after allegations of antisemitism were made against the professor. *See Hochschule streicht Seminare nach Antisemitismus-Vorwürfen*, Hannoversche Allgemeine (Aug. 5, 2016), https://www.haz.de/Nachrichten/Der-Norden/Uebersicht/HAWK-Hildesheim-streicht-Seminare-nach-Antisemitismus-Vorwuerfen. *See also*, the statement of the Berlin Graduate School regarding a cancelled talk of Prof. Lila Sharif at the Free University of Berlin: *Statement by the Berlin Graduate School Muslim Cultures and Societies on the cancellation of Professor Lila Sharif's talk on 23 November 2017*, http://www.bgsmcs.fu-berlin.de/dates/Ressourcen/BGSMCS_statement_Sharif.pdf [link no longer working].

## A    *Access to Public Venues*

On March 27, 2019, the Higher Administrative Court of Lower Saxony ruled that the local commune of Oldenburg had no right to withhold public rooms from BDS activists.[25] This judgment is one among a couple of major achievements for BDS activists in Germany who have suffered from exclusion from access to rooms to present their work and organize.

Prior to the judgment, the commune of Oldenburg refused to rent out its publicly-owned room to BDS activists. The activists had planned to hold events during International Anti-Apartheid Week in 2019. Four events were supposed to take place in this regard: (1) a film presentation titled "Roadmap to Apartheid" following a presentation of the BDS initiative; (2) a workshop with local and international BDS activists to develop strategies of implementing international and human rights; (3) a lecture with Prof. Dr. Norman Paech about "Apartheid, settler-colonialism, and freedom of speech;" (4) and a lecture titled "Human rights under attack?" targeting the question of defamation of BDS activists.

The legal framework allows citizens of the city of Oldenburg to use public rooms for their activities so long as these activities do not violate Germany's "free and democratic order" – a vague legal term referring to the constitutional order of Germany. The constitutional order is based first and foremost on German Basic Law, Grundgesetz (GG) article 1, establishing that human dignity is inviolable, and that all public authorities are obliged to respect and protect it. This means that the access to public rooms is also bound by that core principle of the German GG. It is an established finding determined by the Constitutional Court of the Federal Republic of Germany that the protection of human dignity results in outlawing anti-Semitic and racist discrimination.[26] Therefore, access to public rooms is shaped by the question "Is the planned event or usage of the room compatible with the German constitutional order?;" *i.e.* is the event planned anti-Semitic or racist?

The city of Oldenburg answered that question by claiming that BDS violates that constitutional order because it comprises an "anti-Semitic concept." Following that decision, BDS activists went to court demanding their right to access to the public rooms. In the first instance, the Administrative Court of Oldenburg ruled against that right, without elaborating on how or why it

---

25    10 ME 48/19, Higher Administrative Court of Lower Saxony, Judgment, Mar. 27, 2019 (Ger.), https://www.rechtsprechung.niedersachsen.de/jportal/?quelle=jlink&docid =MWRE190001146&psml=bsndprod.psml&max=true.

26    *See, e.g.,* 2 BvB 1/13, Bundesverfassungsgericht (Constitutional Court of Germany), Judgment, Jan. 17, 2017 (Ger.), https://www.bundesverfassungsgericht.de/SharedDocs/ Entscheidungen/DE/2017/01/bs20170117_2bvb000113.html.

WILL THE GERMAN JUDICIARY PROTECT THE RIGHT TO BDS? 187

reached that conclusion.[27] Rather, the court avoided a clear position by claiming that both sides did not offer enough evidence for or against the criterion of violating Germany's free and democratic order, but that the burden of proof for being *not* anti-Semitic lies on the BDS activist. The court said that it could not rule in favor of the applicant by essentially hiding behind arguments such as "the complex nature" of the conflict and the ambiguous definition of antisemitism (the city of Oldenburg referred to the International Holocaust Remembrance Alliance's working definition, while the BDS activists contested the usefulness and validity of this definition). The activists appealed against that decision. Indeed, in the second instance, the Higher Administrative Court of Lower Saxony ruled in favor of the right to access the public room. The judgment is based on two arguments.

*Firstly*, the Higher Administrative Court established that in light of the right to hold and express an opinion (GG article 5) the onus of proof lies with the state. This means that should the BDS initiative contain anti-Semitic positions, it is the state that has to prove it and not the other way around. *Secondly*, the Higher Administrative Court criticizes the judgment of the first instance by arguing that it is not possible to justify the claim of anti-Semitism. The BDS movement worldwide is a heterogenous campaign, meaning that a sweeping designation as "anti-Semitic" is untenable. Interestingly, the court based its conclusion on material that has already been lodged by both sides in the first instance. Particularly, the court referred to reports of the federal parliament and parliament of Lower Saxony about BDS. Even these reports tiptoe around the question whether BDS is anti-Semitic or not. Numerous academic publications, news articles, and parliamentary inquiries are cited in these reports that all come to the same conclusion: BDS is controversial, yet not clearly anti-Semitic. The latter is being defined by using the working definition of the International Holocaust Remembrance Alliance (IHRA).[28] Moreover, there are no findings that BDS activities threaten Germany's free and democratic order to lead to monitoring by domestic intelligence services.

The Administrative Court of Cologne handed down a second important judgment with regards to access to public rooms on September 12, 2019.[29] This judgment is crucial, not only because it builds on the work that has been

---

27     3 B 709/19, Administrative Court Oldenburg, Judgment, Mar. 21, 2019 (Ger.) [unpublished (on file with authors)].

28     For the development of the antisemitism cases and the use of the EUMC/FRA/IHRA definition until 2017, *see* Ahmed Abed, *Antisemitismus im Spiegel des Rechts*, INAMO (Winter 2017), https://www.inamo.de/project/inamo-heft-92-antisemitismus-dirskurse/.

29     14 L 1765/19, Administrative Court Köln, Judgement, Sep. 13, 2019 (Ger.), https://www.justiz.nrw.de/nrwe/ovgs/vg_koeln/j2019/14_L_1765_19_Beschluss_20190912.html.

achieved in Lower Saxony, but also because it underlines a central argument. In its ruling, the Administrative Court of Cologne clarified the status of this and other anti-BDS motions:

> The motions of the Bonn City Council, as well as the motions of the parliament of North-Rhine Westphalia (20 September 2018) and the German Bundestag (17 May 2019), do not constitute legislative acts, but are political resolutions or expressions of political will. These motions alone cannot justify, from any legal perspective, the restriction of an existing legal right.[30]

The facts of the case concern the German-Palestinian Women's Association and the Palestinian Society Germany – Bonn. They filed a case after the City of Bonn excluded the Association from the "Vielfalt! Bonner Kultur und Begegnungsfest" (Diversity! Bonn's Culture and Encounter Festival) that was supposed to take place on September 29, 2019. The festival is a public event that highlights the city's cultural and linguistic diversity and where intercultural organizations as well as cultural, musical, and dance groups present their work and activities.

The city council argued that due to its support for BDS, the German-Palestinian Women's Association supported an anti-Semitic campaign and thus had to be excluded. The council based its decision, *inter alia*, on the Bundestag and a similar motion of the parliament of North-Rhine Westphalia,[31] but also on its own motion adopted on May 14, 2019 named "No place for the anti-Semitic BDS movement in Bonn."[32] The motion calls upon all municipal institutions in Bonn to deny facilities to BDS groups and to refrain from supporting events of the BDS campaign, or of groups pursuing BDS goals.

However, the Administrative Court of Cologne ruled in the first instance that the City of Bonn has "not even remotely" demonstrated that any justification for this exclusion exists. The Court stated that the exclusion of the Women's Association from the festival on the grounds of its support for the BDS Movement constitutes "unequal treatment," which is "not even remotely justified." The court thus found the conduct of the City of Bonn breached the

---

30  *Id.*

31  In Nordrhein-Westfalen ist kein Platz für die antisemitische BDS-Bewegung, Beschluss vom 14.09.2018, 17/3577 (Ger.), https://www.landtag.nrw.de/portal/WWW/dokumentenarchiv/Dokument/MMD17-3577.pdf.

32  *See* full text of motion adopted by the City Council of Bonn: http://www2.bonn.de/bo_ris/daten/0/pdf/19/1911513EB2.pdf.

principle of equality set out in GG article 3, and violated the Association's right to freedom of opinion and expression under GG article 5.

Two other local organizations, the German-Palestinian Society and the Palestinian Community of Bonn, were excluded from the festival on the same grounds as the German-Palestinian Women's Association. They also sued the City of Bonn, but only the Palestinian Community of Bonn won the case, because the German-Palestinian Society did not meet the criteria of being "based" in Bonn, a pre-condition of gaining access to the festival.[33]

It is worth mentioning that the City of Bonn, organizers of the festival, asked another Palestinian cultural association, that has no ties whatsoever with BDS, to sign a statement against BDS and against anti-Semitism.[34] Not only is this practice unlawful, as the judgments show, but it highlights the discriminatory and prejudiced nature behind the city council's action: none of the other participants reported that they were asked to sign a statement distancing themselves from BDS. It seems that only Palestinian organizations were targeted. Such targeting leaves a bitter aftertaste: it seems that the "Palestinian-ness" of the cultural group was enough to be targeted, requiring it to explain itself. The judgments, of course, do not address this issue.

After losing at the Administrative Court of Munich and three years of trial, the Higher Administration Court of Bavaria gave a plaintiff the right to host an event on the threat of freedom of expression by the anti-BDS motion of the City of Munich.[35] The judges made very clear that the 2017 anti-BDS motion of the City of Munich could not restrict prior-ranking communal law nor the freedom of expression or the principle of equality of the plaintiff. Though the decision is well-reasoned, and therefore the chances to tackle the ruling are very low, the court allowed the City of Munich to appeal to the Federal Administrative Court since the issue on limiting access to public facilities based on of unconstitutional expressions has yet to be decided yet by any supreme court.

---

33 European Legal Support Center, *Another German Court rules in favor of supporters of BDS Movement*, Press Release (Sep. 16, 2019), https://rightsforum.org/wp-content/uploads/2019/09/2019-09-16-ELSC-Press-release-Bonn.pdf?fbclid=IwAR0ljYV4WuQ1w%20picP8 wgaBGGLrvqjEcctWTAjqzpEQvbt3iQRPqLtPoyZYw.

34 *See Meinungsfreiheit ... gibt es nicht geschenkt*, Bündnis für Gerechtigkeit zwischen Israelis und Palästinensern (Blog) (Sep. 22, 2019), https://bibjetzt.wordpress.com/2019/09/22/meinungsfreiheit/.

35 4 B 19.1358, Higher Administration Court of Bavaria (pending) (Ger.), https://www.vgh.bayern.de/media/bayvgh/presse/4_b_19-1358_bds.pdf. Von Jacob Wetzel, *Stadt darf Diskussionen über die BDS-Kampagne nicht verhindern*, Süddeutsche Zeitung (Nov. 19, 2020), https://www.sueddeutsche.de/muenchen/muenchen-gericht-bds-anti semitismus-urteil-1.5120642.

The latter ruling was followed up by an equal decision in a summary proceeding before the Hessian Higher Administrative Court.[36] The Palestinian-Jewish-German initiative "Bundestag 3 for Palestine" (BT3P), who are suing the German Bundestag for their anti-BDS motion,[37] and a supporter of the initiative tried to book a city-owned hall to introduce their case to the public on December 5, 2020. First, they received a reservation for the hall. Three days before the event, the reservation was cancelled based on the reason that the speakers were suing against the anti-BDS motion of the Bundestag. The city argued that the 2017 anti-BDS motion of the City of Frankfurt forbids any BDS supporters in city-owned halls. Yet the Hessian Higher Administrative Court gave the initiative and their supporters the right to speak in the city-owned hall. Implicitly, the court even repealed the anti-BDS resolution of the City of Frankfurt.[38]

The judicial record, however, is inconsistent. Unlike the positive outcome of the previous cases, the Administrative Court of Düsseldorf ruled in a summary proceeding that the German-Palestinian Woman's Association is not negatively impacted by mentioning the BDS movement in the report of the secret service because they are not named in the report.[39] The latter argument is rather tenuous since the Constitutional Tribunal of North-Rhine-Westphalia pointed out, in its September 22, 2020 decision, that it is sufficient to bring legal action to court if you were identified as BDS supporter.[40] Although the Constitutional Tribunal ruled that the lawsuit against the North-Rhine-Westphalia parliament's motion is inadmissible because the legal recourses have yet to be exhausted, the eight judges made the important assessment that BDS activists are generally affected by legally non-binding motions even if they or their organization are not named and the violation of constitutional rights can be reviewed by the courts.

## B    *Access to Private Venues*

Under contract law, the parties must be held to account according to what has been agreed upon. The principle of freedom of contract does not allow

---

36    8 B 3012/20, Hessian Higher Administration Court, Judgement, Dec. 4, 2020 (Ger.).

37    Updated information can be found at: www.bt3p.org.

38    Bundestag 3 for Palestine, *Stadt Frankfurt am Main muss Veranstaltung der BT3P im Saalbau Gebäude stattfinden lassen*, Press Release (Dec. 5, 2020), https://www.frankfur ter-info.org/news/stadt-frankfurt-am-main-muss-veranstaltung-der-bt3p-im-saalbau -gebaeude-stattfinden-lassen.

39    20 L 1432/20, Administrative Court of Düsseldorf, Judgement, Nov. 13, 2020 (Ger.) [still pending at the Higher Administrative Court of North-Rhein-Westphalia: 16 B 1906/20].

40    VerfGH 49/19.VB-2, Constitutional Tribunal of North-Rhein-Westphalia, Judgement, Sep. 22, 2020 (Ger.) [soon to be released on www.vgh.nrw.de].

changes after the contract has been signed, except in the event of extraordinary circumstances.

A case from Munich manifests this principle. The Jewish-Palestinian Dialogue Group (JPDG) planned to hold an event with a Der Spiegel journalist. A contract to use the church-owned room was first signed and subsequently terminated. The lessor argued that the JPDG had ties with BDS and went on to explain that due to the anti-BDS motion passed by the Bundestag, the contract was no longer binding.

The District Court of Munich, however, clearly stated that the termination of the contract on the given grounds constitutes a violation of freedom of speech, and that the Bundestag motion was not enough to justify such an act.[41] Conflicts between obligations under contract law and public authorities' conduct emerged in October 2019 when the mayor for finance of the City of Frankfurt am Main, Chairman of the German-Israel Society Uwe Becker, put pressure on the private tenant for a civil society event titled "Freedom of Expression instead of Censorship." The mayor, known for promoting settlement products, threatened the tenant with withdrawing public finances if they didn't cancel the contract for the venue. He even released a press release with the title "Unacceptable for Frankfurt: Mayor Becker demanded the cancellation of the planned sympathizers' meeting of the anti-Semitic haters of Israel."[42] The press release compared the supporters of the BDS campaign, and the invited Jewish speaker Judith Bernstein of the JPDG and the Palestinian speaker, with Nazi anti-Semitism and the City of Halle murderer who attempted killing 60 Jews in a synagogue. Again, the tenant cancelled the contract, and the venue could only happen by recourse through an urgent judicial procedure.[43] Afterwards, the civil society organizations that organized the event pressured the mayor to withdraw his threats. Even when a councilor addressed the City of Frankfurt am Main with the recent court decisions of the Higher Administrative Court of Lower Saxony and the Administrative Court of Cologne, the City rejected the legal comparison and held their ground. In the pending case against the City of Frankfurt am Main by Judith Bernstein that aims to forbid the press release that smeared her as anti-Semitic, the City's main argument is that Judith Bernstein is not affected by the smearing as anti-Semitic but only the BDS-campaign.[44] The mayor was not the only one

---

41  12 O 13183/19, District Court Munich I, Judgment, Sep. 23, 2019 (Ger.).

42  City of Frankfurt am Main, Press Release (Oct. 11, 2019), https://frankfurt.de/sixcms/detail.php?id-2855&ffmpartidinhaltl=36159609 [link no longer working].

43  2-32 O 126/19, District Court Frankfurt am Main, Judgement, Oct. 16, 2019 (Ger.).

44  7 K 851/20.F, Administrative Court Frankfurt am Main, Pending (Ger.).

to justify his actions by explicitly invoking the Bundestag motion. Other private persons followed a similar tactic. For instance, a board member of the German-Israeli Society was sentenced by the District Court of Oldenburg for insulting a BDS-activist as "anti-Semitic pig" and "shitty anti-Semite" in a public event and for trying to forcefully throw him out.[45] Ultimately, the organizers and the viewers threw out the attacker himself. But in trial, the attacker explicitly justified his actions with the Bundestag resolution and said that he didn't regret his actions and announced that he would do it again.

Moreover, the Bundestag motion was used to cancel an event with a former member of the Central Council of Jews in Germany, Prof. Rolf Verleger, in the City of Mannheim. The hotel that cancelled the room made it clear that it would not rent a room to people who are affiliated with the BDS movement.

## III    Visa Withdrawal and Ban of Political Activities

The cases of Rasmea Odeh and Khaled Barakat are certainly among those that represent the most flagrant violations of civil and human rights. In both cases, visa or residency permits were revoked, deportations were ordered, and bans on political activities were issued.

### A    *The Case of Rasmea Odeh*

On March 15, 2019, the Berlin police stopped well-known Palestinian organizer and feminist Rasmea Odeh from speaking at a public event on the occasion of the International Women's Day in Berlin. Mrs. Odeh was supposed to talk about women's struggle in Palestine alongside the Palestinian poet Dareen Tatour. Mrs. Odeh was given two documents: the first announced the immediate withdrawal of her Schengen visa, and the second contained a temporary ban on political activities in Germany.

Prior to that, the event's organizers faced an intense public smear campaign orchestrated by local tabloids, the mayor, and the interior ministry of the federal state of Berlin.[46] This campaign focused on events that took place in Palestine more than 50 years ago, when Mrs. Odeh was accused of participating

---

45    5 O 1380/19, District Court, Dec. 4, 2019 (Ger.).

46    Noa Landau, *Germany Deports Palestinian Convicted of Terror, Cancels BDS Event at Israel's Request*, Ha'aretz (Mar. 16, 2019), https://www.haaretz.com/israel-news/.premium -germany-deports-palestinian-terrorist-cancels-bds-event-at-israel-s-request-1.7023689; Berlin senate for domestic affairs, Press Release (Mar. 15, 2019), https://www.berlin.de/ sen/inneres/presse/pressemitteilungen/2019/pressemitteilung.793082.php.

WILL THE GERMAN JUDICIARY PROTECT THE RIGHT TO BDS?

in a bombing campaign. Following her arrest by Israeli soldiers in 1969, Mrs. Odeh was severely tortured and forced to confess.[47]

Mrs. Odeh spent her entire life peacefully campaigning for the rights of women, migrants, Palestinians, and other marginalized groups. Yet, such activities were not taken into account; rather, she was designated a "terrorist." The fact that the local BDS group re-posted the event where Mrs. Odeh was supposed to speak provided the missing link for the German security authorities. Now, the opponents of the event could claim that not only was Mrs. Odeh a convicted "terrorist" (albeit convicted by a draconian Israeli military court), but that she was an anti-Semite too, because of her affiliation with BDS.

Mrs. Odeh went to the Administrative Court of Berlin against the withdrawal of her visa and the ban on political activities. Since the visa withdrawal had an immediate effect, Mrs. Odeh lodged an urgent application where the court would not decide and argue the case in depth, but instead would undertake a summary examination only. Hence, the benchmark is whether, according to a summary examination, the state authorities (in this case the immigration authorities) made any obvious error in forecasting any danger for public order and security.

The Administrative Court of Berlin then handed out a judgment based on the summary examination that no obvious errors were made by the authorities.[48] The court's preliminary decision stated that the criterion of "danger" also includes "potential danger," a term so limitless that any legal remedies of foreign visa holders are effectively barred.[49] The authorities' margin of discretion is expanded to such an extent that the court cannot undertake its own evaluation. Rather, the court is limited to an assessment of: whether the underlying facts have been investigated correctly; whether the acting authorities applied the legal terms correctly; and whether the authorities' decision was arbitrary or not.

The court then stated:

> The defendant's [i.e. immigration authorities'] assessment that the applicant's [i.e. Mrs. Odeh's] presence in Germany is suitable to pose a danger for the international relations of the Federal Republic of Germany *inter alia* with Israel and the peaceful co-existence within Germany is not obviously wrong.

---

47    *See Report of the Special Committee to investigate Israeli Practices affecting the human rights of the population of the occupied territories*, U.N. Doc. A/34/631 (Nov. 13, 1979).

48    VG 8 L 96.19 V, Administrative Court Berlin, Judgment, Mar. 21, 2019 (Ger.), https://www.juris.de/jportal/prev/JURE190004005.

49    The Administrative Court of Berlin refers to a controversial judgment of the European Court of Justice: Case C-544/15, *Fahimian v Bundesrepublik*, 2017 E.C.R. (Apr. 4).

Moreover,

> The defendant was allowed to take public reactions to the applicant and her planned participation in the event into account which is under suspicion of abetting anti-Semitism.

The court acknowledges the conflict with the constitutional right of holding and expressing an opinion. However, the court accepts the authorities' claim that Mrs. Odeh is

> an icon of the Palestinian movement that glorifies a violent approach to Israel, and who cooperates with anti-Semitic groups such as BDS ... In light of the applicant's controversial vita, especially because of her conviction for participating in a terror attack, this conclusion is not arbitrary.

Mrs. Odeh's appeal against the decision of the Administrative Court of Berlin was unsuccessful. The Higher Administrative Court of Berlin confirmed the decision of the first instance, claiming that it found no errors in the application of the law.[50] Odeh left Germany in early April 2019, after a second ban on political activities in the context of a planned second event was issued,[51] and after a pro-Zionist organization had pressed criminal charges against her for violating the ban.[52]

The case against the ban on Mrs. Odeh's right to publicly express her opinion is still pending. The immigration authorities explicitly referred to the Bundestag motion to argue that Mrs. Odeh's positions are anti-Semitic and thus constitute a danger to public order and security.

## B  *The Case of Khaled Barakat*

The case of Khaled Barakat differs with regard to the fact that he holds a residency permit for free-lancers and has been living in Germany over the last couple of years. On June 22, 2019, the immigration authorities presented several arguments why a revocation of his residency was justified, among them

---

50  3 S 20.19, Higher Administrative Court Berlin-Brandenburg, Judgment, Mar. 29, 2019 (Ger.) [unpublished, on file with authors].

51  Invitation to the event "Rasmea speaks," and letter of support undersigned by several Berlin-based organizations, dated Mar. 26, 2019, available at: https://ilmr.de/2019/rasmea -spricht-palastinensische-frauen-werden-nicht-zum-schweigen-gebracht-veranstaltung -mit-rasmea-odeh-am-27-marz.

52  *See* Jüdisches Forum für Demokratie und gegen Antisemitismus (undated), https://www .jfda.de/blog/2019/03/29/strafanzeige-gegen-rasmea-odeh [link no longer working].

his BDS affiliation. The authorities also issued a ban on political activities that lasted for more than one month.[53]

Mr. Barakat challenged the decision in the Administrative Court of Berlin and started an urgent procedure against both the revocation of his residency and the ban on political activities. Again, the immigration authorities argued that according to the Bundestag motion, Mr. Barakat's positions were anti-Semitic and thus dangerous. This is troubling, not only because the authorities used an explicitly non-binding expression of the parliament's political will, but also because it used it to justify a major violation of Mr. Barakat's political and civil rights. The immigration authorities are using §47 Aufenthaltsgesetz (Act on the Residence, Economic Activity and Integration of Foreigners in the Federal Territory, or "Residence Act"), which in and of itself is considered to be on the fringes of the constitution. It is law only to be used *ultima ratio*, namely if the foreigner's political activities

1. impair or endanger the development of informed political opinion in the Federal Republic of Germany, the peaceful co-existence of Germans and foreigners or of different groups of foreigners in the federal territory, public safety and order or any other substantial interests of the Federal Republic of Germany,

2. may be counter to the foreign policy interests of the Federal Republic of Germany or to the obligations of the Federal Republic of Germany under international law,

3. contravene the laws of the Federal Republic of Germany, particularly in connection with the use of violence,

4. are intended to promote parties, other organisations, establishments or activities outside of the federal territory whose aims or means are incompatible with the fundamental values of a system of government which respects human dignity.[54]

In the past, this law was used only a few times, and in most cases the immigration authorities were unsuccessful in proving at court an appropriate and constitutional usage of the ban. Cases in the past have dealt with Kurdish

---

53 FIDH, Association of Democratic Lawyers (Germany), European Association of Lawyers for Democracy & World Human Rights, *EJDM, VDJ und Internationale Liga für Menschenrechte fordern Redefreiheit für den palästinensischen Journalisten Khaled Barakat*, Joint Press Release (July 12, 2019) [*hereinafter* Barakat Press Release], https://ilmr.de/2019/ejdm-vdj-und-internationale-liga-fuer-menschenrechte-fordern-redefreiheit-fuer-den-palaestinensischen-journalisten-khaled-barakat.

54 German Residence Act (in English), available at: https://www.gesetze-im-internet.de/englisch_aufenthg/englisch_aufenthg.pdf.

activists who had been affiliated with the PKK[55] or those affiliated with the Hizbullah.[56] While both of these organizations are designated as terrorist, BDS certainly is not. This is clear to the authorities, which is why in Mr. Barakat's case they had to add another argument: his actual or seeming affiliation with the Popular Front for the Liberation of Palestine (PFLP) – which, however, is not a listed terrorist organization either. It thus seems unconvincing, and politically motivated, that such a legal provision would be applied to a non-violent grassroots campaign like BDS.

What happened next was rather unusual: the judges, who were supposed to rule on the issue, "sat out" a decision to avoid taking a stance. Because the ban was intact for a month, the court prolonged its decision-taking (albeit in an urgent procedure) until the phase of the ban was over. It is open to speculation whether this delay was an attempt of the court not to obstruct the authorities' designs, or whether the court attempted to avoid making a decision on a controversial issue.

As a form of compensation, however, the court offered guarantees by the immigration authorities that Mr. Barakat was allowed to continue giving interviews and gain public attention about his case.[57] The judicial delay and avoidance of decision-making notwithstanding, the effect of the ruling is that the ban went unchallenged and achieved its effect of silencing political speech.

At the time of writing, the case is still pending. However, it became clear from the material presented before the court that there is another aspect of the attempt to repress BDS: Mr. Barakat and other activists have been monitored by the intelligence services. This is a disturbing development, especially because the Berlin senator for domestic affairs announced this after a visit to Israel.[58] It is thus likely that the surveillance results concerning German residents might be shared with foreign authorities.[59] It would also pose a *novum* because BDS, as such, has at no point been described as a security threat, as violent, or unconstitutional.

---

55    11 S 1581/12, Administrative Court of Baden-Württemberg, Judgment. Jan. 8, 2013 (Ger.).

56    24 L 3189/04, Administrative Court of Düsseldorf, Judgment. Dec. 23, 2004 (Ger.).

57    Barakat Press Release.

58    Andreas Geisel, *Besuch in Tel Aviv – Gespräch mit dem israelischen Minister für öffentliche Sicherheit*, Press Release (Jan. 10, 2020), https://andreas-geisel.de/besuch-in-tel-aviv-gespraech-mit-dem-israelischen-minister-fuer-oeffentliche-sicherheit/.

59    The case material also makes clear that the immigration authorities based their decision on a report by the "NGO Monitor," a pro-Israeli NGO with possible ties to the Israeli government.

# WILL THE GERMAN JUDICIARY PROTECT THE RIGHT TO BDS? 197

## C *International Reactions to the Bundestag Motion*

The problematic and objectionable nature of the Bundestag motion is illustrated by the joint reaction of five United Nations (UN) Special Rapporteurs.[60] The rapporteurs sharply criticized the continuing human rights violations against BDS activists by the Bundestag resolution of May 17, 2019.[61] In their public letter, dated October 18, 2019, they state:

> We wish to express our concern that the motion sets a worrying trend of unduly limiting the rights to freedom of opinion and expression, peaceful assembly and of association in its call for governmental bodies, as well as German states, cities and municipalities and other public actors, to refuse financial support, premises or facilities to projects or events organized by the BDS movement or by groups pursuing its aims. Accordingly, the motion unduly interferes with the right of people in Germany to engage in political speech, namely, to express support for the BDS movement.[62]

Furthermore, the rapporteurs recognized the anti-racist human rights agenda of the BDS campaign, rejecting the general suspicion of anti-Semitism and recommend that actions should be taken against racism in the case that it occurs instead of postulating general and false allegations.

Explicit reference is made to the above-mentioned decisions of the Administrative Court of Cologne and the District Court of Munich which sought to secure the above-mentioned human rights. The rapporteurs expressly demanded the answer to their questions on how the government intends to comply with its international human rights obligations as BDS activities are attacked in consequence of the Bundestag resolution.

The Permanent Mission of the Federal Republic of Germany to the UN and other international organizations in Geneva answered on January 14, 2020, making clear that it has not considered the anti-BDS motion as a violation of human rights. In its Note Verbale it states:

---

60    *Mr. David Kaye, Special Rapporteur on the promotion and protection of the right to freedom of opinion and expression; Mr. Clement Nyaletsossi Voule, Special Rapporteur on the rights to freedom of peaceful assembly and association; Mr. Michael Forst, Special Rapporteur on the situation of human rights defenders; Mr. Michael Lynk, Special Rapporteur on the situation of human rights in the Palestinian territory occupied since 1967, and Mr. Ahmed Shaheed, Special Rapporteur on freedom of religion and belief,* U.N. OHCHR, Ref. No. AL DEU 3/2019 (Oct. 18, 2019), https://spcommreports.ohchr.org/TMResultsBase/DownLoadPublicCommunicationFile?gId=24834.

61    *Id.*

62    *Id.*

At the outset, it should be noted that as a principle, mere political motions adopted by the German Bundestag cannot – as such – impair individual rights, as they do not affect the rights of an individual. Rather, specific decisions by a governmental body (e.g., a German city or municipality) on requests by supporters of the BDS movement for financial support or for the use of facilities could have such an effect.

If, however, in the context of BDS activities or purported affiliation with BDS, an individual or a group perceives his or her rights violated by such an individual decision, it is always possible to take legal action. It is then the responsibility of the German judiciary to determine whether the activities in question are within the scope of the aforementioned rights and whether they were violated.[63]

Effectively, the government delegates all responsibility to the German judiciary system and offers no thorough response to any of the Special Rapporteurs' demands.

## IV    Outlook: The Defamation of BDS as a Matter of Constitutional Rights

The German response to the Special Rapporteurs' concerns may leave the reader disillusioned; or, it may raise the expectations with regards to the German courts. Reposing the question that has been raised at the beginning of this contribution, it might well be that it will eventually be the German judiciary that comes to the protection of the right to advocate for BDS. Germany's Note Verbale indicates that BDS activists must rely on the German judiciary, because no other German institution will step up to protect their rights.

Contrasting the judgments on access to public rooms with the judgments regarding the ban on political activities and visa revocations, it shows that the authorities will try to find ways to add the notion of "security threat" to obscure access to the right to BDS. The analysis of the judgments shows that in some cases, it is merely a matter of details and the right legal structuring of the margin of discretion which lead to upholding the right to advocate BDS. To carve out settled case law, more cases have to be brought forward, and BDS activists and organizers going to court will have to show patience and courage.

---

63    Federal Republic of Germany, Ref.: Pol-10–381.70 PSE, Note Verbale, Note No. 7/2020, available at: https://spcommreports.ohchr.org/TMResultsBase/DownLoadFile?gId=35109.

WILL THE GERMAN JUDICIARY PROTECT THE RIGHT TO BDS? 199

As legal representatives in BDS cases, it has become clear to the authors of this contribution that the stigmatization and consequent silencing of BDS is a broader issue. It needs to be understood in the context of an illiberal attack on human rights and democratic principles.[64]

Since the hegemonic political position in Germany demands that any party aiming at governing must have a pro-Zionist agenda,[65] the fight against BDS is the only issue that all parties, with the exception of the leftist party DIE LINKE, agree on: in all parliaments, local ones and the Bundestag, the motions discrediting BDS have been passed mainly with great majority. Yet, this should not blind us to the fact that right-wing parties and organizations are the ones promoting an alliance between anti-democratic, racist, and Zionist ideas. In Germany, the right-wing AfD ("Alternative for Germany") has been at the forefront of anti-immigration and anti-Muslim policies, while simultaneously founding an association called "Jews in the AfD" which states in its declaration of principles, that UNRWA ought to be dismantled, and argues against the "influx of young men coming from the Islamic cultural area" because "Muslim antisemitism" is perceived to be the biggest threat to Jewish life in Germany.[66]

Therefore, the authors of this contribution are challenging the anti-BDS motion of the Bundestag at the Administrative Court of Berlin,[67] along with the Palestinian-Jewish-German initiative "Bundestag 3 for Palestine."[68] The arguments put forward is that the motion violates German constitutional law and the European Convention on Human Rights. The violations are not justified, because they have no legal basis: the motion is cited by authorities to violate the rights of individuals even though the motion is clearly a non-law and therefore not binding. Furthermore, the suit filed argues that the motion is based on insufficient facts because it is based on an unsubstantiated definition of anti-Semitism (namely the IHRA definition), and a false application of it to BDS. The lawsuit is supported by the international law experts Prof. Eric David, Prof. Xavier Dupré De Boulois, Prof. Richard Falk (former UN Special Rapporteur), and Prof. John Reynolds, along with the European Legal Support

---

64 *See* Palestine Legal, *The Palestine Exception to Free Speech: A Movement Under Attack in the US* (Sep. 30, 2015), https://palestinelegal.org/the-palestine-exception. *See also* Ed Pilkington, *Revealed: right-wing push to ban criticism of Israel on US campuses*, Guardian (Oct. 17, 2019), https://www.theguardian.com/us-news/2019/oct/16/conservative-activists-want-to-outlaw-antisemitism-in-public-education-why-is-that-a-bad-thing.

65 *See* Leandros Fischer, *Deciphering Germany's Pro-Israel Consensus*, 49 J. Palestine Stud. 26, 27 (2019).

66 Grundsatzerklärung der Juden in der AfD (undated), available at: https://j-afd.org/grundsatzerklaerung.

67 VG 2 K 79/20, Administrative Court Berlin (pending, filed in May 2020) (Ger.).

68 Updated information available at: www.bt3p.org.

Centre.[69] It is yet to be seen how the court will deal with the challenge of the motion altogether in the light of the decision of the European Court for Human Rights on *Baldassi* and others against France of June 11, 2020.[70]

The German courts' decisions so far have been mixed, but the effects of an ostensible non-binding motion have taken an unprecedented toll on democracy and basic rights in Germany. The challenge of the motion altogether, if successful, might turn the tide towards a more democratic and peaceful Europe. After all, the benchmark for democracy is the treatment of the marginalized and unpopular speech.[71]

---

69   *See, generally*: https://elsc.support.

70   *Baldassi et al. v. Fra*, Case No. 15271, 169 Eur. Ct. Hum. Rts. (2020), http://hudoc.echr.coe.int/fre?i=003-6718555-8953654.

71   *See* Nikole Hannah-Jones, *America Wasn't a Democracy until Black Americans Made it one*, N.Y. Times (Aug. 14 2019), https://www.nytimes.com/interactive/2019/08/14/magazine/black-history-american-democracy.html.

# PART 3

## *Review Essays*

# A Hundred Years of Settler-Colonialism: History, Law, Horizons Beyond

*Rashid Khalidi, The Hundred Years' War on Palestine: A History of Settler Colonialism and Resistance, 1917–2017 (2020) & Noura Erakat, Justice for Some: Law and the Question of Palestine (2019)*

John Reynolds

### Contents

I   History
II  Law
III Horizons Beyond

The Balfour Declaration in 1917 marked the beginning of what Rashid Khalidi describes as the "hundred years' war" on Palestine. A century of settler-colonialism brought us from Balfour's steal of the century to Trump-Netanyahu's so-called "deal of the century." The public agent and author of that deal was American property developer – and Trump's son-in-law and advisor-of-sorts – Jared Kushner. There are certain parallels with Balfour here – "Bloody Balfour" as he is remembered in Ireland – whose appointment to the position of Chief Secretary for Ireland and subsequent rise through the ranks of British imperial government was ascribed to the nepotism of his uncle, three-time Prime Minister Robert Cecil. From which, Khalidi reminds us, derives the expression "Bob's your uncle."[1]

Bob's your uncle. Don's your father-in-law. Of course, when questioned about his credentials for the job of leading a global superpower state's work on one of the world's longest-running situations of colonial occupation and intransigence, Kushner claimed it was based on merit not marriage. His infamous response was that he had read 25 books on Palestine-Israel. We do not know what these books are, or what he took from them. The act of reading itself was presented as feat and qualification. What did emerge from some

---

[1] Rashid Khalidi, The Hundred Years' War on Palestine: A History of Settler Colonialism and Resistance 266 (2020) [*hereinafter* Khalidi].

inside reports suggests that his insights on Palestine were gleaned less from any Palestinian perspectives and more from the work of neo-con pundits like Jonathan Schanzer (of the Washington-based think-tank Foundation for Defense of Democracies). Such erasure is indicative – the omission of Palestinian scholarship and writing on the very question of Palestine is all-too pervasive across academic, policy, and legal institutional spaces.[2] Kushner's patronizing rhetoric towards Palestinians reflects this. His assertions that the Palestinians "are not yet capable of governing themselves" are a reminder that the ghost of civilizing missions and Mandates past is very much still with us.[3]

I think we can safely assume that Palestinian scholars Rashid Khalidi and Noura Erakat[4] were unlikely to have been on Kushner's reading list. Certainly, any vision of future horizons in Palestine informed by their recent books would be worlds apart from the recipe for further Israeli colonization and control that Kushner's plan cooked up.

## I    History

In their respective texts, Khalidi and Erakat both retrace the arc of modern Palestinian history since the Balfour Declaration – bending as it has done towards injustice, shaping the terrain in which a Trump-Netanyahu axis could fuse with such ease as the latest layer of an ever-deepening apartheid structure. The two books differ significantly in their methods and disciplinary lenses but overlap almost exactly in the timelines they cover and are sketched on parallel but often converging tracks in the stories they tell.

Khalidi has been one of the leading historians of Palestine over recent decades, described by one writer as "the intellectual heir to Edward Said."[5] This is likely a moniker and a weight of expectation that Khalidi himself would eschew and, while Said is inimitable, Khalidi's scholarship on Palestinian

---

2   *See, e.g.*, Victor Kattan, *Palestinian Scholarship and the International Criminal Court's Blind Spot*, Third World Approaches Int'l L. Rev.: Reflections (Feb. 20, 2020), https://twailr.com/palestinian-scholarship-and-the-international-criminal-courts-blind-spot/.

3   *Kushner: Palestinians not yet capable of governing themselves*, Al-Jazeera (June 3, 2019), https://www.aljazeera.com/news/2019/6/3/kushner-palestinians-not-yet-capable-of-governing-themselves. *See also Kushner recommends "foolish" Palestinians take "cold shower" before rejecting sham peace plan'*, New Arab (Jan. 30, 2020), https://english.alaraby.co.uk/news/kushner-calls-palestinians-foolish-rejecting-farcical-peace-plan.

4   Noura Erakat, Justice for Some: Law and the Question of Palestine (2019) [*hereinafter* Erakat].

5   David Gardner, *The Hundred Years' War on Palestine – how to reconcile equality and a single state*, Financial Times (Feb. 28, 2020), https://www.ft.com/content/229342a8-532f-11ea-8841-482eed0038b1.

A HUNDRED YEARS OF SETTLER-COLONIALISM

identity and nationhood has been of profound impact in its own right.[6] *The Hundred Years' War on Palestine* is his eighth book, and knits together strands from some of his previous, more time-specific or theme-specific works to draw out a big-picture but sharp-focused panorama of events in Palestine over the last century. It should endure as one of the definitive generalist histories of this period. The particular innovation that Khalidi brings with this book is the weaving of family history and personal anecdote through the historical narrative. This is a potentially perilous move, but it works in Khalidi's case – because of the proximity of members of multiple generations of his (elite) family to key historical moments, and because he avoids the trap of self-indulgence. He writes them into his account where pertinent, but in a sparing and understated way.

Erakat is one of an emerging generation of Palestinian socio-legal scholars who have been pushing the boundaries of intellectual engagement while significantly augmenting the Palestinian canon.[7] *Justice for Some* is her first book, rich with the conceptual tools of critical legal thinking and imbued with the political clarity and urgency of an anti-imperial internationalist lens. The book is a story about Palestine, but is also a story of international law itself. Some of its most important insights are more universal than specific and make major contributions with value well beyond the question of Palestine. In terms of emancipatory knowledge production from the Palestinian perspective, Erakat provides some invaluable materials and insights through the book's small but significant set of interviews with Palestinian legal and political protagonists, as well as her own theoretical innovations.

*The Hundred Years' War on Palestine* is structured by what Khalidi presents as six declarations of war on Palestine: by Britain and the League of Nations (1917–39); by Zionist paramilitary and political forces, plus the United Nations (UN) (1947–48); by Israel with the support of the United States (US) and the silence or connivance of Arab regimes in the West Bank and Gaza (1967); in Lebanon (1982); from the occupied territories to Oslo (1987–1995); and from

---

6 Perhaps most notably: Rashid Khalidi, Palestinian Identity: The Construction of Modern National Consciousness (1997).

7 *See, e.g.*, Noura Erakat, *Litigating the Arab-Israeli Conflict: The Politicization of U.S. Federal Courtrooms*, 2 Berkeley J. Middle East & Islamic L. 27 (2009); Noura Erakat, *Operation Cast Lead: The Elusive Quest for Self-Defense in International Law*, 36 Rutgers L. Rec. 164 (2009); Aborted State? The UN Initiative & New Palestinian Junctures (Noura Erakat & Mouin Rabbani eds., 2013); Noura Erakat, *Whiteness as Property in Israel: Revival, Rehabilitation, and Removal*, 31 Harvard J. Ethnic & Racial Just. 69 (2015); Noura Erakat, *Taking the Land Without the People: The 1967 Story As Told by Law*, 47 J. Palestine Stud. 18 (2017); Noura Erakat, *The Sovereign Right to Kill: A Critical Appraisal of Israel's Shoot-To-Kill Policy*, 19 Int'l Crim. L. Rev. 783 (2019); Noura Erakat, *Geographies of Intimacy: Contemporary Renewals of Black Palestinian Solidarity*, 72 Am. Q. 471 (2020).

Camp David to the Jabaliya refugee camp (2000–2014). This largely mirrors Erakat's organization of *Justice for Some* into five key historical junctures: the "colonial erasures" that the Balfour Declaration set in train (1917–1966); the "permanent occupation" of the remaining Palestinian territory (from 1967); the engagement in international arenas by Palestine Liberation Organization's (PLO) "pragmatic revolutionaries" through the 1970s–1980s; the "ghettoized sovereignty" they ended up accepting in Oslo process capitulation in the 1990s; and Israel's shifts in strategy and legal discourse "from occupation to warfare" in the post-2000 conjuncture. Both texts are defined by their emphasis on the settler-colonial nature of Zionism as foundational to understanding the question of Palestine. Both also highlight – in Khalidi's case, more obliquely and sporadically; in Erakat's case, front and center – the shape-shifting complicity of international law.

Khalidi begins his account with reference to the exchange of letters in 1899 between his own great-great-great uncle, Yusuf Diya al-Din Pasha al-Khalidi – who had been mayor of Jerusalem, among other positions of authority – and Theodor Herzl, founder of the World Zionist Organization. Herzl had made his sole visit to Palestine in 1898 and was continuing to ramp up his diplomatic initiatives in support of colonization. Yusuf Diya would have been familiar with Herzl from his own stint in Vienna as a university professor and was well aware of the scope of Herzl's ambition for his political project. He advised Herzl that while he of course understood the need for Jews being persecuted in Europe to find refuge, it would be "pure folly" for Zionism to plan to take over Palestine: the "brutal force of circumstances had to be taken into account ... Palestine is an integral part of the Ottoman empire, and more gravely, it is inhabited by others." On this basis, Yusuf Diya urged Herzl in no uncertain terms to "let Palestine be left alone."[8] In his prompt response, Herzl, "with the smug self-assurance so common in nineteenth-century Europeans," sought to reassure Yusuf Diya by deploying the classic colonial trope that colonization would benefit rather than harm the native population. The chilling reality of Herzl's vision lurks between the lines of his response to a question that Yusuf Diya himself had not asked: "You see another difficulty, Excellency, in the existence of the non-Jewish population in Palestine. But who would think of sending them away?"[9] We know that Herzl himself, of course, was thinking specifically of that – expressing it elsewhere in terms of a "process of expropriation and removal [which] must be carried out discreetly and circumspectly," and of the need to "spirit" the native Palestinians "across the border"

---

8  Quoted in: Khalidi, at 5.
9  Quoted in: Khalidi, at 7.

A HUNDRED YEARS OF SETTLER-COLONIALISM 207

through forced unemployment and impoverishment.[10] Khalidi emphasizes this as foundational to Zionism ("the coddled stepchild of British colonialism")[11] as a very particular settler-colonial project: "Herzl grasped the importance of 'disappearing' the native population of Palestine in order for Zionism to succeed."[12]

Herzl's language in his correspondence with Yusuf Diya is also revealing of the line that runs directly from Zionist thought to British foreign policy and international institutions. Herzl's "existence of the non-Jewish population in Palestine" would become the "existing non-Jewish communities in Palestine" of the Balfour Declaration and the League of Nations Mandate for Palestine. The Palestinians were not positively defined by any aspect of their own identity or sense of belonging in their homeland, but instead negatively marked only by their non-Jewishness. This is what Erakat characterizes as the "juridical erasure"[13] of the Palestinians by the League of Nations, necessary to facilitate the self-determination of a settler population in their place. This tied international law into a knot in 1922 which has not been undone since.

The dynamics of imbalance and structural bias were evident from the outset. Khalidi shows that the Palestinian leadership pursued a "fruitless legalistic approach for over a decade and a half" after the Balfour Declaration – "elite-led initiatives" that engaged in "a dialogue of the deaf" with British officials who refused to recognize the representative authority of the Palestinian Arab congresses.[14] The Brits preconditioned any engagement on Arab acceptance of the Balfour Declaration and the terms of the League of Nations Mandate, knowing it was an impossible concession for the Palestinians to make. This tactic of demanding that the Palestinians retroactively agree to their own dispossession – and refusing to recognize them when they fail to do so – continues to serve Israel (and the US) well a century later. Khalidi characterized the Trump-Netanyahu "deal" in January 2020 as the logical continuation of this trajectory: "the erasure of Palestinians on display" as Trump and Netanyahu "unveiled a one-sided 'vision for peace' might have been an unusually blatant act of disregard, but it was in no way new. The omission is the essence of the conflict."[15] A year later, in the early phase of the Biden presidency, Erakat

---

10   Theodor Herzl, Complete Diaries 88–89 (Raphael Patai ed., 1960).
11   Khalidi, at 13.
12   *Id.*, 7.
13   Erakat, at 16.
14   Khalidi, at 31.
15   Rashid Khalidi, *The Erasure of Palestinians from Trump's Mideast "Peace Plan" has a Hundred-Year History*, The Intercept (Feb. 1, 2020), https://theintercept.com/2020/02/01/hundred-years-war-palestine-book-rashid-khalidi/.

makes clear that while the tone and optics may have softened, there is – unsurprisingly – no sign of any meaningful change to US-Palestinian policy.[16]

In an internal British government cabinet memo written in 1919, Balfour was explicit that "in Palestine we do not propose even to go through the form of consulting the wishes of the present inhabitants of the country" – the Allied powers of the post-World War I conjuncture were "committed to Zionism ... be it right or wrong, good or bad."[17] This effectively remains true of the West's relation to Israel today, performative expressions of concern over its more egregious violence notwithstanding. *The Hundred Years' War on Palestine* gives us a thorough rendition of the major events and structures that have unfolded and embedded in the intervening century. From an international law perspective, Khalidi's telling of the diplomatic story of UN Security Council Resolution (UNSC) 242 is an interesting one. His father was working in the UN in New York at the time, in a role in the division of Political and Security Council Affairs which involved him attending any UNSC meetings relevant to the Middle East. The nineteen-year-old Khalidi sat in the visitors' gallery and hung around his father's office in June 1967 as the Six-Day War unfolded – increasingly incredulous and outraged as he witnessed the dark art of the US ambassador providing diplomatic cover and extra time for Israeli aggression to continue. Khalidi provides some telling insights into the sausage-making process which eventually produced UNSC Resolution 242 later that year. This resolution (which Erakat also deconstructs convincingly in her analysis, more on which below) made a pivotal contribution to sidelining the Palestinians from their own situation. It treated the conflict and the new occupation as purely as an issue of state relations between Israel and other Arab states, failing to even mention the Palestinians or acknowledge most of the fundamental elements of the question of Palestine. With this, Khalidi argues persuasively, "a whole new layer of forgetting, erasure and myth-making was added to the induced amnesia that obscured the colonial origins of the conflict between Palestinians and the Zionist settlers."[18]

---

16  *See* Noura Erakat, *Biden's early Israel policies show he won't be much better for Palestinians than Trump*, NBC (Feb. 9, 2021), https://www.nbcnews.com/think/opinion/biden-s-early-israel-policies-show-he-won-t-be-ncna1257146.

17  Documents on British Foreign Policy, 1919–1939 340–348 (E.L. Woodward & Rohan Butler eds., 1952).

18  Khalidi, at 107.

## II    Law

The role and complicity of international law is dealt with more comprehensively as the central theme of Erakat's compelling text. *Justice for Some* builds on, but also departs in crucial ways from, the existing literature on the relationship between international law and Palestine. The book's timeline overlaps slightly with, and follows on from, Victor Kattan's *From Co-existence to Conquest: International Law and the Origins of the Arab-Israeli Conflict 1891–1949*.[19] Erakat is indebted to Kattan's archival work, legal history, and textual analysis, while at the same time adopting a more explicitly critical methodology. In this sense, her approach aligns with critical and socio-legal scholars who have produced significant work on (international) law and Palestine such as Lisa Hajjar, George Bisharat, and Richard Falk, as well as with the position of "cynicism about the law" to which renowned Palestinian human rights lawyer Raja Shehadeh ultimately arrived.[20] Erakat does also acknowledge and value the more doctrinal work on international law and Palestine produced by scholars like John Quigley, Susan Akram, and Michael Lynk,[21] positioning herself as building on their work though not attempting to advance a particular legal argument as practical solution in the ways that they do.

Ultimately, much of the mainstream literature on international law and Palestine is premised on the idea that "the conflict" has not been "resolved" because international law has been ignored or insufficiently applied, whereas Erakat subjects international law itself to deeper critique. She shows that the Israeli state project has of course been consolidated and expanded on a platform of might making right since 1948 – but that the law has been very much bound up in that. Israeli governments have actively sought to craft legal justifications for the conquest and colonization of territory, and to harness international law in their favor. They have been able to do this – successfully, in many instances – because the law cannot provide predetermined and definitive outcomes; it can only promise a contest over an outcome. Legal outcomes are ultimately determined in the historical and political contexts in which the law is being mobilized and applied. This is a fluid process; the law is continuously

---

19    Victor Kattan, From Co-existence to Conquest: International Law and the Origins of the Arab-Israeli Conflict 1891–1949 (2009).

20    Erakat, at xii.

21    *See, e.g.,* John Quigley, The Case for Palestine: An International Law Perspective (2005); International Law and the Israeli-Palestinian Conflict: A Rights-Based Approach to Middle East Peace (Susan M. Akram, Michael Dumper, Michael Lynk, & Iain Scobbie eds., 2010).

sculpted over time and reshaped from new vantage points as historical processes unfold or new protagonists emerge. These political struggles over law in the Palestinian context have produced both "anti-colonial legalities"[22] and "settler-colonial legalities."[23]

Erakat traces this story – against the shifting backdrops of colonial maneuvering, Third World revolt and US empire-building – through her five key historical junctures over the hundred-year arc. She begins in 1917 with Balfour's single but weighty sentence, with which the British government gave the promise of a Jewish national home in Palestine to the Zionist Federation. The Palestinians were reduced to Herzl's "existing non-Jewish communities," to be granted some civil rights protections but not necessarily any sovereignty or self-determination. International law and its institutions soon became complicit in the dispossession of the Palestinians – first by incorporating the Balfour Declaration into the League of Nations Mandate, and later with the UN proposing a partition of Palestine and recognizing an Israeli state created in 1948 on the back of mass displacement of Palestinians. From the outset, that state subjected the Palestinians who had managed to stay in their homes to a racialized emergency law regime of military rule,[24] instituting a system of "internal colonialism."[25] International law was silent in its consent.

The UN subsequently sought to prohibit colonialism "in all its forms and manifestations," through a string of resolutions advanced by the Third World bloc from 1960. Yet Israel further expanded its colonial jurisdiction and military regime through the occupation of the remaining Palestinian territories after the 1967 war. The UNSC eventually issued a call on Israel to withdraw its occupation forces later that year. Like Khalidi, however, Erakat is rightly skeptical of UNSC Resolution 242. Her analysis shows us that even iterations of international law like this one which may appear favorable to Palestinians on the surface are often the product of, and platform for, extensive "legal work" by Israel.[26] Erakat draws on the scholarship of Duncan Kennedy for her conceptualization of "legal work" as a form of tactical intervention "to transform an initial apprehension of what the system of norms requires, given the facts,

---

22  *See* John Reynolds, *Anti-Colonial Legalities: Paradigms, Tactics & Strategy*, 18 Palestine Y.B. Int'l L. 8 (2015).

23  *See* Markus Gunneflo, *Settler-Colonial and Anti-Colonial Legalities in Palestine*, 20 Palestine Y.B. Int'l L. 171 (2019).

24  For analysis, *see, e.g.*, John Reynolds, Empire, Emergency and International Law 221–229 (2017).

25  Elia Zureik, The Palestinians in Israel: A Study in Internal Colonialism (1979).

26  *See* Duncan Kennedy, *A Left Phenomenological Alternative to the Hart/Kelsen Theory of Legal Interpretation*, in Legal Reasoning: Collected Essays 158 (Duncan Kennedy, 2008).

A HUNDRED YEARS OF SETTLER-COLONIALISM 211

so that a new apprehension of the system, as it applies to the case, will correspond" to one's own political preferences. At the UNSC, Resolution 242 normalized Israel's regime within the 1948 borders, and its language regarding the 1967 occupation was toned down and rendered deliberately ambiguous. Erakat shows that it was no accident that "Israel strategically deployed Resolution 242 to justify is territorial encroachments"[27] and has been able to continue the occupation to this day without legal sanction.

While the "content" (rules and provisions) of international law might appear to prescribe a certain position, its "form" (structural and institutional) is just as much a part of the legal order and illustrates the book's core argument about law and politics being inseparable. Early in the book, to visualize this law-politics entanglement, Erakat invites the reader to:

> Think of the law as like the sail of a boat. The sail, or the law, guarantees motion but not direction. Legal work together with political mobilization, by individuals, organizations, and states, is the wind that determines direction. The law is not loyal to any outcome or player, despite its bias towards the most powerful states. The only promise it makes is to change and serve the interests of the most effective actors. In some cases, the sail is set in such a way that it cannot possibly produce a beneficial direction, and the conditions demand either an entirely new sail, or no sail at all.

The metaphor works well in presenting the law as a subordinate part of a bigger dynamic rather than an autonomous entity in itself, and in highlighting the agency of political actors as the force needed to propel and direct the law. It is a useful way of thinking about the relation between the two and their interdependency. I would consider another layer to this, stemming from the distinction between law's content and form. The sail as the law can be deconstructed further by understanding the physical fabric of the sail as its content, whereas control over the very means of production of the sail is the form. So, while the direction that the boat takes is never absolutely fixed or predetermined, some sails may be loaded with certain weights or steering limitations to orient them in a particular direction – regardless of how progressive the political mobilization may be. In this sense, the "no sail at all" scenario may need to be deployed more readily than it has been to date.

Erakat is acutely conscious of this reality – that the law is not a level terrain and that its default position will tend to favor the ruling class. However, she argues that this is the case for all sites of political struggle, which are all

---

27    Erakat, at 87.

also interconnected, and the legal terrain cannot be abandoned any more than political economy, culture, or social struggle. She gestures to productive precedents to suggest there can still be grounds for optimism in thinking about Palestine from the perspectives Third World Approaches to International Law (TWAIL) and the capacity of social movements in the global South to shape and transform international law from below,[28] as well from perspectives in the Marxist tradition thinking through the lens of strategy and tactics.[29] Erakat is adamant that law can be a source of emancipatory politics where it is "wielded in the sophisticated service of a political movement that can both give meaning to the law and also directly challenge the structure of power"[30] which has hitherto steered the law to obstruct justice. She narrates the period where the Palestinians did so most effectively in a powerful chapter on the PLO operating as "pragmatic revolutionaries" through the 1970s – the book's third juncture. This was a time when Third World nations and the Non-Aligned Movement were attempting to radically transform the international political, legal, and economic orders. In that environment, the PLO made significant inroads through their own legal work at the UN. They gained international legal recognition of the Palestinians as a people with the right to self-determination (not just a refugee population). They overcame staunch Western opposition to assert their alliance with the anti-apartheid struggle in South Africa, culminating in the UN condemning Zionism as a form of racism. The Palestinians were also central to the recognition of national liberation movements as legitimate combatants with rights and duties under international law in 1977. This was all done in pursuit of a clear political strategy at the time to democratize the governance structures of Israel and the occupied territories in a single democratic state.

As Erakat points out, there has been no shortage of Palestinian legal initiatives, and no shortage of good Palestinian lawyers. What there has been a shortage of since the late 1980s, when the single democratic state project was formally abandoned, is political vision from the Palestinian leadership. The Palestinian Authority (PA) was formed out of the Oslo "interim agreements" as a temporary governing entity in the West Bank and Gaza and has been fixated on securing recognition of a partitioned state in fragmented territories. Meanwhile, Israel continues to expand its settlement construction and moves towards annexing more Palestinian land while excluding its people. Erakat provides a cutting critique of both the Oslo process and the PA's more recent

---

28  *See* Balakrishnan Rajagopal, International Law from Below (2003).
29  *See* Robert Knox, *Strategy and Tactics*, 21 Finnish J. Int'l L. 193 (2010).
30  Erakat, at 4.

A HUNDRED YEARS OF SETTLER-COLONIALISM

"haphazard" legal initiatives and obsession with the symbols of statehood rather than the substance of equality and justice.

Here, the contrasts with Namibia[31] are important, not least because of the extent to which international legal initiatives against Israel's occupation of Palestinian territory have recently been analogized to the situation in South West Africa under South African occupation. Advocates for Palestinian rights understandably looked to draw lessons from the Namibia precedent at the UN and the International Court of Justice (ICJ) through the 1950s–70s. This has tended to produce relatively superficial conclusions that pursuit of further ICJ advisory opinions will inherently constitute progress towards Palestinian freedom. The 1971 decision from the ICJ on Namibia was certainly ground-breaking in terms of international law's approach to self-determination. For the South West Africa People's Organisation (SWAPO), however, it was a stepping-stone towards their strategic quest, not the essence of it. SWAPO used the advisory opinion to unify and galvanize the people locally – particularly the labor, student, and church movements – and to mobilize allies internationally. In conceptualizing and narrating the Namibian liberation struggle in *To Be Born a Nation*, SWAPO were remarkably lucid on the law-politics dynamics at play. Their position was explicit: Namibian liberation did not require validation from international law or its institutions. They can be a useful tool towards emancipation but are not definitive of it. For SWAPO, their "right to self-determination" was "quite independent of the niceties of international law," and, equally, "victories in international law alone do not liberate a colonized people from their oppressors." The liberation movement was all too aware that "the legal battles of the past quarter century have often masked the nature of the power struggles which have decided the fate of Namibia."[32]

In the SWAPO analysis, the most crucial development in 1971 was not the ICJ decision itself, but the political action that provided the launchpad for a general strike initiated by the labor movement soon afterwards, which in turn laid the foundations for further years of defiance, civil disobedience and insurrection against: the apartheid regime as a whole; South African attempts to impose a sham peace process; foreign investors and extraction by multinational mining companies; and the UNSC when all three Western permanent powers used their veto to block sanctions against South Africa. Ultimately, the Namibian legal-diplomatic initiatives also carved out the space for SWAPO to harness Cuba's support and leverage the struggle in Angola against the US and

---

31    Erakat, at 224–228.

32    SWAPO of Namibia, Department of Information and Publicity, *To Be Born A Nation: The Liberation Struggle for Namibia* (Zed, 1981), at 122.

South Africa. These elements and tactics together, over time, were eventually decisive in ending apartheid South Africa's occupation of Namibia 20 years after the 1971 ICJ decision. The ICJ was certainly a part of the story, but the advisory opinion was received and wielded by SWAPO not as an end in itself, but in the service of the consistently-articulated strategic endgame of a socialist state project rooted in "freedom, not only from oppressive rule of the hated colonial regime but also from the political and economic stranglehold of its imperialist allies, and for the end of class exploitation and all forms of social injustice."[33] Even at that, South Africa and the Western Contact Group managed to ensure that this radicalism was diluted as much as possible in the interests of international capital before independence was achieved.

## III      Horizons Beyond

If we picture the future histories of Palestinian liberation, the question that arises in this light is whether it will be elite judicial institutions like the ICJ that are remembered as central – making history through international law from above. Or whether it will be from the cracks, shadows, and blind spots of international law that people and movements have emerged to make their own history – like the Boycott, Divestment, Sanctions movement and other vital Palestinian activism and global solidarities. As it stands, the most vibrant Palestinian activist initiatives and international solidarity movements are movements of the left with relatively radical visions of freedom, equality, and justice, but these are not the visions of an official Palestinian leadership that has "engaged in a politics of diplomatic respectability and has refrained from cultivating or joining a global movement highlighting the justness of its cause and/or Israel's role as an aggressor."[34]

In this sense, international law – with its indeterminacy tilting in a particular conservative direction due to its structural biases – may be an obstacle more than an aid to Palestinian freedom. Erakat reinforces and augments existing TWAIL scholarship showing that the sovereign exception dynamics within international law have allowed colonial powers to shape and create new doctrine on the basis of supposedly exceptional fact patterns (in ways that weaker states or entities are rarely able to). In similar ways to Samera Esmeir's telling of colonial legal history in Egypt,[35] Erakat shows that the problem in

---

33    *Id.*, at 4.

34    Erakat, at 227.

35    Samera Esmeir, Juridical Humanity: A Colonial History (2012).

A HUNDRED YEARS OF SETTLER-COLONIALISM                                    215

Palestine is not one of lawlessness, but of the fullness of very particular stripes of law. This is the thorny reality for many of those advocating and support- ing Palestinian self-determination. It is not just a case of saying we need more international law, better law, or more law enforcement. For Erakat, it is a case of saying yes; sometimes it may be conducive to use international law – but sometimes not. More importantly, we need principled, coherent, and strategic political mobilization. The Palestinians certainly need better political leader- ship from above, or the supplanting of their leadership structures with mass movement from below. They need their allies around the world to think with them beyond the "sovereignty trap" which Erakat describes. She argues persua- sively that for a future of Palestinian freedom, the kind of limited autonomy or truncated statehood currently being pursued by the PA is not nearly enough. By the same measure, a vision based only on international law principles is by itself also not enough, where international law's post-1960 articulation of self-determination does not challenge pre-existing colonial partition lines or settler-colonial sovereignty.

This brings us to Erakat's final section on "Horizons of Freedom Beyond the State," which is, in many ways, the most fascinating and provocative part of her book. She pushes us here to think beyond the one-state versus two-state binary and towards more radical imaginations and visions for the future. To do so, she draws on recent Indigenous scholarship which has been grappling with how to move beyond the politics of recognition, how to advance concepts of human and social belonging rather than state sovereignty, and how to make real the idea of decolonization from below.[36]

Erakat trains our sights on the horizons ahead. She is clear that there is no optimal past to return to, but that there are still optimal futures to shape and alternative futures to be forged in Palestine and Israel in terms of belonging, co-existence, and race relations. A Palestinian bantustan state in part of the West Bank will not be sufficient to resolve the situation of exiled Palestinian refugee communities and Palestinian second-class citizens of Israel, never mind building a shared communal future between Jews and Palestinians in the region. For the Palestinian refugees, the journey of return "will, by definition, be a project of building something new. Returning to Palestine will literally be going back to an unknown future."[37] It will be the start, rather than the end, of decolonization. Decolonization does not need to mean the removal of the settler but does at the least require the remaking of the settler as cohabitant

---

36    Here, Erakat draws on the thinking of Indigenous scholars such as Taiaiake Alfred, Glen
      Coulthard, Audra Simpson, Waziyatawin, and others.

37    Erakat, at 238.

rather than conqueror. In Palestine, it will involve Jewish-Israelis becoming part *of* the Middle East, rather than of a colony *in* the Middle East. It will see Mizrahi Jews, for example, as Middle Eastern communities, restoring identities that were deliberately obscured by an Israeli state-building project "modeled on white European values and culture."[38] It will mean dismantling the structures of militarism and racial separation that Zionism has constructed. It will require social solidarities and class alliances between Palestinians, Jews, migrant workers, and refugees in their collective struggles for justice.

It is in this light that we see the limitations of the vision of Palestinian self-determination as a partitioned national state in the West Bank and Gaza. But that vision is international law's vision, which the PLO's "pragmatist" camp was convinced to subscribe to. This reflects the dilemma that Erakat ultimately finds herself in. As a "movement lawyer," she retains a conviction in the capacity of the law to serve as a vehicle for progressive political action that can transform power structures and reshape societal visions. As a researcher, she finds some evidence of this having been proved to work where the law is harnessed in a savvy and strategic way. As a critical thinker and liberation theorist, however, she sees that if we are to ultimately escape the deep, labyrinthine social and political holes we have dug ourselves into, law is not the answer.

If freedom is ultimately contingent on thinking beyond the state, as Erakat suggests, this has implications for an international law system which is so intimately tied to the idea and status quo apparatus of the state. If the optimal futures are not defined by or restricted by law, and may ultimately be obstructed by law, is it wise to rely on the law to get there – even as a tactical bridge? If the Palestinians have survived and resisted a century's worth of imperial attempts at erasure, as documented by Khalidi and Erakat, despite – rather than because of – international legal instruments and institutions, what does this say about international law? If social and political movements are committed to the kind of radical visions of freedom and justice – economic justice, racial justice, gender justice, ecological justice – that Erakat urges us to imagine, they may need to divest from the unfreedoms and injustices of law.

38   *Id.*, at 239.

# The "Visible" and "Invisible" College of Legal Advisers

Andraž Zidar and Jean-Pierre Gauci eds., "The Role of Legal Advisers in International Law" (2016)

Ata R. Hindi

## Contents

I   Introduction
II  The Colonial and Imperial Legacies of International Law
III The "Invisible" College of International Lawyers
IV  The Interplay Between Law and Politics
V   The Palestinian Legal Adviser
VI  Conclusions

## I   Introduction

*The Role of Legal Advisers in International Law*, edited by Andraž Zidar and Jean-Pierre Gauci, is an appealing, cautious look into the roles and responsibilities of those persons engaged in international law work as advisers — primarily those persons attached to respective ministries of foreign affairs.[1] As explained by the editors, the text "seeks to address some of the issues surrounding this role by bringing together a wide range of perspectives from legal advisers to national governments and international organisations."[2] The text is a project of the British Institute of International and Comparative Law, published in 2016 by Brill.

This review essay attempts to discuss a number of themes including: the colonial and imperial legacies of international law and its effect on the contributions to the volume; the "invisible" college of international lawyers and the shortcomings of more diverse geographic and thematic contributions; and the

---

1   The Role of Legal Advisers in International Law (Andraž Zidar & Jean-Pierre Gauci, eds., 2017) [*hereinafter* Zidar & Gauci].
2   *Introduction*, in Zidar & Gauci, at 1.

interplay between law and politics. Finally, it provides some perspective of the roles and responsibilities of Palestinian legal advisers in international law, and the diverse places that he/she works in.

## II    The Colonial and Imperial Legacies of International Law

The text attempts to find a balance between being "international and comparative in its format and scope" and being part of a series on "British Influences on International Law."[3] The editors explain that "[i]t is widely acknowledged that British Legal Advisers have had a leading influence in the development of international law and that they enjoy an excellent reputation among their international peers."[4]

In the preface, Rosalyn Higgins praises British contributions. She expects that those contributions will continue and further influence the future. There are many ways in which one may address her statement, keeping in mind that at the time of writing, for the first time in the storied history of the International Court of Justice (ICJ), there is no British judge on the Court.[5] It is difficult to reconcile her view with some of the questionable legal positions taken by the British in recent years, including via the European Court of Human Rights in several key cases,[6] the ICJ,[7] treaty-making (such as shunning the recent nuclear

---

3    *Id.*, at 2.

4    *Id.*

5    *See* Owen Bowcott, *No British judge on world court for first time in its 71-year history*, Guardian (Nov. 20, 2017), https://www.theguardian.com/law/2017/nov/20/no-british-judge -on-world-court-for-first-time-in-its-71-year-history.

6    *See, e.g.*, Al-Skeini et al. v. U.K., App. No. 55721/07, 2011-IV Eur. Ct. H.R. 99; Al-Jedda v. U.K., App. No. 27021/08, 2011-IV Eur. Ct. H.R. 305. In *Skeini*, the UK argued that "[t]he essentially territorial basis of jurisdiction reflected principles of international law and took account of the practical and legal difficulties faced by a State operating on another State's territory, particularly in regions which did not share the values of the Council of Europe member States" (para. 109).

7    *See, e.g.*, Written Statement of the United Kingdom of Great Britain and Northern Ireland (Legal Consequences of the Construction of a Wall in the Occupied Palestinian Territory, Advisory Opinion, 2004 I.C.J. Rep. 136 (July 9)). In the *Wall*, the UK argued that the ICJ should decline to answer the question posed by the UN General Assembly on various basis including that it would likely "hinder, rather than assist, the peace process" and that it was "essentially a dispute between two parties one of which has clearly not consented to the jurisdiction of the court" (at 2, para. 1.6). *See also* Written Statement of the United Kingdom (Legal Consequences of the Separation of the Chagos Archipelago from Mauritius in 1965, Advisory Opinion, 2019 I.C.J. Rep. 95 (Feb. 25)), https://www.icj-cij.org/public/files/case -related/169/169-20180215-WRI-01-00-EN.pdf. In *Chagos*, the UK argued similarly that it was essentially a "dispute" between two parties (at 1, para. 1.3.), while going so far as to argue that the right to self-determination "had not crystallized by 1968" (at 119, para. 8.3). The UK

# THE "VISIBLE" AND "INVISIBLE" COLLEGE OF LEGAL ADVISERS          219

ban treaty in the present or voting against the anti-apartheid convention in the past), or the legal justification to attack and invade Iraq in 2003, leaving in its wake today one of world's greatest humanitarian and political crises.

Such perceptions do not properly consider the "expansion" (rather than "development") of international law, in the course of European colonialism and imperialism. No attempt is made at underlining international law's origins as a means of control and domination, neither within the introduction nor the preface. After all, colonies were founded in law, and the relationship between colonizers were governed by law.[8] Law did not provide a means for colonies to operate as sovereign equals on the international plane.[9]

This ahistorical and uncritical approach does not fully contextualize the forces which challenged the Euro-centric, colonial, and imperial origins of the discipline. Where Higgins gives credit to the Americans, Germans, and French, none is properly given to the formidable institution of international lawyers and jurists behind the codification and progressive development of international law today, including the scores coming from a decolonized and decolonizing world. The driving forces behind the rules prohibiting apartheid and aggression, for example, did not come from the efforts of the British or their Western counterparts – but from a world beyond Europe, no longer operating under the guns of Western colonial and imperial armies.[10] At least one contributor to the volume, Sarak McCosker, provides some consolation in discussing Indian international law scholarship's role in the development of a distinct approach of the Global South to the discipline, including the emergence of what is now called the "Third World" approach.[11] There, she points out that "several current or former international law advisers in the Indian government have been actively engaged in international law scholarship, and/in

---

snubbed the ICJ and refuses to apply its advisory opinion. *See British Indian Ocean Territory: Written statement – HCWS90*, Made by: Christopher Pincher (Minister of State for Foreign and Commonwealth Affairs), Foreign and Commonwealth Office, www.parliament.uk (Nov. 5, 2019), https://questions-statements.parliament.uk/written-statements/detail/2019-11-05/HCWS90.

8   *See, generally*, Martti Koskenniemi, The Gentle Civilizer of Nations: The Rise and Fall of International Law 1870–1960 (2009).

9   *See, generally*, Anthony Anghie, Imperialism, Sovereignty and the Making of International Law (2012).

10  On the history behind the Anti-Apartheid Convention, *see* John Reynolds, *Third World Approaches to International Law and the Ghosts of Apartheid*, in The Challenge of Human Rights: Past, Present and Future 194–218 (David Keane & Yvonne McDermott eds., 2012). On aggression, *see* Charles De Bock, *The Crime of Aggression: Prospects and Perils for the Third World*, 13 Chinese J. Int'l L. 91–131 (2014).

11  Sarah McCosker, *The Intersecting Professions of the International Law Adviser and Diplomat in a Rising Asia: Australia, India and Malaysia*, in Zidar & Gauci, at 115 [*hereinafter* McCosker].

activities of international law associations."[12] However, overall, the visibility of one world's college of international lawyers leaves another world's college invisible.

## III    The "Invisible" College of International Lawyers

The absence of a discussion on the colonial and imperial legacies of international law, then, goes hand in hand with an insufficiently representative group of contributing authors to the volume. Without prejudice to its unique contributions and some range of diversity, the text doesn't fully represent the contemporary college of international lawyers, who form an "invisible" rather than "visible" college of international lawyers/jurists.[13] In essence, the text could have benefitted tremendously from the contributions of a more diverse group of legal advisers, as well as non-traditional experts – making the "invisible" legal adviser "visible."

Contributions from the Global South (and East) are few. Africa[14] and Latin America[15] are each represented by one opinion, and the Arab World by none. Asia as a whole is represented by Japan[16] as well as Malaysia and India (although by an Australian; and one of the more fascinating pieces in the volume).[17] It is unfortunate that more views from what was disdainfully known as the "Third World" were not included. The same could have been done for regional organizations, such as the League of Arab States, African Union, or Association of Southeast Asian Nations. These perspectives would have provided valuable contributions to the text, including understanding their thematic interests and their perceptions on the interplay between politics and law, while equally inviting critique. The same can even be said for the legal advisers from the other United Nations (UN) Security Council (UNSC) member states (China and Russia). It may also have been possible to discuss the role of the Non-Aligned Movement (NAM), and how states perceive their past and present roles vis-à-vis NAM, a movement that was at the forefront of international law's progress and development.

---

12    *Id.*, at 116.

13    *See Introduction*, in Zidar & Gauci, at 3.

14    Dire Tladi, *Reflections on Advising the South African Government on International Law*, in Zidar & Gauci, at 167 [*hereinafter* Tladi].

15    Eugenia Gutiérrez Ruiz, *The Experience of Legal Advisers in Costa Rica: A Case for Peaceful International Law*, in Zidar & Gauci, at 87 [*hereinafter* Ruiz].

16    Yasuo Kita, *The Legal Advice System of the Ministry of Foreign Affairs of Japan: Between Legal Advisers and Foreign Policy Makers*, in Zidar & Gauci, at 128.

17    McCosker, at 96.

THE "VISIBLE" AND "INVISIBLE" COLLEGE OF LEGAL ADVISERS 221

The views of "non-traditional" legal advisers – those not attached to the state or to international organizations – are also underrepresented; one such example being legal advisers coming from NGOs (although the conference preceding the text did include Amnesty International). NGO legal advisers are engaged in a wide variety of tasks including research, analysis, and advocacy for a wide range of stakeholders, including those working in a similar capacity to several authors in the text. Those representing international arbitration and adjudication bodies – such as the ad hoc or hybrid international criminal tribunals, or the regional human rights courts – would have also provided interesting perspectives. These perspectives would have delivered intriguing contributions to the volume, especially given that many of the legal advisers showcased their interactions with such bodies.[18]

One particularly refreshing contribution comes with Eugenia Gutiérrez Ruiz's Costa Rican perspective, where "international law can be seen as both an arm of a State with no army and as a more general *modus vivendi*."[19] Relying on "international law as a real and effective mechanism to uphold norms and principles"[20] is certainly a perspective shared by legal advisers in Palestine, for one. Here, Costa Rica exhibits its legal advocacy on a number of progressive and meaningful initiatives, including the establishment of the International Criminal Court (ICC), as well as the Arms Trade Treaty, while also playing a "leading role in securing regional support towards nuclear disarmament and non-proliferation."[21] The dichotomy between a defense-driven foreign policy, and a rule of law-driven foreign policy, tips in favor of the latter, and certainly has its enthusiasts.

Another refreshing contribution comes from Dire Tladi, on advising the government of South Africa. Tladi explains the difficult balance between being an academic and possessing the independence to express one's views as such, and working as a legal adviser for the government, which necessarily involves restrictions on independent public declarations of any sort.[22] On "consistency" between the two, he explains the efforts to "reshape current global power dynamics" such as through UNSC reform. On "divergence," and although not in complete disagreement, Tladi employs the example of when he was personally against the insinuation of the ICC as a "neo-colonial project" while

---

18  *See, e.g.*, François Alabrune, *The Case of the Legal Advisor to the French Ministry of Foreign Affairs*, in Zidar & Gauci, at 181 [*hereinafter* Alabrune].

19  Ruiz, at 87.

20  *Id.*, at 88.

21  *Id.*, at 89–90.

22  *Id.*, at 174.

agreeing with a narrow interpretation of Article 98 of the Rome Statute in that there was a duty not to arrest Sudan's Omar Bashir.[23]

Overall, despite many interesting contributions to the text, the text would have benefitted tremendously from greater diversity which could have, in turn, invited more inclusive perspectives.

## IV    The Interplay between Law and Politics

The conference report touches upon the interplay between law and politics, including a view that the law is "politics in technical specialist language."[24] What may be considered as an existential crisis to some, is how the interplay between law and politics deals affects issues of "principle." How do legal advisers deal with government positions that may challenge efforts to respect core rules and principles of international law (*e.g.* peremptory international law norms like the prohibition on the use of force, or the denial of the right to self-determination)? This theme, exploring the ethical and moral considerations of the international law, is common to several pieces within the volume.

Zidar's discussion of professional ethics explains that legal advisers "find themselves in a position both of upholding the interests of their institution (a foreign ministry or an international organisation) and of safeguarding the values and integrity of the system of international law as a whole."[25] In turn, James Kingston differentiates between "hard" legal advice – as to whether a particular course of action or non-action may be lawful – as opposed to advice that is not legal in nature at all; where "hard" legal advice is given and not followed – using the examples of questions of human rights or *jus cogens* – he boldly offers that "the ultimate step of resigning may well be an opinion the legal adviser ought to consider very carefully."[26] Sir Michael Wood then quotes Richard Bilder: "[w]here government lawyers exceed the bounds of honest and responsible argument – functioning purely as apologists or 'hired guns' ... they betray not only their responsibilities but their vocation."[27] These views expressing ethics and morals in its purest form can be differentiated from François Alabrune's more nuanced approach, quoting Sir Gerald Fitzmaurice

---

23    *Id.*, at 166–167.

24    Jean Pierre-Gauci and Kate Jones, *Conference Report: The Role of Legal Advisers in International Law* 378, in Zidar & Gauci.

25    Andraž Zidar, *Legal Advisers and Professional Ethics*, in Zidar & Gauci, at 315.

26    James Kingston, *Organisation and Context for the Work of the Legal Adviser: The Legal Division of the Department of Foreign Affairs and Trade of Ireland*, in Zidar & Gauci, at 81.

27    Sir Michael Wood, *Legal Advisers*, in Zidar & Gauci, at 64–65.

who in turn explains that the legal adviser's duty "is to advise as to the means, within the law, whereby his government can achieve its aims, if these are legally achievable."[28] For Alabrune, politics is adapted to law. This is distinguished from Harold Koh's understanding of the "duty to explain," which entails the use of law to justify to others why the legal adviser's country takes a specific course of action.[29] Koh's "duty to explain" describes the ability to "explain in public the international legal basis supporting what action their government has taken."[30] For Koh, law is adapted to politics. In either approach, ethical and moral considerations are, unfortunately, limited.

In many legal fora (those fixed like the UN General Assembly's Sixth Committee, or temporary like treaty-making), legal advisers may very well contribute to the *regression* rather than the *progression* of international law based on this interplay. Many states, for example, have led numerous efforts to stifle the law, its application, and operation. Some historical examples include efforts undermining: justice and accountability in certain contexts (*e.g.* Palestine and Yemen); a prohibition on nuclear weapons; defining aggression and its inclusion into the Rome Statute; or the criminalization of apartheid. The text provides some indication of these dilemmas in actual practice. Anders Rönquist, for one, alludes to the challenges towards achieving principled language with his counterparts on the situation in Ukraine.[31] Hans Correll then explicates the self-imposed restraint (if I may call it that) in legal advocacy while working in the public service.[32] Lucio Gussetti discusses coordination of European Union (EU) positions, raising the example of the COJUR,[33] which has been, in many ways, a target of civil society in dealing with matters including, but not limited to, international humanitarian law (IHL) and the ICC. He explains that cooperation between EU legal advisers "may contribute to the progressive convergence of the practices of the Member States and of the EU Institutions."[34] Yet it may also have the opposite effect. The Palestinians, for example, cannot typically hope for a coordinated, principled, EU stance. Common ground may result in abstentions on UN Human Rights Council resolutions on Palestine.

---

28    Alabrune, at 181.

29    Harold Hongju Koh, *The Legal Adviser's Duty to Explain*, in Zidar & Gauci, at 290.

30    *Id.*, at.

31    Anders Rönquist, *The Role of Legal Advisers in International Law: The Swedish Experience*, in Zidar & Gauci, at 184.

32    Hans Corell, *Personal Reflections on the Role of the Legal Adviser: Between Law and Politics, Authority and Influence*, in Zidar & Gauci, at 197–198.

33    Lucio Gussetti, *Legal Advisers and the European Union: A New Perspective to Cooperation in International Law*, in Zidar & Gauci, at 212.

34    *Id.*

For civil society, targeting a split-vote may be preferable to highlight principled EU member state positions, while exposing the flaws and double standards of others.

Adding to this debate, Iain Macleod discusses the scope of contemporary challenges faced by the United Kingdom (UK) Foreign and Commonwealth Office (FCO) legal adviser. He explains the ongoing and developing work on topics ranging from the use of force, to Middle East issues, to others. It is not entirely clear as to whether such issues concern the UK directly or perhaps indirectly, in a manner where the UK is interested in bringing the law and its interpretation to fit UK interests (with the caveat that different governments have different interests, of course). For example, on legal immunities in the UK, how would the FCO legal adviser have formulated an argument for granting Tzipi Livni "special mission" status in the UK on two occasions and on questionable, and clearly political, grounds – all in order to avoid soft questioning on her role in the commission of war crimes in the Gaza Strip?[35] How would they reconcile those caveats with its arguments against the immunities of *actual* state officials being investigated for international crimes, such as Omar Al-Bashir?[36] A human rights NGO legal adviser would expect a more consistent position against immunities for international crimes; at the very least, that one position would be preferred either for or against, and not the operation of double standards (although NGOs themselves may also be selective). One would expect clarity about the underlying foundations they are working with. Steven Hill's discussion of the role of the NATO's legal adviser also alludes to these discrepancies.[37] For example, with respect to NATO's communications with the UN Human Rights Council-mandated Libya Commission of Inquiry, NATO challenged the commission's mandate[38] and bluntly asked that "... in the event the Commission elects to include a discussion of NATO actions in Libya, its report clearly state that NATO did not deliberately target civilians and did not commit war crimes in Libya."[39] Would NATO member states have

---

35    *See* Harriet Sherwood, *Israeli minister Tzipi Livni given diplomatic immunity for UK visit*, Guardian (May 13, 2014), https://www.theguardian.com/world/2014/may/13/israel-tzipi-livni-diplomatic-immunity-uk.

36    *See Foreign Office Minister comments following President al-Bashir's visit to Malawi*, GOV.UK (Oct. 14, 2011), https://www.gov.uk/government/news/foreign-office-minister-comments-following-president-al-bashir-s-visit-to-malawi.

37    Steven Hill, *The Role of NATO's Legal Adviser*, in Zidar & Gauci, at 213.

38    *Report of the International Commission of Inquiry on Libya*, U.N. Doc. A/HRC/19/68 (Mar. 2, 2012), at Annex 2, at 201 (arguing that the Commission's mandate was to investigate violations international human rights law, not international humanitarian law).

39    *Id.*, at 212.

THE "VISIBLE" AND "INVISIBLE" COLLEGE OF LEGAL ADVISERS                225

welcomed the same arguments from Libya, or from a non-NATO member in a different context?

Martii Koskeniemmi then provides a bleak, yet fitting, set of conclusions. In discussing the role of the legal adviser in "collective security" and examining the UNSC's role in reacting to Iraq's attack on Kuwait, Koskeniemmi offers a harsh critique.[40] His reflection, based on his own experience, is this: "It is perhaps a truism that delegations couch decisions in legal garb to make them look more respectable. That is the point of law."[41] While differentiating between the realist (coming from a balance of power perspective) and institutionalist (deferring to international legal institutions) approaches in dealing with international peace and security issues, he maintains that "both imagine the law as an instrument for political purposes."[42] He concludes that "[e]ngaging in the formalism of the legal argument inevitably makes public the normative basis and objectives of one's actions and assumes the actor's communal accountability for what it is that one is justifying. It is the antithesis of a culture of secrecy, hegemony, dogmatism and unaccountability."[43] In the process of articulating a legal argument (which is politics in disguise), both schools are not much different[44] – for Koskeniemmi, they still reach the same course of action.

## V     The Palestinian Legal Adviser

Above, I have considered the following themes: the colonial and imperial legacies of international law; the "invisible" college of international lawyers and the shortcomings of more diverse geographic and thematic contributions; and the interplay between law and politics. Drawing from these themes, I would like to provide a contribution on the roles and responsibilities of Palestinian legal advisers, as an example of Global South engagement with international law and in a colonial context. Here, somewhat departing from the format of the text, I do not speak about Palestinian legal advisers as monolith or being attached to a specific institution (although some will be mentioned), but as attached to a cause. They can be found in a number of places. They may be attached to the government, international or national NGOs, or to no

---

40    Martti Koskenniemi, *The Place of Law and the Role of Legal Advisers in Collective Security*, in Zidar & Gauci, at 327.
41    *Id.*, at 332.
42    *Id.*, at 336.
43    *Id.*
44    *Id.*, at 335.

institution at all. This short part will largely reflect on my time working on international law in relation to Palestine and the Palestinian people over the course of several years (largely with the NGO sector and in academia).[45]

The majority of contributions within the text covers those legal advisers attached to their respective foreign ministries (or equivalent). In Palestine, within the government, the Palestinian Ministry of Foreign Affairs and Expatriates does not have the benefit of an organized legal department with the ranks of legal advisers (or as falling within Wood's above-mentioned categories).[46] International law work is primarily delegated to the "Multilateral Sector," consisting primarily of a small collective of career diplomats with limited international law expertise. A number of graduates from Palestinian law faculties (and graduate law programs abroad) have been hired in recent years, although their tasks are limited, including to human rights treaty body reporting in light of Palestine's accession to a number of international human rights treaties. Within the Ministry, and important delegations abroad, a number of diplomats working on international law issues are not trained in either domestic or international law *per se*, but employ their practical experience developed from their valuable time in the diplomatic service at home and abroad. This has led to significant problems at times, in terms of the capacity and resources of the Palestinian government to handle complex international law issues in global fora. Yet, they are also supported by formidable actors within the ranks abroad, such as in Geneva and New York – some of them part of a Palestinian diaspora at the forefront of handling Palestine's most contentious battles, such as working for Palestine's observer state status at the UN. Generally, the Palestinian diaspora has amongst its ranks a formidable line of international lawyers, principled and passionate, romanticizing the freedom of their homeland and people.

There are also legal advisers in other parts of the government, such as in the President's Office, who may be tasked with handling international law issues.

---

45 Some prominent Palestinian international lawyers and jurists in the past and present include Noura Erakat, Ardi Imseis, Anis Kassem, and Victor Kattan, to name a few. Due regard is also given to those international lawyers who have dedicated much of their lives working in solidarity with Palestine and the Palestinian people, such as John Dugard, John Quigley, and Richard Falk, to name a few.

46 Wood, at 60 ["where the lawyers in the office of the legal adviser at the foreign ministry are all professional lawyers, whose career is wholly or largely spent within the legal office rather than on regular diplomatic assignments.... where the legal adviser's office within the foreign ministry consists largely, if not entirely, of regular diplomats with a legal background or even professional legal training ... [where] the foreign ministry receives legal advice from outside sources, typically from an Attorney General's Office/Ministry of Justice."]

THE "VISIBLE" AND "INVISIBLE" COLLEGE OF LEGAL ADVISERS 227

The Palestine Liberation Organization's Negotiations Affairs Department has also employed a number of legal advisers within its Negotiations Support Unit – coming from within Palestine, the diaspora, and internationals. However, over time, the unit has been weakened through the shrinking of its staff and budget. As a whole, the Department has also had its fair share of troubles, including its problematic concessions in discussions with Israeli government officials. However, the unit has, in the course of its existence, included some bright Palestinian international law minds that have been behind some of Palestine's more prominent work in a number of international organizations.

At times, there have been significant communications problems and disagreements between the government (the Ministry in particular) and civil society, the latter being a driving force behind international law and human rights work in Palestine. In the past, there have been instances where the Ministry's decisions were based primarily on policy (or political) considerations, in order to avoid the disruption of relationships with third states. While the Palestinian government has changed course and become more proactive (such as in its actions in various international fora like the ICC and ICJ), in the not-too-distant past, politics certainly led to detrimental decisions obstructing efforts towards justice and accountability. Then, decision-making processes were at times considered arbitrary, discretionary, and reactionary. For example, the Palestinian government almost ended the adoption of the report of the UN Fact-Finding Mission on the Gaza Conflict in 2009; only reversing after protests from the Palestinian public,[47] then calling for an emergency session to adopt the report.[48] Similarly, it was reported that the government attempted to obstruct international investigations of the attack on the Gaza flotilla.[49] The Palestinian government continuously refused calls for Palestine's accession to the Rome Statute of the ICC, and undermined civil society efforts towards that end before it reversed its position with its accession on January 2, 2015.

With respect to civil society, over the years, the national scene has housed and produced distinguished Palestinian international lawyers and jurists (legal advisers in the non-traditional sense). Organizations such as Al-Haq, the Palestinian Center for Human Rights, and others have created spaces for Palestinians – as well as internationals sympathetic to the cause – to thrive as

---

47   *See: Video: Palestinian anger at Abbas*, Al-Jazeera (Oct. 5, 2009), https://www.aljazeera .com/news/2009/10/5/video-palestinian-anger-at-abbas.

48   *See: UN agrees to 'Goldstone session,'* Al-Jazeera (Oct. 14, 2009), https://www.aljazeera .com/news/2009/10/14/un-agrees-to-goldstone-session/.

49   *See* Asa Winstanley, *Exclusive: Leaked documents show PA undermined Turkey's push for UN flotilla probe*, Electronic Intifada (June 22, 2010), https://electronicintifada.net/content/ exclusive-leaked-documents-show-pa-undermined-turkeys-push-un-flotilla-probe/8888.

legal advisers. These organizations have provided a means for Palestinians to work on the cause through international law. This has been evident in work on the ICC, as well as the formidable work in the UN in Geneva (such as the establishment of several fact-finding missions/commissions of inquiry). Within these organizations, Palestinians have come home from the diaspora, or have pursued studies abroad to return, and serve the cause from within these organizations. They operate under a wide range of difficulties, ranging from death threats, to arrests, to being banned from reentry into Palestine (for those without Palestinian IDs) by the Israelis. They operate on fascinating and complex issues of international law. Some examples include, but are not limited to: international humanitarian law and law of occupation; the extraterritorial applicability of human rights obligations; peremptory norms of international law such as the prohibitions on the forcible acquisition of territory, denial of the right to self-determination, and racial discrimination and apartheid; and third state obligations vis-à-vis Common Article 1 of the four Geneva Conventions and the rules on state responsibility.

After some time spent in these places, it may eventually lead to (at least temporary) exile. There are many reasons for this. Some become frustrated with the lack of progress. Some find it difficult to bear the double standards of foreign states, who fall within the "progressive except Palestine" category, such as with the EU and its member states. Some find it difficult to operate due to the involvement of foreign donors into the work and activities of the organization, whether directly (such as asking that they not work on the ICC), or indirectly (such as shifting core funding into project funding envelopes). Others have been caught on occasion in situations where foreign legal advisers, who do not share the same principled positions as their Palestinian counterparts, undermine the work and advocacy. In my own experience, this has included specifically: demanding that the names of companies involved in war crimes be removed from publications; undermining support for the Boycott, Divestment, and Sanctions (BDS) movement; and refraining from engaging in legal analysis that is deemed too "sensitive" (such as working on legal analysis of racial discrimination and apartheid). The large part of Palestinian legal advisers, committed to the cause, will not give up his or her principles for the purposes of future employment or acceptance from a community which seeks to weaken any effort towards justice and accountability. For Palestinian legal advisers, upholding his/her principles is an existential matter. They are committed to a cause, carefully drawing their arguments from conventional and customary law, but also understanding of the bounds of the law (for example, operating within the context of the "two-state solution"). They also quite naturally have grown to understand the politics undermining that cause (for example, denying Palestine's full membership into the UN).

THE "VISIBLE" AND "INVISIBLE" COLLEGE OF LEGAL ADVISERS          229

Palestine and the Palestinian people are, very much, the litmus test for double standards in international law, its application, and interpretation. Politics drive the efforts of other states in undermining Palestine and the Palestinian people. For example, when working on the ICC, it was typical for the community of Palestinian legal advisers, throughout the spectrum, to be told that it wasn't in our best interests, and to refrain from such work. When working on the UN Human Rights Council-mandated database on business vis-à-vis Israeli settlements, there were similar pronouncements.[50] When calling for the complete dismantling of illegal Israeli settlements, or the right of return of all refugees, we were told by some that these claims were not "practical." It is, in fact, situations like these that lead many Palestinians to believe that international law may not only be unavailable for the Palestinians, but that it actively works against them. At times, those undermining forces refuse to accept the Palestinian's presentation of the law, no matter how well articulated.

Since Israel occupied the remainder of historic Palestine in 1967, there have been continuous IHL violations, including instances of grave breaches of the Fourth Geneva Convention, such as willful killings, torture, unlawful deportations, and extensive destruction of property. Palestinian legal advisers will typically invoke Common Article 1, calling for third states to ensure respect for IHL, and remind those states of their obligations pertaining to the grave breaches regime. Palestinian legal advisers will argue for stronger third state measures, given that the Common Article 1 isn't entirely clear as to what measures the state can take. States would often resort to soft measures like diplomatic dialogue, or perhaps even public denunciation, while resorting to stronger measures in other country situations. What about something more "severe," like Israel's annexation of East Jerusalem? There, third states would generally prescribe measures that amount to non recognition, and non aid and assistance, but will argue against direct action against their companies operating in East Jerusalem, or against the obligation to cooperate to bring to an end, through lawful means, such breaches. For example, with respect to the EU, the language on Palestine is much different than the language used on Ukraine – both suffering from the "occupation to annexation" paradigms.[51]

---

50    *See, e.g.,* the views of Switzerland and the UK upon adoption of the Human Rights Council resolution establishing the database on settlement business: *Human Rights Council adopts six resolutions and closes its thirty-first regular session,* UN OHCHR (Mar. 24, 2016), https://www.ohchr.org/EN/NewsEvents/Pages/DisplayNews.aspx?NewsID=18535&LangID=E.

51    *See* Council of the EU, *Illegal annexation of Crimea and Sevastopol: EU extends sanctions by one year,* Press Release (June 20, 2019), https://www.consilium.europa.eu/en/press/press-releases/2019/06/20/illegal-annexation-of-crimea-and-sevastopol-eu-extends-sanctions-by-one-year/#.

On one occasion, I was told by an international law professor from a prestigious European institution that I, as a Palestinian, should not reference Palestine in my work – because I was Palestinian. I responded by stating that, for some odd reason, there is a platform for Israelis undermining international law to fit Israeli interests. The same goes for the Americans, and every other country – a platform is provided to present the law according to their own interests. Yet Palestinian legal arguments are received with skepticism. It can hardly be said, however, that only Palestinian or Third World experts are subjective or politicized, whereas those from the Global North are objective and disinterested. Yet this view is not peculiar: the erasure of Palestinians voices and the over-representation of Israeli experts is quite prominent in international legal debates and proceedings, as pointed out by Victor Kattan.[52]

Palestinian legal advisers understand the discipline of international law, and that it is drawn from the histories of nations and peoples, structured in colony and empire, and managed through gunpowder and bondage. The Palestinian legal adviser has learned the language, and improved it through progress, skill, and principle – much like his/her counterpart in the decolonized world. As such, they understand history's effects on both the bounds of the law itself, as well as its role in the interplay between law and politics. They thus operate in two alternate dimensions: one that is positivistic (although positivists disagree on what this actually means), and one that is critical. Nevertheless, while they employ "positivist" international law in their work, they also critically engage the law, its interpretation, and application. The endeavor requires due consideration from critical legal studies, particularly those voices emanating from TWAIL. Considering this history and the two effects described above, when it comes to situations like in Palestine, critical engagement is a necessary exercise. Drawing from Koskeniemmi and applying that argument vis-à-vis Palestine, the end result of the different approaches is the same – politics is dressed up as law, and third states and Parties find a way to undermine Palestinian positions.

Palestinian legal advisers seek what is just for their country and people, like: ending the unlawful occupation; equality for Palestinian citizens of Israel; and the right of return for all Palestinian refugees. In order to achieve these aims, the role of Palestinian legal advisers is to do just that – advise, whenever and wherever possible. The adviser advises proactively and reactively. Unfortunately, due to the never-ending cycle of challenges that Palestinians

---

52    *See* Victor Kattan, *Palestinian Scholarship and the International Criminal Court's Blind Spot,* TWAILR (Feb. 20, 2020), https://twailr.com/palestinian-scholarship-and-the-international-criminal-courts-blind-spot/.

THE "VISIBLE" AND "INVISIBLE" COLLEGE OF LEGAL ADVISERS          231

face, much of the work is done on the reactive end. Nevertheless, they are constantly looking for different means and methods towards achieving those aims. Today, Palestinian legal advisers across the spectrum are heavily engaged with international judicial and semi-judicial bodies. Some examples include: the ICC; the ICJ (Palestine v. the US); or the inter-state complaint against Israel with the UN Committee on the International Covenant on the Elimination of Racial Discrimination.

Across that spectrum, international law has become an arm of Palestine's foreign policy and its social justice project. Palestine does not enjoy military power and does not thrive on the idea of such. Palestinian legal advisers approach international law as progressives, fighting to ensure compliance not only with areas of law they typically have to deal with, but on other critical issues – like banning nuclear weapons and fighting against climate change. Over the past decade in particular, it is amazing to see how Palestine's small capacity and few resources have been put to work on the most complex issues of international law, in contrast to those powers that pay little more than lip service to the primacy of the international law in the conduct of their international relations.

## VI      Conclusions

The volume is a fascinating overview of the work of legal advisers in international law. For those working on international law, in any capacity, it is a necessary read. It provides insights into the roles and responsibilities of certain legal advisers which can be of considerable benefit, especially from a comparative lens. Yet it is not without its shortcomings. As this review has attempted to explain, it does not provide due regard for the colonial and imperial origins of international law, and the "Third World" forces which challenged those origins and made significant contributions to its progress and development. In turn, while noting certain contributions from states like Costa Rica and South Africa, it does not sufficiently offer diversity in contributions. Finally, the contributions vary in their positions, and personal experiences, on the interplay between law and politics. This is arguably one of the most interesting aspects of the text. Of course, it must be recognized that the position of legal advisers, and the affiliation that comes with it, seems to constrain some contributors, as opposed to others.

This review also offers my own personal reflections on being a Palestinian legal adviser and working with fellow Palestinian legal advisers. These reflections reflect a broad notion of Palestinian legal advisers, ranging from those affiliated with the government in various capacities, those working for civil society, and others. While brief, I hope that this short reflection provides some insight into our work, principles, and cause. It is further hoped that the three themes described above will be more prominent in future discussions on the work of legal advisers working on international law. The work of Palestinians legal advisers offers some insight into their perspectives on the colonial and imperial legacies of international law; their existence in the college of international lawyers as one that could provide a more diverse geographic and thematic perspective; and their profound experience in dealing with the interplay between law and politics. As such, I think that the Palestinian experience provides lessons that are relevant to other Global South and (de-)colonized nations' engagements with international law.

# PART 4

## *Book Reviews*

Rouba Al-Salem, "Security, Rights and Law: The Israeli High Court of Justice and Israeli Settlements in the Occupied West Bank"

In 2003, the Palestine Liberation Organization (PLO) took the unprecedented step of seeking legal redress before the International Court of Justice (ICJ). The matter concerned Israel's 8-meter-high, 680-km-long separation wall ["Wall"] which snakes through the West Bank, trapping Palestinians on one side and stealing Palestinian land on the other. The unique circumstances of Palestine's non-state status mandated that the ICJ's opinion would be an advisory one only, yet nonetheless indicative of the ICJ's opinion of the legality of Israel's Wall. In its July 2004 opinion, the ICJ overwhelmingly determined that the construction of Israel's Wall and its associated regime are contrary to international law.[1]

In the decades prior to the ICJ opinion, and in the years since, legal practitioners, international donors, and members of the diplomatic community urged Palestinians to seek redress in Israeli courts for Israel's human rights and humanitarian law violations. Underlying this urge was an assumption that the Israeli legal system was neutral and capable of overseeing the practices of the Israeli government and of the army. Those who have advocated this position view Israel as a democracy which, like other democracies, has a system of checks and balances. Diplomats, donors, and scholars point to a number of decisions that have been issued by Israeli courts over the years, including, for example, various decisions purportedly limiting torture, purportedly limiting the confiscation of Palestinian land for the purpose of building settlements, and cases relating to women's rights in Israel.

For their part, the PLO and numerous Palestinian human rights organizations have refused to resort to Israeli courts, holding the position that doing so would be tantamount to recognizing Israeli jurisdiction and accordingly its "right" to adjudicate over such matters. Others, including several local NGOs adopted a more nuanced (some would say pragmatic) approach in which suits are brought before Israeli courts to either "buy time" in the hopes of a "peace agreement" or diplomatic pressure, or in the belief that there is no other alternative available. Whatever the motivation for pursuing action before Israel's courts, Rouba Al-Salem's book, *Security, Rights and Law: The Israeli High Court*

---

1  See Legal Consequences of the Construction of a Wall in the Occupied Palestinian Territory, Advisory Opinion, 2004 I.C.J. Rep 136 (July 9).

236 BOOK REVIEWS

*of Justice and Israeli Settlements in the Occupied West Bank*, provides an interesting analysis of decisions before the Israeli High Court of Justice (HCJ).[2]

The book begins with an overview of the legal and political landscape of Israel's occupation of the West Bank. It sets out the framework in which the Israeli HCJ purports to have the right to adjudicate over the West Bank and over the actions of Israel's Military Commander, providing an overview of both the international and Israeli domestic law framework. Noting the HCJ's position that Israel's military occupation is considered to be "temporary," the author then examines how the inherently *not* temporary measures – such as the construction of Israel's Wall – have been treated by this court. Other chapters focus on the regime surrounding the "seam zone" which prohibits Palestinian movement except for those who reside in these zones, as well as the various petitions that have sought to challenge the legality of Israeli measures restricting Palestinian movement inside the West Bank. Chapter 4 deals with the HCJ's handling of petitions involving the construction of Israel's Wall in and around Jerusalem while the final chapter focuses on some of the petitions challenging Israel's "unauthorized outposts."

In each of these chapters, Al-Salem methodically highlights the arguments put forth by Palestinian petitioners and the responses by the various organs within the Israeli state machinery, providing a "roadmap of the elements that have influenced the manner in which the HCJ has adjudicated security-based measures in relation to the security of settlements and settlers."[3] Ultimately, Al-Salem's analysis concludes that the HCJ "has provided a limited domestic judicial venue for Palestinian petitioners to effectively challenge alleged violations of their rights, which are first and foremost protected under international law."[4]

Al-Salem notes that this is due to the fact that the HCJ has employed a number of different tools to effectively limit successful challenges by Palestinian petitioners, including: refusing to recognize the West Bank and Gaza Strip as an occupied territory (despite the ruling of the ICJ in 2004); declaring that the situation in the occupied West Bank is that of "an armed conflict short of war;" selectively applying international treaties and the Geneva Conventions (accepting the state's argument that only the "humanitarian provisions" of the Conventions apply) thereby transforming Israel's settler-colonial rule into a "humanitarian" case; its treatment of many issues as "non-justiciable" owing to

---

2  Rouba Al-Salem, Security Rights and Law: The Israeli High Court of Justice and Israeli Settlements in the Occupied West Bank (2020) [*hereinafter* Al-Salem].

3  *Id.*, at 232.

4  *Id.*

BOOK REVIEWS 237

their political nature despite its willingness to rule on many other issues; and its refusal to deal with "general" issues, instead preferring to focus on singular issues such as *one* portion of the Wall or *one* unauthorized settlement.

In his 2014 article, *Activism and Legitimation in Israel's Jurisprudence of Occupation*, Nimer Sultany similarly cites the above-noted "tools" to effectively block Palestinian court challenges, adding that while the HCJ's refuses to investigate "security" considerations, it intervenes only when there is an "excess of military power," *i.e.* when "the focus is not on colonial occupation per se as a form of systemic violence and systemic violation of rights."[5] Al-Salem's work provides additional examples of Sultany's conclusions regarding the methods used to limit Palestinian challenges. In short, Israel has created a "balancing" hand-wringing approach to addressing Palestinian rights which has served to both maintain the power in place and legitimate its actions under the guise of law.

As an example, to highlight the various mechanisms used to limit successful challenges, Al-Salem contrasts the ICJ's Advisory Opinion with that of the HCJ in relation to parts of the Wall, demonstrating that Palestinian complainants have

> ... little chance of convincing the [HCJ] that any considerations other than security have influenced the route chosen by authorities for the Wall's construction. Nevertheless, they continue to gather as many facts and indicators as possible to substantiate their claims that political considerations are the driving force behind the respondents' decision to route the Wall along a certain way, hoping it would then be 'easier [for the HCJ] to decide on the proportionality which it so loves', to strike down the route as illegal.[6]

While the book provides an excellent analysis of the decisions of the HCJ, part of Al-Salem's conclusions stands out as incongruous with the work of the rest of the book:

> By subjecting the actions of Israeli military authorities to judicial review in 'real time' the Israeli [HCJ] has demonstrated that Palestinians stand a real chance of compelling Israeli officials to reconsider the effects of their proposed measures and the rights and interests of affected individuals.

---

5 Nimer Sultany, *Activism and Legitimation in Israel's Jurisprudence of Occupation*, 23 Soc. & Legal Stud. 315, 323 (2014) [*hereinafter* Sultany].

6 Al-Salem, at 81.

Often, the mere possibility of 'going to court' to challenge these measures, has ensured that Israeli government and military authorities are
aware they are acting 'in the shadow' of the potential judicial decisions of
the HCJ, and that they may be required to defend their actions in court,
including on the basis of the norms of international law.[7]

Al-Salem similarly adds that,

> ... in the meantime, the need to provide effective judicial remedy goes
> hand in hand with the need to ensure accountability for wrongful acts
> committed by or on behalf of State organs. Together, they constitute a
> central requirement for satisfactory adherence to the international RoL
> (Rule of Law), including in situations of occupation. As the 'gatekeeper'
> straddling the interface between international and domestic law, the HCJ
> must not lose sight of those requirements ... all the while it still can.[8]

Unlike the approach presented in the two paragraphs cited above, the works
of other scholars such as Sultany[9] and Hajjar[10] highlight that Palestinian life
under occupation has *not* been positively transformed following judicial
intervention. Instead, the HCJ has served to "accommodate occupation more
than the occupation has adjusted to accommodate legal restraints."[11] These
paragraphs also seem inconsistent with the remainder of Al-Salem's book
in which she highlights just how ineffective the legal system has been for
Palestinians.

Indeed, while Al-Salem highlights the ineffectiveness of the system, her
approach differs from scholars like Sultany,[12] Jabareen,[13] and Masri.[14] Al-Salem
repeatedly refers to "Israel proper" – a term that has no legal or political foundation given that Israel has never formally declared its borders and continues

---

7    *Id.*, at 232.

8    *Id.*, at 242.

9    *See* Sultany.

10   *See* Lisa Hajjar, Courting Conflict: The Israeli Military Court System in the West Bank and
     Gaza (2005).

11   Sultany, at 321 [*citing* Guy Harpaz & Yuval Shany, *The Israeli Supreme Court and the
     Incremental Expansion of the Scope of Discretion under Belligerent Occupation Law*, 43 Isr.
     L. Rev. 514 (2019)].

12   *See* Sultany.

13   *See* Hassan Jabareen, *How the Law of Return Creates One Legal Order in Palestine*, 21
     Theoretical Inquiries L. 459 (2020).

14   *See* Mazen Masri, *Colonial Imprints: Settler-Colonialism as a Fundamental Feature of Israeli
     Constitutional Law*, 13 Int'l J. L. Context 388 (2017).

BOOK REVIEWS

to apply, as Al-Salem notes, Israeli law to the West Bank. The difference is not merely a semantic one but one of approach, with the above-mentioned scholars examining Israeli HCJ decisions not in light of a system created to accommodate Israel's actions, but in light of Israel's colonial system. The difference is important: focusing on the system from *within* the settler-colonial created logic risks not only distorting the legal analysis, but also legitimating the racist colonial system in place by limiting analysis to the confines that the system itself posits.

As we have witnessed, particularly since the ICJ ruling in 2004, scholars and the United Nations have questioned the use of Israel's legal framework and its interpretation of international humanitarian law (IHL) to address Palestinian rights. During this time, we have witnessed attempts, including by those formerly wedded to the IHL framework, to reframe the analysis to focus on "long-term occupation"[15] and the subsequent labeling of Israel's military occupation into an "illegal occupation"[16] and an "apartheid,"[17] to break away from the limited IHL framework.

Through the use of Israel's courts, it has become clear that, like other colonial systems, the Israeli system is incapable of providing a legal "knock-out" to its regime. Instead, the system works tirelessly to accommodate the regime. Even for those cases where the HCJ disagreed with the state, these disagreements have often been minor in nature and have only served to provide a means of "legitimating" the HCJ.[18] In the words of Audre Lorde, "For the master's tools will never dismantle the master's house. They may allow us temporarily to beat him at his own game, but they will never enable us to bring about genuine change."[19]

In short, by examining cases through the inner logic created by the Israeli courts, Al-Salem's work lends credibility to the position of Palestinian legal NGOs not to use the Israeli legal system to seek redress. The author, however, neither takes nor examines this position. Thus, while the book is a welcome

---

15 *See* Michael Lynk, *Prolonged Occupation or Illegal Occupation*, EJIL: Talk! (May 16, 2018), https://www.ejiltalk.org/prolonged-occupation-or-illegal-occupant/.

16 *See* Orna Ben-Naftali, Aeyal M. Gross, & Meren Michaeli, *Illegal Occupation: Framing the Occupied Palestinian Territory*, 23 Berkeley J. Int'l L. 551 (2005).

17 *See* Richard Falk & Virginia Tilley, *Israeli Practices Towards the Palestinian People and the Question of Apartheid*, U.N. Doc. E/ESCWA/ECRI/2017/1 (2017) [this report was censored by the UN but was published by the Palestine Yearbook of International Law. *See* 20 Palestine Y. Int'l L. 201 (2019)].

18 *See* Ronen Shamir, *"Landmark Cases" and the Reproduction of Legitimacy: The Case of Israel's High Court of Justice*, 24(3) Law & Soc. Rev. 781 (1990).

19 Audre Lorde, *The Master's Tools Will Never Dismantle the Master's House*, in Sister Outsider: Essays and Speeches 110–114 (2007).

contribution to the study of the Israeli legal system, it could have benefitted from additional analysis focusing on these larger trends that view the Israeli legal system more accurately and critically – in particular, the function of self-legitimation that the system plays by addressing both the Israeli public and the international community in order to provide an aura of "justice" all while supporting its colonial regime.

Future work in this area may wish to focus on two aspects: why Palestinians have resorted to using these courts (briefly touched upon in the book); and how the Israeli HCJ treats petitions by Israeli settler petitioners. The latter, a rising (and well-funded) legal phenomena as Israeli settlers now similarly resort to the HCJ to compel the state to carry out demolitions of Palestinian homes.

*Diana Buttu*

BOOK REVIEWS                                                               241

Marco Longobardo, "The Use of Armed Force in Occupied Territory" (2018)

Marco Longobardo, a lecturer in international law at the University of West-minster, United Kingdom, wrote his PhD on the law relating to the prolonged occupation of Palestine.[1] Along the way, he published articles on Palestinians' right to exploit the Dead Sea coastline for tourism amidst the occupation[2] and state responsibility for natural resource exploitation in occupied territories by private actors.[3] He bills this work as the first comprehensive study on the regulation of the use of force in occupied territory.[4]

By "comprehensive," Longobardo means an account that brings together three bodies of international law – the rules governing the use to force (*jus ad bellum*), international humanitarian law (IHL) (*jus in bello*), and international human rights law (IHRL) – and considers the use of force by all relevant actors: the occupying power, the ousted sovereign, and the local population of the occupied territory. The book is divided into seven chapters, with the first two chapters surveying the law of occupation and the substance of his enquiry set forth in chapters 3–6.

Chapter 3 examines whether *jus ad bellum*, in particular the justification of self-defense, applies to the occupying power's use of force in occupied territory. Longobardo concludes, from state practice and the International Court of Justice's (ICJ) rejection of the Israeli claim of self-defense in the *Wall* advisory opinion, that it does not. However, he finds the three rationales generally offered for this conclusion to be unsatisfactory.[5] First, the claim that self-defense cannot be invoked against non-state actors is controversial and unsettled as a matter of state practice. Second, the claim that armed attacks originating in occupied territory lack an international character, and thus do not implicate rules governing resort to force, fails to honor the integrity of the occupied territory and its distinction from the occupying power's own territory. Third, the argument that the law of occupation, as *lex specialis* governing the

---

1  Marco Longobardo, The Use of Armed Force in Occupied Territory xiv (2018) [*hereinafter* Longobardo].

2  *See* Marco Longobardo, *The Palestinian Right to Exploit the Dead Sea Coastline for Tourism*, 58 Ger. Y.B. Int'l. L. 317 (2015).

3  *See* Marco Longobardo, *State Responsibility for International Humanitarian Law Violations by Private Actors in Occupied Territories and the Exploitation of Natural Resources*, 63 Neth. Int'l. L. Rev. 251 (2016). Since publishing the reviewed volume, Longobardo has written on the occupation of maritime territory, with special focus paid to Gaza; *see* Marco Longobardo, *The Occupation of Maritime Territory under International Humanitarian Law*, 95 Int'l. Legal Stud. 322 (2019).

4  Longobardo, at 4.

5  *Id.*, at 118 et seq.

© KONINKLIJKE BRILL NV, LEIDEN, 2021 | DOI:10.1163/22116141_022010_010

242 BOOK REVIEWS

use of force in occupied territory, displaces the rules governing resort to force runs afoul of the principle of separation between *jus ad bellum* and *jus in bello*.

Instead, Longobardo concludes that *jus ad bellum* rules are inapplicable because the occupation "inherently preserves" a state of armed conflict in the occupied territory, even in the absence of actual hostilities.[6] He acknowledges that his theory swims against the current of international law, which, confronted with the "war on terror" and open-ended international interventions, has good reason to break free of the state-of-war/state-of-peace dyad. But Longobardo sets aside any normative commitments in assembling state practice and commentary in support of his theory. He relies on Israel's claims of ongoing armed conflicts to justify military action against Iran, Lebanon, and Syria, while noting the United Nations (UN) Security Council "has often condemned these episodes under *jus ad bellum*."[7] Tortured claims that the 1990–1991 Gulf War never ended and obviated the need to justify anew the United States (US)-led invasion over a decade later get the same purely descriptive treatment. He also relies on black-letter recitals that IHL applies from the start of hostilities until the occupying power relinquishes or loses effective control.[8]

In essence, Longobardo offers a rigidly doctrinal solution to a problem resulting from a rigidly doctrinal interpretation of the concept of *lex specialis*. The *jus ad bellum*/*jus in bello* dichotomy exists to ensure respect for IHL "in all circumstances"[9] and "without any adverse distinction based on the nature or origin of the armed conflict or on the causes espoused by or attributed to the Parties to the conflict."[10] The pre-emptive effect or *lex specialis* force of *jus in bello* certainly must be defined as broadly as necessary to achieve that objective. But as the International Law Commission made clear in its final report on the fragmentation of international law, determining the degree to which *lex specialis* (here, *jus in bello*) pre-empts the general law (*jus ad bellum*) is an exercise in pragmatic decision-making:

---

6   *Id.*, at 126. Longobardo calls his theory a "novel explanation" (at 89) while later acknowledging that a majority of experts participating in a 2012 International Committee of the Red Cross conference on occupation shared this view (at 131, n300) [*citing* Int'l Comm. Red Cross, *Expert Meeting: Occupation and Other Forms of Administration of Foreign Territory* (Tristan Ferraro ed., 2012), at 111.].

7   Longobardo, at 129.

8   *Id.*, at 128–130.

9   Common Article 1 to the four Geneva Conventions of 1949.

10  Protocol Additional to the Geneva Conventions of 12 August 1949, and relating to the Protection of Victims of International Armed Conflicts pmbl., June 8, 1977, 1125 U.N.T.S. 3. *See also* Jenny Martinez & Antoine Bouvier, *Assessing the Relationship between Jus in Bello and Jus ad Bellum: An "Orthodox" View*, 100 Proc. Ann. Meeting (Am. Soc. Int'l L.) 109, 110 (2006).

BOOK REVIEWS 243

The example of the laws of war focuses on a case where the rule itself identifies the conditions in which it is to apply, namely the presence of an "armed conflict". Owing to that condition, the rule appears more "special" than if no such condition had been identified. To regard this as a situation of *lex specialis* draws attention to an important aspect of the operation of the principle. Even as it works so as to justify recourse to an exception, what is being set aside does not vanish altogether....

The important point to retain here is that when *lex specialis* is invoked as an exception to the general law then what is being suggested is that the special nature of the facts justifies a deviation from what otherwise would be the 'normal' course of action. This highlights again the operation of *lex specialis* as an aspect making pragmatic judgements about relative 'generality' and 'speciality', about what is 'normal' and what 'exceptional'.[11]

Such pragmatic judgements require considering the nature and objective of the occupation, something Longobardo is unwilling to entertain, despite his demonstrated familiarity with the relevant contexts. He admits as potential aggression only the initial seizure and occupation of territory and not further acts of force used to maintain the occupation regime[12] or even to pursue objectives antithetical to the supposedly temporary character of the occupation.[13]

Consider, in this vein, the contemporary Israeli governmental discourse that constructing and annexing settlements – *i.e.* forcibly acquiring more Palestinian territory – is an "appropriate Zionist response" to acts of violence by Palestinians against Israelis (combatants or civilians) in the occupied territory.[14] By using settlements as a form of reprisal, state policy merges

---

11    U.N. Int'l L. Comm., *Fragmentation of International Law: Difficulties Arising from the Diversification and Expansion of International Law*, Final Report, at 57, para. 104–105, U.N. Doc. A/CN.4/L.682 (Apr. 13, 2006) [*hereinafter* ILC Fragmentation].

12    Longobardo, at 120–121.

13    Longobardo observes that while the ousted sovereign's right of self-defense is "not renounceable because of its inherent character," the world community disfavored armed resistance in self-defense once an occupation becomes "firmly established" (at 120–121).

14    For example, members of the governing coalition, including the Israeli justice minister, demanded that the government retroactively "legalize" unauthorized settlement construction after a 2018 shooting attack by a Palestinian in the West Bank settlement of Ofra. *See* Lahav Harkov & Tovah Lazaroff, *Netanyahu: Israel Will Build West Bank Settlements Despite ICC Pressure*, Jerusalem Post (Dec. 10, 2018), https://www.jpost .com/Israel-News/Politics-And-Diplomacy/Netanyahu-Israel-will-build-West-Bank-settle ments-despite-ICC-pressure-573970. This discourse is not limited to acts of violence. When the Palestinian Authority and Hamas tried to form a national reconciliation government in 2014, Israel responded by advancing construction on 1,500 new housing units in West Bank settlements. The Israeli housing minister, Uri Ariel, declared settlement

*ad bellum* and *in bello* principles. In Longobardo's account, settlement construction clearly violates the *jus in bello* but flatly does not implicate *jus ad bellum*. The danger of this siloed view – "the loss of an overall perspective on the law"[15] – is well-documented in international law generally and as applied to the law of occupation specifically.[16] Against this growing critical literature and calls for an integrated approach to the law of occupation, Longobardo's dismissal of *jus ad bellum* seems regressive.

The better view is that of Victor Kattan, who has concluded that a territory under the effective control of another state, whether through occupation, annexation, or other forms of external control, may also be subject to aggression, with the gravity of the military offensive distinguishing an "exceptional" act of aggression from the occupying power's "normal" use of force in the occupied territory.[17]

Additionally, Longobardo's "inherently preserves" argument rests on a war/peace dichotomy that not only belies the complexities of contemporary occupations, but is also incongruent with his nuanced assertions about, *inter alia*, the effect of the Oslo Accords on the Palestinian right of armed struggle against the occupying power. It is reductionist to describe the average day in the life of the occupation as a "state of war." Whereas Longobardo claims "the existence of an ongoing armed conflict is *presumed* in situations of occupation," the existence of the Palestinian Authority (PA) – which allows the local population to

---

      expansion "an appropriate Zionist response to the establishment of the Palestinian terror government." *See* Isabel Kershner & Jodi Rudoren, *New Israeli Settlement Plans Draw Swift Condemnation*, N.Y. Times (June 5, 2014), https://www.nytimes.com/2014/06/06/world/middleeast/new-israeli-settlement-plans-draw-swift-condemnation.html.

15    ILC Fragmentation, at 11, para. 8.

16    *See, e.g.*, Aeyal Gross, The Writing on the Wall: Rethinking the International Law of Occupation (2017); Hanne Cuyckens, Revisiting the Law of Occupation (2017). In a different vein, *see* Eyal Benvenisti, *Rethinking the Divide Between Jus ad Bellum and Jus in Bello in Warfare Against Nonstate Actors*, 34 Yale J. Int'l L. 541 (2009).

17    Victor Kattan, *Operation Cast Lead: Use of Force Discourse and Jus ad Bellum Controversies* 15 Palestine Y.B. Int'l. L. 95 (2009), adding that "geographic and political entities entitled to self-determination, or whose legal status is controversial due to a lack of recognition from other states, can be subject to acts of aggression" (at 113). Kattan identified "several instances of state practice both prior to and after the Definition of Aggression was adopted by the UNGA in 1974, where it had been claimed by states that acts of aggression had been committed by or against political entities that were not recognised as states or whose sovereign status was controversial under international law" (at 112, (citing G.A. Res 3314 (XXIX) (Dec. 14, 1974))). He relied on statements made by various state representatives before the UNSC in contexts ranging from the North Korean invasion of South Korea while the latter remained under UN supervision, India's invasion of Portuguese colonies on the Subcontinent, and Indonesia's invasion of East Timor following Portugal's withdrawal.

BOOK REVIEWS

245

deal only indirectly with the "hostile authority" – is predicated on the *absence* of hostilities, as evidenced by Israel openly considering whether to eliminate the PA during periods of hostilities.[18]

Chapter 4 sets out to define the legal framework governing armed resistance against the occupying power. Longobardo starts by explaining the historic "disagreement among states" that has thwarted the establishment of principles in this area. He turns to Karma Nabulsi's theory of a "Grotian tradition" of codifying the laws of war, one which sought to mediate the "martialist" conception of war amongst powerful states with the republican visions of smaller states, as the potential victims of occupation.[19] This mediation, exemplified by the Martens Clause,[20] yielded laws of war which honored the martialist vision by prioritizing state interests and upholding the distinction between soldiers and civilians.[21] But in keeping with the doctrinal nature of the volume, Longobardo gives the traditional narrative of this period. For example, while he recounts the controversy over the status of *francs-tireurs*,[22] he does not incorporate recent critical scholarship, which illustrates that *class interests* – the preservation of sovereign authority, free trade, and private property – motivated denying combatant status to *francs-tireurs*, who had shown themselves willing in the Franco-Prussian War to keep fighting in defiance of their sovereign's surrender.[23]

Longobardo considers the true reason why *levée en masse* – spontaneous, unorganized resistance to invading forces – has long been deemed legitimate is the "metalegal consideration that the defence of the homeland should be considered just for patriotic reasons."[24] But *levée en masse* as codified in article 2 of the Hague Regulations only offers combatant status on this basis to "the inhabitants of a territory which has not been occupied." Longobardo considers that international law fails to provide "any satisfactory answer" for differentiating resistance against invading forces from that against an occupying power.[25]

---

18  Longobardo, at 130–131.

19  *Id.*, at 136. *See also* Karma Nabulsi, Traditions of War: Occupation, Resistance and the Law (1999).

20  Longobardo, at 142–143.

21  *Id.*, at 136. For a critical re-examination of whether the Martens Clause represented genuine mediation of these competing visions and the valorized discourse which surrounds the clause and Martens personally, *see* Rotem Giladi, *The Enactment of Irony: Reflections on the Origins of the Martens Clause*, 25 Eur. J. Int'l. L. 847, 850–855 (2014).

22  Longobardo, at 141–143.

23  *See, e.g.*, Eyal Benvenisti & Doreen Lustig, *Monopolizing War: Codifying the Laws of War to Reassert Governmental Authority, 1856–1874*, 31 Eur. J. Int'l L. 127 (2020).

24  Longobardo, at 137.

25  *Id.*

With that discrepancy as his charge, Longobardo traces tentative developments in the law towards recognizing a right of resistance in occupied territory. He rejects the notion, still advocated by certain states, that the local population of the occupied territory owes a duty of obedience to the occupying power, such that would prohibit armed resistance as a matter of international law.[26] He recounts the deadlock over the right of resistance in occupied territory at the 1874 Brussels Conference and the Hague Peace Conferences, and the 1907 Hague Regulations' resulting silence on the issue. Recognizing the role of armed resistance to the occupations of the Second World War, the Geneva Conventions of 1949 recognized for the first time that IHL does not *per se* prohibit such resistance, provided the resisters satisfy the conditions for combatant status under article 4 of the Third Geneva Convention. Article 44(3) of Additional Protocol I to the 1949 Conventions relaxed the conditions for combatant status when necessitated by "the nature of the hostilities" – foremost in cases of occupation. But here the development stops, as persistent and vehement objection to article 44(3) by certain non-party states, most prominently the US, deny it the status of customary international law.[27] IHL thus regards armed resistance in occupied territory as espionage: neither *per se* prohibited nor worthy of protection beyond the minimum standards of treatment prescribed in common article 3 to the Geneva Conventions.[28]

At this point, Longobardo hints at a normative turn in his work. The law of occupation is concerned principally, and nearly exclusively, with the conduct of the occupying power. Its near silence on the local population's right of resistance thus cannot be read as a prohibition; rather, IHL "*acknowledges* the fact of armed resistance *without regulating* it."[29] Suggesting that the contours of such a doctrine might be found elsewhere, Longobardo surveys the law of self-determination[30] and the historic demands of certain Arab states for a proviso concerning armed resistance against occupation in international conventions against terrorism.[31]

But the normative turn never materializes. Singularly focused on state practice, Longobardo finds debate on the interplay between self-determination and armed struggle "monopolised" by the question of Palestine.[32] A review of "state practice" built on a single case study leads him to some questionable

---

26   *Id.*, at 137–141.
27   *Id.*, at 146.
28   *Id.*, at 147.
29   *Id.*, at 148–149.
30   *Id.*, at 149–159.
31   *Id.*, at 159–162.
32   *Id.*, at 156.

BOOK REVIEWS

conclusions, such as the dated claim that "the principle of self-determination may be invoked only by those armed resistance groups operating under the umbrella of a national liberation movement recognised as such" by the UN General Assembly (UNGA).[33] Whatever practical impact the normative force of decolonization ever had on the rules governing the use of force is now surely lost.[34] Similarly, UN recognition of national liberation movements today seems like a historical curiosity of the decolonization era, with a questionable place in contemporary international law.[35] Further, Longobardo's claim that only recognized liberation movements can invoke self-determination to justify their armed resistance to occupation seems ahistorical: the UNGA only recognized the Palestine Liberation Organization after the latter signaled its willingness to compromise with Israel and to use means *other than armed struggle* to liberate Palestinian territory. The UNGA likewise admitted the Polisario into the Western Sahara *political* process after it made peace with Mauritania.[36] Chapter 4 thus concludes with the rather anodyne conclusion that IHL "offers a source of legitimacy, even if not a proper right, to armed resistance against the occupying power."[37]

The volume's high point comes in Chapter 5, which examines the interplay of the law enforcement and hostilities paradigms governing the use of force in occupied territory. Longobardo argues that the conservationist principle embodied in article 43 of the Hague Regulations and article 64 of the Fourth Geneva Convention, as a "principle of continuity" between ousted sovereign and occupying power, regulates the interplay of the two paradigms. On this basis, he concludes that "the law of occupation prescribes the law enforcement paradigm as long as the ousted sovereign would have employed that paradigm."[38]

---

33    *Id.*

34    *See* Nico Schrijver, *The Ban on the Use of Force in the UN Charter,* in The Oxford Handbook of the Use of Force in International Law 465, 474 (Marc Weller ed., 2015) ("The struggle of peoples to liberate themselves from colonial or foreign domination was regarded as a legitimate exception to the prohibition of the use of force. Currently, this exception has lost much of its relevance.").

35    Case C-104/16P *Council v. Front Polisario,* Opinion of Advocate General Wathelet (Sept. 13, 2016), paras. 184–185 (where the Advocate General of the Court of Justice of the European Union interpreted UN recognition of the Frente Polisario as representative of the Sahrawi people for purposes of efforts towards a "political solution" in Western Sahara to give the Polisario a role "only in the *political* process" without endowing it with the right or obligation to "defend the commercial interests of Western Sahara." Notably, the Advocate General denied that UN recognition established "an absolute identity" between the territory and recognized entity.).

36    G.A. Res 34/37, pmbl. & para. 7 (Nov. 21, 1979).

37    Longobardo, at 163.

38    *Id.,* at 166.

248                                                                      BOOK REVIEWS

Thus, the law enforcement paradigm applies unless the conflict (which the occupying power confronts) features the levels of intensity and organization characteristics (in the "normal" sovereign order) of a non-international armed conflict. The tipping point between the two paradigms, he suggests, is revealed by observing the role of the local police in the occupied territory during an occupation's "peacetime."[39] Here Longobardo is again descriptive to a fault, finding state practice in the use of local police drawn from the occupied territory in East Timor, Palestine and Iraq, while eliding over the very different purposes and means of delegating the maintenance of public order to local authorities in each context.[40] Also, his fulsome understanding of the duty to maintain public order arguably puts more weight on article 43 than it can reasonably bear.[41] Nevertheless, his characterization of the delegation to local forces – as both an expression of the continuity between the ousted sovereign and the occupying power *and* the latter's conservationist duty to maintain

---

39    *Id.*, at 188–194. As Longobardo notes (at 188), the occupying power must respect and preserve the status of local police, as public officials in the occupied territory (Fourth Geneva Convention art. 54), but their service must be maintained on a voluntary basis (First Geneva Convention art. 51(2)).

40    *Id.*, at 190. This decontextualization can be quite jarring, as where Longobardo cites the findings of the East Timor truth and reconciliation commission that Indonesia recruited East Timorese civilians into "conventional territorial security roles, combat, surveillance, and intelligence tasks" (*id.*), without noting this recruitment extended to child soldiers, paramilitaries units, and death squads.

41    Longobardo's expansive reading of article 43 involves questionable methodology in places. For example, he asserts "the fact that Article 43 HR embodies an obligation is also confirmed by the possibility to seek compensation for violations of the duty to restore and ensure public order," citing only a decision of the Governing Council of the UN Compensation Commission (UNCC) (at 171). Notably, given his sensitivity to *lex specialis* in other contexts, he fails to identify the UNCC's liability principles as a special regime built on the "basic premise" set in UNSC Resolution 687 that Iraq was "liable under international law for any direct loss ... or injury to foreign Governments, nationals and corporations as a result of [its] unlawful invasion and occupation of Kuwait." S.C. Res 687 (Apr. 3, 1991), para. 16. While the UNCC governing council decision notes article 43 of the Hague Regulations, its definition of a "direct loss" under Resolution 687 goes far beyond the confiscation of private property (article 46 of the Hague Regulations) to include business losses occurring because company personnel had been detained by Iraqi personnel or fled Kuwait in anticipation of the Iraqi invasion. *See* U.N. Comp. Comm'n, *Propositions and Conclusions on Compensation for Business Losses: Types of Damages and Their Valuation*, U.N. Doc. S/AC.26/1992/9 (Mar. 6, 1992), at 4, para. 14–15. The clearly mistaken notion that Iraq could be liable under article 43 (*jus ad bello*) for the circumstances surrounding its threat or initial use of force (*jus ad bellum*) is a giveaway to the special nature of the UNCC compensation regime.

BOOK REVIEWS

public order through the techniques of law enforcement whenever the ousted sovereign would – is a novel and compelling one.[42]

It should not detract from this contribution that Chapter 6 shows that this novel framing, in practice, does not compel significant rethinking of the interplay between the law enforcement and hostilities paradigms. Longobardo gives adequate, if characteristically doctrinaire, explanations of the two paradigms[43] and the relationship between IHL and IHRL, generally and as applied to occupied territory.[44]

Elsewhere, this volume has been lauded for its "clear decision ... to largely avoid passing judgment against individual regimes and their use of force during occupation."[45] The problem is rather that Longobardo avoids differentiating between the occupation regimes he analyzes, the nature and objectives of which vary in ways which should be crucial to that analysis. Nowhere does he distinguish his primary case studies: the settler-colonial Israeli occupation of Palestine and the US-led occupation of Iraq, which had transformative but not territorial ambitions.[46] Since the volume takes a binary approach to normativity as either "binding" or "soft law,"[47] state practice as demonstrated in these case studies dominates the analysis. The failure to identify the objectives of the occupation regime and account for how those specific objectives shape state practice devalues, rather than enhances, that analysis.

In the context of Palestine, that failure to define the occupation regime's objectives causes the analytical dominoes to fall as follows. The legality of settlements, and thus the presence of settlers, in occupied territory under Israeli law is axiomatic and non-justiciable.[48] The demands of military necessity and of "public order and civil life" under article 43 of the Hague Regulations, as interpreted by the Supreme Court of Israel, are therefore shaped by the interests of

---

42   Longobardo, at 192.

43   *Id.*, at 258–261.

44   *Id.*, at 261–268.

45   Caleb H. Wheeler, *Book Review*, 24 J. Conflict & Security L. 642 (2019) [*reviewing* Marco Longobardo, The Use of Armed Force in Occupied Territory (2018)].

46   Indeed, Longobardo all but invites one to read his analysis with the occupying power's objectives in mind on the volume's very first page, where he references the unrest in occupied Palestine following the US decision to recognize Jerusalem as the Israeli capital (Longobardo, at 1).

47   *Id.*, at 185.

48   *See* David Kretzmer, The Occupation of Justice: The Supreme Court of Israel and the Occupied Territories 78 (2002) (citing HCJ 4481/91 *Bargil v. Government of Israel* 47(4) PD 210 (1991) (Isr.)).

the settler population.[49] This move is justified through the fiction that settlers form part of the local population protected by IHL. That fiction is weaponized to justify infringements on the rights of the Palestinian population, either by invoking the settlers' fundamental rights under Israeli law or by merging the settlers' interests into a broad national security concept (supplanting military necessity, because military needs and settler interests in the occupied territory blur together). Thus, where Longobardo relies on Israeli jurisprudence to elaborate the duty under article 43 to restore and ensure public order and civil life,[50] what passes for neutrality is in fact decontextualization.

Compiling the black-letter law governing the use of force in occupied territory is a considerable task, and as such it is certainly a worthy addition to the literature. But given its normative feints, the volume seems out-of-step with critical scholarship on the law of occupation, which takes aim at the fragmented normative framework that Longobardo chronicles. For this reason, one is left wanting more from a scholar with an evident grasp on the relevant doctrine and intimate knowledge of its practical failings.

### Acknowledgments

The views expressed are those of the author and do not necessarily reflect the view of the UN.

*Omar Yousef Shehabi*

---

49 *See* Guy Harpaz & Yuval Shany, *The Israeli Supreme Court and the Incremental Expansion of the Scope of Discretion under Belligerent Occupation Law*, 43 Isr. L. Rev. 514 (2010).

50 Longobardo, at 171–173.

BOOK REVIEWS

Angélica Maria Bernal, "Beyond Origins: Rethinking Founding in a Time of Constitutional Democracy" (2017)

Angélica Bernal's theoretically rigorous *Beyond Origins: Rethinking Founding in a Time of Constitutional Democracy* provides a well-documented and novel theory that challenges the deeply entrenched foundationalist view underpinning the dominant scholarly understanding of constitutional democratic founding. Foundationalism posits founding as a single, authoritative moment that constitutes democratic states and fixes in its constitution the principles, rights, and values that will guide its people in the future. This paradigm grounds the way we think about how constitutions are made: at a particular point in time, the constituent power, expressing the will of the people, creates the constitution that will govern the new democratic polity. Founding is thus conceived as a superlative moment in time that provides legitimacy for a newly adopted constitution. Bernal argues that this conception has deep empirical and normative implications, as it "distorts the past, masks undemocratic politics in the present, and obscures the multiplicity of founding action and actors across time."[1] Not only is it poor history, since it erases the political contingency of founding, but it serves to obscure political disputes for the future.

Throughout the book, Bernal proposes an "antifoundationalist vision," developing a framework of "founding-beyond-origins." For Bernal, founding is not a fixed moment in time where principles and values emerge *ex nihilo*, but is instead characterized by political action and struggle situated within existing institutions that impact the founding process itself. In addition to this, while foundationalism conceives foundings as moments of authorizations, where the people or their representatives are authorized in making the fundamental law (the constitution), Bernal argues that foundings are marked by "underauthorization": "the foundations of political orders, including importantly their sense of authority and legitimacy, are necessarily incomplete and open to unsettlement"[2] leading to the fact that founders' "authority is itself in question and whose own political efficacy and legality may be shaky."[3] Bernal conceives the politics of founding as encompassing a wide array of actors immersed in a historically situated environment, grounded by the concept of "underauthorized authorizations," which are "claims and political actions that challenge the unstable and incomplete authority of an existing political

---

1 Angélica Maria Bernal, Beyond Origins: Rethinking Founding in a Time of Constitutional Democracy 4 (2017) [*hereinafter* Bernal].

2 *Id.*, at 11.

3 *Id.*, at 13.

order, often from a precarious or insufficiently authoritative place within it."[4] Through this conceptual framework, Bernal not only broadens the scope of the actors involved in foundings, but serves to shed light on actors that have hitherto been invisibilized through ex-post sacralized accounts of foundings.

Founding beyond origins is explored via a series of case studies that span time and geography. Bernal engages in classical and modern discussions on founding, traversing the works of Plato to Thomas Jefferson, travelling from the United States (US) to Haiti to Ecuador, and inviting the reader to question the conventional understanding of founding in constitutional democracies.

The first section of the book highlights the three main problems with the current conception of foundationalism by providing a meticulously documented historical analysis of founding. First, Bernal addresses the problem of original authority, which understands current political legal claims as grounded on a founding authority that emerged in a single moment in time. This issue is explored through close examination of the US civil rights movement and the conservative constitutional thought of the "Tea Party." Bernal argues that while these two movements are ideologically opposed, they share similar visions of founding as a singular superlative moment that is set in stone and must not be transformed or challenged. Turning to discuss Plato's *Laws*, Bernal highlights the problems surrounding the myth of the lawgiver that continues to capture Western political imagination. Foundationalism is characterized by the problem of democratic self-constitution: how can the people constitute themselves democratically when the people are not yet constituted? This question is examined in depth through both the US and Haitian revolutions.

The second section of the book develops the "founding beyond origins" framework. The first case brings us to an alternative narrative of Rome's founding through the work of Titus Livy. Bernal points to the crucial role played by underauthorized actors "from the Sabine women in Rome's first founding as a monarchy, to Lucretia and Junius Brutus in its refounding as a republic."[5] The second case centers on contemporary Latin American constitution-making processes led by social movements and characterized by affirmation of cultural diversity. Bernal examines the dilemma surrounding a particular agent of founding in these processes, presidents, and, more specifically, the role that Hugo Chávez, Evo Morales, and Raffael Correa played in Venezuela, Ecuador, and Bolivia, respectively. The final two chapters address the issue of democratic self-constitution, by first offering a sympathetic interpretation of Jefferson's letter to Madison regarding regenerative founding, which asked the question whether through a written constitution a generation of men can bind another; and finally, by examining the 1947 case *Méndez vs Westminster School*

---

4  *Id.*
5  *Id.*, at 17.

BOOK REVIEWS 253

*District,*[6] where Mexican-American parents challenged segregationist policies in California. Bernal emphasizes the fluidity of founding not as a phenomenon fixed in one moment in time, but as a dynamic and multifaceted process where "underauthorized actors" play a significant role.

Bernal's theory has important empirical and normative implications for constitutional scholars. In line with Third World Approaches to International Law (TWAIL) scholarship,[7] Bernal recognizes the historical contingencies that predate the adoption of a specific kind of norm: the constitution. She urges the reader to consider the politics of founding as a historically situated event, as opposed to the abstract, disembodied accounts of constituent power that ground a large part of constitutional scholarship. By extending the scope of founding, she supports constitutional legal scholars who seek to move away an approach to the law as "neutral" or divorced from politics,[8] as it is understood by mainstream legal positivists. The case studies included in the book not only bring to light new cases that constitutional legal scholars consistently under-study – such as Latin American constitution-making cases – but further debunk the bad history that pervades the field. For instance, Bernal shows how constitutional originalists engage in "historical fundamentalism" as she unpacks the deep disagreements surrounding the founding of the US Constitution, which is treated by the public and scholars alike as sacred and ageless.

Beyond the theoretical depth of the book, Bernal fills a gap in the field of constitutional legal theory that is pervaded by ethnocentrism and discounts non-Western cases as not worthy of theorization.[9] Against the French and US cases that are often held up as paradigmatic references to examine

---

6   *Mendez v. Westminster School District, et al.,* 64 F. Supp. 544 (S.D. Cal. 1946).

7   *See, generally,* James Thuo Gathii, *TWAIL: A Brief History of its Origins, its Decentralized Network, and a Tentative Bibliography,* 3 Trade L. & Dev. 26 (2011); Antony Anghie, *TWAIL: Past and Future,* 10 Int'l Comty. L. Rev. 479 (2008); Luis Eslava & Sundhya Pahuja, *Beyond the (Post) Colonial: TWAIL and the Everyday Life of International Law,* 45 Verfassung und Rechg in Übersee/L. Politics Afr., Asia Latin Am. 195 (2012). Specifically regarding the constitution, *see* Vidya Kumar, *Towards a Constitutionalism of the Wretched: Global Constitutionalism, International Law and the Global South,* Völkerrechtsblog (July 27, 2017), https://voelkerrechts blog.org/de/towards-a-constitutionalism-of-the-wretched; Vijayashri Sripati, Constitution-Making under UN Auspices: Fostering Dependency in Sovereign Lands (2020).

8   *See* Zoran Oklopcic, *The South of Western Constitutionalism: A Map Ahead of a Journey,* in Third World Approaches to International Law on Praxis and the Intellectual (Usha Natarajan et al. eds., 2016).

9   *See* Daniel Bonilla Maldonado, Constitutionalism of the Global South: The Activist Tribunals Of India, South Africa, And Colombia (2013); Maxim Bönnemann, Laura Jung, *Critical Legal Studies and Comparative Constitutional Law,* in Max Planck Encyc. Comp. Const. L. (Rainer Grote et al. eds., 2017); Günter Frankenberg, *Critical Comparisons: Re-thinking Comparative Law,* 25 Harv. Int. Law J. 411 (1985); Günter Frankenberg, Comparative Constitutional Studies: Between Magic and Deceit (2018).

contemporary democratic constitutional founding, this book provides new cases to aid contemporary thought on constitution-making, such as Latin American presidential foundings. Bernal's treatment of the Haitian revolution is particularly enlightening in this regard as she points out how the Haitian case is perhaps the most relevant in thinking about contemporary foundational constitution-making. She underlines the foundational paradox at the heart of constitutional democracies, questioning where a set of actors derive their authority to adopt a new constitution: "[if] it is because they speak in the name of the 'people,' then where does 'the people' get its legitimate authority?"[10] These questions are often evaded by invoking the mythical figure of the nation exercising its constituent power, but Bernal invites us to dive deeper into the uncomfortable paradox of democratic founding. The case of Haiti has much to tell us regarding the dilemma of democratic founding – the struggle of the former French colony of Saint-Domingue that against all odds defied the all-powerful French Army towards independence, and adopted of a new constitution.[11] Unlike the thunderous "We the People" in the US Constitution, the Haitian case points out the paradox of founding in a more acute way, questioning how people who were enslaved can constitute themselves as free people. As Bernal notes, this case emphasizes how the figure of "the people" as an authorizing force is explicitly ambiguous. The 1804 Haitian Declaration of Independence is "an appeal to its people to constitute themselves as free subjects within a context of uncertain freedom where the threat of reenslavement remained."[12] The 1804 Declaration of Independence captures the idea that the people's freedom is not already present: "We have dared to be free, let us be thus by ourselves and for ourselves."[13]

The preamble of the 1805 Haitian Constitution includes another innovation. Unlike the US preamble where there is an implied unity between the constitution's drafters and the people, the Haitian preamble makes explicit the distance that existed between the people and its drafter: "As well in our name as in that of the people of Hayti, who have legally constituted us."[14] Bernal argues that the Haitian case does not solve all the dilemmas of democratic founding, as the question of how the drafters have been legally constituted remains,

---

10   Bernal, at 76.

11   *See* Philip Kaisary, *Hercules, the Hydra, and the 1801 Constitution of Toussaint Louverture*, 12 Atl. Stud. 393 (2015).

12   Bernal, at 93.

13   Haitian Declaration of Independence (1804), available at: https://mjp.univ-perp.fr/con stit/ht1804.htm.

14   Haiti Const. (1805), available at: http://faculty.webster.edu/corbetre/haiti/history/early haiti/1805-const.htm.

BOOK REVIEWS                                                                255

but it makes them more visible and thus open to analysis and critique. The book's discussion of the Haitian case provides a better theoretical lens to examine the problem of democratic founding as it occurs in the context of constitution-making in democratic transitions, which in most cases is evaded by resorting to the abstract notion of constituent power.

Bernal's theoretically robust and useful concept of "underauthorized authorization" allows her to unpack the monolithic category of "the people" by identifying the political struggle that is key to any case of constitutional founding. Her framework is a call to study *in concreto* the difficult questions that foundings in constitutional democracy entail, with a particular emphasis on including in the scope of analysis actors that are generally disregarded, such as social movements. Bernal's theory of founding-beyond-origins offers the conceptual tools not only to avoid bad history and ideological understandings of founding that obscure power struggles, but further to stimulate the political imagination beyond the conventional and ahistorical accounts of mythical lawmakers and superlative moments. Instead, the reader is forced to confront the messy indeterminacy and contingency of founding, which brings into question the role that foundings and constitutions can play in settling contemporary legal and political disputes.

*Alicia Pastor y Camarasa*

# Index

Abed, Ahmed    vii, 179–200
academic freedom    185
Act on the Residence, Economic Activity
    and Integration of Foreigners in the
    Federal Territory (Aufenthaltsgesetz;
    Germany)    195
"Activism and Legitimation in Israel's
    Jurisprudence of Occupation"
    (Sultany)    237
acts of aggression    31n109
    *see also* force, use of/aggression
Adalah (Legal Center for Arab Minority
    Rights in Israel)    13
Administrative Court of Berlin    193–194,
    195, 199
Administrative Court of Cologne    187–189,
    191, 197
Administrative Court of Düsseldorf    190
Administrative Court of Munich    189
Administrative Court of Oldenburg    186–187
AfD (Alternative for Germany; political
    party)    199
Africa    37, 220
    *see also under specific states*
aggression
    definition of    31
    *see also* force, use of/aggression
agriculture, in oPt    118, 121n51
Akram, Susan    209
Alabrune, François    222–223
Alawites    78, 101, 103, 110
Aliyah    66
Alternative for Germany (AfD; political
    party)    199
A-Mandates    100
Amnesty International
    in general    8, 221
    on Israeli nation-state law    66
    self-determination and    63, 70
    UK branch of
        distorted focus of    5, 15, 63–64
        IHRL and    5, 15
        UDHR and    15, 64
Anderson, Benedict    80
annexation
    in general    6–7
    of Crimea    9, 19

disassociation from    55–56
of East Timor    9, 19, 43–44
erosion of legal standards and    68–71
force-enabled, illegality of    21–24
lack of enforcement and    24
law on the use of force and    21–22
or occupation of oPt    13, 19–20, 23–24,
    40–41, 60–61, 67, 68–69, 72, 156–158,
    229, 236
prohibition of    12n31, 73
right to self-determination and    40–41,
    59–60
    *see also* Crimea; Golan heights;
        occupation; Timor Leste; Western
        Sahara
anti-normalization laws    139
anti-Semitism
    BDS campaign as    180–182, 186–187,
    191–192, 194
    *see also* smear campaigns
    German Basic Law and    186, 187
    IHRA definition of    187, 199
    of Muslims    199
apartheid
    as crime against humanity    160
    definitions of    158, 160–161
    Israeli occupation as form of
        in general    20, 32, 117, 155, 161,
        174–176
        arbitrariness and    169–172
        compared to South African model
        of    156, 162
        exclusion and    165–166
        geographic fragmentation
        and    161–164
        harassment/humiliation and    172–174
        legal consequences of    175
        non-annexation and    156–158
        purpose of
            domination and    167–172
            oppression    172–174
        racial groups and    158–159
        segregation and    161–165
        surveillance and    166–169
    in South Africa    156, 162, 212, 213–214
Apartheid Convention (International
    Convention on the Suppression

INDEX
257

and Punishment of the Crime of
Apartheid)  158, 159, 160–161, 165–166, 172
arbitrariness  169–172
ARISWA (Responsibility of States for
Internationally Wrongful Acts)  124–125,
127, 136
armed conflicts
laws on  *see* occupation, law on; use of
force, law on; *under specific laws*
Arms Trade Treaty  221
Asia  220
Assad family  78
assimilation  91, 109
Assyrians  102–103
Aufenthaltsgesetz (Act on the Residence,
Economic Activity and Integration
of Foreigners in the Federal Territory;
Germany)  195
Austro-Hungarian Empire  83
authorization, underauthorized  255

Ba'ath party  78, 103, 105
*Baldassi et al. v. France* case  200
Balfour, Arthur  203, 208, 210
Balfour Declaration  23n77, 203, 207, 210
Bantusans  156
bantustanization  162
Barakat, Khaled  194–196
al-Bashir, Omar  222, 224
*Basic Principles and Guidelines on the Right
to a Remedy and Reparation for Victims of
Gross Violations of International Human
Rights Law and Serious Violations of
International Humanitarian Law*  127
Beck, Volker  185
Becker, Uwe  191
Ben-Naftali, Orna  47, 50, 53
Benvenisti, Eyal  11–12n31, 16n51, 22–23n75,
25n84, 27–28, 30–31, 40n137, 47–49,
52n174
Benvenisti, Meron  157
Berlin  182n13, 184, 185n24, 192
Bernal, Angélica Maria  251–255
Bernstein, Judith  191
*Beyond Origins: Rethinking Founding in
a Time of Constitutional Democracy*
(Bernal)  251–255
Bilder, Richard  222
Birzeit University  3

Bisharat, George  209
blockade, of Gaza  61, 117, 123–124
Bonn  188–189
Boogert, Maurits H. van der  98–99
Boycott, Divestment, and Sanctions (BDS)
campaign
in Germany
activists of  *see under* Bundestag
motion against BDS
as anti-Semitic  180–182, 186–187,
191–192, 194
Bundestag motion against  *see*
Bundestag motion against BDS
federal parliaments motions against
in general  181–182
cases against  190
status of  189
human rights agenda of  186, 197
intelligence service and  183, 196
smear campaigns against  179–180,
182, 185, 191–192
breaches  *see* violations
British Institute of International and
Comparative Law  217
B'Tselem  172–174
Bundestag 3 for Palestine (BT3P)  190, 199
Bundestag motion against BDS
in general  180–181
effects on BDS activists of
in general  182–183
on access to venues
in general  185
private  190–192
public  186–190
on job applications and funding
of  183–185
on political activities  192–194
protection of rights of  198
security threats and  196, 198
violation of human rights of
197, 199
on visas/residency permits
for  192–196
international reactions on  197–198
lawsuits against  189, 199–200
legal status of  188, 199
UN Special Rapporteurs on  197
businesses  *see* corporations
Buttu, Diana  vii, 235–240

Cassese, Antonio 38, 42–43, 47, 49
Castellino, Joshua 95, 102
Cavanaugh, Kathleen 102
Cecil, Robert 203
CESCR (United Nations Committee on Economic, Social and Cultural Rights) 65–66, 70–71
checkpoints 143, 164, 169–170, 172–173
Christians
  in Iraq 104, 106, 108
  in Ottoman Empire 88
  Treaty of Westphalia and 87
citizens, of nation-states 84–85
Clause, Martens 245
Coalition Provisional Authority (CPA) 9, 17–18, 44, 105
COJUR (Working party on public international law) 223
collective punishments 123–124, 152
colonialism/imperialism
  international law and 5–6, 218–220
  minority rights and 76, 86–90, 102–103
  nation-states and 77–78
  prohibition of 210
  statehood and 36–37
  trusteeship and 49–50, 54–56
compromise, self-determination and 45
Constitution (1788; USA) 253
Constitution (1805; Haiti) 254–255
Constitution (2005; Iraq) 107
Constitutional Tribunal of North-Rhine-Westphalia 190
constitutions
  founding and 252–254
  see also under specific constitutions
contract, freedom of 190–191
corporations
  codes of conduct for
    1988 proposed code 129–130
    UNGPS 130–132
    of UNHRC 133–135
  involved in Israeli settlements 134–135
  responsibility to protect of 127–129, 130, 140
Correll, Hans 223
Costa Rica 221
CPA (Coalition Provisional Authority) 9, 17–18, 44, 105
Crawford, James 36n124, 38, 47

Crimea 9, 19
crimes against humanities see apartheid
crimes of aggression 31n109
  see also force, use of/aggression
cuius regio, eius religio principle 87

danger/potential danger, criterion of 193
database, on businesses involved in Israeli settlements 134–135, 229
David, Eric 199
"deal of the century" 69, 203, 207
de-ba'athification 105
Depagine, Vincent 82–83
Department for Research and Information on Antisemitism Berlin (RIAS Berlin) 179n1
Diakonia (Swedish NGO) 10–11, 51
discrimination
  legal framework for 158–160
  of non-Jewish people in Isreal 66
  of non-Muslim people in Ottoman Empire 98–99
  of Palestinians in West Bank 153–155
  see also apartheid
displacements, of Palestinian peoples 4, 14, 38, 65–66, 122, 210
District Court of Munich 191, 197
due diligence 131–133, 135
Dugard, John 150–151, 158–159, 172, 226n45
Dupré De Boulois, Xavier 199

East Jerusalem
  access to 162
  Israeli occupation/annexation of 13, 20, 60–61, 68–69, 229
East Timor 9, 19, 43–44
economical harm, systemic
  in general 112–113
  in occupation of Palestine
    in general 113, 115, 116
    economic agreements and 119
    empirically identification of 117–124
    normative identification of 124–127
    redress for 127–139
      in general 139
      business and human rights framework 128–135
      third states and 135–139
  in occupations, in general 113–114, 116
education, right to 149

# INDEX

enforcement
 lack of
  of minority rights 76
  of right to self-determination 73
 of law, use of force in 247–249
Erakat, Noura 203–216, 226n45
Esmeir, Samera 15, 39, 214
ethnic groups 159
EU (European Union) 132, 223, 229
European Commission 139
European Convention of Human Rights 199
European Court of Human Rights 145n12,
 200, 218
European Court of Justice 139
European Legal Support Centre 199–200
European Union (EU) 132, 223, 229
expression, freedom of 189, 197
extraterritoriality 133–134

fact-finding missions 227, 228
Falk, Richard 163n88, 164n93, 172, 199, 209,
 226n45
Fanon, Franz 36
Federal Administrative Court (Germany)
 189
Ferrando, Costanza vii, 141–176
Fitzmaurice, Gerald 222–223
force, law on use of
 in general 4, 6–7, 8
 acquisition of territory and 21–22
 erosion of legal standards and 68
 Israeli occupation of oPt and
  in general 24–26
  applicability of 241–243
  peace agreements and 27–28, 29–30
  self-defense and 24–26, 29–30,
   34–35
  self-determination and 42–43
  violations of IHL and 32–34
 jurisprudence on self-determination
  and 62–63
 Palestinian Statehood and 72
 pre-emptive self-defense and 27, 30
 withdrawal from occupied territory
  and 27n95, 28
force, use of/aggression
 Kattan on 244
 in occupied territory 241–250

prohibition of 219
in Rome Statute 31
UN Human Rights Committee on 70
UNGA on 25n84, 26
 see also force, law on use of
Foundation for Defense of Democracies
 204
foundationalism 251–252
founding
 in general 251–252
 beyond origins theory 251–255
 constitutions and 252–254
 democratic 254–255
 historical analysis of 252
Fourth Geneva Convention (1949)
 applicability of, to oPt 146–147, 155
 on collective punishment 123
 on law enforcement and hostilities
  247
 on occupation 28, 146, 147
 violations of 229
fragmentation, geographic 161–164
France 89, 93
Franco-Prussian War (1870) 245
francs-tireurs 245
Frankfurt am Main 190, 191
freedom
 academic 185
 of contract 190–191
 of expression 189, 197
 of movement see movement, freedom
  of
 of opinion 189, 197
 religious 87
 of speech 191
Frente Polisario 247
*From Co-existence to Conquest: International
 Law and the Origins of the Arab-Israeli
 Conflict 1891–1949* (Kattan) 209

GATT (General Agreement on Tariffs and
 Trade) 137
Gaza
 blockade of 61, 117, 123–124, 174n125
 development projects in 119
 Israeli occupation of 13, 19
General Agreement on Tariffs and Trade
 (GATT) 137

# INDEX

Geneva Conventions (1949)
  contracting partners of  147
  on duration of occupation  28
  Fourth  *see* Fourth Geneva Convention
  humanitarian paradigm shift and  56
  occupation law and  9–10, 11n31
  on right of resistance  246
  violations of  32, 229
geographic fragmentation  161–164
German Basic Law (Grundgesetz; GG)  186, 187, 189
German Federal Ministry for Education and Research (BMBF)  185
German Rectors' Conference  185
German-Israel Society  191
German-Palestinian Society  189
German-Palestinian Women's Association  188–189, 190
Germany
  Israel and
    in general  179–180
    *see also* Boycott, Divestment, and Sanctions (BDS) campaign
Gerson, Allan  52n174
Glahn, Gerhard von  52n174
Glatung, John  114–115
Global East  220
Global South  129, 130, 212, 219, 220, 225
Golan heights (Syria)  8, 9, 69
Göttinger Peace Award  180n2
Gray, Christine  23n76, 26
"Green Line"  13, 14, 23, 143
Gross, Aeyal  47, 50, 53, 147, 155
Gussetti, Lucio  223
Gutiérrez Ruiz, Eugenia  221

*Haaretz* (newspaper)  167
Hague Regulations (1899 & 1907)
  on law enforcement and hostilities  247
  on *levée en* masse  245
  on military necessity and public order  249
  on occupation law  10, 28, 52n174, 116
  on rules of usufruct  119
  on taxation in occupied territory  121
Haiti  254–255
Hajjar, Lisa  209, 238
Hammouri, Shahd  vii, 112–140
Al-Haq  3, 4, 16, 227
harassment  172–174

Hashhash, Abu  172–174
Hass, Amira  167
health, right to  149
Herik, Larissa van den  114
Herzl, Theodor  206–207, 210
Hessian Higher Administrative Court  190
Higgins, Rosalyn  218, 219
Higher Administration Court of Bavaria  189
Higher Administrative Court of Berlin  194
Higher Administrative Court of Lower Saxony  186, 187, 191
Hill, Steven  224–225
Hindi, Ata R.  vii, 217–232
Hizbullah  196
human rights
  applicability of  144–145
  due diligence and  131–133, 135
  identifying risks related to  131–132
  minority rights and  91
  violations of  122, 149, 197, 199
Human Rights Watch  8, 63, 70
humiliation  172–174
*The Hundred Years' War on Palestine: A History of Settler Colonialism and Resistance, 1917–2017* (Khalidi)  203–216
  in general  203–204
  author of  204–205
  content of  206–208
  structure of  205–206
Hussein, Sadam  78, 103

ICC (International Criminal Court)  221–222, 229
  *see also* Rome Statute
ICCPR  *see* International Covenant on Civil and Political Rights
ICERD (International Convention for the Elimination of All Forms of Racial Discrimination)  158, 159, 160–161
ICESCR (International Covenant on Economic, Social and Cultural Rights)  57
ICRC (International Committee of the Red Cross)  10, 147–148
ID cards  167–168
identity
  conflicts and  96
  Iraqi national  103, 107–108, 110
Identity Card Carrying and Displaying Act (1982; Israel)  168

INDEX

IDF (Israeli Defense Forces)   164, 169, 172
IGC (Iraqi Governing Council)   105–106
IHRA (International Holocaust
   Remembrance Alliance)   187, 199
illegality
   of annexation   21–24
   of Gaza blockade   123, 174n125
   of Israeli settlements in oPt   122, 136–137,
      249
   of occupation   16, 30, 33–34, 72
imperialism   see colonialism/imperialism
Imseis, Ardi   7, 46, 49, 50, 226n45
India   219–220
individualism, methodological   125–126
individuality, right to   75
Indonesia   9, 19, 43–44
Initiative GG 5.3 Weltoffenheit   181
injustice, structural   113, 115–116, 139–140
intelligence service (Germany)   183, 196
International Anti-Apartheid Week (2019;
   Germany)   186
International Committee of the Red Cross
   (ICRC)   10, 147–148
International Convention for the Elimination
   of All Forms of Racial Discrimination
   (ICERD)   158, 159, 160–161
International Convention on the Suppression
   and Punishment of the Crime of
   Apartheid (Apartheid Convention)   158,
      159, 160–161, 165–166, 172
International Court of Justice (ICJ)
   Advisory Opinion
      on Chagos Archipelago   62
      on the Wall   25–26n86, 38, 61–62,
         218n6, 235, 241
      on Western Sahara   41
   on applicability of fundamental human
      rights   145
   on applicability of Geneva Convention
      147
   harmonization of law and   138
   Namibia precedent at   213–214
International Covenant on Civil and Political
   Rights (ICCPR)
   on freedom of movement   144, 148
   on minority rights   93–94, 108, 109
   on racial discrimination   153
   on right to life   70
   on self-determination   57, 58–59, 94

International Covenant on Economic, Social
   and Cultural Rights (ICESCR)   57
International Criminal Court (ICC)   221–
      222, 229
   see also Rome Statute
International Holocaust Remembrance
   Alliance (IHRA)   187, 199
International Human Rights Law (IHRL)
   in general   5, 8
   Amnesty International and   5, 15
   applicability of
      in general   94
      to oPt   143, 144–146
   combining of IHL and
      harmful effects of   147
      mutual exclusivity   144
   condition of occupation and   58–59, 64
   minority rights in   90
   self-determination in   56–57, 72
   violations of   33, 142
International Humanitarian Law (IHL)
   in general   4, 6
   applicability of, to oPt   143–144, 155, 239,
      241–243
   combining of IHRL and
      harmful effects of   147
      mutual exclusivity   144
   occupation in
      in general   10–11
      focus on condition of   13–15, 51, 64
      fundamental rights and   147
      legality of   16
      right to resistance and   246–247
   violations of   31–34, 142, 174, 229
international law
   colonialism and   5–6, 218–220
   freedom of movement in   see under
      movement, freedom of
   harmonization of   137–138
   legal advisers in   see legal advisers
   legitimacy of   138
   minority rights in   see minority rights
   politics and   211–212, 222–225, 253
   responsibility in   125–126, 127
   scholarship in India on   219–220
   systemic economical harm in   see
      systemic economical harm
   violations of   117, 124–125, 127, 136, 139
      see also under specific laws

International Law Commission 127, 138
*International Law* (Oppenheim & Lauterpacht) 28, 48–49
International Territorial Administration (ITA) 50, 54, 55
International Women's Day (2019) 192
Interpretative Notice on the Indication of Origin of Goods from the Territories Occupied by Israel since June 1967 (EU) 139
Iraq
    attack on Kuwait by 225
    Constitution of 107
    continued military presence in 19n65
    CPA and 9, 17–18, 44, 105
    de-ba'athification of 105
    independence of 102
    Iraqi Governing Council of 105–106
    main communal groups 106–107
    mandatory rule of 101–102
    minorities in
        in general 109–110
        in aftermath of 2003 104–108
        protection of
            in general 101, 102
            in Constitution of 2005 107
        Saddam Hussein's use of 103–104
        *see also under specific minorities*
    national identity and 103, 107–108, 110
    occupation of 9, 17–19, 44
    Organic Law of 1924 102
    orientalist understanding of 97, 105
    sectarianism as state policy in 104
    Transitional Administrative Law of 104
Iraqi Governing Council (IGC) 105–106
Ireland 203
Islamophobia Report 179n1
Israel
    Germany and
        in general 179–180
        *see also* Boycott, Divestment, and Sanctions (BDS) campaign
    Jahalin Bedouins and 3–4, 14, 32, 38, 65, 66
    migration to 65
    nation-state law of 2018 66
    non-Jewish people in 66
    occupation of oPt *see* Israeli occupation of oPt

security needs of 19, 26, 34–35, 144, 154, 164, 169, 173
statehood of, as a given and
    annexation and 23
    occupation law and 11–12, 13, 14, 15
    Palestinian self-determination and 37–38, 64, 71
    status of 37n128
    wrongful acts and 124–125
Israeli Defense Forces (IDF) 164, 169, 172
Israeli High Court of Justice 235–240
Israeli Ministry for Strategic Affairs 179–180, 183
Israeli nation-state law (2018) 66
Israeli occupation of oPt
    in general 71
    or annexation of 19–20, 23–24, 40–41, 60–61, 67, 68–69, 72, 156–158, 236
    apartheid and *see* apartheid
    beginning of 21, 25
    ending of
        law on the use of force and
            in general 24–26
            peace agreements and 27–28, 29–30
            self-defense and 24–26, 29–30, 34–35
            self-determination and 42–43
            violations of IHL and 32–34
        self-determination of Palestinians and
            in general 35, 37–43
            delayed approach to 46–49
            trusteeship system and 50, 51–52, 53–54
    erosion of legal standards and 67–70
    land confiscation in 60, 118, 122, 163
    security as justification of 144, 148–151, 154, 164, 169, 173
    settlements in *see* Israeli settlements in oPt
    systemic economical harm and *see* systemic economical harm
Israeli settlements in oPt
    in general 117
    database on businesses involved in 134–135, 229
    illegality of 122, 136–137, 249
    road network for 143, 150, 163
    third states and 136–138

INDEX 263

violations of IHL and 32–34
on West Bank 3–4, 235–240
Israeli-Palestinian Interim Agreement on the
West Bank and the Gaza Strip (1995) 120
ITA (International Territorial
Administration) 50, 54, 55

Jabareen, Hassan 13–14
Jahalin Palestinian Bedouins 3–4, 14, 32,
38, 65, 66
Jennings, Robbie 22–23nn75–77, 24, 40n138,
68, 70
Jerusalem, US embassy in 69, 73
Jessup, Philip C. 119
Jewish Museum Berlin 179n1
Jewish Voice for Peace 179–180n2
Jewish-Palestinian Dialogue Group (JPDG)
191
*jizya* tax 99
JPDG (Jewish-Palestinian Dialogue Group)
191
*jus ad* bellum *see* use of force, law on
*jus in* bello *see* International Humanitarian
Law
*Justice for Some: Law and the Question of
Palestine* (Erakat) 203–216
in general 203–204
author of 205
conclusion of 214–216
content of 209–214
structure of 206

Kassem, Anis 226n45
Kattan, Victor 169n106, 209, 226n45, 230,
244
Kennedy, Duncan 208
Khalidi, Rashid 203–216
al-Khalidi, Yusuf Diya al-Din Pasha
206–207
Khan al-Ahmar 3, 23, 32
Kingston, James 222
Klabbers, Jan 57–58n190
Koh, Harold 223
Koskeniemmi, Martii 225
Kunsthochschule Weißensee 185
Kurdistan 106, 108
Kurdistan Workers' Party (PKK) 196
Kurds 101, 102–103, 105–106, 107, 195–196
Kushner, Jared 203–204

Kuwait 225
Kweli, Talib 184

Lagerquist, Peter 119
land confiscation 60, 118, 122
land tax 121n51
Latin America 220, 253
Lauterpacht/Oppenheim principle 28,
48–49
law enforcement 247–249
law of self-determination *see*
self-determination, law on
law on title to territory 23, 40
League of Nations
A-Mandates of 100–101
Mandates system of 23n77, 49–50, 54
minority protection clauses in 88–90
legal advisers
in general 217–218
colonialism and 218–220
invisibility of non-traditional 220–222
Palestinian 225–232
politics and 222–225
Legal Center for Arab Minority Rights in
Israel (Adalah) 13
legal standards, erosion of 68–71
legitimacy
of constitutions 251
of international law 138
of occupation 6–7, 21, 33–34, 61–62
of states
popular sovereignty as 84–86, 87
religion as 82–83, 97–98
of UK authority over Chagos
Archipelago 62
*levée en* masse 245
*lex* specialis 241–243
liability models 125
liberation movements 245–247
Libya Commission of Inquiry 224
life, right to 70
Linarelli, John 114
Lingaas, Carola 158
DIE LINKE (Left Party; Germany) 179n1, 199
Livni, Tzipi 224
lobbying, of Bundestag MPs 181
Longobardo, Marco 241–250
Lorde, Audre 4, 6, 71, 239
Lynk, Michael 209

MachsomWatch 170n109
Macleod, Iain 224
majoritarianism 85, 87–88, 91, 92
majorities
   use of term 77
      *see also* minority/majority dichotomy
Makdisi, Ussama 100
Malabo Protocol 128
Mandate Agreement for Palestine 23n76
Mandatory Palestine
   Israeli statehood and 37–38, 71
   status of 40
Mandeans 104, 108
Mannheim 192
*Mara'abe v. Prime Minister of Isr.* case
   145n12
Mbembe, Achille 184
McCosker, Sarak 219–220
*Méndez vs Westminster School District* case
   252–253
Mendivíl, Roldán 182n12
Meron, Theodor 147
Michaeli, Keren 47, 50, 53, 155
Middle East
   minority/majority dichotomy in 78–79
   orientalist understanding of 96–97,
      100–101, 105
Miller, Zinaida 114
*millet* legal system 98–99, 101, 102
minorities
   in general 109
   assimilation of 91, 109
   defining who belongs to 80–82, 95
   etymology of 77, 79–80
   intrastate conflicts and 96
   in Iraq *see under* Iraq
   linguistic 81
   national 88
   as perpetrators of violence 90
   religious 87, 101
   rights of *see* minority rights
   in Syria *see under* Syria
      *see also* minority/majority dichotomy;
         *under specific minorities*
minority rights
   in general 75–76
   in international law
      in general 76, 86, 109
      colonialism and 76, 86–90, 102–103

effects of 90–91
human rights and 91
ICCPR 93–94, 108, 109
IHRL 90
League of Nations 88–90
obstacles in 95
UDHR 92, 108
UNGA 92
United Nations Charter 92
United Nations Human Rights
   Committee and 92, 93–94
intersectional issues and 77
in Iraq
   in Organic Law (1924) 102
   UK's interests and 102–103
lack of enforcement of 76
in power-sharing arrangements 77
minority/majority dichotomy
emergence of 85–86, 87
entrenchment of 89–90
in Ottoman Empire 98–99
in sectarian conflicts 77–78
MINURSO (United Nations Mission for the
   Referendum in Western Sahara) 44, 45
Mizrahi Jews 216
Moernhout, Tom 136–138
Morocco
   Western Sahara and
      occupation/annexation by 8–9, 19,
         44–46
      sovereignty over 69
movement, freedom of
   as human right 144
   in international law
      in general 144–146
      as security precaution 147–148
   restriction on Palestinians' *see under*
      Gaza, blockade of; West Bank
Munich 189
Mutua, Makau 36–37
Muwatin Institute 3

Nabulsi, Karma 245
NAM (Non-Aligned Movement) 212, 220
Namibia 213–214
nationalism, methodological 126
nation-states
   citizens of 84–85
   colonialism and 77–78

INDEX

emergence of 88
majoritarianism and 87–88, 91, 92
reformulation of 91
NATO (North Atlantic Treaty
Organization) 224–225
Negotiations Affairs Department (of PLO)
227
Nelly-Sachs prize 184
neo-colonialism 55
Netanyahu, Benjamin 203, 207
Ní Aoláin, Fionnuala 53
Non-Aligned Movement (NAM) 212, 220
non-discrimination clauses 137
non-Jewish people 66
non-Muslim people 98–99
North Atlantic Treaty Organization
(NATO) 224–225
Nusseibeih, Munir 16

occupation
benefits to occupier of 17–20
of East Timor 9, 19, 43–44
ending of 20, 28, 31, 41, 46–48
freedom of movement in see
movement, freedom of
in IHL see International Humanitarian
Law
illegality of 16, 30, 33–34, 72
of Iraq 9, 17–20, 44
justification of, self-defense as 24–26,
29–30, 34–35, 241
law on see occupation, law on
legality of 11, 16
legitimacy of 6–7, 21, 33–34, 61–62
of Palestine see Occupied Palestinian
Territories
right of resistance in 245–247
sovereignty and 12
structural injustice and 116
systemic economical harm in see
economical harm, systemic
use of force and 241–250
of Western Sahara 8–9, 19, 44–46
see also annexation
occupation, law on
in general 4–5, 6–9
benefits to occupier and 17–20
definition of occupation in 11–12

focus on conduct of occupier in
in general 10–11, 64, 71, 246
effects of 13–15
Geneva Conventions and 9–10, 11n31
IHL and 10–11
Israeli statehood and 11–12, 13, 14, 15
Palestinian Statehood and 72
time limits on occupation in 16–18, 28
trusteeship system and 51–52
violations of 33
occupation of, territory 56
Occupied Palestinian Territories (oPt)
agriculture in 118, 121n51
or annexation of 13, 19–20, 23–24, 40–41,
60–61, 67, 68–69, 72, 156–158
corporations' social role and 130
economy of 118–119, 139
Israeli occupation of see Israeli
occupation of oPt
Israeli settlements in see Israeli
settlements in oPt
Israeli taxation policies in 121
land confiscation in 60, 118, 122
quarrying businesses in 121
status of 39–40
water resources in 120
see also East Jerusalem; Gaza; West
Bank
Odeh, Rasmea 192–194
Oldenburg 186–187
opinion, freedom of 189, 197
Organic Law (1924; Iraq) 102
Orientalism 96–97, 100–101, 105
Oslo Accords 119, 163, 212–213, 244
othering 82, 103
Ottoman Empire
in general 83
Christians in 88
millet legal system of 98–99, 101, 102
religion as legitimation of 97
social composition of 97
Tanzimat reforms of 86n47, 100

PA (Palestinian Authority) see Palestine/
Palestinian Authority
Packer, John 81
Palestine Liberation Organization (PLO)
212, 227, 235, 247

## 266 INDEX

Palestine/Palestinian Authority
  existence of   244–245
  forming of   212–213
  government of   227
  one-state versus two-state
    binary   215–216
  statehood of   39, 41, 71–72, 215
    *see also* Palestine Liberation
      Organization; Palestinian peoples
Palestinian Center for Human Rights   227
Palestinian Community of Bonn   188–189
Palestinian Ministry of Foreign Affairs
  226
Palestinian peoples
  displacement of   4, 14, 38, 65–66, 122,
    210
  economic impoverishment of   118–119,
    139
  negative definition of   206–207, 210
  refugees   39, 215
  right of return of   14, 64–65
  right to self-determination of   *see under*
    self-determination, right to
  self-administration of   53–54
Palestinian refugees   39, 215
Paris Protocol   119
Pastor y Camarasa, Alicia   vii, 251–255
peace agreements
  occupations and   27–28, 29–31
  for sectarian conflicts   77
  self-determination and   44–47, 72
Permanent Mission of the Federal Republic
  of Germany to the UN   197–198
permit system   151–152, 167, 171
PFLP (Popular Front for the Liberation of
  Palestine)   196
PKK (Kurdistan Workers' Party)   196
PLO (Palestine Liberation Organization)
  212, 227, 235, 247
Polisario Front   247
politics, international law and   211–212,
  222–225, 253
poll-tax   99
Popular Front for the Liberation of Palestine
  (PFLP)   196
Portugal   43–44
post-colonialism   37, 54, 55–56, 63
President's Office   226
private-public distinction   126

prohibition
  of annexation   12n31, 73
  of colonialism/imperialism   210
  of use of force   219
proportionality, security and   148–151
punishments, collective   123–124, 152

quarrying businesses   120
Quigley, John   209, 226n45

Raad, Walid   184
racial groups   158–159
redress
  of systemic economical harm in
    oPt   127–139
    in general   139
    business and human rights
      framework   128–135
    third states and   135–139
religion
  as legitimation of states   83–84, 97–98
  sovereign's influence on   83, 87
    *see also* Christians; Shi'a Muslims;
      Sunni Muslims
religious freedom, right to   87
Reshaq, Amran   4
Residence Act (Aufenthaltsgesetz;
  Germany)   195
Resolution 31/36 (UNSC)   134
Resolution 242 (UNSC)   28, 30, 208, 210–211
Resolution 465 (UNSC)   136
Resolution 1541 (UNGA)
  on ending colonialism   41, 46
  repudiation of trusteeship-over-people
    in   50, 54
  on statehood   36n124
Resolution 2334 (UNSC)   136
responsibility
  of corporations   128–135, 140
  in international law   125–126, 127
  of third states   135–139, 140
Responsibility of States for Internationally
  Wrongful Acts (ARISWA)   124–125, 127,
    136
return, right of   14, 64–65
Reynolds, John   vii, 158–159, 199, 203–216
RIAS Berlin (Department for Research
  and Information on Antisemitism
  Berlin)   179n1

# INDEX

right of resistance 245–247
right of return 14, 64–65
right of self-determination *see*
  self-determination, right to
right to safe and clean water 120
road networks 143, 150, 163
Roberts, Adam 11n31, 52n174, 55
"The Role of Legal Advisers in International
  Law" (eds. Zidar & Gauci) 217–232
  in general 217–218
  colonial legacies and 218–220
  conclusions on 231
  invisibility of non-traditional legal
    advisors in 220–221
  law and politics in 222–225
Rome Statute (of ICC) 31, 127, 133, 160, 172,
  222
Rönquist, Anders 223
Ruhrtriennale 184
Russell Tribunal 165
Russia 9, 19

Sahrawi 7, 44–46, 247n35
Said, Edward 204
Al-Salem, Rouba 235–240
Salomon, Margot E. 114
Samhouri, Mohammad 119
Samour, Nadija vii, 179–200
Sayed, Hani 11, 20n70, 154
Schäfer, Peter 179n1
Schanzer, Jonathan 204
Schwebel, Stephen 25n85, 27n95, 29n101,
  138
secession 55
sectarianism
  conflicts and 77–78, 96, 99
  state structure and 100, 104
  weaponization of 104
secularism 83–84
security
  BDS as threat to 196, 198
  Israel's need 19, 26, 34–35, 144, 154, 164,
    169, 173
  proportionality and 148–151
  restrictions on movement and 147–148
  *see also* self-defense
*Security, Rights and Law: The Israeli
  High Court of Justice and Israeli*

*Settlements in the Occupied West Bank*
  (Al-Salem) 235–240
segregation 161–165
self-administration 41, 44, 49, 53, 54
self-defense
  as justification for occupation 24–26,
    29–30, 34–35, 241
  pre-emptive 27, 30
  *see also* security
self-determination, law on 7, 35–37, 42–43,
  61, 62–63, 68, 72
self-determination, right to
  in general 5, 7–8
  annexation and 40–41, 59–60
  colonialism and 36–37
  compromise and 45
  delayed approach to
    in East Timor 43–44
    in Iraq 44
    in oPt 46–49
    in Western Sahara 44–46
  as human right
    in general 56–58
    as group not as individual 58–59, 61
    jurisprudence on 59, 61–63
  implementing of 41
  of Palestinians
    in general 35
    delayed approach to 46–49
    ICCPR and 58
    ignoring/downgrading of 67, 72–73
    Israeli nation-state law and 66–67
    lack of enforcement and 73
    peace agreement and 72
    as right of non-domination 115
    support of human rights NGOs
      for 63–64
  territory of 37, 71
  through statehood 37–43
  trusteeship system and 50, 53–54
  US' position on Golan, East Jerusalem
    and Western Sahara and 69–70,
    73
  violations of 42, 43, 61, 70, 94, 117
  peace agreements and 44–47, 72
  relevance of 63
  right of resistance and 246–247
  trusteeship systems and 50–56

268 INDEX

Separation Wall
in general 143
ICJ Advisory Opinion on 25–26n86, 38, 61–62, 218n6, 235, 241
Israeli HCJ handling petitions involving 236–238
settler-colonialism 203
Sfard, Michael 157
Shah, Samira 150
Shammas, Sally vii, 75–111
Shamsie, Kamila 184
Sharif, Lila 185n24
Shehabi, Omar Yousef vii, 241–250
Shehadeh, Raja 209
Shi'a Muslims 78, 99, 101, 104, 105–106, 107
*Al-Skeini et al. v. U.K.* case 218n6
smear campaigns
against BDS/BDS activists 179–180, 182, 185, 191–192
against Jewish Voice for Peace 179–180n2
against Rasmea Odeh 192–193
social connections model 114, 115–116, 127, 136, 138, 139
Sornarajah, Muthucumaraswamy 114
South Africa
apartheid in 156, 162, 212, 213–214
legal advisors in 221–222
South West Africa People's Organisation (SWAPO) 213–214
sovereignty
change in conception of 83–84, 87
legitimation of states and 84–86, 87
occupation and 12
over Western Sahara 69
Special Tribunal for Lebanon 128
speech, freedom of 191
*Der Spiegel* (magazine) 181
standard of living, right to adequate 149
statehood
collective identity and 36–37, 38
colonialism and 36–37
of Israel
annexation and 23
occupation law and 11–12, 13, 14, 15
status of 37n128
of Palestine 39, 41, 71–72

states
legitimacy of
popular sovereignty as 84–86, 87
religion as 82–83, 97–98
occupation laws and 11–12
secularism and 83–84
systemic harm in occupation and
in general 135–136
in oPt 136, 140
structural injustice 113, 115–116, 139–140
Sub-Commission on Prevention of Discrimination and Protection of Minorities (of UN) 92, 93
Sultany, Nimer 237, 238
Sunni Muslims 78, 99, 101, 104, 105–106, 107
surveillance 166–169
SWAPO (South West Africa People's Organisation) 213–214
Syria
minorities in
Alawites 78, 101, 103, 110
reconstruction and 110–111
sectarian conflicts in 78

Tatour, Dareen 192
*terra* nullius 22–23n75, 39, 40
territory
acquisition of 21–22
annexation of *see* annexation
occupation of *see* occupation
title to
in general 24
law on 23, 40
*see also* colonialism/imperialism
"The School for Unlearning Zionism" (art lectures) 185
Third World Approaches to International Law (TWAIL) 212, 214, 219–220, 253
Tilley, Virginia 155, 157
Timor Leste 9, 19, 43–44
Tladi, Dire 221–222
*To Be Born a Nation* (SWAPO) 213
transformatory occupations 17–20
Transitional Administrative Law (2004; Iraq) 104
Trump, Donald 46, 69, 203, 207

INDEX     269

trusteeship-over-people systems
  colonial/post-colonial context of   49–50,
    54–56
  law of occupation and   51–52
  occupation of oPt and   50, 51–52, 53–54
Turkmen   104, 106, 108
TWAIL (Third World Approaches to
  International Law)   212, 214, 219–220, 253

UDHR   *see* Universal Declaration of Human
  Rights
Ukraine   223, 229
UNCTAD (United Nations Conference for
  Trade and Development)   117–118, 120
underauthorized authorization   255
UNGA   *see* United Nations General
  Assembly
UNGPs (United Nations Guiding Principles
  on Business and Human Rights)   130–132
UNHRC (United Nations Human Rights
  Council)   132, 133–135, 149, 224, 229
United Kingdom Foreign and
  Commonwealth Office (FCO)   224
United Kingdom (UK)
  authority over Chagos Archipelago   62
  mandatory rule of Iraq by   101–102
  occupation of Iraq by   9, 17–19, 44
United Nations (UN)
  in general   8
  fact finding missions of   227, 228
  regime for Non-Self-Governing
    Territories   50
  Trusteeship system of   50, 54
    *see also under specific committees,*
      *conferences, declarations etc.*
United Nations Centre for Transnational
  Corporations   129
United Nations Charter
  article 103   18
  minority rights in, lack of   92
  objectives of   44–45
United Nations Committee on Economic,
  Social and Cultural Rights (CESCR)
    65–66, 70–71
United Nations Committee on the
  Elimination of Racial Discrimination   161
United Nations Conference for Trade and
  Development (UNCTAD)   117–118, 120

United Nations Declaration on the Rights of
  Persons Belonging to National or Ethnic,
  Religious or Linguistic Minorities   92–93
United Nations General Assembly (UNGA)
  on aggression   25n84
  on applicability of fundamental human
    rights   144–145
  on applicability of Geneva
    Convention   146
  on Israeli occupation of oPt   26
  liberation movements and   247
  on minority rights   92
  on Palestinians right of return   64
  Resolution 1541   *see* Resolution 1541
United Nations Guiding Principles
  on Business and Human Rights
  (UNGPS)   130–132
United Nations Human Rights Committee
  on extraterritoriality of IHRL   146
  on freedom of movement   148
  on Gaza blockade   61
  on Israeli nation-state law   66
  minority rights and   92, 93–94
  Palestinians right of return and   65, 66
  on right to life   70
  on self-determination
    comment on ICCPR article   57
    as group not as individual   58–59
    of Palestinians in oPt   59–61
United Nations Human Rights Council
  (UNHRC)   132, 133–135, 149, 224, 229
United Nations Mission for the Referendum
  in Western Sahara (MINURSO)   44, 45
United Nations Office of the High
  Commissioner for Human Rights
  (OHCHR)   242
United Nations Relief and Works Agency
  for Palestine Refugees in the Near East
  (UNRWA)   199
United Nations Security Council (UNSC)
  on acquisition of territory   22
  on applicability of Geneva
    Conventions   145
  CPA and   105
  diplomatic story of Resolution 242   208
  on Israeli justification of military
    actions   242
  on Israeli settlements   134, 136

United Nations Security Council (cont.)
 on occupation 28, 30, 208, 210–211
 occupation of East Timor and 43–44
 occupation of Iraq and 17–18, 44
 occupation of Western Sahara
  and 44–46
United Nations Special Rapporteurs 197
United Nations Transitional Administration
 in East Timor (UNTAET) 44, 50
United States of America (USA)
 constitution of 253
 diplomacy of 139
 embassy of 69, 73
 occupation of Iraq by 9, 17–19, 44
 occupation of Western Sahara and 46
 Palestine policy of
  in general 207–208
  on the Golan, East Jerusalem, and
   Western Sahara 8, 69–70, 73
Universal Declaration of Human Rights
 (UDHR)
 in general 4
 adoption of 9, 56
 Amnesty International UK and 15
 applicability of 94
 on freedom of movement 144
 minorities and 92, 108
 self-determination omitted from 57, 64
UNRWA (United Nations Relief and Works
 Agency for Palestine Refugees in the Near
 East) 199
UNSC *see* United Nations Security Council
UNTAET (United Nations Transitional
 Administration in East Timor) 44, 50
*The Use of Armed Force in Occupied Territory*
 (Longobardo) 241–250
use of force, law on *see* force, law on use of
usufruct, rules of 119–120
*uti possidetis juris* 36

Verleger, Rolf 192
victims, definition of 127
violations
 of freedom of movement *see under*
  freedom of movement
 of freedom of speech 191
 of Geneva Conventions 32, 229
 of human rights 122, 149, 197, 199

 of IHL 32–34, 142, 174, 229
 of IHRL 33, 142
 of international law 117, 124–125, 127,
  136, 139
 of right to self-determination 42, 43, 61,
  70, 94
 of rules of usufruct 120
violence, Glatung's definition of 114–115
voluntarism 132

Wall *see* Separation Wall
war, martialist vision of 245
war crimes 32
water, right to safe and clean 120
weaponization, of sectarianism 104
Weber, Max 125–126
Werteinitiative 181
West Bank
 development projects in 119
 Israeli-only roads in 143, 150, 163
 Jahalin Bedouins in 3–4
 occupation of
  or annexation 19–20, 24, 69
  benefits of 19–20
  occupation law and 13, 19
  as self-defense 24
 quarrying businesses in 120
 restrictions on movement in
  in general 141–142
  as apartheid
   in general 161, 174–176
   arbitrariness and 169–172
   exclusion and 165–166
   geographic fragmentation
    and 161–164
   harassment/humiliation and
    172–174
   non-annexation and 156–158
   purpose of 167–174
   segregation and 161–165
   surveillance and 166–169
  discriminatory system behind
   in general 153
   institutionalized aspect
    of 154–155
   impacting fundamental rights
    142–143, 148
   insecurity and 150–151

INDEX 271

legal analysis of 143–144
as security precaution 144, 148,
149–151, 153–154
as systematic mechanism of
exclusion 151–153
water resources in 120
*see also* Separation Wall
Western Sahara
Morocco's occupation/annexation
of 8–9, 19, 44–46
Morocco's sovereignty over 69
Westphalia, Treaty of 83, 86–87
White, Benjamin 81–82
Wilde, Ralph vii, 3–74
Wilson, Arnold 52n174
Wood, Michael 222
work, right to 149

Working party on public international law
(COJUR) 223
World Trade Organization (WTO) 137
World Zionist Organization 206
wrongful acts 124–125
WTO (World Trade Organization) 137

Yack, Bernard 84–85
Yanagihara, Masaharu 22–23n75
Yezidis 104, 108
Younes, Anna 179n1
Young, Iris Marion 114, 115–116, 132, 138

Zeitoun, Mark 120
Zionism 206–208, 210, 212
Zreik, Raef 156

Printed in the United States
by Baker & Taylor Publisher Services